RONALD REAGAN AND THE POLITICS OF FREEDOM

Andrew E. Busch

ROWMAN & LITTLEFIELD PUBLISHERS, INC.

Lanham • Boulder • New York • Oxford

ROWMAN & LITTLEFIELD PUBLISHERS, INC.

Published in the United States of America
by Rowman & Littlefield Publishers, Inc.
4720 Boston Way, Lanham, Maryland 20706
www.rowmanlittlefield.com

12 Hid's Copse Road
Cumnor Hill, Oxford OX2 9JJ, England

British Library Cataloguing-in-Publication Information Available

Library of Congress Cataloging-in-Publication Data

Busch, Andrew.
  Ronald Reagan and the politics of freedom / Andrew E. Busch.
    p. cm.
  Includes bibliographical references and index.
  ISBN 0-7425-2052-8 (alk. paper)—ISBN 0-7425-2053-6 (pbk. : alk. paper)
    1. United States—Politics and government—1981–1989. 2. Reagan, Ronald—Political
and social views. 3. Liberty—Political aspects—United States—History—20th century. 4.
Liberty—Social aspects—United States—History—20th century. I. Title.

E876 .B858 2001
973.927—dc21

                                                                            2001019405

Printed in the United States of America

⊗™ The paper used in this publication meets the minimum requirements of American National
Standard for Information Sciences—Permanence of Paper for Printed Library Materials, ANSI/NISO
Z39.48–1992.

To Janusz and Betty

Contents

Tables

Charts

Acknowledgments

I WOULD LIKE TO THANK, first and foremost, my loving and patient wife Melinda, who proofread, assembled the bibliography, saved me from Microsoft Excel, watched the kids, and endured long days and longer nights of waiting for me to finish this project. I owe a debt to a number of undergraduate research assistants who have helped with this project, including Kari Anderson, Sean Kalic, and James Meyer. I would also like to thank Steve Wrinn, Mary Carpenter, Ginger Strader, Pelham Boyer, and the rest of the hardworking staff at Rowman & Littlefield, as well as Dave Weiden and several anonymous reviewers whose comments were collectively invaluable. Finally, I am grateful to friends who provided suggestions and encouragement over the course of years.

Introduction

"My fellow citizens, our nation is poised for greatness. We must do what we know is right, and do it with all our might. Let history say of us, 'These were golden years—when the American Revolution was reborn, when freedom gained new life, and America reached for her best.'"

Ronald Reagan, Second Inaugural Address

IN 2001, RONALD REAGAN CELEBRATED his ninetieth birthday and the twentieth anniversary of his inauguration as president of the United States. As Reagan's unofficial biographer Lou Cannon argued, "Since the turn of the century, no president save FDR defined a decade as strikingly as Ronald Reagan defined the 1980s."[1] In the last twenty years, there has been no shortage of commentary on Reagan. Journalists, scholars, and political participants have all contributed, and their works have generally fallen into one of a handful of categories.

Some have been biographical in nature, such as Cannon's *President Reagan: The Role of a Lifetime*, Garry Wills's *Reagan's America*, and the official biography *Dutch*, published in 1999 by Edmund Morris. Others have focused on specific areas of Reagan administration policy. Most notably, economic policy has garnered great attention from friendly authors like Paul Craig Roberts (*The Supply-Side Revolution*), Martin Anderson (*Revolution*), and Lawrence Lindsey (*The Growth Experiment*); neutral scholars like John W. Sloan (*The Reagan Effect*); and a multitude of critics exemplified by Anthony S. Campagna (*The Economy in the Reagan Years*), David Stockman (*The Triumph of*

Politics), and Kevin Phillips (*The Politics of Rich and Poor*). Reagan's foreign policy has been the other major area of interest, though almost every distinct policy realm has been the subject of at least some study. Many works with a focused policy emphasis, as well as many general memoirs, have been produced by former Reagan administration officials, often praising Reagan, sometimes condemning him.

Another line of inquiry has examined Reagan's presidential style and capacities. In *Ronald Reagan: How an Ordinary Man Became an Extraordinary Leader*, Dinesh D'Souza wove a study of Reagan's leadership around a discussion of foreign and economic policy, while many political scientists and historians like Stephen Skowronek, Sidney Milkis, and Robert Dallek have tried to assess the quality and impact of his leadership against some more academic standard.

Despite the large number and wide variety of works on Reagan, there have been surprisingly few attempts to offer a broad judgment of just exactly how Reagan defined the 1980s—or, to put it another way, exactly what defined his presidency and what that meant, and continues to mean, for America, not just economically but politically and socially. The nearest approach to such a global interpretation has been the attempt by some to label the 1980s the "decade of greed." To many of these critics, like author Jack Mitchell, "There's no question that the Reagan team was ultimately responsible for the floodtide of greed that dominated the decade of the Eighties"[2]—a decade when Donald Trump became a popular figure, BMWs were the rage, and Wall Street financier Ivan Boesky proclaimed in a commencement address that "Greed is healthy." As early as 1984, columnists were labeling the 1980s the "GOP 'Me Decade.'"[3] In the 1990s, television anchors like Bryant Gumbel routinely referred to the "greedy excesses of the Reagan years";[4] filmmakers (while grossing millions of dollars on such films) described their latest productions as morality plays about the "greed and conspicuous consumption that characterized the 1980s."[5] Public-policy textbooks declared, "The 1980s was a time of expansion, careless spending, and greed."[6] Even home-decorating supplements in local newspapers explained changes in carpet fashion from red to earthtones by reference to the end of the conspicuous consumption of the 1980s. When Volkswagen reintroduced the legendary "VW Bug" in 1998, it marketed the vehicle by proclaiming, "If you sold your soul in the 1980s, here's your chance to buy it back."

In a complementary vein, journalist Haynes Johnson accused Americans (and Reagan) of "sleepwalking through history," while two well-known social commentators alleged that "the placid, self-involved decade of the 1980s" had been characterized by an "abandonment of concern for public causes."[7] To many the 1980s were a decade of social neglect—the years of homelessness,

AIDS, budget reductions in education, increasing poverty, and the collapse of the middle class. Along these lines, *CBS Sunday Morning* critic John Leonard indicted the "plague years of the 1980s—that low decade of denial, indifference, hostility, opportunism, and idiocy."[8] To Barbara Ehrenreich, the 1980s were simply "the worst years of our lives."[9]

Cornel West's critique of the 1980s in *Newsweek*'s sixtieth-anniversary edition neatly summarized this position:

> The 1980s were not simply a decade of glitz and greed. . . .
> The major economic legacy of Reaganomics was to increase the disparity between rich and poor and to downsize the American middle class. . . . [A]n undeniable decline in the quality of life set in—with increased crime, violence, disease (e.g., AIDS), tensions over race, gender, and sexual orientation, decrepit public schools, ecological abuse and a faltering physical infrastructure. In short, Reaganomics resulted in waves of economic recovery, including millions of new jobs (many part-time), alongside a relative drop in the well-being of a majority of Americans. . . .
> The unintended cultural consequence of this economic legacy was a spiritual impoverishment in which the dominant conception of the good life consists of gaining access to power, pleasure and property, sometimes by any means. . . .
> A creeping zeitgeist of coldheartedness and mean-spiritedness accompanies this full-blown market culture.[10]

This interpretation is now repeated even in children's summaries of the twentieth century found in pediatricians' offices. One such magazine declares, "In the 1980s, the rich got richer and the poor got poorer. Under President Ronald Reagan, the government cut taxes on the rich, lifted many regulations on business, and spent billions on the military. The national debt tripled. . . . Homelessness and a deadly new virus called AIDS worried many. . . . African Americans made few economic gains."[11]

The "decade of greed" interpretation is bolstered, in the view of its adherents, by the record of scandal in the 1980s. Private scandals included such headline-grabbing trials as Ivan Boesky's for insider trading, Michael Milken's for improper junk-bond sales, and Leona Helmsley's for tax evasion. In the public sector, journalist John Judis has argued that "the Reagan administration was easily the most corrupt administration since that of Warren Harding."[12] By some estimates, approximately two hundred Reagan administration officials were indicted or investigated, most for questionable financial dealings in office (though many of these were later cleared of wrongdoing).[13] To many the Reagan years were epitomized by the savings and loan fiasco, in which federal taxpayers ultimately paid approximately $150 billion in deposit insurance and other costs to cover losses attributed by the popular press to crooks and "quick-buck artists."

However, the "decade of greed" interpretation of Reagan's significance is severely limited by the relative lack of evidence supporting it, the logical leaps that must be made by its adherents, and the ad hominem nature of much of the argument. For example, while there clearly was greed in the 1980s, there is little evidence that greed was more common in that decade than others. From the "Gilded Age"[14] to the "Roaring Twenties,"[15] from the "selfish, indifferent, commercial" fifties[16] to the hedonistic sixties[17] to the "Me Decade" of the seventies,[18] almost every decade since the Civil War has been seen by contemporary critics as marked by excess, materialism, and selfishness. The Whiskey Ring and Crédit Mobilier, the "Black Sox" scandal, war profiteering, Teapot Dome, Works Progress Administration corruption, the Truman scandals, Sherman Adams, Bobby Baker and Billy Sol Estes, the milk lobby scandals, Abscam, and Koreagate seem to show that greed marks every era.[19] Indeed, congressional scholar David Mayhew has demonstrated that major congressional hearings related to financial scandal in the executive branch (defined as hearings from 1946 to 1990 that rated twenty or more front-page stories in the *New York Times*) were not more common in the Reagan years than the Carter years, Kennedy-Johnson years, Eisenhower years, or Truman years (see table I).[20]

The 1990s did not escape the opprobrium of materialism, either. Indeed, the very trends that critics said indicated greed and consumerism in the 1980s accelerated in the 1990s: the personal savings rate fell, personal debt increased, the number of millionaires and billionaires multiplied, income inequality grew, and the stock market quintupled (after merely tripling in the 1980s). More than a dozen major financial scandals entangled hundreds of government officials, businessmen, and fundraisers.[21] Such new game shows as *Who Wants to Be a Millionaire?* and *Greed* emerged. Books like *The Courage to Be Rich* and *Greed Is Good* drew significant readership, and some became bestsellers. In 1999, *Newsweek* devoted a cover story to "The Whine of the '90s: Everyone's Getting Rich but Me"; its author, Adam Bryant, complained that

TABLE I
Major Congressional Investigations of the Executive Branch
Related Primarily to Financial Wrongdoing, 1946–1989

Administration	Number of Investigations
Truman	6
Eisenhower	2
Kennedy/Johnson	2
Nixon/Ford	1
Carter	2
Reagan	2

Source: Adapted from David Mayhew, *Divided We Govern* (New Haven, Conn.: Yale University Press, 1991), 13–25.

"nobody's really countering the money hype." Greed was more widely accepted than ever, Bryant contended; he labeled the 1990s "the Age of Outlandish Expectations." Indeed, Bryant remarked, "Now it seems as if the list of seven deadly sins has been shortened to six."[22] Others suggested the 1990s should be labeled the "Go-Go-Go-Some-More-'90s," the "Greed is Good Again—Just Don't Tell Anyone—Decade," and, reflecting the conspicuous consumption of the time, the "Age of Showing Off."[23] In the view of one Wall Street analyst, "The '90s make the '80s seem quaint."[24]

Furthermore, advocates of the "decade of greed" interpretation have failed to provide a compelling connection between Reagan and the greed that was present, often seeming to rely instead on the proposition that he transmitted nebulous signals indirectly advancing greed through rhetoric or the misdeeds of associates. Of course, symbolism and rhetoric are powerful presidential tools for good and ill, and consequently should never be discounted, but they do not quite seem up to the task assigned to them in this case. In any event, there were good reasons to believe that Reagan's critics overstated the absolute, not just relative, level of greed in the 1980s. Research by economist Richard McKenzie and others shows that a large and unexpected increase in charitable giving by Americans took place in the 1980s.[25] Likewise, there were numerous indicators of an upsurge in voluntarism. It is difficult to reconcile the picture of an era defined by extraordinary selfishness with a population that was *more* generous with its time and money.

Therefore, we must continue searching for the significance, the defining tendency, and the overarching theme of the Reagan presidency. This book proposes an alternative approach to that question based on the view that Reagan's significance can be found by assessing him in light of his own standard—found in his second inaugural address—of promoting the freedom of Americans. Since the goal was self-imposed, no one can object that Reagan is being held to an unfair, externally imposed standard. More importantly, no one can complain that the standard itself—national liberty—is substantively trivial, an unworthy object of statesmanship or subject of study.

It should be clear that there are several things this book is *not*. It is not a biography of Ronald Reagan or a chronological history of his presidency. It is not a detailed examination of his leadership style. It is not even a comprehensive review of every aspect of public policy under Reagan. It is, rather, an attempt to lay out an argument focusing on the effects of Reagan's presidency on American freedom.

That argument is that Reagan, for the most part, passed the test established by his standard. In a variety of ways, Reagan sought to enhance the freedom of Americans, and he largely succeeded. Furthermore, no other objective defined as many areas of Reagan administration activity; no other goal came close to serving as a common theme or a glue holding together large and disparate swaths of policy. Consequently, Reagan's presidency must be seen, above all, as engaging in the politics of freedom.

Before embarking upon that argument, several questions must be addressed. For example, how did Reagan conceive of freedom? Why was it, for him, such a paramount issue? As he sought to promote it, what were his general goals and by what strategy did he advance them?

To Reagan, freedom was the most fundamental American principle, the cause that "allowed individuals to make America great."[26] As early as 1952, he argued in a commencement address that America was ultimately defined by

> Nothing but the inherent love of freedom. . . . It is simply the idea, the basis of this country and of our religion, the idea of the dignity of man, the idea that deep within the heart of each one of us is something so God-like and precious that no individual or group has a right to impose his or its will upon the people, that no group can decide for the people so well as they can decide for themselves. . . . I, in my own mind, have thought of America as a place in the divine scheme of things that was set aside as a promised land.[27]

Political scientist Walter Dean Burnham has called Reagan "the most ideological president, and the leader of the most ideological administration, in modern American history."[28] As many observers (both sympathetic and unsympathetic) have noted, Reagan was no intellectual in the mold of a Woodrow Wilson, who served as president of Princeton University before he became president of the United States. He was not an original theorist or a "social philosopher."[29] He was a practical politician—but his politics were driven by a clear set of interlocking ideas, supported by an even more fundamental set of moral and religious convictions.

Reagan's philosophy of government and his understanding of liberty rested on several strands of complementary thought. First and foremost, Reagan was more consistently and self-consciously grounded in the philosophy of the Founders of the American Republic than any president since the New Deal. As we will see in chapter 1, he spoke the language of Thomas Jefferson and Alexander Hamilton, of the Declaration of Independence, *The Federalist*, and, not infrequently, the antifederalists. He consulted the Founders as the primary source of guidance for American statesmanship. In applying the principles of the founding to modern issues of the welfare state, Reagan was also heavily influenced by the rise of the conservative movement, whose de facto leader he became after Barry Goldwater's 1964 defeat. As a perusal of *The Conscience of a Conservative* will verify, Reagan's views paralleled Goldwater's on topics as wide-ranging as taxes and economic growth, welfare, federalism, education, and foreign policy.[30] Though Goldwater's political prominence preceded Reagan's, Reagan had been speaking on similar themes for at least a decade before Goldwater's nomination, even noting in his memoirs that Goldwater's book "contained a lot of the same points I'd been making in my speeches."[31] Reagan, and certainly the policies of his administration, were also influenced by trends in intellectual conservatism that gained prominence in the 1970s and 1980s in the areas of economics, social policy, and foreign affairs.

Reagan was attached as well to the thinking of Alexis de Tocqueville, whose ideas on the political and social bases of free society are found in his two-volume *Democracy in America*. Political analyst Michael Barone has frequently remarked on the degree to which the America forged in the 1980s and 1990s largely returned to its Tocquevillian roots.[32] In the view of Reagan speechwriter William Ker Muir Jr., Tocqueville exerted a "powerful influence" on the Reagan White House, as "Reagan's public philosophy echoed Tocqueville's personal sentiments."[33] Even Soviet foreign minister Eduard Shevardnadze complained that Reagan bombarded him with quotations from the Frenchman.[34] (It also bears pointing out that Goldwater cited Tocqueville's fear of "democratic despotism," discussed below, in *Conscience of a Conservative*.)[35] According to the *Public Papers of the Presidents*, from January 1981 through January 1989 Reagan cited Tocqueville no fewer than fifty-eight times in public remarks.

Finally, Reagan's own personal experience was important to his views. His economic views, for instance, had been shaped by his college education. As an economics major at Eureka College before the rise of Keynesianism, Reagan received a training in classical economics. As a Hollywood figure who found himself in the 91 percent income-tax bracket, Reagan developed a firsthand opinion about the moral and economic deficiencies of extremely high marginal tax rates. As a Screen Actors Guild representative, he witnessed the deception and ruthlessness of the Hollywood communists who sought to control the guild in the late 1940s, an experience not dissimilar to the accumulated experiences that turned most of organized labor in America into devout anticommunists.[36] As an eyewitness to World War II, Reagan, like most Americans of his generation, was convinced of the futility of appeasement and isolationism. Reagan's experience on the speaking circuit was, in his words, "almost a postgraduate course in political science for me"; he heard complaints from hundreds of people across America about "how the ever-expanding federal government was encroaching on liberties we'd always taken for granted."[37] Finally, there can be little question that Reagan's personal religious faith significantly affected his view of the world and man's place in it. Not least, that faith shaped Reagan's belief both in the "divine spark" that was the source of human dignity and in the imperfectability of human beings and the human condition.[38]

Guided by this combination of influences, Reagan aimed in his presidency at strengthening what could be called the "architecture" of American freedom: the political, economic, and social framework that gives concrete meaning to liberty and makes it sustainable. Reagan paid special attention to four components of that architecture. First, as the Founders noted, there must be a political structure to support freedom. That structure must achieve a combination of consent of the governed and the protection of fundamental rights—a combination resting on the rule of law, equally applied. Because of human imperfection, such a combination cannot be secure without limitations upon government; any free society must guard against excessive or unaccountable concentrations of power in either government in general or any branch or level of government. The importance of this structure in Reagan's thinking cannot be overstated. Indeed, he repeatedly argued that the American Revolution did not really start until 1787: "It was with the writing of the Constitution, setting down as it were the architecture of American democracy, that the fine words and brave rhetoric of 1776 took on substance."[39] The structure, to be effective, must be buttressed from above by a political discourse that consistently reaffirms the centrality of liberty. Likewise, from below, "Active and informed citizens are vital to the effective functioning of our constitutional system," as are patriotism and love of country.[40]

The second component of the architecture of a free society is a substantial degree of economic freedom. This principle is closely tied to the right to be secure in the property that one has earned, a right that John Locke and the American Founders thought essential. As Nobel-winning economist Friedrich Hayek argued in *The Road to Serfdom*, any government that fundamentally disrespects that right or assumes too much power over the economic well-being of a nation—whether through overregulation, overtaxation, extreme redistributionism, or direct ownership of the means of production—threatens the independence and liberty of its citizens. Reasonable people can debate the precise point at which governmental control over the economy becomes inconsistent with free society, but Reagan had no doubt that there is such a point. As Reagan pointed out, the Founders believed that private property is "one of the most important of civil rights, the most fundamental protection of the individual and the family against the excessive and always growing demands of the state. They knew that without economic liberty, political freedom may be no more than a shadow."[41]

Third, certain preconditions of free society are social in nature, imbedded in social practices and social institutions that Americans often do not view as political in either nature or consequence. Taken together, this complex constitutes the social infrastructure of democracy, or what Tocqueville referred to as the "customs and manners of the people."[42] To Tocqueville, there were numerous social characteristics of American democracy, ranging from the strength of religion and family to the abundance of voluntary civic associations, that were essential to its maintenance. Indeed, Tocqueville held these social underpinnings of democracy to be even more important than laws and the political structure, because they informed the lives of Americans and made them worthy citizens of a free society. That Reagan fundamentally concurred can be seen in his descriptions of religion, the family, and voluntarism, as outlined in chapter 6.

Finally, the survival of free society in the twentieth century required Americans to meet the challenge of a variety of antidemocratic and antiliberal forces, culminating in the military and political threat posed by the Marxist-Leninist states, led by the Soviet Union. Failure in the struggle against totalitarianism would have meant the destruction of liberal democracy in America and around the world. Thus, Reagan saw a national security policy capable of maintaining national safety and independence as indispensable to American freedom.

Reagan understood these components of freedom to be practically intertwined. Concentration of economic power in the state, while often economically inefficient, is most troubling because of the way that it can so easily be translated into awesome political power. An overactive state, no longer bound by the strictures of limited government, likewise has a tendency of intruding deeply into the social connections of civil society. Perhaps the most perceptive analysis of this question was offered in *Democracy in America*, where Tocqueville described the potential for "democratic," or "soft," despotism. In this condition, citizens become perpetual children—corrupted, enervated, and ultimately enslaved by a benevolent but all-encompassing government that leaves no sphere for freedom. To Tocqueville, the democratic passion for equality, combined with inattention to the social supports of democracy, could lead to extreme centralization, ending with the loss of liberty. This despotism would be "more extensive and more mild" than the despotism of the caesars and would be carried out by a power standing above the people, a power "which takes upon itself alone to secure their gratifications and to watch over their fate." To avoid this condition of dependence, the principles of limited, constitutional, decentralized government had to be preserved, and efforts had to be made to increase the people's ardor for freedom.[43] To Tocqueville, social and civic institutions, as well as strong local self-government, were crucial to liberty.

Echoing Tocqueville's fear of "democratic despotism," Reagan argued that America was at a crossroads. One choice led "down through the welfare state to statism, to more and more government largesse accompanied always by more government authority, less individual liberty and, ultimately, totalitarianism, always advanced as for our own good." The other choice led up to the

Founders' vision of "the ultimate in individual liberty compatible with an ordered society."[44]

Of course, Reagan's notion of liberty was not the only one possible. Many libertarians reject it as allowing for too much government, too much law, and too much concern with social structure. The above vision, though individualistic, is not one of atomistic individuals with complete freedom; it is, rather one of what has alternately been referred to as "ordered liberty," "liberty under law," or "liberty, not license." On the other hand, some reject this vision of liberty for allowing for too little government. At the extreme, adherents of Marxism-Leninism, fascism, and national socialism have each contended that liberal democracy is a sham; that "true" freedom is not an individual good but solely a collective one, to be enjoyed on the basis of class, nation, or race; and that only an all-encompassing state can bring it about. A milder version of this same critique is found on the Left, among adherents of "positive government," who contend that limited government, especially economic freedom and property rights, effectively enslave all but the privileged few. In this view, government must take on a dominant role to regulate, redistribute income, and ensure "positive rights" to certain economic goods. Real freedom here is freedom from inequality and the vicissitudes of nature, freedom promised and delivered by the state.

Needless to say, Reagan's framework provoked no small amount of criticism from positive-government egalitarians. In a sense, however, their argument was less with Reagan than with the long-standing American political tradition of ordered liberty. Indeed, Reagan's concept of liberty closely paralleled what political scientist Hugh Heclo called "The enduring verities of the American consensus," including the ideas that "individual freedom is the touchstone of good government; government power, especially when it is centralized in Washington, is to be distrusted; free enterprise is the key to economic progress and personal liberty; the role of government is to assure equal opportunity, not to mandate particular results."[45]

Reagan's attention to the question of liberty took on particular urgency in the context that surrounded his presidency. Reagan had long contended that these "enduring verities of the American consensus" were in fact in growing danger of breaking down. In the 1950s, Reagan was already warning of growing "collectivism" and "the tendency to center the power of all initiative in one central government." The hour was late, he said, in the "day of decision."[46] When Reagan spoke for Barry Goldwater in October 1964, he reiterated his belief that Americans had "a rendezvous with destiny," in which the choice would soon be made whether to preserve America's freedom or lose it.[47] As Reagan later explained it,

Our federal bureaucracy expanded relentlessly during the post-war years and, almost always with the best of intentions, it began leading America along the path to a silent form of socialism. Our government wasn't nationalizing the railroads or the banks, but it was confiscating a disproportionate share of the nation's wealth through excessive taxes, and indirectly seizing control of the day-to-day management of our businesses with rules and regulations that often gave Washington bureaucrats the power of life and death over them.[48]

By the time Reagan was elected in 1980, events had seemed to validate his concerns. America faced a crisis that was rapidly coming to a head, a crisis that was fundamentally about the question of whether free nations could continue to make freedom work—politically, economically, socially, and internationally. As Reagan began his presidency, the economy was reaching a crisis point, as the federal government's size, scope, and intrusiveness continued to expand. Many observers were asking whether the free-market economic system could (or should) survive. Government had become increasingly centralized; federal authority continued to grow at the expense of state and local institutions of government, and there appeared to be no end to that trend in sight. Indeed, several important constitutional principles aimed at limiting government seemed increasingly irrelevant to actual practice. The traditional discourse of American liberty had been largely supplanted by a technocratic and lifeless discourse, leading some political scientists to argue that America no longer enjoyed a public philosophy. Popular confidence in American institutions in general had reached a low point. Numerous scholars were suggesting that the American presidency was unworkable and that the entire American system had become incapable of action. A variety of negative social trends that originated or accelerated in the 1960s—including dramatically higher crime rates, signs of family breakdown, drug abuse, declining school test scores, and a weakening of religion and civil society—raised questions about the future of American society. Not least, the crisis of 1980 was one of foreign affairs; American weakness was displayed in the Iranian hostage seizure, and Soviet totalitarianism advanced on almost every continent. When the Soviets occupied Afghanistan in December 1979, it was the tenth country in five years to have fallen into their orbit.[49]

Altogether, in the crisis of 1980, each element that Reagan saw as central to the preservation of free society seemed to be—and in fact almost certainly was—endangered. He identified the economic, national security, and confidence crises as the most urgent,[50] but he and his administration developed a strategy to address every front. Reagan's approach was built around three fundamental components—philosophy, policy, and politics. This book examines each in turn, arguing that Reagan:

- Reoriented political discourse in a way that emphasized themes of freedom, in an attempt to build a foundation for the establishment of a post–New Deal public philosophy. Far from empty rhetoric, this discourse served as the philosophical glue that held together the rest of Reagan's strategy (chapter 1).

- Revived a more traditional conception of American constitutionalism, including reintroducing the idea of the federal government as a limited government of enumerated powers, strengthening the principles of separation of powers and equality under the law, restoring federalism to greater prominence, and seeking a more restrained role for the federal judiciary (chapter 2).
- Directly and indirectly bolstered crucial institutions of American democracy, like the presidency and the political parties, as well as public confidence and patriotism (chapter 3).
- Helped overcome the economic crisis of the late 1970s and early 1980s and contributed to the expansion of the 1990s, through policies of tax cuts, restrained federal spending, deregulation, and free trade—policies characterized by a consistent preference for more rather than less economic freedom (chapter 4).
- Put the U.S. government on the road to renewed fiscal health, despite record deficits in the 1980s, by focusing on federal spending control and economic growth (chapter 5).
- Contributed to the strengthening of civil society and a partial recovery of important social indicators in the 1980s, a recovery that was potentially as important as the economic recovery but was little noted at the time (chapter 6).
- Developed a strategy in world affairs that led to the liberation of Eastern Europe and the collapse of the Soviet regime only months after he left office (chapter 7).
- Constructed a political coalition for limited government that remains strong today, a coalition capable of counterbalancing the already existing, well-organized one advocating the expansion of government (chapter 8).

The conclusion will bring these points together and assess Reagan's legacy, especially within the framework offered by his standard of promoting freedom.

Reagan's politics of freedom—a philosophy and discourse of limited government, policies aimed at enhancing freedom and strengthening free society, and attempts to build an electoral coalition supporting those policies—constituted the central story of his presidency. The consequences of his politics of freedom were, in turn, the central story of the 1980s, and perhaps the 1990s as well. The story begins where many analyses of Reagan end, in his role as the "Great Communicator."

Notes

1. Lou Cannon, *President Reagan: The Role of a Lifetime* (New York: Simon and Schuster, 1991), 831.

2. Jack Mitchell, *Executive Privilege: Two Centuries of White House Scandals* (New York: Hippocrene, 1992), 393.

3. Sidney Blumenthal, *Our Long National Daydream* (New York: Harper and Row, 1988), 107.

4. Quoted in Lorrin Anderson, "Good Intentions," *National Review*, June 21, 1993, 57.

5. Clifford D. May, "In the Post-Greed Era: A Varoom at the Top," *Rocky Mountain News*, July 18, 1993, 3A.

6. Lawrence G. Brewster and Michael E. Brown, *The Public Agenda*, 3rd ed. (New York: St. Martin's, 1994), 39.

7. Marvin Cetron and Owen Davies, *American Renaissance: Our Life at the Turn of the 21st Century* (New York: St. Martin's, 1989), 94, 92.

8. Leonard made these comments on September 5, 1993. Cited in "Notes and Asides," *National Review*, December 31, 1999, 12.

9. Barbara Ehrenreich, *The Worst Years of Our Lives: Irreverent Notes from a Decade of Greed* (New York: Pantheon, 1990).

10. Cornel West, "The '80s: Market Culture Run Amok," *Newsweek*, January 3, 1994, 48–49.

11. See *20th Century* (New York: Kids Discover, 1999), 7.

12. John B. Judis, "Conservatism and the Price of Success," in *The Reagan Legacy*, ed. Sidney Blumenthal and Thomas Byrne Edsall (New York: Pantheon, 1988), 162.

13. William E. Pemberton, *Exit with Honor: The Life and Presidency of Ronald Reagan* (Armonk, N.Y.: M. E. Sharpe, 1998), 146.

14. Dubbed such because of the material extravagance of the "robber barons," the Gilded Age is held by historians to have lasted from 1865 to as late as the turn of the century (depending on which historian one consults). The era was declared by one student of the subject "one of the most corrupt in American history." Abraham S. Eisenstadt, "Political Corruption in American History," in *Political Corruption*, ed. Arnold J. Heidenheimer, Michael Johnston, and Victor T. Levine (New Brunswick, N.J.: Transaction, 1989), 552.

15. The 1920s earned the appellation "The Roaring Twenties" for the conspicuous consumption, wild living, frantic speculation, and corruption of the time. *The Great Gatsby*—a portrayal of a nouveau riche hustler—was for many Americans emblematic of the 1920s. As one example of speculation and hucksterism, a massive real estate bubble abruptly inflated in Florida before popping just as abruptly, leaving thousands of individuals and numerous communities destitute. Dana L. Thomas, *Lords of the Land: The Triumphs and Scandals of America's Real Estate Barons: from Early Times to the Present* (New York: Putnam, 1977), 176–208. Adam Smith, host of PBS's *Adam Smith's Money World*, even compared Ivan Boesky to Gatsby. Adam Smith, *The Roaring '80s* (New York: Summit, 1988), 210.

16. Adlai Stevenson, Dwight D. Eisenhower's two-time presidential election opponent, also said that America in the 1950s was "stifled with complacent self-confidence. . . . Americans seemed content to satisfy their wants at ever higher standards of material luxury." The 1950s were the age of "The Man in the Gray Flannel Suit" and of Willy Loman, whose greedy and empty life was set forth by Arthur Miller in *Death of a Salesman*. Eisenhower was accused of fostering greed as much as Reagan would later be. According to one critic, "The stridently pro-business attitude of the Eisenhower White House created a laissez-faire atmosphere in the capital in which corporate America could do no wrong." The generation

coming of age in the 1950s was criticized as the "politically comatose" and passive "Brain-Washed Generation," among which "Chamber of Commerce morality is flourishing as never before." In the view of John Updike, "As in the 1920s, business interests reasserted control over government. Idealism retreated from the public sector; each man was an island. . . . The citizens of the '50s were relatively docile." Stuart Gerry Brown, *Conscience in Politics: Adlai E. Stevenson in the 1950s* (Syracuse, N.Y.: Syracuse University Press, 1961), 245–46, 249, 252; Mitchell, *Executive Privilege*, 210; Karl Shapiro, in *The 1950s: America's "Placid" Decade*, ed. Joseph Satin (New York: Houghton Mifflin, 1960), 25–26; John Updike, "The '50s: Each Man Was an Island," *Newsweek*, January 3, 1994, 36–37.

17. The 1960s were criticized strongly from two opposing perspectives. Contemporary America, said the New Left and Students for a Democratic Society, was greedy, materialistic, and empty. SDS declared in its 1962 "Port Huron Statement" that "our own upper classes revel in superfluous abundance." In the words of Herbert Marcuse, "The people recognize themselves in their commodities; they find their soul in their automobile, hi-fi set, split-level home, kitchen equipment." On the other hand, the counterculture itself came under attack for heavy doses of narcissism, nihilism, and hedonism. As Newt Gingrich would later argue, the counterculture "taught self-indulgent, aristocratic values without realizing that if an entire society engaged in the indulgences of an elite few, you could tear the society to shreds." Contemplating the 1960s, social commentator Dinesh D'Souza asked whether 1980s yuppies were really "more selfish than all those young men who fled to Canada or Sweden so that the Vietnam War wouldn't interrupt their lifestyles of sex, drugs and rock 'n' roll?" Herbert Marcuse, "Dehumanization and Repression," in *American Political Radicalism*, ed. Gilbert Abcarian (Lexington, Mass.: Xerox College, 1971), 150. Fred Barnes, "Revenge of the Squares," *New Republic*, March 13, 1995, 29; Dinesh D'Souza, "The Decade of Greed That Wasn't," *Forbes*, November 3, 1997, 123.

18. Tom Wolfe dubbed the 1970s "The Me Decade," a time representing an "unprecedented American development: the luxury, enjoyed by so many millions of middling folk, of dwelling upon the self." Social critic Christopher Lasch argued that the seventies saw the onset of "the culture of narcissism," in which "to live for the moment is the prevailing passion—to live for yourself, not for your predecessors or posterity." Others at the time decried the seventies as "decadent" and "self-absorbed," devoted to "the denial, in the name of higher truth, of the claims of others upon the self." In short, the "search for fulfillment" characteristic of the 1970s was said by critics "to divide individuals against one another, to intensify loneliness, and to promote greed." Tom Wolfe, "The Me Decade," *New York*, August 23, 1976, 40; Christopher Lasch, *The Culture of Narcissism* (New York: W. W. Norton, 1978), 5; Peter Marin, "The New Narcissism," *Harper's*, October 1975; Jim Hougan, *Decadence: Radical Nostalgia, Narcissism, and Decline in the Seventies* (New York: Morrow, 1975); Peter Clecak, "Saved from the Sixties," *Commonweal*, May 7, 1982.

19. The most serious of these was probably the scandals of the Truman years. It is often forgotten that Truman left office in 1953 under a cloud of financial impropriety that had ensnared the head of the Reconstruction Finance Corporation; the chairman of the Democratic National Committee; the attorney general and assistant attorney general in charge of the Tax Division; the White House personnel director; the president's personal physician, appointment secretary, and military adviser; and nearly two hundred employees of the Bureau of Internal Revenue, including the commissioner, assistant commissioner, and legal counsel. If this were not enough, the Department of Agriculture discovered that the sum of ten million dollars was "missing and presumed stolen." See Jules Abels, *The Truman Scandals* (Chicago: Regnery, 1956); Mitchell, *Executive Privilege*, 188–90. Shelley Ross, *Fall*

from Grace: Sex, Scandal, and Corruption in American Politics from 1702 to the Present (New York: Ballantine, 1988), 182.

20. David R. Mayhew, *Divided We Govern* (New Haven, Conn.: Yale University Press, 1991), 13–25.

21. George H. W. Bush's chief of staff, John Sununu, resigned for personal use of government transportation. A massive scandal surrounded the Bank of Credit and Commerce International (BCCI), while the House bank and post office scandals entangled literally hundreds of members of Congress. A federal investigation was launched into the trading practices of thirty mutual funds; a major bond trading scandal erupted at Kidder, Peabody and Co.; and several defense firms probably defrauded the government of at least six billion dollars. President Clinton's commerce secretary, agriculture secretary, and interior secretary were investigated for financial corruption. The Clintons' Whitewater cover-up held the nation's attention intermittently through the 1990s. Questions surrounded Speaker of the House Newt Gingrich's book deal and college course. A spate of presidential appointments collapsed in the face of financial irregularities. Campaign finance violations in 1996 touched both the Dole and Clinton-Gore campaigns, including the prospect that Clinton had allowed the transfer of sensitive missile technology to China in exchange for large, open contributions from the chairman of Loral Corporation and large, laundered contributions from officers of Chinese military intelligence.

22. Adam Bryant, "They're Rich (and You're Not)," *Newsweek*, July 5, 1999, 37–43.

23. Fred Vogelstein, "Greed Is Good Again. Just Don't Tell Anyone," *U.S. News & World Report*, December 15, 1997, 60; Marilyn Geewax, "Class Distinctions Making Unwelcome Return to U.S.," *Rocky Mountain News*, April 8, 1998, 40A.

25. Richard B. McKenzie, *What Went Right in the 1980s* (San Francisco: Pacific Research Institute for Public Policy, 1994), chap. 3.

26. "Radio Address to the Nation on Independence Day and the Centennial of the Statue of Liberty, July 5, 1986," *Public Papers of the Presidents: Ronald Reagan 1986* (Washington, D.C.: Government Printing Office [hereafter GPO], 1988), 925.

27. Pemberton, *Exit with Honor*, 49.

28. Walter Dean Burnham, "The Reagan Heritage," in *The Election of 1988: Reports and Interpretations*, ed. Gerald M. Pomper (Chatham, N.J.: Chatham House, 1989), 1.

29. Hugh Heclo, "Reaganism and the Search for a Public Philosophy," in *Perspectives on the Reagan Years*, ed. John L. Palmer (Washington, D.C.: Urban Institute, 1986), 40.

30. Barry M. Goldwater, *The Conscience of a Conservative* (Shepherdsville, Ky.: Victor, 1960).

31. Ronald Reagan, *An American Life: The Autobiography* (New York: Simon and Schuster, 1990), 138–39.

32. Michael Barone and Grant Ujifusa, *The Almanac of American Politics 1998* (Washington, D.C.: National Journal, 1997), 26–30.

33. William Ker Muir Jr., *The Bully Pulpit: The Presidential Leadership of Ronald Reagan* (San Francisco: ICS, 1992), 61.

34. Eduard Shevardnadze, *The Future Belongs to Freedom* (New York: Free Press, 1991), 81.

35. Goldwater, *Conscience of a Conservative*, 21–22.

36. Edmund Morris, *Dutch: A Memoir of Ronald Reagan* (New York: Random House, 1999), 230–46.

37. Reagan, *An American Life*, 129.

38. On the latter point particularly see Muir, *The Bully Pulpit*, 65–76.

39. "Remarks to the Winners of the Bicentennial of the Constitution Essay Competition, September 10, 1987," *Public Papers of the Presidents: Ronald Reagan 1987* (Washington, D.C.: GPO, 1989), 1016.

40. "Remarks at the Bicentennial Celebration of the United States Constitution, September 16, 1987," *Public Papers of the Presidents: Ronald Reagan 1987* (Washington, D.C.: GPO, 1989), 1040.

41. "Remarks at a White House Briefing for the American Legislative Exchange Council, December 12, 1986," *Public Papers of the Presidents: Ronald Reagan 1986* (Washington, D.C.: GPO, 1988), 1624.

42. Alexis de Tocqueville, *Democracy in America* (New York: Vintage Books, 1945), vol. 1, 310–42.

43. Tocqueville, *Democracy in America*, vol. 2, 334–39.

44. "Remarks Accepting the Presidential Nomination of the Republican National Convention in Dallas, Texas, August 23, 1984," *Public Papers of the Presidents: Ronald Reagan 1984* (Washington, D.C.: GPO, 1987), 23. This theme had been voiced by Reagan for many years prior to his presidency. Almost identical wording can be found in Reagan's October 1964 nationally televised address on behalf of Barry Goldwater. See Reagan, *An American Life*, 142.

45. Heclo, "Reaganism and the Search for a Public Philosophy," 39.

46. Morris, *Dutch*, 309–10. Excerpts from a Reagan address to the California Fertilizer Association, November 10, 1958.

47. Reagan, *An American Life*, 142.

48. Reagan, *An American Life*, 120.

49. For an academic commentary on this multifaceted crisis, see Burnham, "The Reagan Heritage," 4–6.

50. See Reagan, *An American Life*, 217–19.

1

Reagan and American Political Discourse

IN 1978, HARVARD POLITICAL SCIENTIST Samuel Beer wrote an essay—which, though important, was little noted outside of academic circles—asserting the rather startling claim that America faced political "equilibrium without purpose. . . . We do not enjoy a public philosophy."[1] Since the mid-1960s, Beer argued, political philosophy had been supplanted by a "technocratic takeover," grounded in the Great Society hope of a "scientifically managed" polity.[2]

This claim was startling because the United States, as is often remarked, was the first country explicitly founded, sustained, and developed on account of a political idea. The Declaration of Independence and Constitution established the American civic creed, a creed based in natural rights and consisting of liberty, equality, limited government, and consent of the governed. The first party system and much of subsequent American political discourse was shaped by the Jeffersonian-Hamiltonian dialogue of the 1790s, pitting states' rights against nationalism, strict constitutional interpretation against broad interpretation, legislative supremacy against presidentialism, and idealism against realism on the world scene. To historian Daniel Boorstin, "We are either Jeffersonians or Hamiltonians. In no other country has the hagiography of politics been more important."[3] Yet by the mid-1960s, in the view of scholar Albert Fried, the politically preponderant new liberalism had "prided itself on its abandonment of ideology—its transcendence of both Hamiltonianism and Jeffersonianism."[4]

Beer and Fried were addressing two distinct but overlapping concerns. The first was that American political discourse, the language framing concrete political choices, was bankrupt, leaving Americans with a debate disconnected from the rich heritage of American political thought and history.

The second was that New Deal liberalism was no longer the dominant public philosophy—defined as the dominant political discourse plus a policy regime, control of the terms of debate, and consistent public support—but had not yet been replaced by a coherent alternative.

From another point of view, this era did not really signify the end of ideology, only its submersion. An alternative ideology—one that replaced the limits of the nation's founding with boundless confidence in the right and ability of central government to work its will in society—had become so imbedded in the political culture that most of the time it was effected without serious question. As a result, the philosophical big picture was largely removed from view, leaving only a series of incremental choices framed within the context of "compassion" and "problem solving." This incrementalism had arguably led Americans into a government far larger and more powerful than anything they would willingly have chosen had they been shown it in its entirety in 1932, when the Democratic platform called for a 25 percent cut in federal spending, a balanced budget, and states' rights. Furthermore, the incremental process was in many ways an automatic one, for which there seemed to be no single point of responsibility. By this interpretation, a fundamental transformation in the nature and ends of American government had taken place, without serious reference to the first principles of American politics. The theory of the Constitution had been changed, the traditional understanding supplanted by a new version not through formal amendment but through practical action and judicial redefinition. This new substantive version, which had left the old form deceptively intact, had been undertaken by politicians and activists who replaced one philosophy with another while touting the end of philosophy itself.

Whichever interpretation was correct, the implications were troublesome for American politics, which depends to no small degree on the legitimacy and structure conferred by its connection to the past. To be sure, the bankruptcy of political discourse under technocratic liberalism never went completely unchallenged; Barry Goldwater in 1964 and the New Left in the late 1960s each confronted it in their own ways. But Goldwater lost badly, and the New Left, representing what Samuel Beer called "the romantic revolt," was even farther removed than its target from the discourse with which most Americans were familiar and comfortable. Gerald Ford occasionally warned against overweening government, but he served only two years in an accidental presidency. Individual court justices and members of Congress fought rear-guard actions to keep traditional American political discourse alive, while the conservative intellectual movement labored for decades to lay the groundwork for a resurgence of that discourse. Yet there was no really powerful challenge to technocratic liberalism until Reagan.

When Ronald Reagan took office in January 1981, he and his supporters set for themselves no less a goal than to establish the dominance of a new public philosophy, a conservative philosophy in which the federal government would take a smaller role in American life and in which individuals, families, civil society, and state and local government would play a larger role. Political scientists observed in the 1980s that "the Reagan administration has been engaged in a whole-hearted effort to change the prevailing directions of thought about American domestic government."[5] A key element in this effort was Reagan's attempt to revive classical American political discourse, which he supplied to an extent not seen for a generation or more. Samuel Beer had concluded in his essay, published two years before Reagan's election, that "a great hinterland of common belief, the American political tradition, helps to hold conflicts within manageable limits and to enable exchange, economic and political, to flourish. The question is whether the nation will be able to elicit from this body of belief the forces of renewal constituting a new public philosophy."[6] Reagan's objective was to answer that challenge, to revitalize the discourse of the American political tradition in order to lead Americans to a new public philosophy.

Reagan's Political Discourse

Communication is of supreme importance to the modern presidency in general—Mary Stuckey refers to the office as the nation's "interpreter-in-chief"[7]—and it was central to Reagan's politics of freedom, for a variety of reasons. First, an appropriate political discourse is in itself an important part of the architecture of freedom that Reagan sought to bolster. As Reagan speechwriter William Ker Muir Jr. explained, "The fabric of a free society had constantly to be backed up with understanding."[8] Free societies have to be reminded of the importance of freedom and its prerequisites, a task that recent presidents had largely neglected. Furthermore, Reagan's rhetoric established the philosophical grounding for the policies his administration hoped to enact, and it held those policies together as a more or less coherent project. No attempt to promote a new public philosophy could succeed without such a framework. Finally, rhetoric was the one element of Reagan's strategy that he could carry out by himself. As Muir pointed out, "His messages to the people did not have to be authorized by Congress, or upheld by the Supreme Court, or executed by the bureaucracy."[9] Indeed, sometimes Reagan's rhetoric had to serve as a substitute for policy, when political resistance was too great to achieve more. No matter how Reagan's fortunes waxed or waned in other respects, rhetoric was the one constant. Altogether, Reagan sought to change the way Americans thought about government and society, a goal that could not be accomplished without a transformed discourse.

Reagan took great personal interest in the crafting of his public addresses, believing that words formulate ideas and that ideas drive politics. Indeed, "White House professional speechwriters found that Reagan remained the best craftsman among them."[10] He set basic rules for his speechwriters and did not hesitate to make revisions in their drafts. For example, Reagan extensively edited his speech of October 1983 on the Grenada and Lebanon crises, adding nine pages of handwritten changes, and he almost entirely rewrote the speechwriters' draft of his remarks on the destruction of KAL 007 by a Soviet warplane.[11] The ideas illuminated in Reagan's speeches were Reagan's own, which he had expressed consistently in a variety of venues for thirty years before he acquired a White House speechwriting staff. Any remaining doubts on that score were erased when a volume of Reagan's radio speeches was released in 2001 showing his personal drafts and extensive editing.[12] Indeed, one of his speechwriters, Tony Dolan, would remark that "the Reagan speechwriters' major function is to plagiarize the president's old speeches and give them back to him to say."[13]

Reagan made a concerted effort to promote entrepreneurship as a new kind of heroism. He once remarked that his greatest hope was "that this country remains a country where someone can always get rich"[14]—a comment cited by his opponents whenever they wanted to prove that his rhetoric encouraged greed, though it could also be interpreted as a call for opportunity. However, freedom remained to him, in his presidency no less than on the speaking circuit three decades before, the defining principle of America.[15] Reagan expressed his freedom-centered vision of the good life in his second inaugural address: "From new freedom will spring new opportunities for growth, a more productive, fulfilled, and united people, and a stronger America—an America that will lead the technological revolution and also open its mind and heart and soul to the treasures of literature, music, and poetry, and the values of faith, courage, and love."[16] Furthermore, Reagan's conception of freedom was neither the one offered by radical libertarians nor the one espoused by "positive government" egalitarians. Rather, his discourse sought to apply traditional American political discourse to modern problems.

Though it is not possible to precisely quantify the extent to which traditional discourse recovered in the 1980s from the depths of the technocratic takeover diagnosed by Samuel Beer, some rough measurements can be taken. The tables below help to illuminate the degree to which recent presidents took seriously the statesmen and ideas that had shaped the American republic.

A review of major Reagan addresses shows that they frequently included four or five references each to the American political tradition; in fourteen major addresses, he averaged more than three and a half such references. No other president in the previous quarter-century came close, with the exception of Gerald Ford's brief stint, coinciding with the bicentennial celebration. This statistical comparison conceals even greater qualitative differences: Most of Lyndon Johnson's, and many of Richard Nixon's and Ford's, references were perfunctory and vague. Johnson, for example, frequently mentioned pioneers as examples of hardiness who offered no concrete political guidance, while Nixon and Ford sprinkled their speeches with passing references to the upcoming bicentennial. Reagan was much more likely to use his references to the American political tradition to buttress specific positions of policy or philosophy. In his autobiography, Reagan mentions Thomas Jefferson, Abraham Lincoln, James Madison, and George Washington a total of eighteen times. Jimmy Carter in his memoirs refers to them seven times; Nixon, five times; and Johnson, a total of three times. Similarly, the index of Reagan's autobiography contains entries referring to the Constitution or constitutional principles ten times; the others alluded to them not once between them (see table 1.1).[17]

Altogether, in the words of his speechwriter Muir, Reagan was "seeking a rebirth of the idea of liberty in this country."[18] Ultimately, restoring the nation's habits of ordered liberty was the chief goal of his rhetoric. Consequently, Reagan systematically used his "bully pulpit" in the presidency to revitalize the traditional American political discourse of limited government, constitutionalism, democratic accountability, and individual responsibility—collectively the political foundation on which he believed free government and free society stand.

Limited Government

The theme of limited government was the most central to Reagan's discourse. Jefferson had asked in his first inaugural address, "What more is necessary to make us a happy and prosperous people?" His answer was "a wise and frugal government, which shall restrain men from injuring one another, which shall leave them otherwise free to regulate their own pursuits of industry and improvement,

TABLE 1.1
Presidential References to the American Political Tradition, 1963–1989

President	References per Major Address	"Big Four" in Memoirs*	Constitution in Memoirs
Johnson	1.2	3	0
Nixon	.9	5	0
Ford	3.3	10	0
Carter	.5	7	0
Reagan	3.7	18	10

*Washington, Jefferson, Madison, and Lincoln.
Source: *Public Papers of the Presidents of the United States*, presidential memoirs.

and shall not take from the mouth of labor the bread it has earned."[19] Reagan approvingly quoted Jefferson and consistently defended his own policies on similar philosophical grounds: The purpose of government, as the Declaration had said, was to protect life, liberty, and the pursuit of happiness. Government activity outside of that realm was at worst illegitimate, and at best a luxury that had to be justified by its proponents. He typically explained his abandonment of the Democratic Party, made formal in 1962, by reference to the Democrats' abandonment of Jeffersonian principles of limited government.[20]

Announcing his candidacy for the presidency in 1979, Reagan expressed his belief that the nation hungered "to see government once again the protector of our liberties, not the distributor of gifts and privilege."[21] For Reagan, to create a new government program or to expand an existing one was not an isolated decision but part of a broader question of the proper size and role of government in American society. "We must have the clarity of vision," Reagan said at the 1980 Republican convention, "to see the difference between what is essential and what is merely desirable; and then the courage to use this insight to bring our government back under control and make it acceptable to the people."[22] Reagan's goal was to stop the momentum of incrementalism and to force the polity to make a conscious, deliberate choice about how much government it wanted—not just in a particular case but in the aggregate. The growth of government had first been justified in the progressive era as a "countervailing power" to protect citizens against big business; Reagan proposed that new countervailing action might not be necessary to protect Americans against the big government that had resulted.

Reagan had mixed success promoting limited government in practice, as we will see in future chapters. This result owed itself in part to congressional resistance but also to Reagan's accommodation with many aspects of the welfare state; his limits were clearly less stringent than, say, Calvin Coolidge's or Herbert Hoover's. Nevertheless, it was a notable departure from the practice of recent presidents that Reagan, with considerable success, systematically sought to revise Americans' expectations from government in a downward direction; he aimed to convince Americans to depend less on the government and more on themselves and on each other, by reorienting Americans' view of themselves from beneficiaries to taxpayers.[23]

The rhetoric of limited government was applied to issues like tax cuts, deregulation, privatization of government services, selected spending projects, land management, and many others. In abolishing energy price controls, for example, Reagan remarked that "government exists to protect us from each other," not to allocate fuel or dictate prices.[24] Reagan's doctrine of limited government was not the same as anarchism or libertarianism, in that it conceded vigorous government to be necessary; that vigor, however, was to be circumscribed and ordered by reference to the proper functions of government. Consequently, increased defense spending could be promoted during the 1980s while cuts were being sought in many other programs. There was a genuine military threat emanating from the Soviet Union; further, Reagan (in the tradition of the Founders) argued that the defense of the nation was one of the core functions of an appropriately limited government, indeed its "prime responsibility."[25]

Ultimately, Reagan repeatedly argued, the burden of proof rested on those supporting larger and more powerful government. Further, limited government was both historically and logically connected to freedom and to a prosperous political economy, hence ultimately to human happiness, not only in America but as a universal principle. The idea of limited government was, for Reagan, to be supported for reasons both moral and practical, both political and economic, both positive and negative. Throughout his speeches, it appears as the surest guarantee of liberty, the best prospect for progress, and a necessary prerequisite for social strength and happiness. Only it could ensure sufficient room for individual development and produce consistent economic prosperity, dynamism, and social mobility. Limited government prevented bad things (tyranny and a corruption of both government and society chief among them) and promoted good things—like wealth, meritocracy, a strong civil society, and a hardy popular spirit. In the words of Reagan's 1988 State of the Union address, "We're for limited government, because we understand, as the Founding Fathers did, that it is the best way of ensuring personal liberty and empowering the individual so that every American of every race and region shares fully in the flowering of American prosperity and freedom."[26] Limited government could not promise utopia, nor did it seek to; precisely because it did not, it was less likely than unrestrained government to do harm and more likely to permit good.

Constitutionalism

Reagan's rhetorical theme of limited government was closely connected to the theme of constitutionalism. Reagan reintroduced to the public debate the idea that the federal government is a constitutional government of enumerated powers. He explicitly challenged the elite understanding of the Constitution that had dominated for decades—in essence, that the federal government could do anything that it considered prudent and desirable.

This emphasis on constitutionalism took several forms. One was a renewed consideration of the proper place of the federal government in the federal system—or, as James Madison had called it, the "compound republic."[27] This concern was very much a feature of Jeffersonianism; in his surreptitiously written Kentucky Resolutions, Jefferson had argued that the federal government was a creation of—and hence subordinate to—the states. Reagan made the argument that the states were constitutionally entitled to the powers not specifically enumerated to the federal government, pointing to the Tenth Amendment as evidence.

This important place of the states in the American system was called in *The Federalist* a "double security to the rights of the people."[28] Yet as Alexis de Tocqueville foresaw a century and a half before Reagan took office, centralization was the natural tendency of democracy. In his view, centralization would proceed more or less automatically, whereas decentralization could only survive as the "products of art."[29] By the end of the 1960s, the process of centralization in America was well advanced. Richard Nixon made a halfhearted effort at decentralization, but he justified it more on the basis of governmental efficiency than of constitutional imperative.

In contrast, Reagan threw the force of his rhetoric behind not only a practical but moral and constitutional defense of federalism.[30] In his view, "The federal government," in contravention of the Tenth Amendment, "has taken on functions which it was never intended to perform and which it does not perform well."[31] It was time to "restore constitutional government. Let us renew and enrich the power and purpose of States and local communities and let us return to the people those rights and duties that are justly theirs."[32] In short, Reagan announced, "This Administration has faith in State and local governments and the constitutional balance envisioned by the Founding Fathers."[33]

Reagan also voiced a more traditional constitutional view of rights. The view of rights predominant at the time of the founding had been that only the things with which a person is born—his life, his liberty, and his ability to acquire property through his labor—are natural rights. These rights are to be protected by government—indeed, this is the chief object of government—but government does not "grant" them through positive action, except perhaps through laws that formalize and facilitate property rights. Those property rights are central to liberty; the ability to acquire property through one's own labor, and to be secure in that property, is one of the most fundamental of human rights, the absence of which makes one in effect a slave.[34] Furthermore, to the Founders, rights inhered in individuals, not in groups. Equality under the law meant that each individual would be treated by the law as an individual, according to his own deserts. There would be no aristocracy but the "natural aristocracy of merit," no titles or curses to be handed down from father to son, and no collective guilt.

A competing conception of rights now holds that rights include an array of policy preferences that require positive governmental action to bring into being—the right to a job, a guaranteed income, housing, and health care, for example. These are sometimes referred to as "positive rights." This new view often sees property rights not as one of the fundamental human rights but as existing only in competition with them. Further, it holds rights to inhere largely in groups rather than individuals. Unlimited government, policies of group preference, and a condition of widespread popular dependence on the largesse of the state become, in this view, not threats to rights but collectively the very definition of them.[35] Reagan rejected this new vision of rights in favor of the old.

Civil rights was one area in which Reagan took an approach indicative of the older view of rights. Reagan was often criticized for being "anticivil rights," but in reality what he opposed was the group-based version of civil rights, favoring instead the more traditional version emphasizing the protection of individuals. To Reagan, "Their [the Democrats'] government sees people only as groups; ours serves all the people of America as individuals. . . . We believe in the uniqueness of each individual."[36] In this respect, his rhetoric was in the tradition of Justice John Marshall Harlan's celebrated dissent in *Plessy v. Ferguson*:

> There is no caste here. Our Constitution is color-blind, and neither knows nor tolerates classes among citizens. In respect of civil rights, all citizens are equal before the law. . . . The sure guaranty of the peace and security of each race is the clear, distinct, and unconditional recognition by our governments, national and state, of every right that inheres in civil freedom, and of the equality before the law of all citizens of the United States without regard to race.

In 1896, the issue was segregation; in the 1980s, it was a variety of affirmative action efforts that offered preferential treatment to women and racial minorities. Reagan voiced a commitment to a civil rights policy that punished specific acts of discrimination by individuals against individuals.

Since the issues of rights and of constitutional structure so often go to the courts, the judiciary and judicial philosophy became another arena for Reagan's rhetoric of constitutionalism. Reagan vowed to appoint judges who would fill what he considered their proper roles as interpreters of the Constitution rather than act as legislators who would reinvent the Constitution to suit their personal policy preferences.[37] Throughout the 1980s, Reagan's position stimulated a debate over the choices between judicial restraint and judicial activism, original meaning and judicial creativity. This debate forced Americans to consider not only the meaning of the Constitution but the role of the courts in their system, as well as the proper locus of constitutional interpretation. The bicentennial of the Constitution produced an long-running exchange between Attorney General Edwin Meese and Justice William Brennan over just these questions.[38]

Overall, Reagan emphasized the language and spirit of political self-restraint. As he argued, "It's time for Washington to show a little humility."[39] There were some things government should not do, even if they were tempting in the short term; there were some things the federal government should not do, because they were the province of the states; there were preferences or wants that should not be elevated to the status of rights; there were some things courts should not do, like exercising the policy-making powers of the elected branches. Ultimately, Reagan treated political self-restraint as the essence of constitutionalism, without which the words of the Constitution were only "parchment barriers." In doing so, he promoted with his rhetoric a certain kind of statesmanship that was as important as it was difficult to sustain, a statesmanship that ran counter to the self-indulgent tendencies of the modern era.

Democratic Accountability and Self-Government

The third overlapping theme of Reagan's presidential rhetoric was a return to democratic self-government. Reagan argued that the hidden, bureaucratic government of the administrative state, the centralization of governmental power in Washington, and the increasing tendency of courts to act as legislatures had combined to reduce seriously the control that the American people had over their own government. Democracy was being eroded; as Reagan argued in 1986, "Government growing beyond our consent had become a lumbering giant."[40] Reagan accordingly attempted to bolster the principle of consent of the governed and to enhance the American people's taste for self-government. In his 1980 campaign for the presidency, Reagan vowed to bring the unelected bureaucracy under control:

> Our leaders attempt to blame their failures on circumstances beyond their control, on false estimates made by unknown, unidentifiable experts. . . . I will not accept the supposed "wisdom" which has it that the federal bureaucracy has become so powerful that it can no longer be changed or controlled by any administration. As President I would use every power at my command to make the federal establishment respond to the will and the collective wishes of the people.[41]

The emphasis on decentralization was connected to this theme as well as to the theme of constitutionalism—that government closer to the people was more accessible to them. Reagan claimed when proposing his "new federalism" to Congress in 1982 that the program would strive to "make government again accountable to the people," by "mak[ing] our system of federalism work again."[42] Likewise, his emphasis on judicial restraint would restore the centrality of the elected branches. Further, Reagan, unlike his recent predecessors, urged constitutional amendment as a popular check on questionable judicial decisions. In general, he expressed a Jeffersonian faith in the ability of the people to govern themselves successfully. Reagan repeatedly quoted the maxim that "the people were not made to serve government; government was made to serve the people."

This call for a renewal of self-government did not consist only of an attack on bureaucrats, activist judges, and excessive centralization. It was also a positive call to the American people to "recapture our destiny, to take it into our own hands."[43] This summons was, in the broadest sense, a challenge to Americans to embrace the art of self-government at all levels of society: the nation, the state, the city, and the local school district, and also in the community and neighborhood, the church, the charity, and the other private associations that constitute civil society. It was, as his speechwriter Muir said, a call for Americans to participate in the "partnership" of their society.[44] Thus Reagan extolled not only limited government but its necessary corollary, a strong civil society and what he called a "community of shared values": religion, the family, work, neighborhood.[45]

Perhaps the most human manifestation of this rhetorical theme was Reagan's practice, begun in 1983, of introducing a citizen hero at his State of the Union address. One year the hero was a man who had swum through freezing water to rescue passengers of a crashed airliner; another year it was a soldier who had helped liberate Grenada; yet another year, a woman who started a home for infants of heroin addicts. This presentation of heroes helped to remind Americans that they were not passive extras in a drama the course of which was predetermined by insular elites or impersonal forces of history. Ordinary Americans made their own history, Reagan was saying. Their country was what they made of it.

Of course, democratic accountability taken to an extreme can conflict with constitutionalism and limited government. The Founders well understood and feared this tension between democracy and liberalism classically defined, but they believed it possible—indeed necessary—to construct a balance between them in which government was grounded in the people but subjected to limitations. They also believed (at any rate, hoped) that the constitution that emerged from the federal convention of 1787 had found that balance. As Reagan saw it at the beginning of the 1980s, the problem was not that one element was overcoming the other but that both were breaking down in favor of a third, alien principle—unlimited government run by "experts." Reagan thus sought to underscore rhetorically both original principles—democracy and classical liberalism.

Individual Responsibility

Finally, Reagan's rhetoric was aimed at restoring to the nation's discourse the notion of individual responsibility. People were to be freed from excessive and centralized government, but Reagan did not view liberty as license. He called repeatedly for a return to the traditional moral virtues that underpinned limited government in America but had been downplayed since the 1960s. Specifically, he extolled the importance of religion to American life, arguing (like George Washington, John Adams, and many others) that religion was an irreplaceable source of the morality necessary if a free society is to avoid self-destruction.[46] In 1984, Reagan argued that "without God, there is no virtue, because there's no prompting of the conscience. Without God, we're mired in the material, that flat world that tells us only what the senses perceive. Without God, there is a coarsening of the society. And without God, democracy will not and cannot long endure."[47] For this viewpoint he was scolded by critics like Sidney Blumenthal, who (when not attacking him for promoting materialism) derided Reagan for believing that "the crisis in the material world was only a manifestation of a spiritual crisis."[48]

Reagan eschewed the sociological behavioralism that had dominated discussion of morality for years, preferring instead more traditional notions. Those notions might be summarized in this way: Human beings have souls. The foundation of political liberty is a recognition that those souls have free will and must be allowed to exercise it. Human dignity requires us to consider those souls responsible for their choices, good and bad—and there *is* good and bad, not just value-neutral, situational alternatives. Ultimately, a polity cannot relieve its citizens of responsibility for the course of their own lives without losing its freedom and their dignity.

Accordingly, Reagan sought to "reinvigorate the assumption of individual responsibility."[49] Thus Reagan infused his language with insistence on individual responsibility and the nurturing of a common moral sense. He foreshadowed this theme of his presidency when he announced his candidacy: "We will uphold the principles of self-reliance, self-discipline, morality and—above all—responsible liberty for each individual."[50] Reagan "reinfused American discourse with 'the phenomenology of evil,'" and "made [Americans'] political and economic institutions understandable" again, by emphasizing the imperfection and imperfectibility of man.[51] At the same time, he saw as well the other side of free human will: the dignity inherent in the "divine spark," the capacity of man for heroism, goodness, and glory in the choices and acts of life.[52] Reagan rhetorically applied this understanding of the nature and meaning of human life to issues as wide-ranging as work and welfare, crime and punishment, the family, and relations with the Soviet Union. His speechwriter Muir felt that Reagan sought to use rhetoric to strengthen the "moral institutions" that nourish freedom.[53] George Will's view was that "rhetoric has been central to Reagan's presidency because Reagan has intended his statecraft to be soulcraft. His aim has been to restore the plain language of right and wrong, good and evil, for the purpose of enabling people to make the most of freedom."[54]

Social commentator Michael Novak, writing in 1985, contended that "the discussion of character was missing from American life for more than a generation. The nation's return to this discussion is one of the decisive events of the last 20 years."[55]

Reagan's Discourse of Liberty: Evaluations

Despite the broad appeal and evident influence of Reagan's political discourse, not all Americans were enamored of it. In a thoughtful academic critique, Jeffrey Tulis criticized Reagan's use of oratory as another step in the direction of a plebiscitary rather than constitutional presidency. A critique not so much of Reagan as of the whole development of the American presidency since at least Woodrow Wilson, Tulis's *The Rhetorical Presidency* raised the important question of whether the very use of presidential rhetoric, regardless of its content, undermines limited constitutional government.[56] Political scientist Hugh Heclo argued that the same attribute that made Reagan's rhetoric so widely appealing—his ability to tap into many varying strands of the American tradition—made it unlikely that an enduring public philosophy could be constructed from it. As Heclo saw him, Reagan stood for "antigovernment nationalism," "communitarian individualism," and "free market radicalism." If to a supporter these were only complexities and nuances, to a skeptic they were outright contradictions; in any event, they were not easy to hold together.

For some Americans Reagan's presidency was an exercise in empty rhetoric. "Great Communicator" became a form of backhanded compliment, implying sophistry or lack of substance. To Michael Riccards, Reagan was "the ultimate media president," whose success was attributable to "substituting images for ideas."[57] In this view, Reagan led the nation with a silver tongue that offered fantasy and myth as substitutes for reality. To some extent this is true of all gifted orators, one of whose chief characteristics is the ability to lift their listeners out of the gloom of crisis by offering a compelling picture of what could (and should) be. "Reality," after all, hardly provided fertile ground for the optimism of Franklin Roosevelt, the defiance of Winston Churchill, or the magnanimity of Abraham Lincoln. In any case, national and international events since 1980 do not provide much evidence that those making this charge had a stronger grip on reality than did Reagan.

On the other hand, some analysts of Reagan's rhetoric had no doubt that it was embued with substance; they simply did not like the substance. For example, Robert E. Denton and Dan F. Hahn accused Reagan of contributing to the supposedly unique greed and selfishness of the era, arguing that his metaphorical language appealed to "a selfish, narcissistic, yuppie-dominated

society where everybody is looking out for self."[58] As a *New Republic* columnist, Sidney Blumenthal endorsed that line of argument by asserting that
"[Reagan's] free-market rhetoric gives a license to unfettered consumption."[59]
However, as has been discussed, there is little reason to believe that the era was
uniquely selfish or greedy. Indeed, it is hardly unusual for presidential candidates to emphasize economic issues in their campaigns. Bill Clinton won in
1992 by promising improved economic performance; he won reelection in
1996 by claiming credit for a strong economy. His strategists in the 1992 campaign made a point of reminding each other that the overriding issue was "the
economy, stupid." In fact, for more than a century, presidential contests have
ridden at least partially on the question of which candidate the voters thought
most likely to maintain or regain national prosperity. To the extent that Reagan's successful appeal *was* an economic appeal in 1980 or 1984, it was no
more indicative of national greed than William McKinley's appeal in the
1890s (the "full dinner pail" for every working man), Herbert Hoover's in
1928 (two cars in every garage and a chicken in every pot), Franklin D. Roosevelt's in the 1930s (which certainly did not downplay issues of personal finance), Harry S Truman's in the 1940s, John F. Kennedy's in the 1960s, Jimmy
Carter's in the 1970s, or Clinton's in the 1990s. In any event, as we have seen,
prosperity was not the chief subject of Reagan's rhetoric.

A more serious criticism is that Reagan's "attack on government" was (in
the words of historian Arthur M. Schlesinger Jr.) "a disaster for the Republic."[60] Correspondent Elizabeth Drew claimed that with Reagan's leadership
came "an antigovernment mood, a negativity about government itself, for
which the country is still paying a price."[61] Haynes Johnson charged more directly that Reagan's deprecation of the ability of government to solve problems "contributed to more cynicism."[62] Yet such a cost is easier to assert than
to identify. As we will see in chapter 3, cynicism and distrust of government
went down, not up, in the 1980s, by virtually every measure. Indeed, some analysts have suggested that people had *more* confidence in government precisely
because they could be more certain that government leaders had regained
some much-needed humility. This line of attack is really an argument that
Reagan was wrong: wrong about the nature of freedom, wrong about the limited capacities of government, wrong about the dangers of centralization,
wrong about looking to our "anachronistic" political tradition for solutions. It
was not likely Reagan's rhetoric these critics found most worrisome but the
prospect of a new public philosophy growing from the soil of that rhetoric.

In truth, Reagan's rhetoric was not opposed to government per se but to
what he perceived to be the excessive growth and illegitimate scope of government. In rejecting the overgrown claims of the federal government before
1980, Reagan's discourse was firmly in keeping with the tradition of Patrick

Henry, Thomas Paine, Samuel Adams, Thomas Jefferson, and indeed virtually the entire leadership of the American Revolution. He held, as they did, that liberty depends in no small measure on a healthy skepticism of the capacities of government; power, once delegated by the people to the state, is rarely reclaimed. In the end, what observers like Schlesinger and Drew disliked about Reagan's rhetoric was exactly what made it so important to Reagan's project: It asserted the primacy of freedom, and it bypassed the proposition that the Founders had little of worth to tell us today.

Indeed, much of Reagan's political success can be attributed to the way in which he wove together strands of the Jeffersonianism and Hamiltonianism that constitute the bedrock of American political thought. If Reagan was a Jeffersonian in his emphasis on limited government, states' rights, and free trade, he was a Hamiltonian in his exaltation of a dynamic commercial society, his respect for tradition and religion, and his vigorous use of the presidency to promote a legislative agenda and safeguard the nation's interests abroad. In the conduct of foreign affairs, as we will see, Reagan adopted Hamilton's hard-headed, power-oriented means, but he largely put them to the service of Jefferson's ends and frame of analysis. Reagan, like Jefferson, believed that bad regimes rather than mere struggles of interest were the source of conflict in the world, and that the gradual extension of the realm of freedom was the best hope for peace. On balance, Reagan tilted toward Jefferson, but he embraced the most popular aspects of Hamiltonianism, like dynamic commerce, vigorous presidential leadership, and tempered traditionalism.[63] Ultimately, Reagan had a greater affinity for both Jefferson and Hamilton than the "new liberals" of the Great Society had for either.

As Reagan challenged the technocratic ethos, he produced a political and intellectual debate over first principles that American politics had long been missing. Even the skeptic Hugh Heclo conceded that "Reaganism appears to tap the essential consensus in our long-standing political tradition. It seems to dispel the mood of impending disintegration in the country's political ideas. And in between the tradition and the mood, Reaganism seems to offer a more structured sense of the argument between individualistic and communitarian visions."[64] As Reagan speechwriter Peggy Noonan argued, "Ronald Reagan spent the eighties reminding us of things we used to know and had forgotten, and telling much of the world what it didn't quite know and might find useful. . . . The eighties marked a revolution in thought, a re-finding of old truths."[65]

In the end, Reagan returned the traditional discourse of American liberty to the realm of everyday politics, and he substantially reconnected that discourse to policy, as we will see in subsequent chapters. As William Ker Muir argued, the president "set out to define a philosophy of freedom, to distinguish it from a philosophy of equality [of condition], and to plant it in the soul of the nation. Virtually all of Reagan's domestic policy achievements either ended in that moral goal or proceeded from it."[66] This translation of discourse into popular debate and practical policy will now be examined, starting with Reagan's approach to constitutionalism.

Notes

1. Samuel Beer, "In Search of a New Public Philosophy," in *The New American Political System*, ed. Anthony King (Washington, D.C.: American Enterprise Institute [hereafter AEI], 1978), 44.

2. Beer, "In Search of a New Public Philosophy," 18–22.

3. Daniel J. Boorstin, *The Genius of American Politics* (Chicago: University of Chicago Press, 1953), 16–17.

4. Albert Fried, *The Jeffersonian and Hamiltonian Traditions in American Politics* (Garden City, N.Y.: Doubleday, 1968), 503.

5. Hugh Heclo, "Reaganism and the Search for a Public Philosophy," in *Perspectives on the Reagan Years*, ed. John J. Palmer (Washington, D.C.: Urban Institute, 1986), 31.

6. Beer, "In Search of a New Public Philosophy," 44.

7. Mary Stuckey, *The President as Interpreter-in-Chief* (Chatham, N.J.: Chatham House, 1991).

8. William Ker Muir Jr., *The Bully Pulpit: The Presidential Leadership of Ronald Reagan* (San Francisco: ICS, 1992), 11.

9. Muir, *The Bully Pulpit*, 13–14.

10. William E. Pemberton, *Exit with Honor: The Life and Presidency of Ronald Reagan* (Armonk, N.Y.: M. E. Sharpe, 1999), 204.

11. Pemberton, *Exit with Honor*, 204; Ronald Reagan, *An American Life: The Autobiography* (New York: Simon and Schuster, 1990), 246, 583–84.

12. Kiron K. Skinner, Annelise Anderson, and Martin Anderson, eds., *Reagan in His Own Hand: The Writings of Ronald Reagan That Reveal His Revolutionary Vision for America* (New York: Free Press, 2001).

13. Quoted in Muir, *The Bully Pulpit*, 74.

14. R. W. Apple Jr., "New Stirrings of Patriotism," *New York Times Magazine*, December 11, 1983, 140.

15. On this point, see Muir, *The Bully Pulpit*, 143–55.

16. "Inaugural Address, January 21, 1985," *Public Papers of the President: Ronald Reagan 1985* (Washington, D.C.: Government Printing Office [hereafter GPO], 1988), 56.

17. See Reagan, *An American Life*; Jimmy Carter, *Keeping Faith* (New York: Bantam, 1982); Gerald R. Ford, *A Time to Heal* (New York: Harper and Row, 1979); Richard M. Nixon, *RN: The Memoirs of Richard Nixon* (New York: Grosset and Dunlap, 1978); and Lyndon Baines Johnson, *The Vantage Point: Perspectives on the Presidency, 1963–1969* (New York: Holt, Rinehart and Winston, 1970).

18. Muir, *The Bully Pulpit*, 177.

19. See "First Inaugural Address," March 4, 1801, in *The Portable Thomas Jefferson*, ed. Merrill D. Peterson (New York: Viking, 1975), 293.

20. Reagan, *An American Life*, 119, 134–35, 325.

21. Ronald Reagan, address announcing his candidacy for the presidency, New York, November 13, 1979.

22. "Acceptance Speech by Governor Ronald Reagan," Republican National Convention, Detroit, Michigan, July 17, 1980.

23. See Benjamin Ginsberg and Martin Shefter, "The Presidency, Interest Groups, and Social Forces: Creating a Republican Coalition," in *The Presidency and the Political System*, ed. Michael Nelson, 3rd ed. (Washington, D.C.: Congressional Quarterly, 1990), 341–43.

24. Reagan, address announcing his candidacy for the presidency.

25. "Address before a Joint Session of Congress on the State of the Union, January 25, 1984," *Public Papers of the Presidents: Ronald Reagan 1984* (Washington, D.C.: GPO, 1987), 88.

26. "Address before a Joint Session of Congress on the State of the Union, January 25, 1988," *Public Papers of the Presidents: Ronald Reagan 1988* (Washington, D.C.: GPO, 1990), 85.

27. James Madison, *Federalist* 39.

28. *Federalist* 51. While the Founders rejected the proposal that the Tenth Amendment include the phrase "expressly" delegated to the federal government, several of the Federalist Papers clearly state that the federal government will be one of enumerated powers and that all other responsibilities will be left to the states, leaving the states in a very strong position in the system. See *Federalist* 14, 17, 39, 45.

29. Alexis de Tocqueville, *Democracy in America* (New York: Vintage , 1945), vol. 2, 313.

30. On both occasions in Reagan's autobiography that he discusses the general topic of the role of the states, it is in terms of "the rights and powers granted to them in the Constitution." Reagan, *An American Life*, 198, 220.

31. Reagan, address announcing his candidacy for the presidency.

32. "Remarks in Atlanta, Georgia, at the Annual Convention of the National Conference of State Legislatures, July 30, 1981," *Public Papers of the Presidents of the United States: Ronald Reagan 1981* (Washington, D.C.: GPO, 1982), 683.

33. "Address before a Joint Session of Congress Reporting on the State of the Union, January 26, 1982," *Public Papers of the Presidents: Ronald Reagan 1982* (Washington, D.C.: GPO, 1983), 76.

34. Thomas G. West, *Vindicating the Founders: Race, Sex, Class, and Justice in the Origins of America* (Lanham, Md.: Rowman & Littlefield, 1997), 37–70.

35. For a candid exposition of this new view, see Jennifer Nedelsky, *Private Property and the Limits of American Constitutionalism* (Chicago: University of Chicago Press, 1990). A good example of this view of rights in action would be the dissent offered by Justice Thurgood Marshall in *Harris v. McRae* (1980), in which he argued that federal funding for abortions was a constitutional right.

36. "Remarks Accepting the Presidential Nomination of the Republican National Convention in Dallas, Texas, August 23, 1984," *Public Papers of the Presidents: Ronald Reagan 1984* (Washington, D.C.: GPO, 1986), 1174, 1179.

37. Ronald Reagan, "At the Investiture of Chief Justice William H. Rehnquist and Associate Justice Antonin Scalia at the White House, September 26, 1986, Washington, D.C.," in *The Great Debate: Interpreting Our Written Constitution* (Washington, D.C.: Federalist Society, 1986), 53–56.

38. *The Great Debate*, 1–25.

39. "State of the Union, January 25, 1988," 87.

40. "Address before a Joint Session of Congress on the State of the Union, February 4, 1986," *Public Papers of the Presidents: Ronald Reagan 1986* (Washington, D.C.: GPO, 1988), 126.

41. Reagan, address announcing his candidacy for the presidency.

42. "State of the Union, January 26, 1982," 75.

43. "Acceptance Speech by Governor Ronald Reagan."

44. Muir, *The Bully Pulpit*, chap. 5.

45. See Reagan, address announcing his candidacy for the presidency; "Acceptance Speech by Governor Ronald Reagan."

46. Muir, *The Bully Pulpit*, 125–41.

47. "Remarks at an Ecumenical Prayer Breakfast in Dallas, Texas, August 23, 1984," *Public Papers of the Presidents: Ronald Reagan 1984* (Washington, D.C.: GPO, 1986), 1167–68.

48. Sidney Blumenthal, *Our Long National Daydream* (New York: Harper and Row, 1988), 123.

49. Muir, *The Bully Pulpit*, 69.

50. Reagan, address announcing his candidacy for the presidency.

51. Muir, *The Bully Pulpit*, 74–75.

52. Muir, *The Bully Pulpit*, chap. 6.

53. Muir, *The Bully Pulpit*, chap. 10.

54. George F. Will, "How Reagan Changed America," *Newsweek*, January 9, 1989, 17.

55. "The State of American Values," *U.S. News & World Report*, December 9, 1985, 58.

56. Jeffrey L. Tulis, *The Rhetorical Presidency* (Princeton, N.J.: Princeton University Press, 1987).

57. Michael Riccards, *The Ferocious Engine of Democracy: A History of the American Presidency* (New York: Madison, 1995), vol. 2, 344.

58. Robert E. Denton Jr. and Dan F. Hahn, *Presidential Communication: Description and Analysis* (New York: Praeger, 1986), 70.

59. Blumenthal, *Our Long National Daydream*, 107.

60. Arthur M. Schlesinger Jr., "The Ultimate Approval Rating," *New York Times Magazine*, December 15, 1996, 51.

61. Elizabeth Drew, *The Corruption of American Politics* (Secaucus, N.J.: Birch Lane, 1999), 159.

62. Haynes Johnson, *Sleepwalking through History: America in the Reagan Years* (New York: W. W. Norton, 1991), 455.

63. For example, Reagan cites Jefferson nine times in his autobiography *An American Life*, but Hamilton not at all. For an extensive treatment of this subject, see Andrew E. Busch, "Ronald Reagan's Public Philosophy: Strands of Jefferson and Hamilton," in *Ronald Reagan's America*, ed. Eric J. Schmertz, Natalie Datlof, and Alexej Ugrinsky (Westport, Conn.: Greenwood, 1997), vol. 1, 41–53.

64. Heclo, "Reaganism and the Search for a Public Philosophy," 48.

65. Peggy Noonan, *What I Saw at the Revolution: A Political Life in the Reagan Era* (New York: Random House, 1990), 344.

66. Muir, *The Bully Pulpit*, 14.

2

Reagan and the Constitution

A T THE CENTER OF RONALD REAGAN'S VIEW of limited government and American freedom lay his conception of the Constitution and what had happened to it in the twentieth century. To Reagan, the Constitution of 1787 was
an inspired document establishing the indispensable political framework for
a free society.[1] Indeed, he often used architectural language to describe the
Constitution—it was "the architecture of democratic government," "the very
foundation of our Republic," and "our blueprint for freedom."[2] It formed a
system, comprising several key components, for constraining the power of
government. Separation of powers aimed at preventing an excessive concentration of power within the federal government. Provisions guaranteeing individual rights were found in both the Bill of Rights and the main body of the
Constitution. The idea of enumeration of powers, found in Article I, Section
8, established the specific areas reserved for federal action, and by implication
it limited federal action to those areas. What the enumeration of powers did
not grant to the central government—and much of what governments do was
not granted—was reserved to the states within the federal system. The federal
judiciary existed to interpret the Constitution as it was written and intended
(otherwise, Reagan reasoned, why have a written Constitution?), to exercise—
as Alexander Hamilton had said—"judgment, not will."

As Reagan and other conservatives saw it, this constitutional order had been
significantly weakened. The emerging administrative state had often subsumed
democratic accountability and self-government under the claims of expert
competence. Separation of powers was weakened, as administrative agencies
like the Federal Trade Commission, the Environmental Protection Agency, and

the Occupational Safety and Health Administration were increasingly given effective power to legislate. Congress assumed the role of administrative ombudsman; indeed, by the 1970s, a common explanation given for the increased advantage accruing to incumbency was that members of Congress had largely traded legislating for constituency service.[3] Federal courts had increasingly substituted their wills for those of elected representatives on matters that were arguably more of a policy than constitutional character, ranging from school integration to abortion. Both federalism and the doctrine of enumerated powers suffered, as the federal government expanded with little concern for legitimate constitutional authorization. In Reagan's view,

> We had strayed a great distance from our founding fathers' vision of America: They regarded the central government's responsibility as that of providing national security, protecting our democratic freedoms, and limiting the government's intrusion into our lives—in sum, the protection of life, liberty, and the pursuit of happiness. They never envisioned vast agencies in Washington telling our farmers what to plant, our teachers what to teach, our industries what to build. The Constitution they wrote established sovereign states, not administrative districts of the federal government.[4]

Both Reagan's interpretation of the Constitution and his interpretation of the decline of constitutionalism in the 1900s were, of course, open to dispute. Constitutional-law scholars and historians could point out that the Constitution of 1787 had represented a shift to a stronger central authority than had existed before, in the Articles of Confederation. They could, indeed, argue persuasively that Reagan's view of the origin of the Constitution—the essentially Jeffersonian conception that it was a compact among sovereign states— was incomplete, omitting the important ways that state governments were downgraded in the Constitution and were bypassed in the ratification process. For that matter, the doctrine of original intent was often easier to support than to apply, given the variety of viewpoints held by the Founders themselves on a number of issues. Nevertheless, fundamentally, Reagan had the better argument. The federal convention had proposed, and the nation had ratified, a constitution that was clearly conceived to be a document expressing a limited grant of power from the people to the central government. In the form of the so-called Virginia and Hamilton Plans, the convention was twice given the opportunity to propose a new system that would have radically expanded the power of the center, effectively reduced the states to complete subservience, and left to Congress alone the determination of how far to extend its own legislative reach. Both times it declined. A measure of the degree to which Reagan was right about the original meaning of the Constitution could be found in the nature of many of the arguments against him—essentially, that the original intent of the framers was irrelevant, because the Constitution was a "living document."

To Reagan, the Constitution was indeed a living document but could only remain so if its meaning was predictable from day to day. Though it had to be flexible enough to meet unforeseen circumstances, a basic document without a reasonably fixed meaning could hardly be called basic and would be unable to constrain government and establish the rule of law. Indeed, Reagan quoted James Madison as declaring that if "the sense in which the Constitution was accepted and ratified by the nation is not the guide to expounding it, there can be no security for a faithful exercise of its powers."[5] Furthermore, Reagan believed—consistent with views held by Thomas Jefferson and Abraham Lincoln—that the Supreme Court is not the sole expositor of the meaning of the Constitution. Rather, each branch has a right and duty to participate in constitutional interpretation.[6] Consequently, throughout his presidency, Reagan sought in the realm of policy to rebuild the essential principles of constitutionalism as he saw them. He had mixed results, but overall, his attempt to put constitutionalism back on the public agenda had the effect of revitalizing important constitutional principles.

Enumerated Powers

In the broadest sense, Reagan attempted to restore a constitutional view of the United States government as a limited government of specifically enumerated powers that would concentrate its efforts upon subjects of undoubted national scope, like defense, diplomacy, and the facilitation of commerce. Reagan aimed at relegitimizing this conception, which had been out of favor since at least the New Deal. In his view, fidelity to the enumerated powers was what made America's constitution unique. In other constitutions, "the government tells the people what they can do." Ours, on the other hand was "one in which we the people tell the Government what it can do, and it can do nothing other than what is prescribed in that document."[7] Implicit in this emphasis was a nonjudicially driven mode of constitutional interpretation; Reagan was, in essence, calling on the elected branches to enforce the enumeration of powers by self-restraint.

If measured simply by the absolute size and scope of federal activity at the end of his presidency—or a decade later—this project was a clear failure. No one could argue that Congress or Reagan (much less his successors) operated in practice as if the doctrine of enumerated powers offered a literal guide to action. Yet this abject failure should not obscure important successes achieved by Reagan. It was one thing to restore American government to the shape that it might have taken had enumerated powers been faithfully observed in the half-century before he took office. That reconstruction would have been painful and probably politically suicidal, as Reagan understood. It was quite another to apply the logic and the metaphor of enumerated powers to proposals for additional government, or to relatively recent and unentrenched accretions to federal power. It was the latter task that Reagan sought to, and substantially did, achieve.

First and foremost, he accomplished this through the domestic spending reductions that he achieved in his first year and the spending restraint that was applied thereafter. Few significant reductions were achieved (or even sought) in the large and popular entitlement programs. Other programs—especially the recent social welfare programs of the Great Society—were targeted, and some were trimmed significantly. The logic of the doctrine of the enumeration of powers also guided the reordering of federal spending priorities. Defense—to Reagan, the most crucial function of any limited government—was given a larger share of the federal pie, while domestic spending (especially the discretionary domestic spending, within relatively easy political control) fell as a percentage of federal spending. Finally, the limitation of federal revenue achieved through tax cuts and tax reform, though not as severe as claimed by critics who blamed it for the federal deficits of the 1980s, nevertheless forced something of a prioritization of federal programs. No longer were proponents of spending able to escape the burden of defending it in reference to the essential functions of government.

Taken together, these three elements of fiscal policy partially revived the spirit, though not the letter, of enumeration of powers, by changing the rules of the game. Before 1980, the burden of proof was on those resisting the expansion of the federal government; during the Reagan years, it was on those seeking the expansion. In this respect, as political scientist James Ceaser has pointed out, the Reagan administration installed a new theory of governance: Refraining from acting was a legitimate, and often preferable, option for the federal government.[8] The elections of 1994 and the budget-cutting efforts of the 104th Congress demonstrated not only that the vision of a limited government of enumerated powers that Reagan had resuscitated was still alive, but also that it still faced enormous obstacles in moving from theory to practice.

Better evidence that Reagan started a meaningful reconsideration of enumerated powers lay in the gradual movement of the Supreme Court toward his view in the years after he left office. In two major cases, *United States v. Lopez* (1995) and *United States v. Morrison* (2000), the Court ruled that Congress had overstepped its bounds by passing federal laws that stretched the commerce clause of the enumerated powers beyond recognition.[9] In his *Lopez* decision, Chief Justice William Rehnquist argued that it was a "first principle" that "the Constitution creates a federal government of enumerated powers." Though only a tentative step, *Lopez* represented the first time since the 1930s that the Supreme Court had read Article I, Section 8, of the U.S. Constitution as a meaningful limitation on the scope of federal authority.[10]

Separation of Powers

"The accumulation of all powers, legislative, executive, and judiciary, in the same hands," James Madison intoned in *Federalist* 47, "may justly be pronounced the very definition of tyranny."[11] With that dictum in mind, Reagan and his administration attempted to strengthen the fundamental principle of separation of powers. They took as their starting point the belief that Congress in the 1970s had replaced the formerly "imperial" presidency as the source of hegemonic impulses in American politics. As evidence, they pointed to congressional enactments like the War Powers Act of 1973, which sought to constrain presidential use of military force; the Budget and Impoundment Control Act of 1974, which asserted greater congressional control over the budget process; and various intrusions of Congress into the foreign-intelligence-gathering process.[12] More general evidence might have been the degree to which numerous commentators had declared the presidency to be in a state of decline (a phenomenon that will be discussed in greater detail in chapter 3). For their part, the congressional majorities that had chosen to challenge the presidency in the 1970s had argued that they were merely re-asserting legitimate congressional prerogatives that Congress had forsaken from the 1930s on.

Given both an institutional divide and a partisan divide, Reagan vigorously sought to exert presidential authority. As we will see in the next chapter, he was largely successful at restoring the prestige of the presidency. In domestic affairs, Reagan often tried to bypass Congress with an "administrative presidency" strategy that relied heavily on executive orders and bureaucratic decision making. In foreign policy, like his predecessors and successors, Reagan mostly refused to acknowledge the binding nature of the War Powers Act; on several occasions he sent U.S. forces into harm's way without effective congressional consultation. Reagan also successfully insisted, for the first time, on the inclusion of presidential signing statements in the official legislative records used for later judicial interpretation of statutes. To his defenders, this pattern demonstrated a Reagan who was merely acting in the mold of strong presidents who refused to allow Congress to define unilaterally the nature of their relationship.[13] However, the most egregious case, the Iran-Contra episode, revealed a troubling willingness simply to overrule Congress administratively. In that instance, both the president's critics and many of his supporters agreed that his administration had gone beyond the legitimate defense of presidential prerogatives—an essential underpinning of separation of powers—to a trivialization of the legislative branch that if generalized would tend toward the destruction of separation of powers. Some critics, like Nancy Kassop, went farther, accusing Reagan and his administration, on the basis not just of Iran-Contra but its entire separation-of-powers policy, of instituting "The Arrogant Presidency" and "wag[ing] war on the separation of powers principle and its corollary of checks and balances."[14]

To Reagan, separation of powers also meant encouraging the federal judiciary to perform its proper constitutional role rather than encroaching on the lawmaking and enforcement duties of the legislative and executive branches. To this end, he adopted a judicial strategy (to be discussed in detail below) that produced substantial and ongoing results. At the same time, he sought to limit the power of the judiciary, by invoking one of the few constitutional checks that exist against judicial power: the Constitutional amendment. Reagan supported a number of proposed amendments, many (though not all) of which were intended to undo a variety of socially liberal court decisions, like the ban on school prayer and the *Roe v. Wade* abortion case. In these attempts, which were uniformly unsuccessful, Reagan departed from the practice of most recent presidents.

Reagan's administration also had an important long-term impact on the theory of separation of powers. Three major separation-of-powers cases were decided in the 1980s, and in each the administration sought to bolster a more traditional view of the subject based on a more distinct separation of branches. In two of the three cases, the administration pressed and won arguments before the Supreme Court arguing that Congress had overstepped its bounds by intertwining itself too much with the executive role.[15] In the third case, the administration lost in the Court but won in the long run in Congress itself.

That third issue was the independent-counsel provision of the 1978 Ethics in Government Act, a provision that the administration believed was an unconstitutional breach of separation of powers. In words that later echoed loudly at the height of the Clinton impeachment fight, Reagan's second attorney general, Edwin Meese III, warned that the independent-counsel statute was a "major threat to constitutional government" and a "bureaucratic Frankenstein," with "its unprecedented statutory scheme and its breaching of the traditional separation of powers." Meese contended that

> once set up in business, independent counsels are effectively answerable to no one. They are free to spend millions of dollars of taxpayers' money to see if they can find any grounds whatever for prosecuting a given individual, or group of individuals, on an open-ended basis. . . . The post of independent counsel thus

hangs in organizational space—supposedly tied to other agencies of government, but in practical reality responsible to no one. . . . Government by independent counsel is clearly akin to government by judiciary—an effort to rule outside the normal framework of our constitutional system, beyond the limits of accountability.[16]

Other administration officials, including Reagan's first attorney general, William French Smith, also spoke out against the provision.[17] Partly because so many Reagan administration officials had run afoul of the Ethics in Government Act, reducing the administration's credibility on this issue, and partly because the Democrats who then controlled Congress suffered a lack of imagination in perceiving how the law might someday be turned against them, such warnings fell on deaf ears; Congress reauthorized the act in 1987. When Reagan signed the reauthorization, he noted that the independent-counsel provision "raises constitutional issues of the most fundamental and enduring importance to the Government of the United States. . . . I am taking the extraordinary step of signing this bill despite my very strong doubts about its constitutionality."[18] One year later, despite the arguments of the administration's solicitor general, the Supreme Court ruled in *Morrison v. Olson* that the independent-counsel provision did not violate separation of powers. However, in 1999, after the national trauma of impeachment, Congress quietly allowed the statute to expire, amidst a general consensus that Reagan had, after all, been right.

Altogether, Reagan enjoyed considerable success in promoting his conception of separation of powers, though some of that success did not come until after he left office. To the extent that Congress had overstepped its bounds in the 1970s, Reagan restored balance, but in at least one case and possibly others his administration arguably went too far in denying Congress its proper role. The administration's more traditional theory of separation of powers was increasingly ascendant. Even its critique of the independent-counsel statute, which failed to have any impact in the short term, laid the groundwork for changes a decade later, as did Reagan's large number of judicial appointments.

Individual Rights

The administration's approach to issues concerning the protection of individual rights consisted of support for rights clearly anchored in the Constitution, substantial skepticism toward the new rights discovered by courts in the recent past, and outright hostility toward the group orientation that the administration believed had supplanted individual rights in contemporary civil rights policy. Consequently, Reagan came under sustained fire from both civil libertarians and civil rights organizations.

Those individual rights the administration saw as grounded in the text and philosophy of the Constitution and the traditions of the United States received stronger support from Reagan than from most recent presidents. Those included, for example, property rights, freedom of religious expression, and Second Amendment rights to keep and bear arms. Freedom of the press was also strengthened by an administration decision to end the "fairness doctrine," by which radio and television stations that aired editorials were required to air opposing views as well.[19] Many of these rights had been conceived by the framers as having a dual significance. On their faces, they were guarantees of individual rights; at the same time, they were also parts of the structural architecture of freedom. For example, a free press helps maintain governmental accountability, while property rights, aside from protecting the fruits of an individual's labor, promote a decentralized society.[20] Gun rights, in the view of the framers, were a last line of defense against tyrannical government.[21] In short, the administration gave preference to those rights that most seemed to undergird the architecture of American freedom.

On the other hand, recent innovations in rights imposed by federal courts were generally viewed by the administration as defective in two ways. First, they altered the balance between individual rights and community consent, in favor of a radical individualism. Second, many of them could not actually be found in the text of the Constitution but had come into existence only though judicial fiat and, in Reagan's view, usurpation. Such rights included abortion on demand, First Amendment protections for pornography, and the inadmissibility of confessions obtained without having first informed the suspect of his or her right to remain silent (the Miranda rule). Against these rights Reagan's administration waged a persistent struggle.[22]

His opposition to the *Roe v. Wade* abortion ruling was much remarked upon and does not need much elaboration. In two specific abortion cases, the administration explicitly asked the court (unsuccessfully) to overturn *Roe*.[23] Midway through his presidency, Reagan also appointed a commission to develop federal approaches to fight pornography. The commission's argument that numerous social dangers were associated with pornography led to the creation of an Obscenity Enforcement Unit in the Criminal Division of the Justice Department, as well as to congressional legislation, the development of model statutes for use by the states, and an increase in investigations and prosecutions at all levels of government.[24] At the same time, the administration sought to modify the impact of the rulings on the rights of criminal defendants. As Meese later argued,

The Reagan administration repeatedly tried to combat unreasonable restrictions on the use of truthful evidence in a criminal trial. . . . [B]oth the President and I believed strongly in preserving the rights of all persons accused of crime, and we upheld the constitutional protections against arrogant and arbitrary actions by governmental authorities of any sort. But we believed that this could be effectively accomplished without an endless series of court-invented obstacles that defied common sense, obscured truth, and frustrated justice.[25]

Some analysts ultimately perceived in some decisions by the Rehnquist Court a wholesale assault on the Fourth Amendment itself, an assault that belied Meese's assurances. Even if overstated, those concerns opened the question of whether Reagan may have set in motion a response that went too far in compensating for earlier judicial invention. On this issue alone is Reagan vulnerable to plausible charges that he trespassed on the clear language and intent of the Constitution respecting individual rights. Even here, though, the evidence is not conclusive.

When it came to civil rights, the Reagan administration took a relatively hard line against quotas, set-asides, and timetables. Reagan argued that "any quota system based on race, religion, or color is immoral. . . . I consider quotas, whether they favor blacks or whites, men or women, to be a new form of discrimination as bad as the old ones."[26] Meese expressed the belief that affirmative action, as it had developed, "went directly against two basic principles of a free society: that people are to be treated equally under the law, irrespective of who they are; and that advancement should be based on merit, rather than on racial, ethnic, or other distinctions."[27] William Bradford Reynolds, the controversial Assistant Attorney General for Civil Rights, declared,

I think we should bring the behavior of the government on all levels into line with the idea of according equal opportunity for all individuals without regard to race, color, or ethnic background. In my view this means that we should remove whatever kind of race- or gender-conscious remedies and techniques that exist in the regulatory framework to ensure that the remedies that are put in place are sensitive to the non-discrimination mandate that is in the laws.[28]

In light of this view, Reagan pursued a two-pronged approach to civil rights. The "group rights" approach was downgraded. Reagan supported legislation, which passed the Senate but not the House, that would have severely limited forced busing. Secretary of Labor Raymond Donovan issued new guidelines that had the effect of exempting almost 75 percent of federal contractors from affirmative-action jurisdiction.[29] In more than fifty cases, the Justice Department tried to convince courts to eliminate racial quotas from consent decrees. Simultaneously, the administration reoriented civil rights enforcement to an individual approach. Illegal discrimination by individuals against individuals was investigated and prosecuted. Indeed, the administration noted in 1987 that from 1981 to 1986, the Equal Employment Opportunity Commission had recovered $213 million in damages for individual victims of discrimination, a new record.[30] In the civil rights area, civil lawsuits were less numerous, but criminal prosecutions were more numerous, under Reagan than under Carter. With the aid of Reagan-appointed justices, the short-term crest of this policy was reached in 1989, when the Supreme Court's *Ward's Cove Packing Co. v. Atonio* decision declared that employers could be sued only for specific acts of discrimination, not mere statistical discrepancies in employment patterns. Even critics acknowledged that "probably more than any President, Reagan used public rhetoric to change the public agenda in civil rights"[31] and that Reagan was "winning the war to shape public opinion."[32]

At the time, Reagan enjoyed only modest success in his efforts. Amid a storm of controversy, he was forced to back away from a planned revision of Executive Order 11246, the order signed by Lyndon Johnson (and strengthened by Richard Nixon) that gave affirmative action much of its standing within the executive branch. In the *Bob Jones University* Supreme Court case, the administration lost its argument that the Internal Revenue Service did not have the right to interpret civil rights law; in 1988, the Civil Rights Restoration Act passed over Reagan's veto, which he had wielded due to his perception that the act would impose an extraordinary regulatory burden on educational institutions.[33] Two years after Reagan left office, the Civil Rights Act of 1991 overturned *Ward's Cove*, restoring a group-based policy presuming guilt in cases of statistical discrepancies even when unaccompanied by claims of actual discrimination against any individual.

Many civil rights leaders, black commentators, and white liberals decried Reagan's shift of emphasis. Scholars like Joseph Stewart Jr. claimed that Reagan had led a broad "charge backward" on civil rights, complaining that "the administration pursued only [employment discrimination] cases where it could find 'identifiable victims.'"[34] Norman C. Amaker argued that the Reagan legacy was one of "weakened enforcement of the nation's civil rights laws" and "failure of moral leadership," and he suggested that Reagan's rhetoric and policy was indirectly responsible for incidents of racial violence, perhaps including the 1992 Los Angeles riots.[35] Steven A. Shull all but declared the Reagan civil rights legacy a "kinder, gentler racism."[36] Academic and journalistic critiques of Reagan's civil rights policy often took as their first assumption the proposition that Reagan's position was the result of a cynical calculation aimed at winning the votes of prejudiced working-class whites.[37]

However, such an appraisal does not do justice to either Reagan's character or to the moral, legal, or constitutional logic of his position. Personally, Reagan was neither a bigot nor tolerant of bigotry.[38] Politically, Reagan believed, not without cause, that his new civil rights policy was really the old civil rights policy—what the nation had thought it was adopting in 1964. Not only was his shift consistent with the text and the spirit of the landmark Civil Rights Act of 1964, but it was arguably more consistent with that act than was the policy of group preferences he sought to replace.[39] (Indeed, some scholars suggested that Johnson's Executive Order 11246 was a direct violation of the Civil Rights Act and hence illegal.)[40] The Reagan administration's position on quotas also echoed that of Justice William O. Douglas, who stated in the *Defunis* case in 1974, "There is no constitutional right for any race to be preferred." As Nicholas Laham concluded in his 1998 book *The Reagan Presidency and the Politics of Race,*

> All the documented evidence currently available suggests that Reagan's civil rights policy was motivated by his sincere and genuine desire to achieve colorblind justice and limited government, which served as two core principles of his conservative agenda. . . . Reagan was not a practitioner of the politics of racial division, much less a bigot, but a genuine conservative who opposed racial preferences and quotas, believed in the constitutional principle of equality under the law, and opposed many federal regulations, including some relating to civil rights, which conflicted with his philosophical commitment to limited government.[41]

Furthermore, as Laham could have said but did not, there is not much reason to believe that racial minorities or women were hurt by Reagan's civil rights policy. That point is worth exploring in greater detail, given the heated rhetoric emanating from some quarters (Cornel West, for example, declared that 1980s America was virtually defined by racial and gender divisions— "Race sits at the center of this terrifying moment").[42] In reality, two trends seriously undercut the arguments for preferential treatment throughout the 1980s: the steady improvement of the black condition, and the steady decline of racially prejudiced opinions among whites. Numerous studies have documented that white attitudes on average have become much less prejudiced over the last sixty years and that this shift continued and even accelerated through the 1980s.[43]Indeed, McKee McClendon remarked in 1985 that "improvements in racial attitudes suggest that traditional racial prejudice may no longer be an important factor in perpetuating racial inequality."[44] The percentage of whites who told pollsters that blacks were "lazy" fell from 75 percent in 1933, to 26 percent in 1967, to 4 percent in 1990; the number saying blacks were "superstitious" dropped from 84 to 13 to 3 percent; those who said blacks were "stupid" fell from 22 to 13 to 3 percent. At the same time, studies showed that media portrayals of blacks were much more frequent and more positive.[45] A more focused case study was available at the University of Alabama, where in 1963 only 30 percent of white students at the University of Alabama favored desegregation; by 1982, 72 percent favored desegregation, a figure that climbed to 81 percent in 1988.[46] At the end of the 1980s, polls showed that nine of ten whites believed black and white students should go to the same schools, seven out of ten believed that blacks worked as hard or harder than whites, and almost seven of ten said that landlords should face prosecution if they discriminated on the basis of race.[47] Perhaps most telling of all, the Census Bureau reported one million interracial marriages in 1990, compared with only 310,000 twenty years earlier.[48]

Largely as a result of these changed attitudes, blacks expanded their political power in the 1980s, winning or holding mayorships in Los Angeles, Chicago, Philadelphia, Detroit, the District of Columbia, New Orleans, Atlanta, and New York City. In 1989, Douglas Wilder of Virginia became the first black to be elected to a governorship in the twentieth century, in a state where blacks were only 12 percent of the population. In many of these elections, black victories depended on large numbers of white votes; in virtually all of them, a higher percentage of white voters voted for black candidates than black voters voted for white candidates. On the national level, Jesse Jackson ran two campaigns for the presidency, gaining a significant number of white votes in 1988. Overall, the number of black officeholders increased substantially in the 1980s, providing a foundation for the 50 percent increase in black members of Congress in the 1992 elections. At the same time, Reagan elevated Gen. Colin Powell to the position of National Security Adviser, which became Powell's steppingstone to the chairmanship of the Joint Chiefs of Staff and ultimately a position as George W. Bush's secretary of state.

This process was also aided by the mandates of the Voting Rights Act Amendments of 1982, which required that legislative districts be drawn with the aim of maximizing minority representation. Whether the amendments were good public policy, or even constitutionally permissible, remains a point of contention—the Reagan administration initially opposed them but later agreed to a compromise version—but they almost certainly did contribute to their objective of increasing the number of minority officeholders.

The decline in white prejudice and growth in black political influence was accompanied by a continued and substantial growth in the black middle class (a subject that will be considered in greater detail in chapter 4).[49] A sign of the black community's growing economic and political influence in the 1980s was its political diversity. A significant minority of black intellectuals openly challenged the assumptions of the welfare state and affirmative action: Glen Loury, Thomas Sowell, Shelby Steele, and Clarence Thomas were representative of this new force of black conservatism. The emergence of greater diversity of opinion and debate within the black intellectual community was perhaps the best sign that the position of blacks had improved to the extent that a false front of conformity was no longer necessary.

Altogether, despite the concerns of Cornel West and others, racial tensions in the 1980s were probably at their lowest point in decades. There was, admittedly, an increase in reports of racially motivated criminal incidents and a rise in white political and paramilitary organizations based on racial hatred. Nevertheless, the incidence of racial violence was not large compared to the 1960s, and extremist groups could "count only a few thousand active supporters" in a nation of 250 million.[50] Racial tension was also exacerbated by the rise of black demagogues like Louis Farrakhan, Al Sharpton, and Leonard Jeffries, a black professor at City College of New York who taught that whites were biologically inferior "ice people." Yet it was difficult to argue that such individuals were more prominent in the 1980s than twenty years before, when Malcolm X and the Black Panthers had been major forces. And no incident or issue in the 1980s could compare with the racial discord produced by forced busing in the 1970s. It is worth remembering that 1983 was the year that Martin Luther King Day was made a federal holiday, an event that would have been nearly unthinkable even one decade before.

None of this is to say that racism disappeared in the 1980s. Nor is it to deny the enormous problems faced by the black underclass. But arguments that the progress of blacks stopped in the Reagan years and that the nation experienced a rebirth of racism are not supported by the facts.[51] At the end of the decade, while whites and blacks disagreed over precisely how much equality blacks had achieved, majorities of both races agreed in polls that American society had become less racist in the 1980s, that blacks had the same opportunity that whites did to live a middle class life, and that the gap in living standards between whites and blacks had not widened in the previous ten years (see table 2.1). In 1978, only 38 percent of blacks surveyed said their conditions were excellent or good; by 1990, that figure had risen to 50 percent. Given a hypothetical case of a black and white of equal intelligence and ability applying for the same job, only one-third of blacks said the white would have a better chance at the job (in 1978 one-half had said so).[52] Other minority groups also gained in the 1980s. The Hispanic middle class grew substantially, and Asian immigrants did well enough that part of the racial tension of the 1980s was derived from black hostility to the advances of Asian newcomers.

The story of women in the 1980s similarly contradicts claims that the Reagan administration conspired with other social forces to turn back the clock. In perhaps the best example of such claims, Susan Faludi postulated in *Backlash: The Undeclared War against American Women* that the 1980s had seen a multifaceted counterrevolution against the gains of women.[53] However, after two decades of stagnation, the wage gap between men and women actually declined considerably in the 1980s. At the beginning of the decade, full-time

TABLE 2.1
White and Black Views on Racism and Opportunity, 1987–1988

	Black	White
More	37	20
Less	54	70
No change	6	6
Not sure	3	4

Do Blacks have the same opportunity to live a middle-class life as Whites? (1988)

	Black	White
Yes	50	70
No	46	27
Not sure	4	3

Is the gap in living standards between Black people and White people wider or narrower than ten years ago? (1987)

	Black	White
Wider	39	18
Narrower/no change (vol.)	56	71
Don't know	6	12

Sources: "The Black Middle Class," *Business Week*, March 14, 1988, 65; Diane Colasanto and Linda Williams, "The Changing Dynamics of Race and Class," *Public Opinion*, January/February 1987, 51.

working women were receiving sixty cents for a man's dollar; at the end of the decade, that figure was seventy-one cents, and most of the remaining difference disappeared when controlled for education, work experience, and other such factors.[54] Second, while men's employment in the 1980s increased by 20 percent, women's employment grew by 33 percent; women were integrated ever more fully into the national workforce.

At the end of the decade, plausible claims were made that women faced a corporate "glass ceiling." What was new, though, was not the "glass ceiling" but that for the first time a significant number of women employees were at a high enough level to bump into it. Politically, the first woman Supreme Court justice, Sandra Day O'Connor, was appointed by Reagan in 1981, and like that of blacks, women's influence grew substantially at the state and local levels. It was this success throughout the 1980s that made possible the large gains made by female candidates at the federal level in 1990, 1992, and 1994. Interestingly, at the end of her book, Faludi tacitly admits that the "backlash," if one actually existed, had little real effect.[55] Taking Faludi and like-minded commentators to task, *Detroit News* reporter and feminist Cathy Young responded in her 1999 book *Ceasefire!*

that "the '80s were not a 'backlash decade' but a time of steady progress for women and, generally, of strong support for women's advancement."[56]

On balance, Reagan's constitutional policy toward individual rights was controversial but well grounded in the law and the Constitution. He rejected group rights and recently discovered rights lacking clear connection to the Constitution, yet his support for individual rights was solid. Any suggestion that Reagan was, in some general sense, against individual rights because he was skeptical of the exclusionary rule or of exotic interpretations of speech must come to grips with the obvious fact that there are far more property owners, far more gun owners, and far more religious believers—whose rights he consistently defended—than there are accused felons or distributors of pornography. His general conception of individual rights—that no correct interpretation of them can defy common sense, that they must exist in balance with the principle of consent of the governed, and that they trump any assertions of collective guilt or collective reparation—was well in keeping with the American political tradition and was probably supported by most Americans.

A dozen years after Reagan's presidency ended, his conception was still advancing. Despite the legislative reversal of *Ward's Cove*, by the year 2000 race-based preferences were in political and judicial retreat, in instances ranging from California's Proposition 209 to the Supreme Court's decision in *Adarand Constructors v. Pena*. Forced busing had lost ground almost everywhere. Courts and Congress limited criminal appeals, and a property rights movement grew in intellectual, political, and judicial influence. Movement in the direction of Reagan's view was not uniform: on the subject of gun control, the traditional conception of individual rights was periodically endangered; likewise, federal courts continued to devise more rigorous standards tending to exclude religious expression from public life. On balance, however, Reagan had contributed heavily to what had emerged as a new baseline of constitutional application.

Federalism

Federalism was, it is fair to say, the constitutional lodestar of the Reagan administration. In his first inaugural address, Reagan declared, "It is my intention to curb the size and influence of the federal establishment and to demand recognition of the distinction between the powers granted to the federal government, and those reserved to the states or to the people."[57] This principle was promoted first and foremost because Reagan saw it as essential to the Constitution of 1787. Indeed, though the framers meant to establish a stronger central authority, they had steadfastly denied accusations by antifederalists that the

Constitution would lead to "consolidation," then a shorthand for hyper-centralization and ultimate irrelevancy of the states. Reagan and his allies defended federalism on both philosophical and practical grounds. The decentralization of government provided by the federal system was, in Reagan's view, an important line of defense against overweening government. Merely by preventing all significant governmental power from coming to rest in one set of hands, federalism nurtured liberty. Furthermore, it was a strong guarantee of national diversity. New York and Texas did not have to pursue the same policy on the death penalty; California and Louisiana did not have to share divorce laws. Homogenization is in many ways an enemy of freedom, and federalism acted to restrain the democratic tendency toward homogenization. Because the federal system allowed for the preservation of differences, it also had a practical benefit. States whose policies were not uniformly mandated from Washington could, as it were, experiment, testing a variety of responses to the same problem. They were more likely to find an approach suitable to their locale, and as "laboratories of democracy" the states could contribute greatly to the advance of effective policy. Consequently, Reagan attempted to restore the states to a more prominent position in American government and indeed tried to reestablish decentralization of government as a crucial component of America's real—as opposed to merely written—constitution.

In this goal, Reagan faced several obstacles. Perhaps most importantly, the doctrine of states' rights had been dealt a severe blow in the Civil War and during the civil rights movement of the 1950s and 1960s. During those struggles, "states' rights" had been largely a high-sounding theoretical cover for the defenders of slavery and segregation. Consequently, any states' rights argument, no matter how sincere, was subject to dismissal as a "code word" for racism. Furthermore, centralization had by 1980 reached such an extent that untangling the federal system in order to provide it greater definition was not an easy task. States and municipalities had become highly dependent on federal funds and were reluctant to insist on their prerogatives if it meant forgoing those funds. Additionally, for many years a large number of state governments had seemed to lack the institutional capacity to deal effectively with issues like welfare or environmental protection. Altogether, from the 1930s until the mid-1970s, public confidence in the federal government had been significantly greater than confidence in state governments.

Nevertheless, it was clear by the 1980s that state governments had, on the whole, significantly enhanced their structural capacity for action.[58] Scandals and policy failures at the federal level had also raised doubts about Washington's omniscience, leading to shifts in public opinion; by 1981, Americans believed by a four-to-one margin that states had a better understanding than the federal government's of "people's real needs."[59] From Reagan's perspective, the historical misuse of a constitutional principle did not negate the truth of that principle. In any event, in 1980, the growing concentration of power in Washington seemed a more pressing concern than Confederate secession or Jim Crow. As federalism scholar Martha Derthick argued, progress on civil rights and desegregation established conditions under which "the case for the states can at last begin to be discussed on its merits."[60]

Reagan approached his goal of revivifying federalism with a three-part strategy: administrative, legislative, and judicial. Administratively, as a group, Reagan's appointees understood the importance the issue held for the president and worked within their agencies to promote his views. Broadly speaking, Reagan's was the first administration to recognize that intergovernmental regulation was a distinct form of federal regulation and to seek explicitly to limit that regulation.[61] This often meant interpreting agency rules and regulations in the manner that provided the greatest flexibility to states. In one of the earliest manifestations of this policy, Reagan directed the Environmental Protection Agency in early 1981 to transfer enforcement of significant portions of clean air and other environmental regulations to the states.[62] The presidential Task Force on Regulatory Relief, headed by Vice President George Bush, took action in 1981–83 against twenty-seven intergovernmental regulations, saving state and local governments an estimated 11.8 million work hours per year, two billion dollars a year, and four to six billion dollars in one-time costs.[63]

Formalizing this approach, Reagan issued Executive Order 12372 in 1982 and Executive Order 12612 in 1987. Executive Order 12372 specified a number of federal programs and activities that could not be pursued without "intergovernmental review," meaning a system of consultation with the states. Executive Order 12612 required that the implications for federalism be formally considered before any federal administrative action.

This latter executive order, which attempted to institutionalize what had already become standard practice in many offices, declared that "in the absence of clear constitutional or statutory authority, the presumption of sovereignty should rest with the individual states. Uncertainties regarding the legitimate authority of the national government should be resolved against regulation at the national level."[64] It went on to establish guidelines for executive branch action, including "strict adherence to constitutional principles"; consulting with states; granting to the states the "maximum administrative discretion possible"; refraining from establishing "uniform, national standards"; and deferring to the states to the maximum extent possible. Federal preemption of state regulation was to be considered only when constitutional and statutory justification was clear, and it was then to be undertaken only to the minimum extent necessary. Executive departments and agencies were ordered to refrain from submitting to Congress any legislation that would place extraneous conditions on federal grants or would "directly regulate the States in ways that would interfere with functions essential to the States' separate and independent existence or operate to directly displace the States' freedom to structure integral operations in areas of traditional governmental functions." Finally, Executive Order 12612 required all agency heads to certify in a written "federalism assessment" that these conditions had been met, an assessment that would then become part of the central clearance process for new policies at the Office of Management and Budget.[65]

Legislatively, Reagan proposed a wide variety of policy changes that had the effect of strengthening the role of the states in the federal system. The most comprehensive proposal, his "new federalism" proposal (the title was the media's, not his), failed, but it gives insight into Reagan's understanding of federalism. Closely mirroring a proposal he made on the campaign trail in his unsuccessful 1976 presidential bid, Reagan's 1982 "new federalism" aimed to sort out federal and state responsibilities in domestic policy areas. The plan, announced as the centerpiece of his 1982 State of the Union Address, entailed a complete federal takeover of Medicaid in exchange for states' assuming complete responsibility for Aid to Families with Dependent Children (welfare) and food stamps, as well as forty-four programs mostly in the areas of education, community development, transportation, and social services. The revenues of certain federal excise taxes were to be put into a trust fund to help the states pay for their new responsibilities; the taxes were then to be phased out over a period of eight years.[66] The proposal died in no small part because state governments were reluctant to assume additional responsibilities at that time and voiced doubts that the proposed funding sources were sufficient to meet the need. Reagan himself failed to intervene personally in the negotiations, drawing criticism later for allowing an important opportunity to slip through his fingers.[67]

Nevertheless, Reagan had a series of legislative successes that achieved much of what he wanted. Foremost, the 1980s saw a significant change in the fiscal relationship between Washington and the states. As Reagan saw it,

> Washington, ignoring principles of the Constitution, was trying to turn the states into nothing more than administrative districts of the federal government. And the path to federal control had, to a large extent, become federal aid. . . . Over time, [states and communities] became so dependent on the money that, like junkies, they found it all but impossible to break the habit, and only after they were well addicted to it did they learn how pervasive the federal regulations were that came with the money. . . . As all this was going on, the federal government was taking an ever-increasing share of the nation's total tax revenue and making it more difficult for states and local governments to raise money on their own.[68]

Reagan's policies addressed this situation through a variety of means. First, a number of "block grants"—that is, grants with a fairly broad purpose and few conditions attached—were created to replace narrower and more restricted "categorical grants." As scholar Richard Nathan explained it,

> Four new block grants in the health field were created in the 1981 budget act. They are for alcohol, drug abuse, and mental health (replacing three categorical grants); maternal and child health (replacing seven categorical grants); preventive health services (combined eight separate grants); and primary health care. A block grant for elementary and secondary education was also established consolidating twenty-nine categorical grants. Revisions were made in the existing community development block grant giving states new authority to allocate funds among small cities. States were also given new authority under the community services block grant to allocate funds to community action agencies for services to low-income persons. Other existing broad grants were changed in less important ways and described as new block grants by the administration, notably those for social services and energy assistance to low-income households.[69]

A total of nine new block grants were created in 1981, by consolidating seventy-seven programs and terminating sixty-two.[70] After this first wave of success, the administration won passage of the 1982 Job Training Partnership Act, which revised federal employment training programs by turning them into a block grant and requiring greater state input. Altogether, in his first six years in office, Reagan won enactment of ten major proposals for new or substantially revised block grants, and he unsuccessfully proposed another two for every one that was adopted.[71] His successes in the block grant area should not be exaggerated, but they were important. While state-level assessments did not uniformly support this conclusion, the Office of Management and Budget estimated that the paperwork burden imposed on state and local governments had been cut by 83 percent from 1981 to 1983.[72] Revisions in these programs bolstered the position of the states in another way as well: Rather than bypassing the states by providing aid directly to local units of government, the Reagan approach focused block grants on the states. From 1980 to 1986, the proportion of federal aid going to localities fell by two-fifths.[73]

Part of the 1981 budget plan also provided greater statutory flexibility to states in the design of the Medicaid program. States were given the option of devising "workfare" programs in 1981, and another much-heralded welfare reform, with substantial input from the National Governors Association, passed in 1988. Though the 1988 welfare plan proved not as important as it seemed at the time, it did provide states with greater discretion and served as a way station to the more fundamental welfare reform enacted in 1996.

In addition to changing federal programs to give states more authority, the administration won fiscal changes that reduced the power of the federal government and enhanced the position of the states over the long run. First, the general-revenue-sharing program, initiated during the Nixon administration, was discontinued midway through Reagan's presidency. With the federal government running annual deficits in the two-hundred-billion-dollar range, it was clear to most observers that there was no extra revenue to share. At first glance, revenue sharing would seem to have fit the Reagan administration's criteria for intergovernmental interaction, since the program came with "no strings attached." However, by 1980 general revenue sharing had been redirected solely to local, not state, governments, thus conflicting with Reagan's state-centered constitutional view of federalism. Furthermore, Reagan considered the program to be an unjustified redistributionary scheme from well-off areas to those that were not prospering; in his view, such an approach undermined state and local distinctiveness and made it harder for citizens to "vote with their feet" by leaving one dissolute jurisdiction for a more frugal and better-governed one.[74] Such an open-ended subsidy from the federal government implied that the receiving entity was nothing more than an administrative unit of the federal government. It allowed for no concept of distinction between federal and state or local roles, and it encouraged greater local dependency on the federal government. It was exactly that ethos with which Reagan wished to dispense. Indeed, seeking to reduce the reliance of states on federal largesse—consistent with the goal of providing them greater institutional autonomy—the Reagan administration worked with Congress to reduce the overall level of federal grants to states *or* localities. Combined federal aid to states and localities was reduced for the first time since the 1940s, while the number of federal assistance programs was reduced by one-fourth.[75] In the words of economist Alice Rivlin, one important consequence of fiscal policy in the 1980s was that "the pattern of increasing state and local dependence on federal grants had been broken."[76]

More fundamentally, authors like Richard Nathan have discussed how the "fiscal constitution" of the United States shifted in the 1980s in ways that aided the states. In short, the tax cuts and discretionary domestic spending cuts at the federal level, in combination with the less tangible "signals" of decentralization, left room for states to expand their influence. On the basis of these changes, Reagan told the National Association of State Legislatures in 1981 that "with our economic proposals, we are staging a quiet federalist revolution."[77] In other words, the expansion of state capacities was being facilitated by the overall retrenchment at the federal level. Reagan's belief was that if the federal government did less, the states would do more—a belief that turned out to be essentially correct.[78] As one student of federalism wrote in retrospect, "The really revolutionary feature of Reagan's economic and intergovernmental policies was that few state and local officials by 1988 looked to Washington for solutions to many of their most pressing problems."[79]

The administrative and legislative strategies to promote federalism were complemented by a judicial strategy. The heart of that judicial strategy, as we will see below, lay in attempting to ensure that federal judicial appointments were made only to individuals sharing the president's general conception of the Constitution and the federal system.

Some analysts rightly pointed out near the end of Reagan's presidency that "the administration has not yet lived up to the concept of the 'Reagan revolution' in decentralization" and that the 1980s had been a period of "missed opportunity" for fundamental restructuring.[80] Yet, as James Ceaser suggested, critics may have overstated the importance of that failure: "if adhered to consistently," block grants and the cessation of new federal initiatives "could over a period of years alter fundamental patterns of behavior and accomplish silently as much or more than a 'constitutional' settlement."[81] Other analysts criticized Reagan's federalism initiatives on the grounds that they were politically disingenuous or socially harmful. Interest groups affected by block grants often expressed concern that states would be unable to meet their new responsibilities, a concern that in retrospect seems mostly unfounded. A number of Democratic governors and congressmen accused Reagan of using devolution of programs to the states as a cover for what they considered his real agenda, spending cuts and deficit reduction.[82] While this position was understandable—block grants were typically proposed at a level of spending 25 percent lower than the sum of the categorical grants from which they were fashioned, and the 1982 "new federalism" proposal envisioned a gradual reduction of federal taxing and spending on state and local aid—its adherents had difficulty explaining Reagan's strong rhetorical commitment to federalism over a period of decades prior to his presidency.

Finally, some observers argued that the administration's proclaimed federalism stance was not entirely believable, because not all administration actions were consistent with it. Reagan allowed Congress to force the twenty-one-year drinking age on unwilling states, supported product liability reform that preempted state laws, and imposed uniform trucking standards. In short, as one student of federalism put it, Reagan was willing to "sacrifice his federalism goals whenever they conflict with his other deeply held policy objectives."[83] That objection was valid, as far as it went. Anyone looking for pure consistency in the application of the principles of federalism was likely to be disappointed by a close review of Reagan's record. However, in a political world of multiple (and sometimes conflicting) goals, a fragmented governmental system, and outside pressure groups (like Mothers Against Drunk Driving, which lobbied hard for the federal drinking age), it is not clear that complete consistency is an appropriate standard. A more reasonable question is whether Reagan moved the country substantially in his direction on federalism questions, and whether—on balance—states were in a stronger or weaker position at the end of his term than before he took office.

By this standard, it is evident that the position of the states in the federal system has been enhanced considerably since 1980. Observers like Richard Nathan argued that "Reagan has achieved notable success in the pursuit of his goals for federalism reform" through the indirect and incremental steps outlined above.[84] By 1992, Alice Rivlin had discerned that "in the last decade, the tide of centralization has turned and the balance of power has generally shifted from the federal government toward the states."[85] Analysts began describing a growing diversity of state action in the regulatory field, as well as a growing "judicial federalism" in which state courts were increasingly fashioning their own distinct jurisprudences on the basis of state constitutions. One of the best pieces of inferential evidence that states had regained a place of vigor in policy making was the fact that interest-group activity surged at the state level throughout the 1980s.[86]

That trend continued in the 1990s, even though some elements of the Reagan approach were discontinued by subsequent presidents. President Clinton, for example, rescinded Executive Order 12612, eliminating the requirement that federal executive agencies consider the impact of proposed federal action on the states and the federal system. Legislation frequently ignored the principle of federalism, just as before Reagan. Nevertheless, acting in the spirit of Reagan's profederalism bent, Congress in the 1990s passed laws limiting the federal imposition of unfunded mandates on the states, handed control of welfare back to state governments, and gave states and local school districts greater flexibility in the spending of federal education aid. Likewise, if Reagan's judicial strategy produced a mixed bag in the 1980s—the Supreme Court resolved some cases in favor of the states, and others against—in the 1990s it became much clearer that this strategy was bearing fruit. The Court allowed modestly greater abortion regulations by the states in 1992 and threw out parts of the Brady gun control act in 1996, on the Tenth Amendment grounds that it improperly commandeered state and local law enforcement personnel to carry out federal administrative functions. As mentioned above, the Court also disallowed at least two federal laws for reading too expansively the commerce clause of the enumerated powers in an instance when Congress should instead have deferred to the states.

The Role of the Judiciary

The element that all of the above positions had in common was their reliance, to some degree, on a judicial strategy. This strategy was unusually well crafted and grounded in a particular set of constitutional and policy objectives. As constitutional law scholar David M. O'Brien wrote, "Reagan's administration had a more coherent and ambitious agenda for legal reform and judicial selection than any previous administration."[87]

The first priority of the Reagan administration judicially was a careful screening of judicial appointments. The administration's goal, as Attorney General Edwin Meese described it, was "to institutionalize the Reagan revolution so it can't be set aside no matter what happens in future presidential elections."[88] To attain this goal, Meese explained, "In selecting judges, the administration established a rigorous process of interviews and background-checking" running through the Justice Department. The Office of Personnel Management, housed in the Executive Office of the President, also conducted its own independent reviews. Furthermore, rather than leave nominations of district court and appellate court judges purely in the hands of local Republican senators or House members, as was the tradition, Reagan insisted that they provide a list of options from which he could choose. The ability of the president and his Justice Department to control the judicial selection process was enhanced by ending formal channels of input by organizations representing black and women lawyers, and by downgrading the role of the American Bar Association in rating prospective judges. The president's influence over the process was maximized by his Committee on Federal Judicial Selection—a group including the White House chief of staff, one or more presidential counselors, the president's assistant for legislative affairs, the attorney general, and a handful of other Justice Department appointees—which centralized the final decision process.[89]

Some critics complained that the Justice Department improperly applied a "litmus test" on specific judicial issues, like abortion, gun control, criminal justice, and affirmative action. Meese and other Justice Department officials denied that a "litmus test" was required on any particular issue, insisting instead that potential nominees "were interviewed on their understanding of the Constitution and their philosophy of judicial practice."[90] Reagan himself later wrote that "the only litmus test I wanted . . . was the assurance of a judge's honesty and judicial integrity. As in California, I wanted judges who would interpret the Constitution, not try to rewrite it."[91] Consequently, the president's critics accused him of "politicizing" the judiciary, while his defenders held that he was trying to "de-politicize" it, by trying to restore the judiciary to its proper—that is, nonlegislative—role. Whatever the case may be, there is no doubt that the Reagan administration paid unprecedented attention to the question of ensuring philosophical compatibility among its judicial appointees.

By the end of his presidency, Reagan had appointed 49 percent of the entire federal judiciary, including three Supreme Court justices and the chief justice of the Supreme Court. He counted only a handful of failures, most notably the unsuccessful attempt to nominate conservative jurist Robert Bork to the Supreme Court. Furthermore, according to David O'Brien, "in terms of the ABA's ratings of professional qualifications, Reagan's judges on balance compare favorably with those appointed by earlier administrations."[92] If those ratings are a guide—and the administration was the first to acknowledge that they were an imperfect guide, at best—the Reagan appointment process did not typically sacrifice professional quality for ideological conformity. Altogether, "Reagan indubitably has had a major, lasting impact on the federal judiciary, both in terms of his unrivaled number of appointments and in reinvigorating judicial conservatism on the bench."[93]

Reagan appointees on federal district and circuit appellate courts quickly compiled a distinct pattern of decisions, voting in a fairly consistent conservative direction and often as a bloc. They were typically more restrained and tougher on crime.[94] By the end of his presidency, legal scholars were arguing that the early Rehnquist Court had developed a new guiding standard for itself, that of "reasonableness based on a rough analysis that seeks to fit new policies to the traditional principles and values of economic and social life in America."[95] In the longer term, Reagan's judicial strategy fell short of many of its objectives, particularly in the social realm. Contentious Supreme Court decisions on abortion and school prayer were not overturned, and movement on many other issues seemed to proceed at a glacial pace. Some scholars argued that not much had changed.[96] Nevertheless, it is clear that Reagan's constitutional interpretation of federalism, property rights, and racial preferences has moved, at least for awhile, into the ascendant position in the Supreme Court. Few presidents could claim even that much success in deliberately moving the direction of judicial interpretation of the Constitution. In the words of legal analyst Richard L. Pacelle, "When future scholars and analysts map agenda and doctrinal trends, they may compare the influence of Ronald Reagan to Franklin Roosevelt a half-century earlier."[97]

If judicial appointments were Reagan's long-term judicial strategy, the litigation policy of the Justice Department represented the short-term strategy. In many civil rights, antitrust, and environmental cases, the administration simply refused to litigate when previous administrations would have done so. On certain issues, like forced busing and affirmative action, the Reagan Justice Department took positive action to advance the president's position. In the area of environmental regulation, one study indicated that the number of cases referred by the Environmental Protection Agency to the Justice Department for prosecution fell by 84 percent from June 1981 to July 1982.[98] On a variety of issues, but especially cases with an impact on federalism, the Justice Department also filed briefs in appellate courts supporting the president's position.

The Reagan Justice Department was hence the linchpin of both elements of the judicial strategy, judicial appointments and litigation/briefs. It was able to perform that function because Reagan, his closest advisers, and his attorneys general understood the importance of filling it with appointees who shared a common view of the Constitution. As David O'Brien pointed out:

> Young "movement conservatives" were attracted to the department.... Attorneys were recruited from senatorial staff and the ranks of former law clerks of leading conservative jurists, such as Chief Justice Rehnquist, and law professors such as [Robert] Bork and Antonin Scalia, who were elevated by Reagan to the federal bench. In addition, many were associated with the Federalist Society, a conservative legal fraternity founded in the early 1980s at the University of Chicago and several other law schools.... What they shared was a sense of being in the vanguard of a new conservative legal movement.[99]

In short, Reagan assembled a Justice Department able and willing to focus its considerable energy on the task of implementing his conception of constitutionalism through every available means.

Reagan's Constitutionalism: Evaluations

There can be little doubt that Reagan's administration gave more consideration to the Constitution and to the principles of constitutionalism than any administration in recent history. As T. Kenneth Cribb argued, "The question that President Reagan always asks first is a question that most modern politicians don't ask at all, and it is this: What is the proper role of government under the American Constitution?" Cribb believed that Reagan "saw farther than the common politician," because he "stood on the shoulders of the framers of that Constitution."[100] That accomplishment in itself was notable. Beyond putting constitutionalism back on the public agenda, what did Reagan accomplish?

Criticisms of Reagan's constitutionalism come in two basic types. Some argue that Reagan was right in his interpretation of the Constitution and in his determination to act on that interpretation but failed by not doing enough. Viewed from the standpoint of the high hopes held by Reagan and his supporters in 1980, the constitutional tendencies of 1990 or 2000 might seem disappointingly unchanged. The federal government was not even close to interpreting the enumerated powers literally; no comprehensive reform of federal-state relations had taken place; some of the most controversial examples of alleged judicial overreaching had not been reversed; racial preferences were not undone by a single stroke of the executive pen, as Reagan (in theory) had the capacity to do. Too much was accomplished by unilateral executive action rather than by legislation, leaving the accomplishments vulnerable to the differing predilections of future presidents. Above all, on a range of issues, many saw too large a gap between the boldness of Reagan's rhetoric and the halting, incremental nature of the results.

A different set of critics held him to be substantively wrong, or at least confused and inconsistent. To some, the attempt to restore a constitutionalism of "original intent" or "original meaning" was a thinly veiled assault on social progress, or at best hopelessly incoherent. Attempting to ascertain the original intent is sometimes difficult, and a jurisprudence of original intent is not automatically compatible with a jurisprudence of judicial restraint. Others pointed out important contradictions or inconsistencies between the administration's professed constitutional principles, not to mention between its constitutionalism and other policy commitments. Its conception of individual rights regarding property rights and civil rights frequently came into conflict with federalism, as state and local policies were overruled on issues like tort reform and affirmative action. Likewise, principles of limited government were not always easy to reconcile with the policy of presidential aggrandizement or increased police power.

Nevertheless, Reagan could claim some significant successes in his battle to restore important constitutional principles. He succeeded in bolstering separation of powers by reviving the presidency, restraining Congress and the judiciary, and winning acceptance for a stricter theory of separation of powers. He rendered the metaphor of enumerated powers once again useful for policy makers. He strengthened the status of several traditional individual rights. He also strengthened the status of individual rights generally, by opposing their primary competitor in modern America, the collectivist model of group rights and group identity. In the same way, Reagan defended the principle of equality under the law, arguably one of the most fundamental underpinnings of any free constitutional order. Perhaps most signally, Reagan decentralized power by contributing incrementally but heavily to the revival of federalism. Furthermore, Reagan set in motion a long-term strengthening of many of these principles, ranging from federalism to equal protection to skepticism of unlimited government to, in a very specific case, appreciation for the constitutional flaws of the independent counsel statute.

As Reagan argued, the Constitution is the fundamental political blueprint for the American architecture of freedom. On balance, Reagan advanced key principles of that blueprint in the 1980s and beyond. Perhaps as importantly, he advanced the proposition that government should take seriously the constraints of the Constitution, that it should operate as if the Constitution mattered. In those efforts, he changed the terms of debate significantly, achieving as much as any president is likely to accomplish.

Notes

1. To Reagan, the term "inspiration" was not merely metaphorical. At a celebration marking the two-hundredth anniversary of the completion of the Constitutional Convention, Reagan made extensive remarks attributing the success of the convention to divine inspiration and intervention. See "Remarks at the 'We the People' Bicentennial Celebration in Philadelphia, Pennsylvania, September 17, 1987," *Public Papers of the Presidents: Ronald Reagan 1987* (Washington, D.C.: GPO, 1989), 1042.

2. "Remarks to the Winners of the Bicentennial of the Constitution Essay Competition, September 10, 1987," *Public Papers of the Presidents: Ronald Reagan 1987* (Washington, D.C.: GPO, 1989), 1016; "Radio Address to the Nation on the Federal Judiciary, June 21, 1986," *Public Papers of the Presidents: Ronald Reagan 1986* (Washington, D.C.: GPO, 1988), 818; "Remarks at the Bicentennial Celebration of the United States Constitution, September 16, 1987," *Public Papers of the Presidents: Ronald Reagan 1987* (Washington, D.C.: GPO, 1989), 1040.

3. See Morris Fiorina, *Congress: The Keystone of the Washington Establishment* (New Haven, Conn.: Yale University Press, 1977); and David Mayhew, *Congress: The Electoral Connection* (New Haven, Conn.: Yale University Press, 1974).

4. Ronald Reagan, *An American Life: The Autobiography* (New York: Simon and Schuster, 1990), 197–98.

5. Ronald Reagan, "At the Investiture of Chief Justice William H. Rehnquist and Associate Justice Antonin Scalia at The White House, September 26, 1986, Washington, D.C.," in *The Great Debate: Interpreting Our Written Constitution* (Washington, D.C.: Federalist Society, 1986), 55.

6. This doctrine, known as "departmentalism," is explored by Susan R. Burgess in *Contest for Constitutional Authority: The Abortion and War Powers Debates* (Lawrence: University Press of Kansas, 1992).

7. "Remarks to the Winners of the Bicentennial of the Constitution Essay Competition, September 10, 1987," 1017.

8. James W. Ceaser, "The Theory of Governance of the Reagan Administration," in *The Reagan Presidency and the Governing of America*, ed. Lester M. Salamon and Michael S. Lund (Washington, D.C.: Urban Institute, 1984).

9. In one case, Congress had tried to justify federal penalties on guns in schools on the basis of the commerce clause; in the other, Congress had tried to federalize crimes like rape and domestic violence.

10. Michael S. Greve, *Real Federalism: Why It Matters, How It Could Happen* (Washington, D.C.: AEI, 2000), 25–26.

11. James Madison, *Federalist 47*, in *The Federalist Papers*, ed. Clinton Rossiter (New York: NAL, 1960), 301.

12. See, for example, a number of the essays contained in L. Gordon Crovitz and Jeremy A. Rabkin, *The Fettered Presidency* (Washington, D.C.: AEI, 1989). See also Reagan, *An American Life*, 483, where he complains that congressional Democrats "have been trespassing increasingly across the invisible boundary established by the separation-of-powers principle inherent in our Constitution."

13. On war powers see David Locke Hall, *The Reagan Wars: A Constitutional Perspective on War Powers and the Presidency* (Boulder, Colo.: Westview Press, 1991).

14. Nancy Kassop, "The Rise of the Arrogant Presidency: Separation of Powers in the Reagan Administration," in *Ronald Reagan's America*, ed. Eric J. Schmertz, Natalie Datlof, and Alexej Ugrinsky (Westport, Conn.: Greenwood, 1997), 359, 367.

15. *Immigration and Naturalization Service v. Chadha* (1983) and *Bowsher v. Synar* (1986).

16. Edwin Meese, *With Reagan* (Washington, D.C.: Regnery Gateway, 1992), 322–27.

17. William French Smith, "Independent Counsel Provisions of the Ethics in Government Act," in *The Fettered Presidency*, ed. L. Gordon Crovitz and Jeremy A. Rabkin (Washington, D.C.: AEI, 1989), 253–61; Terry Eastland, *Ethics, Politics, and the Independent Counsel: Executive Power, Executive Vice 1789–1989* (Washington, D.C.: National Legal Center for the Public Interest, 1989).

18. Cited by Kassop, "The Rise of the Arrogant Presidency," 371.

19. See David R. Henderson, *The Truth about the 1980s* (Palo Alto, Calif.: Hoover Institution, 1994), 3.

20. For an excellent discussion of the Founders and property rights, see Thomas G. West, *Vindicating the Founders: Race, Sex, Class, and Justice in the Origins of America* (Lanham, Md.: Rowman & Littlefield, 1997), 37–70.

21. Stephen Holbrook, *That Every Man Be Armed: The Evolution of a Constitutional Right* (Albuquerque: University of New Mexico Press, 1984).

22. Walter F. Murphy, "Reagan's Judicial Strategy," in *Looking Back on the Reagan Presidency*, ed. Larry Berman (Baltimore: Johns Hopkins University Press, 1990), 219.

23. Those cases were *Akron v. Akron Center for Reproductive Health* (1983) and *Thornburgh v. American College of Obstetrics and Gynecology* (1986).

24. Meese, *With Reagan*, 312–13.

25. Meese, *With Reagan*, 305–306.

26. Reagan, *An American Life*, 401.

27. Meese, *With Reagan*, 314.

28. Robert R. Detlefsen, "Affirmative Action and Business Deregulation: On the Reagan Administration's Failure to Revise Executive Order No. 11246," in *Presidential Leadership and Civil Rights Policy*, ed. James W. Riddlesperger and Donald W. Jackson (Westport, Conn.: Greenwood, 1995), 61.

29. Harrell R. Rodgers Jr., "Fair Employment Laws for Minorities: An Evaluation of Federal Implementation," in *Implementation of Civil Rights Policy*, ed. Charles S. Bullock III and Charles M. Lamb (Monterey, Calif.: Brooks/Cole, 1984), 111–12.

30. See *The Reagan Record: Five Years of Continuous Economic Growth* (Washington, D.C.: White House Office of Public Affairs, November 1987), 16.

31. Steven A. Shull and Albert C. Ringelstein, "Presidential Rhetoric in Civil Rights Policymaking 1953–1992," in *Presidential Leadership and Civil Rights Policy*, ed. James W. Riddlesperger Jr. and Donald W. Jackson (Westport, Conn.: Greenwood, 1995), 26.

32. Philip A. Klinkner and Rogers M. Smith, *The Unsteady March: The Rise and Decline of Racial Equality in America* (Chicago: University of Chicago, 1999), 303.

33. For an in-depth review of both of those battles, see Nicholas Laham, *The Reagan Presidency and the Politics of Race: In Pursuit of Colorblind Justice and Limited Government* (Westport, Conn.: Praeger, 1998).

34. Joseph Stewart Jr., "Between 'Yes' and 'But': Presidents and the Politics of Civil Rights Policy-Making," in *The Presidency Reconsidered*, ed. Richard W. Waterman (Itasca, Ill.: Peacock, 1993), 329, 334.

35. Norman C. Amaker, "The Reagan Civil Rights Legacy," in *Ronald Reagan's America*, ed. Schmertz, Datlof, and Ugrinsky, 163–64. See also Norman C. Amaker, *Civil Rights and the Reagan Administration* (Washington, D.C.: Urban Institute, 1988).

36. Steven A. Shull, *A Kinder, Gentler Racism? The Reagan-Bush Civil Rights Legacy* (Armonk, N.Y.: M. E. Sharpe, 1993).

37. For examples, see Klinkner and Smith, *The Unsteady March*, 300–304; John B. Judis, "Conservatism and the Price of Success," in *The Reagan Legacy*, ed. Sidney Blumenthal and Thomas Byrne Edsall (New York: Pantheon, 1988), 150–51.

38. To cite one example of many in Reagan's early years, in December 1945 Reagan addressed a "United America Day" rally in Santa Ana, California, saying "The blood that has soaked into the sands of the beaches is all one color. America stands unique in the world—a country not founded on race, but on a way and an ideal. Not in spite of, but because of our polyglot background, we have had all the strength in the world. That is the American way." Edmund Morris, *Dutch: A Memoir of Ronald Reagan* (New York: Random House, 1999), 228. See also Reagan, *An American Life*, 385, 401–402; Lou Cannon, *President Reagan: The Role of a Lifetime* (New York: Simon and Schuster, 1991), 519–20.

39. For example, the Civil Rights Act of 1964 stated, "It shall be an unlawful employment practice for an employer to fail or refuse to hire or to discharge any individual, or otherwise to discriminate against any individual with respect to his compensation, terms, conditions, or privileges of employment, because of such individual's race, color, religion, sex, or national origin. . . . Nothing in this title shall be interpreted to require any employer . . . to grant preferential treatment to any individual or to any group because of the race, color, religion, sex, or national origin on account of an imbalance which may exist with respect to the total number or percentage" of such persons in the workforce. Title VII, Section 703(a)(1) and 703(j). Additionally, the act declared, "Nothing herein shall empower any official or court of the United States to issue any order seeking to achieve a racial balance in any school by requiring the transportation of pupils or students from one school to another in order to achieve such racial balance." Title IV, Section 407(a)(2).

40. Detlefsen, "Affirmative Action and Business Deregulation," 64–65.

41. Laham, *The Reagan Presidency and the Politics of Race*, 213, 216.

42. West, "The '80s: Market Culture Run Amok," *Newsweek*, 48–49.

43. See Tom W. Smith and Paul B. Sheatsley, "American Attitudes toward Race Relations," *Public Opinion*, October–November 1984, 14–15, 50–53; Howard Schuman, Charlotte Steeh, and Lawrence Bobo, *Racial Attitudes in America* (Cambridge, Mass.: Harvard University Press, 1985), especially chap. 3; *Public Opinion*, July–August 1987, esp. 21–36; Glenn Firebaugh and Kenneth E. Davis, "Trends in Anti-black Prejudice, 1972–1984: Region and Cohort Effects," *American Journal of Sociology* (September 1988), 251–72.

44. McKee J. McClendon, "Racism, Rational Choice, and White Opposition to Racial Change: A Case Study of Busing," *Public Opinion Quarterly* (Summer 1985), 215.

45. James Waller, *Face to Face: The Changing State of Racism across America* (New York: Insight, 1998), 59–66.

46. Donal E. Muir, "'White' Attitudes toward 'Blacks' at a Deep-South University Campus, 1963–1988," *Sociology and Social Research* (January 1989), 84–89.

47. Smith and Sheatsley, "American Attitudes," 15; "Racism on the Rise," Time, February 2, 1987, 21; "The Black Middle Class," *Business Week*, March 14, 1988, 65.

48. Cited in Arthur M. Schlesinger Jr., *The Disuniting of America* (New York: W. W. Norton, 1992), 133.

49. See Robert J. Samuelson, "Racism and Poverty," *Newsweek*, August 7, 1989, 46; "Rethinking Race," *The New Republic*, February 9, 1987, 8; "The Black Middle Class," 62–65.

50. "Sudden Rise of Hate Groups Spurs Federal Crackdown," *U.S. News & World Report*, May 6, 1985, 68; "Is an Ugly Past Returning to Haunt America?" *U.S. News & World Report*, February 21, 1987, 12; "Racism on the Rise," 21.

51. It is interesting, and not a little unnerving, to observe the lengths to which many commentators went to deny that blacks were making significant progress. See Alphonso

Pinkney, *The Myth of Black Progress* (New York: Cambridge University Press, 1984); Waller, *Face to Face*. Waller's 1998 work was particularly mystifying, as he provided voluminous evidence that conditions had improved for blacks and then went on to label that improvement a "myth" and the continued existence of racism "reality." Of course, they were both reality.

52. Waller, *Face to Face*, 66.

53. Susan Faludi, *Backlash: The Undeclared War Against American Women* (New York: Crown, 1991).

54. Steven Rhoads, *Incomparable Worth: Pay Equity Meets the Market* (New York: Cambridge University Press, 1993), 6.

55. As Faludi described it, "And yet, for all the forces the backlash mustered—the blistering denunciations from the New Right, the legal setbacks of the Reagan years, the powerful resistance of corporate America, the self-perpetuating myth machines of the media and Hollywood, the 'neotraditional' marketing drive of Madison Avenue—women never really surrendered. The federal government may have crippled equal employment enforcement and the courts may have undermined twenty-five years of antidiscrimination law—yet women continued to enter the work force in growing numbers each year. Newsstands and airwaves may have been awash with frightening misinformation on spinster booms, birth dearths, and deadly day care—yet women continued to postpone their wedding dates, limit their family size, and combine work with having children. Television sets and movie screens may have been filled with nesting goodwives, but female viewers still gave their highest ratings to shows with strong-willed and independent heroines. Backlash dressmakers couldn't even get women to follow the most trivial of fashion prescriptions; while retailers crammed their racks with garter belts and teddies, women just kept reaching for the all-cotton Jockeys." *Backlash*, 454.

56. Cathy Young, *Ceasefire! Why Women and Men Must Join Forces to Achieve True Equality* (New York: Free Press, 1999), 10. See also 62–81.

57. "Inaugural Address, Washington, D.C., January 20, 1981," *Public Papers of the Presidents: Ronald Reagan 1981* (Washington, D.C.: GPO, 1982), 2.

58. For example, see Larry J. Sabato, *Goodbye to Good-Time Charlie: The American Governorship Transformed*, 2nd ed. (Washington, D.C.: Congressional Quarterly, 1983); U.S. Advisory Commission on Intergovernmental Relations, *The Question of State Government Capability*, Report A-98 (Washington, D.C.: Government Printing Office, 1985); Ann O'M. Bowman and Richard C. Kearney, *The Resurgence of the States* (Englewood Cliffs, N.J.: Prentice Hall, 1986).

59. Timothy Conlan, *New Federalism: Intergovernmental Reform from Nixon to Reagan* (Washington, D.C.: Brookings Institution, 1988), 105.

60. Martha Derthick, "American Federalism: Madison's Middle Ground," *Public Administration Review* 47, no. 1 (January–February 1987), 72.

61. Conlan, *New Federalism*, 200–204.

62. See B. Dan Wood, "Presidential Control of Intergovernmental Bureaucracies," in *The Presidency Reconsidered*, ed. Richard Waterman (Itasca, Ill.: Peacock, 1993), 97–98.

63. Conlan, *New Federalism*, 205.

64. Executive Order 12612 of October 26, 1987, "Federalism," *Federal Register 52*, no. 216.

65. Executive Order 12612, 41686–88.

66. See Richard Nathan, "Institutional Change under Reagan," in *Perspectives on the Reagan Years*, ed. John L. Palmer (Washington, D.C.: Urban Institute, 1986), 125.

67. David B. Walker, *The Rebirth of Federalism: Slouching toward Washington*, 2nd ed. (Chatham, N.J.: Chatham House, 2000), 151.

68. Reagan, *An American Life*, 196–97.

69. Nathan, "Institutional Change under Reagan," 137.

70. Timothy Conlan, *From New Federalism to Devolution* (Washington, D.C.: Brookings Institution, 1998), 95.

71. Conlan, *New Federalism*, 151.

72. David R. Beam, "New Federalism, Old Realities: The Reagan Administration and Intergovernmental Reform," in *The Reagan Presidency and the Governing of America*, ed. Lester M. Salamon and Michael S. Lund (Washington, D.C.: Urban Institute, 1984), 425–26.

73. Richard Nathan, "Federalism: The 'Great Composition,'" in *The New American Political System*, ed. Anthony King, 2nd version (Washington, D.C.: AEI, 1990), 258.

74. Beam, "New Federalism, Old Realities," 431–32.

75. Conlan, *New Federalism*, 151.

76. Alice M. Rivlin, *Reviving the American Dream* (Washington, D.C.: Brookings Institution, 1992), 102.

77. Conlan, *New Federalism*, 147.

78. Nathan, "Institutional Change Under Reagan," 135–41; Nathan, "Federalism: The 'Great Composition,'" 231–61.

79. Walker, *The Rebirth of Federalism*, 150.

80. Jack A. Meyer, "Social Programs and Social Policy," in *Perspectives on the Reagan Years*, ed. John L. Palmer, 79, 88.

81. Ceaser, "The Theory of Governance of the Reagan Administration," 83.

82. See, for example, Conlan, *New Federalism*, 110–11; Beam, "New Federalism, Old Realities," 441.

83. Conlan, *New Federalism*, 218. See generally Conlan, *New Federalism* 211–18; "Twisted Federalism," *Los Angeles Times*, November 16, 1986, section 5, 4.

84. Nathan, "Institutional Change under Reagan," 135–36.

85. Rivlin, *Reviving the American Dream*, 109.

86. "Lobbyists File in with Welcome Mats as State Capitols Take Bigger Role," *Wall Street Journal*, May 30, 1990, A14.

87. David M. O'Brien, "The Reagan Judges: His Most Enduring Legacy?" in *The Reagan Legacy: Promise and Performance*, ed. Charles O. Jones (Chatham, N.J.: Chatham House, 1988), 62.

88. O'Brien, "The Reagan Judges," 62.

89. Tinsley E. Yarbrough, "Reagan and the Courts," in *The Reagan Presidency*, ed. Dilys M. Hill, Raymond A. Moore, and Phil Williams (New York: St. Martin's, 1990); Murphy, "Reagan's Judicial Strategy;" Meese, *With Reagan*, 317–20; O'Brien, "The Reagan Judges," 67.

90. O'Brien, "The Reagan Judges," 68–70; Meese, *With Reagan*, 318.

91. Reagan, *An American Life*, 280.

92. O'Brien, "The Reagan Judges," 78.

93. O'Brien, "The Reagan Judges," 96.

94. W. Gary Fowler, Donald W. Jackson, and James W. Riddlesparger Jr., "Reagan's Judges: A Latent Revolution?" in *Ronald Reagan's America*, ed. Schmertz, Datlof, and Ugrinsky, 343–58; O'Brien, "The Reagan Judges," 82–83.

95. Martin Shapiro, "The Supreme Court from Early Burger to Early Rehnquist," in *The New American Political System*, ed. King, 84.

Chapter 2

96. James F. Simon, *The Center Holds: The Power Struggle inside the Rehnquist Court* (New York: Simon and Schuster, 1995).

97. Richard L. Pacelle, *The Transformation of the Supreme Court Agenda from the New Deal to the Reagan Administration* (Boulder, Colo.: Westview, 1991), 208.

98. Nathan, "Institutional Change under Reagan," 133–34.

99. O'Brien, "The Reagan Judges," 63–64.

100. T. Kenneth Cribb, "Discussant," in *Ronald Reagan's America*, ed. Schmertz, Datlof, and Ugrinsky, 297.

3

Reagan, American Political Institutions, and National Morale

I F THE CONSTITUTION IS THE FUNDAMENTAL BLUEPRINT for American freedom, it is not the only important measure of the institutional health of the polity. One of the most telling moments of the Carter presidency was the day in July 1979 when Jimmy Carter argued in a televised speech that Americans were suffering from a profound "crisis of spirit." In what later became known as his "malaise" speech, Carter decried the lack of unity, lack of direction, and growing lack of confidence that characterized the American condition in the late 1970s. While initial public reaction to the remarks was positive, the speech soon became a metaphor for the gloom and doom of the post-Vietnam, post-Watergate, oil-crisis era.

The "malaise" was more than a fleeting mood. Public confidence in American institutions, both governmental and private, had been falling since the mid-1960s. The presidency—not long before dubbed "imperial" by historian Arthur M. Schlesinger Jr.—had seemingly lost its luster and its capacity for accomplishment. Voter turnout had fallen dramatically since 1960. The political parties were in the midst of a decline that many observers feared was terminal. Least tangibly, but not least importantly, patriotism or an active pride in America had apparently reached a low ebb.

These trends were intertwined, deeply rooted, and highly troubling. They represented the response of citizens whose political leaders had failed them on issues ranging from Vietnam to Watergate, from the War on Poverty to forced busing, and from stagflation to gasoline lines. They posed a variety of dangers to American democracy over the long term. How does a nation maintain a representative democracy in the face of ever-declining participation? How does a political system mediate diverse interests and minimize the risk of personalistic demagoguery in the absence of strong political parties? Can the presidency continue to give voice to the aspirations of the whole American people or deal decisively with foreign threats in a significantly weakened state? How can meaningful politics be conducted without popular confidence in the institutions of government? In the end, how does a free people stir itself to necessary action if it cannot do so out of love of country? These questions, or variants of them, confronted Americans in 1980. To Ronald Reagan, no problem "was more serious than the fact that America had lost faith in itself. . . . We had to recapture our dreams, our pride in ourselves and our country, and regain that unique sense of destiny and optimism that had made America different from any other country in the world."[1] Reagan's approach was to promote stronger feelings of patriotism, and to make government work again. By most possible standards, Reagan's presidency ended the "malaise" and quieted the questions that had troubled Americans in their crisis of confidence. Nor was this development merely a change of atmospherics; rather, it was connected to a very real improvement in the condition of certain American political institutions.

"More and Bigger Flags"

In the 1960s and 1970s, patriotism was widely derided as the province of bigots or naifs, typified by the television character Archie Bunker. Perhaps the most remarked-upon change in American society in the Reagan years was the revival of unabashed patriotism. There had been early signs of this revival in 1976 during the bicentennial of the Declaration of Independence, but these had quickly receded. Then in late 1979 and 1980, the Iranian hostage crisis and the Soviet invasion of Afghanistan ignited a national awakening that was punctuated by the chants of "USA! USA!" at the Lake Placid Winter Olympics when the American hockey team upset the supposedly invincible Soviets.

Promoted by Reagan's oratory, this national spirit continued growing in the 1980s. Reagan took the rejuvenation of national morale to be an important task of presidential leadership, and his administration spared no effort in rhetoric, spectacle, or symbolism to achieve it. He believed in America's ideals, capacities, and Providential purpose—and he did not hesitate to convey that belief from every available forum. Reagan, *Newsweek* said, "made it fashionable again for Americans to show their patriotism."[2] By mid-decade, observers noted that "magazine after magazine, newspaper and TV stories emphasize a rebirth of patriotism, of belief in the nation."[3] This revival of patriotism showed itself in a variety of ways. The flag-waving reception given American athletes at the 1984 Los Angeles Olympics surpassed that of Lake Placid in 1980. Even the procession of the Olympic torch was an occasion for fervent roadside demonstrations throughout its trip across America; the transfer of the torch in Salt Lake City drew a crowd of two hundred thousand.[4] Another sign was the popularity of a large number of explicitly patriotic, promilitary, and anticommunist films (including *The Right Stuff, First Blood* [a "Rambo" movie] and its sequels, *Firefox, Red Dawn, Delta Force, Rocky IV, Top Gun, An Officer and a Gentleman, Invasion U.S.A., Commando, Uncommon Valor, Missing in Action, POW,* and *Heartbreak Ridge*) and songs (Lee Greenwood's "God Bless the U.S.A." for country fans, Twisted Sister's "We're Not Gonna' Take It" for those preferring a harder edge). A Vietnam veterans parade in Chicago in 1986 drew another two hundred thousand marchers.[5] Flag sales rose to record levels, advertising campaigns emphasized patriotism, and even "GI Joe" sales jumped from forty-five million dollars in 1982 to eighty-five million in 1983.[6] Events like the invasion of Grenada, the bombing of the U.S. Marine barracks in Beirut, and the Soviet shooting down of KAL 007 produced a visible "surge of national solidarity," as did the 1986 bombing of Libya.[7] A series of patriotic celebrations added to the spirit, including the bicentennials of the American revolutionary victory at Yorktown (1981) and of the signing of the U.S. Constitution (1987), the centennial of the Statue of Liberty (1986), and the forty-year anniversary of the Normandy invasion (1984).

New York Times correspondent R. W. Apple Jr., returning to the United States after seven years in Europe, noted in late 1983 that he was surprised to find the display of "more, and bigger, flags" than when he left. "Americans seem to be returning after a nightmarish period of confusion," Apple said, to "belief in one's country's intrinsic worth." Furthermore, "Americans of all kinds have pulled the whole question [of patriotism and relation of self to country] out of the backs of their minds and are examining it with some care. That in itself represents a significant change."[8] *Newsweek* columnist Meg Greenfield similarly commented on the "near-universality" of renewed patriotism: "It is there, strong and deep, among practically everyone, including even those who seem somewhat embarrassed to profess it."[9] In the late 1980s, two foreign policy analysts, Tami R. Davis and Sean M. Lynn-Jones, argued that

> during Ronald Reagan's presidency, the United States has rediscovered its faith in itself. Americans once again have begun to feel good about themselves, their country, and their role in the world. The flame of American patriotism, which dimmed and flickered after Vietnam and Watergate, is burning as brightly as ever.[10]

Not all observers found this development equally positive. Some considered the change healthy but found it tiresome or acknowledged it only backhandedly; some dismissed this airy change of disposition in the nation as Reagan's sole accomplishment. Some found it offensive or worrisome. Davis and Jones, for example, expressed fear that overemphasis on American exceptionalism was a poor foundation for a "realistic" foreign policy and could lead to messianism or (more likely) isolationism among Americans.[11] Humorist Russell Baker termed the trend "fanfaronade patriotism," a concoction that was "doubly sweet" because it gave the "opportunity to thump yourself on the chest" and "the thumping doesn't cost you anything." To Baker, real patriotism would consist of "turning over more income to Uncle Sam" and "feel[ing] good about it."[12] Others saw the new patriotism as a vehicle "to shut off the political dialogue,"[13] while respected theologian Martin Marty despaired of "boasting about our boasting" and saw too intimate a connection between the new patriotism and attitudes of superiority, egotism, and militarism.[14] Film critics and social commentators decried the rush of patriotic movies as "neokitsch aesthetic" and the sign of a "coarsened politics. . . . A subordination of thought to knee-jerk emotions."[15] For its part, Moscow did not care for the new atmosphere either. A *Literaturnaya Gazeta* correspondent reported from America that "The 'new patriotism,' which began to blanket the country in the early 1980s, is now the dominant phenomenon of the nation's public life. Even young adults are going mad with patriotic delight, rather than," the correspondent continued wistfully, "burning draft cards."[16]

However, most Americans saw in this turn of events a welcome change. As R. W. Apple Jr. related, most people were "glad to be out from under what they considered to be the humiliation of Vietnam, Watergate, and the Iranian hostages."[17] In any event, hardly anyone argued that the American spirit, however amorphous and difficult to define, was not more confident and vigorous in the eighties than it had been at any time since the early 1960s. The view expressed by *Harper's*—that the "current discovery of patriotism" had less to do with genuine public feeling than with marketing—was in a distinct minority.[18] For the most part, whether they liked it, disliked it, or were ambivalent, observers believed they were witnessing a real phenomenon.

It is reasonable to ask how deep this patriotism actually went. It took little exertion to applaud Rambo's nearly single-handed defeat of the Soviet army in Afghanistan, and if the patriotic revival of the 1980s went only that far, it was shallow indeed. One possible measure of the depth of this patriotic revival was whether Americans were more willing to join the armed forces and risk their lives in the defense of their country.

At the end of the 1970s, recruiters were having a difficult time filling their quotas with high-quality recruits. Shortly after assuming office, Reagan himself had told the Joint Chiefs of Staff that "I wanted to do whatever it took to make our men and women proud to wear their uniforms again."[19] By the mid-1980s, the problem was solved. In 1986, more than 680,000 Americans sought to enlist to fill 325,000 positions.[20] Reserve Officer Training Corps programs also reported great increases in student interest and in the respect shown to ROTC cadets by other students on campuses. In 1984, journalists noted that "campus Reserve Officer Training Corps programs, shunned after Vietnam, are booming."[21] Likewise, the service academies reported an upsurge in applications and a higher academic level of applicants than ever before.[22] Part of this phenomenon, especially in the enlisted ranks, was due to enhanced pay and benefits; a concerted effort was made by the Reagan administration and Congress to make service in the volunteer armed forces more financially attractive. Nevertheless, observers tended to agree that a large portion of this recruiting improvement resulted from an increased sense of national pride and civic duty. As *U.S. News & World Report* surmised in 1984, the armed forces were popular again primarily because "patriotism seems resurgent among the young."[23] Naval Academy admissions officer Capt. Harry Seymour agreed. Patriotism, said Seymour, was the "key *x* factor" explaining the 35 percent increase in applications from 1979 to 1986. "I'm astounded at how much they want to serve their country. It's no curveball, no smokescreen—they want to get in, they want to serve."[24] Consequently, as *U.S. News* put it, "Far from being just a fad, the patriotic stirrings and the popularity of things military have strategic significance for the nation."[25]

As Davis and Lynn-Jones conceded, and despite their concerns, "Patriotism, pride in American principles, and moral vision are all ideals fundamental to American self-identity, and thus they are necessary building blocks for any successful foreign policy."[26] The renewed patriotic fervor not only filled the "hollow army" but stiffened the resolve of American politicians, provided support for the defense buildup, and gave Reagan the freedom to pursue the policies (to be discussed in chapter 7) that were to contribute to the collapse of the Soviet bloc. No doubt guided in part by Reagan's public discourse, a 1983 Roper Poll revealed that 81 percent of Americans believed that America had a "special role" in the world.[27] Indeed, in 1982, a *New York Times* poll found a two-to-one margin (55 percent to 28 percent) preferring to "risk destruction" rather than be "dominated by the Russians."[28] That margin only grew through the decade. By 1985, a *Los Angeles Times* poll showed that by a margin of sixty-one to twenty-eight, Americans would choose to "risk destruction" rather than "be dominated by the Russians," while a February 1987 poll indicated that 72 percent of Americans preferred to fight an all-out nuclear war rather than surrender to Soviet power (only 19 percent preferred surrender).[29]

The patriotism of the 1980s carried over into the early 1990s and ensured that the country was prepared for the crisis with Iraq, both militarily and emotionally. The "high-water mark of protest" against the Persian Gulf war came on the second day after bombing began, as a thousand demonstrators were arrested in San Francisco.[30] From then on, the tide of activism ran in the other direction. The antiwar protests were dwarfed in size and consequence by large and frequent demonstrations in support of the war effort, many by younger Americans. *Newsweek* reported,

> It could have been a scene out of the '60s: hundreds of young people demonstrating in front of the White House as a line of graying veterans march past in opposition. But for this encounter, just days after the Gulf War started, the generations switched sides. The young people—almost all twentysomething—were passionately in favor of the war.[31]

Thousands of prowar demonstrators filled a San Diego parking lot to make an American flag from colored cards. A rally in Lexington, Virginia, drew 1,300 students; Harvard Students United for Desert Storm signed up seven hundred members in one day; student journalists reported that 60 percent of the Kent State student body supported the war effort. In the first month of the war, army recruiting jumped by two-thirds. An air force recruiter explained, "A lot of kids feel it is about time to start standing behind the country."[32]

Domestically, the revival of patriotism also had important consequences. It was tied, as we will see below, to a more general restoration of confidence in national institutions. Some observers also emphasized its importance to national unity in a country that had always been diverse and was growing ever more so. In a decade when fundamentalist and evangelical Christians sought to grasp tightly the mantle of patriotism, even the executive director of the American Humanists Association argued that while patriotism could lead to "fanaticism and bigotry," it was also "the glue that holds this diverse nation together. . . . Americanism, for all its shortcomings, dangers, and new problems, has successfully served as the religious unifying factor thought so necessary for successful governments . . . by America's founders."[33] In his book *Why Americans Hate Politics*, journalist E. J. Dionne looked at the question of national unity from another angle. In Dionne's view, the extraordinary power of patriotism in the 1980s (particularly the 1988 presidential election) was a consequence of its being a metaphor for national unity, as against liberal policies perceived by many Americans as undermining that unity. In 1988, Dionne pointed out,

> Michael Dukakis spoke contemptuously of the Republicans' campaign of "flags and furloughs." But flags and furloughs spoke precisely to the doubts that many Americans developed about liberalism from 1968 onward. In the eyes of many of their traditional supporters, liberal Democrats seemed to oppose the personal disciplines—of family and tough law enforcement, of community values and patriotism—that average citizens, no less than neoconservative intellectuals, saw as essential to holding a society together.[34]

To the extent that this analysis is true, patriotism in Reagan years takes on a much more specific political connotation. In all likelihood, the revival of patriotism was derived from a variety of sources, including a reaction against loss of national pride, purpose, and unity, against specific disintegrative liberal policies, and against global advances by America's totalitarian adversaries. The consequences of that revival were equally varied, ranging from restoration of national resolve to strengthened unity, to greater military readiness, to higher confidence. Not least, the new patriotism served as an instrument by which voters forced the Democratic Party into greater cultural moderation. The most important consequence, however, was the reenergizing of the American people and the relegitimizing of the idea of America. Altogether, the renewed patriotism of the Reagan era was both real and consequential.

The Presidency

As noted presidential scholars like Richard Neustadt, Sidney Milkis, and Michael Nelson saw it, the presidency that Reagan assumed in January 1981 was a presidency in crisis. In 1980, Neustadt was driven to ask, "Is the presidency possible?"[35] Milkis and Nelson would later reflect,

> It seemed during the final days of the Carter administration that the presidency no longer worked, that presidents had become frustrated beyond hope of achievement by an attenuated party system, a hostile press, a congeries of powerful special interest groups, an intransigent bureaucracy, an aggressive Congress, assertive courts, and a demoralized public. From 1961 to 1977, five presidents had come to office. None had completed two terms.[36]

This crisis of the presidency carried with it profound implications for the United States. Since the inauguration of George Washington as the first president under the Constitution of 1787, the presidency had served as a symbol of the unity of the American people. Throughout the twentieth century, the presidency had been the organizing center for the nation's response to foreign danger; as the *Federalist* papers argue, the executive alone had the ability to act with the "secrecy, energy, and despatch" required to meet crises.[37] More than a few political scientists argued that the presidency served a crucial integrative role in an otherwise highly dispersed system.

By the end of the Reagan presidency, most observers agreed that the presidency as an institution had been reinvigorated. Four factors seem to have brought about this change. First, Reagan's legislative successes in 1981—when his budget was adopted that cut taxes, limited domestic spending, and accelerated the defense buildup—represented in the view of many analysts the greatest shift in public policy since Lyndon Johnson's term. Charles O. Jones argued that Reagan's success was "akin to the policy breakthroughs of the Great Society."[38] To Milkis and Nelson, the legislative campaign of 1981 "rivaled the early breakthroughs of the New Freedom, the New Deal, and the Great Society."[39] Reagan personally lobbied undecided congressmen, and his administration made innovative use of an element of the 1974 budget reform act—the "budget reconciliation" process—to maximum tactical effect. Democratic House Speaker Tip O'Neill, a fervent opponent of Reagan's plan, nevertheless acknowledged the competence that had brought its victory: "All in all, the Reagan team in 1981 was probably the best run political operation unit I've ever seen. . . . [T]hey knew where they were going and they knew how to get there."[40] Reagan achieved this "breakthrough" by concentrating his personal energies on a few major priorities—in contrast with Carter, who came to office with an agenda so sweeping that he could not easily focus on any single aspect of it. Though Reagan's success rate with Congress fell significantly after 1981, his first-year victories not only established a reputation for competence that served his administration well but put Reagan in control of the national agenda for the rest of his presidency. This success—which few serious observers had expected, given the recent history of presidential weakness—led to a broad-based reappraisal of the capacities of the modern chief executive.

Second, Reagan remained in control of the agenda, even when he lost specific battles, because he offered a relatively consistent, and consistently delivered, message. Unlike several previous presidents, who were less philosophically grounded and hence more likely to swing unpredictably from one message and one policy to another, Reagan's ideas constituted a clear framework for his administration. On several occasions, Reagan maintained his course despite intense pressure from interest groups, the news media, and even his own advisers. Some observers argued that the revival of public confidence was owed in part to the high level of congruence between what Reagan promised and what he actually did.[41]

Additionally, the first two factors combined to produce an appearance of strength and decisiveness. When Reagan fired the striking air-traffic controllers of the PATCO union in August 1981, he demonstrated to many Americans that he was no Jimmy Carter. He also frequently tapped into popular movies for memorable one-liners that conveyed an image of toughness, such as "You can run, but you can't hide," and "Make my day." Public opinion analysts pointed out that in the 1984 presidential election, Reagan scored more poorly than Walter Mondale on the attribute of compassion (trailing in a poll taken one month before election day by fourteen percentage points) but much better than Mondale on the attribute of strength (on which he led by thirty-one percentage points). Indeed, a full 75 percent of Americans said they thought of Reagan as a "strong leader."[42]

Finally, Reagan rebuilt the strength of the presidency by paying extraordinary attention to subordinating the executive-branch bureaucracy to the preferences of the president. Peter M. Benda and Charles H. Levine argued in 1988 that "from the outset, the Reagan administration pursued a campaign to maximize presidential control over the federal bureaucracy that was more self-conscious in design and execution, and more comprehensive in scope, than that of any other administration of the modern era."[43] The administration undertook a two-pronged strategy. First, it centralized policy design and decision making in the Executive Office of the President, which was under the direct political control of Reagan and his staff. It also attempted to harness the permanent civil service bureaucracy, by ensuring through an elaborate screening mechanism that all political appointments—not only cabinet secretaries but the crucial "subcabinet" of assistants, deputies, and lower officials—were filled with people committed to the president's program.[44] Indeed, a substantial degree of change within agencies was prodded by the subcabinet, which "reflected more the pure Reagan conservative ideology than the views of their generally more conciliatory cabinet chiefs."[45] The conservative administrative apparatus installed by Reagan controlled important budgeting, personnel, and regulatory matters.

Facing some form of divided government for his entire presidency, Reagan also made frequent use of executive orders to impose his agenda to the fullest extent possible without congressional action, especially in the regulatory sphere. Executive Orders 12291 and 12498 mandated "central clearance" of proposed regulations in the Office of Management and Budget; in 1985 and 1986, OMB figures indicated that this procedure resulted in revision of 23 percent of all proposed regulations.[46] For the most part, Reagan's administrative strategy was quite effective. One political scientist reflected in 1990 that "the Reagan presidency impressively demonstrated the potential of the chief executive to reshape both public policy and the modus operandi of the federal bureaucracy."[47]

On the negative side of the ledger, Reagan's management style came under criticism from scholars and commentators. Both supporters and critics of Reagan agreed that the president's management method was heavily weighted toward delegation to subordinates. However, his alleged lack of knowledge about policy details was almost certainly exaggerated by his opponents, as was his fondness for vacations; a *U.S. News & World Report* study published in 1984 showed that Reagan had spent a smaller percentage of time on vacation in his first term than Presidents Nixon, Kennedy, Eisenhower, or Franklin Roosevelt.[48] It was doubtless not a coincidence that in the "kiss-and-tell" memoirs of some Reagan appointees accusing him of laziness and intellectual weakness, he was uniformly at his stupidest when he refused to take the advice offered by the authors. While Reagan did not possess raw brilliance in the manner of the college president Woodrow Wilson or the engineers Herbert Hoover and Jimmy Carter, their examples might encourage greater circumspection about the importance of raw brilliance in the White House.

Nevertheless, it is clearly true that Reagan took less interest in the day-to-day execution of policy, outside of a handful of issues about which he cared passionately, than most recent presidents. This approach contributed to Reagan's success by preventing him from being overwhelmed with details, as Carter had been. Because of his strongly held beliefs, many administrative decisions were never referred to him; lower-level appointees were able to discern his preferences without asking. As one administration aide related, "Through some mechanism I don't pretend to understand, he wouldn't get asked things that he wouldn't agree with. You could say he didn't have to do anything . . . because there was a kind of self-control or self-censorship by the staff. People wouldn't bring him something if they knew he would be averse to it."[49]

On the other hand, Reagan's management style worked against him on more than one occasion, sometimes producing serious consequences. The most obvious of these failures was the Iran-Contra episode. The president's public standing was significantly, if temporarily, shaken when revelations surfaced that the administration had sold arms to Iran in hopes of improving the prospects for the release of hostages held in Beirut by pro-Iranian terrorists, and had then diverted the proceeds to the Nicaraguan Contras fighting the Sandinista regime. An investigative commission appointed under Sen. John Tower reported that a "flawed process" and a "lack of responsibility" from Reagan down had led to the fiasco; the president "did not seem aware of the way in which the operation was implemented and the full consequences of U.S. participation."[50] The Iran-Contra scandal clearly undid some of what Reagan had previously achieved in terms of restoring public confidence in American institutions.

The other genuinely troubling breakdown was Reagan's ineffective response to the savings and loan crisis. As we will see in chapter 4, the savings and loan industry was already facing insolvency when Reagan took office, due to a variety of causes that made deregulation a plausible policy choice. However, the administration did not press for repeal of the two-and-a-half-fold increase in deposit insurance that Congress had passed in 1980, nor did it effectively monitor the foray of the deregulated saving and loan institutions into new lending areas. When it became clear to some administration officials that the crisis had worsened and that the solution was likely to be costly, the administrative "self-censorship" that diverted many issues from cluttering Reagan's desk worked to keep him uninformed. Political appointees calculated whether the president wanted to know, decided he would prefer to leave the problem for his successor, and did not push Reagan for action. The price was twofold: a major financial cost to the nation, and a blow to Reagan's claim of "moral leadership."[51]

These management shortcomings have combined with the political predilections of the academy to produce some highly uncharitable appraisals of Reagan as president. One 1995 textbook ranked him "low" on five of six categories of leadership.[52] At least two surveys of historians taken after his presidency ended ranked him among the mediocre presidents, though the reasons offered seemed to indicate that the rankings were the consequence more of ideological animus than any objective defect. One group of historians explained its 1993 ranking by arguing that Reagan's domestic policy had been "wrongheaded and malignant" and his foreign policy "unnecessarily belliger-ent."[53] Another group, headed by Arthur M. Schlesinger Jr., reported in 1996 that its low ranking of Reagan was based on his "attack on government and his tax reductions."[54]

Nevertheless, it is probably true that more Americans—including many po-litical scientists who study the presidency—believed that Reagan's presidency rejuvenated the institution, rescuing it from the appearance of impotence it had suffered under Jimmy Carter and, to a lesser extent, all the presidents for the previous quarter-century. In this view, which crossed ideological lines, the flaws were outweighed by the strengths. As commentator Richard Reeves pro-claimed in 1984, Reagan "made a mockery of the conventional wisdom that the country was ungovernable."[55] Richard Nathan of Princeton concurred. Writing in 1986, Nathan held that "Ronald Reagan was elected at a time when the presidency was in deep trouble. . . . [T]he executive office needed resusci-tation, and Ronald Reagan, in a way that surprised many observers, has ac-complished precisely that."[56]

This contemporary appraisal has since been bolstered by a number of very prominent presidential scholars, Schlesinger notwithstanding. Indeed, as Prof. Paul Kengor pointed out in an article in late 1999, Reagan is much better treated in academic articles and books than one would have expected, given the overwhelmingly liberal leanings of the universities.[57]

For example, Marc Landy and Sidney Milkis, the latter of whom was among those who feared the presidency had become unworkable prior to Reagan's election, now declare Reagan to stand with Lyndon Johnson as one of only two presidents in the second half of the twentieth century with a plausible claim to greatness. In their view, he fell short in the end, because of "lack of programmatic ambition," exemplified by his unwillingness to risk his popu-larity on behalf of a campaign for change in 1984. Nevertheless, to Landy and

Milkis, Reagan's claim to presidential greatness was "in some ways, more impressive than those of LBJ. Like LBJ, he rhetorically challenged the status quo and engineered some very important changes in the status quo. Unlike LBJ, he served out his two terms and left his party stronger than he found it."[58]

Richard Neustadt, author of the classic *Presidential Power*, first published in 1960, criticizes Reagan for "less intellectual curiosity, less attention to detail than any president since at least Calvin Coolidge." His analysis makes clear his skepticism regarding Reagan policy initiatives. Nevertheless, Neustadt claims that Reagan's presidency "restored the public image of the office to a fair (if rickety) approximation of its Rooseveltian mold: a place of popularity, influence, and initiative, a source of programmatic and symbolic leadership, both pacesetter and tonesetter, the nation's voice to both the world and us, and—like or hate the policies—a presence many of us loved to see as Chief Executive." Reagan's impact on public policy was, "in anybody's reckoning . . . substantial."[59]

In a study of the way modern presidents use public appeals to move policy, Samuel Kernell lauds Reagan's skill in using rhetoric to help negotiate passage of his legislative program. To Kernell, "Ronald Reagan eclipsed all of his predecessors in the quantity of national appeals and outdid most of them as well in the quality of presentation. . . . Will [Reagan's] shadow loom over the next generation of White House occupants? Quite possibly. This is more than idle speculation, for Ronald Reagan relied on going public for his influence in Washington more heavily and more profitably than did his predecessors. His success has forced others in Washington to reevaluate the way they assess the office."[60]

Stephen Skowronek argued, in his widely acclaimed *The Politics Presidents Make*, that Reagan was one of only five "reconstructive" presidents in American history. He was, in Skowronek's view, not as successful as the rest in establishing new regimes for American politics, owing largely to how entrenched and difficult to dislodge bureaucratic power has become. Nevertheless, and despite his obvious distaste for Reaganism, Skowronek places Reagan in the same category as Thomas Jefferson, Andrew Jackson, Abraham Lincoln, and Franklin Roosevelt.[61]

Not least, Aaron Wildavsky—who was relatively sympathetic to Reagan on programmatic grounds—wrote in 1991, "Despite continuous efforts to belie his achievements, Reagan remains the most creative president of recent times and, with Franklin Roosevelt, one of the two most influential of the modern era."[62] In Wildavsky's view, Reagan provided "about as much direction as the existing American antileadership system can support."[63]

These assessments are not universally accepted, and they vary even among themselves about the mix of good and bad in Reagan's presidency. Nevertheless, the fact cannot be easily dismissed that half a dozen of the most distinguished presidential scholars in recent American history have agreed that Reagan was a central figure in the presidency in the last half of the twentieth century. Two new academic surveys, published in early 2000, reflect this growing, if often grudging, respect for Reagan among scholars. Instead of languishing in the middle of the pack of presidents, Reagan moved up to eleventh out of forty-two in one survey, eighth of thirty-nine in the other.[64] It is entirely possible that the future will see further upward revision.

Political Parties

Political scientists have long been supportive of strong political parties. In their near-consensus view, parties serve several crucial functions in the American political system. They are critical actors in the process of interest aggregation; in other words, they constitute the institutional mechanism by which a highly fractured society forms governing coalitions and provides meaningful choices to voters. The parties can also help to create greater collective accountability. Additionally, some scholars argue that the danger of demagoguery is reduced if presidential candidates are answerable to a whole party of citizens and fellow officeholders. In this view, excessive personalism in politics threatens the fabric of freedom, and relatively strong parties can counterbalance such tendencies. Therefore, it was a worrisome trend when the parties experienced a dramatic decline in organizational strength and voter loyalty from the 1960s to the 1980s. In some cases, these trends of decline had started much earlier. By 1972, respected political correspondent David Broder warned that "the party's over" and that American politics could soon suffer from paralysis, if not demagoguery that could shake republicanism to its foundations.[65]

In the 1980s, however, there were several signs of a modest party rejuvenation. In the words of Sidney Milkis, "Under Ronald Reagan . . . the party system showed at least some signs of transformation and renewal."[66] The movement of voters toward self-identification as "independents" halted, and the proportion of voters who identified themselves as "strong" partisans slightly increased for the first time in at least two decades. At the national level of party organization, political scientist James Ceaser noted in 1990 that "both parties have significantly increased their activities since the mid-seventies."[67] With financial assistance from the national parties, state and local parties also engaged in a process of organizational rebuilding in the 1980s.[68] Within Congress, much of the fragmentation produced by the reforms of the 1970s gave way in the 1980s to greater party discipline and a stronger role for the party leadership. In 1990, Ceaser argued, "Both parties today are far more cohesive than they were twenty years ago, as indicated by party unity scores in the Congress. The principal reason for this change almost certainly lies in the associational developments of the decline of radical southerners in the Democratic Party and the emergence of modern conservatism in the Republican Party."[69]

In this process, Reagan's role as party leader was vital. As Paul Allen Beck pointed out, Republican organizational successes were "heightened by a popular Republican occupant in the White House. President Reagan provided a powerful symbolic presence around which his party could rally both activists and rank and file."[70] Indeed, Reagan seemed to relish that role. He broke with the tendency of most recent presidents to minimize identification with their parties, instead consciously seeking to build the Republican Party into a more powerful force. According to his White House political director, Reagan exhibited a "total readiness" to engage in fund-raising and other party-building activities.[71] After cataloguing the list of presidents from Eisenhower through Carter who had neglected their parties, parties expert Larry J. Sabato declared in his 1988 book *The Party's Just Begun,*

> Fortunately, modern chief executives now have an alternative model well worth emulating. Ronald Reagan has been the most party-oriented president of recent times. . . . In 1983 and 1984 during his own reelection effort, Reagan made more than two dozen campaign and fundraising appearances for all branches of the party organization and candidates at every level. More than 300 television advertisements were taped as well, including one for an obscure Honolulu city council contest. Reagan has even shown a willingness to get involved in the nitty-gritty of candidate recruitment, frequently calling in strong potential candidates to urge them to run. During the pitched and ultimately losing battle to retain control of the Senate for the Republicans in 1986, Reagan played the good soldier, visiting twenty-two key states repeatedly and raising $33 million for the party and its candidates. Unlike Eisenhower, Reagan has been willing to attempt a popularity transfer to his party and to campaign for Republicans whether they are strongly loyal to him personally or not; unlike Johnson, Reagan has been willing to put his prestige and policies to the test on the hustings; unlike Nixon, Reagan spent time and effort helping underdogs and long-shot candidates, not just likely winners; unlike Carter, Reagan has signed more than seventy fundraising appeals for party committees and has taken a personal interest in the further strengthening of the GOP's organizational capacity.[72]

At the organizational level, in 1982 Reagan handpicked the chairman of the Republican National Committee, Frank Fahrenkopf, and established a new party post of general party chairman, to be filled by his close friend Sen. Paul Laxalt. This new position allowed a greater coordination among the varying campaign arms of the Republican Party regarding message and strategy.[73] Under Laxalt's and Fahrenkopf's leadership, Republicans also continued a program advanced by former RNC chairman Bill Brock from 1976 to 1980, developing mass-based direct-mail fund-raising and other organizational and technological innovations. From a direct-mail base of twenty-four thousand contributors in 1975, the Republican direct-mail donor list grew to over two million by the mid-1980s, at which point the Republican Party was bringing in three-fourths of its total revenue through direct-mail contributions that averaged under thirty-five dollars each.[74] As Sabato pointed out, the cascade of money allowed Republicans to engage in unprecedented professional party staffing, voter contact, polling, media advertising, candidate recruitment and staff training, research and data sharing, party communication, and outreach.[75] Similar fund-raising strategies and political innovations were used by the Republican congressional election committees (the National Republican Congressional Committee and National Republican Senatorial Committee). In the short term, this drive gave Republicans an advantage. In the longer term, Democratic committees gradually caught up, reducing a six-to-one disadvantage in combined fund-raising in 1982 to 2.5 to one in 1988. Consequently, over time, parties as institutions grew stronger and took increased roles in an otherwise candidate-centered system.[76] David Broder was able to remark in 1983 that "having written at considerable length on the weaknesses of the parties, I am delighted to see that the invalids are sitting up and taking nourishment."[77]

At the level of party voters, Reagan's clear ideology almost certainly led to the growth in numbers of Republicans generally—who inched toward rough parity with Democrats in the mid-1980s—and also of self-identified strong Republicans. It also probably led to the growth among strong Democrats. Offering, as Barry Goldwater had promised in 1964, "a choice, not an echo," Reagan not only sorted out the parties but contributed to the intensity of each side.

Altogether, this party revival was only partial in nature. Partisanship in the electorate, for example, did not regain the position it had held in the 1950s, and split-ticket voting actually increased. Reagan's party building and popularity failed to bring an across-the-board partisan realignment favoring Republicans in the 1980s. The kind of party government mourned by David Broder did not reappear. Indeed, Reagan was accused of separating his presidential reelection campaign from Republican congressional campaigns in 1984, making it difficult for Republican candidates "down the ballot" to benefit from Reagan's coattails in that landslide year. To a large extent, it was also true that the institutional revival that did occur was made possible only by a reorientation of parties toward greater party centralization and greater emphasis on national issues. However, while observers at the end of the 1980s noted simultaneous signs of decline, resurgence, and stabilization in the strength of parties,[78] political parties were on balance stronger at the end of the 1980s than at the beginning.

Public Confidence in Institutions

The growth of patriotic sentiment combined with the increasing effectiveness of key American institutions to produce a rise, beginning in 1982, in the confidence that Americans had in their political and social institutions. During the 1980s, polls showed increased levels of confidence that "government does the right thing most of the time." There was also a rise in public confidence in institutions like public education, the military, and business, which had also suffered in the 1960s and 1970s.[79] As we have seen, confidence in the presidency was substantially restored among citizens and scholars alike, many of whom had begun to wonder whether the office was too difficult for any one man.[80] Confidence in the Supreme Court and even in Congress improved, though possibly on the coattails of the presidency. Some analysts went a step farther, arguing that increased popular confidence in the institutions of government flowed from Reagan's attempts to limit government to a narrower scope of action. In the view of political scientist James Ceaser, the "remarkable shift in both elite and public perceptions regarding the possibility of effectively governing our political system" could be attributed to Reagan's refusal to create unreachable expectations for government.[81] In 1981, surveys showed that by a fifty-four-percentage-point margin Americans thought that the federal government creates more problems than it solves; by 1986, that margin had shrunk to twenty-four percentage points.[82]

Similarly, measures of public cynicism declined in national election studies from 1980 to 1988, in most cases falling sharply by the mid-1980s before moving slightly upward again at the end of the decade (see table 3.1).[83] The key governmental and nongovernmental pillars of American society enjoyed greater popular confidence in the 1980s than at any time in recent history. One analyst of public opinion held in 1985 that "the cynicism about politics that so marked the Johnson, Nixon, Ford, Carter, and early Reagan years seems almost like a bad memory."[84]

Numerous surveys showed that by the mid-1980s this confidence extended to the future of the country. In May 1980, only 21 percent were willing to say that things were going "fairly well" or "very well"; by December 1983, 60 percent said so.[85] To a large extent, this confidence paralleled increasing confidence in the economy, and it was seen as well through much of the 1990s. That explanation, however, is incomplete. Confidence also tracked presidential approval ratings, which were driven by both the economy and several other factors, often related to foreign policy, throughout the 1980s. After the recession of 1981–82, Ronald Reagan's approval ratings broke 50 percent not with the onset of economic recovery but with the invasion of Grenada in October 1983, one of the events that catalyzed the new patriotism.[86] Furthermore, the

TABLE 3.1
Positive Responses to Questions Regarding Cynicism toward Government

	1964	1968	1972	1976	1980	1984	1988
1. Can government be trusted all or most of the time?	78	63	54	35	26	45	41
2. Is government run for the benefit of all?	69	56	41	26	23	41	33
3. Does government waste a lot of tax money?	48	61	67	76	80	66	64
4. Are many in government crooked?	30	26	38	44	49	33	42

Source: National Election Studies, cited in Ruy Texeira, *The Disappearing American Voter* (Washington, D.C.: Brookings Institution, 1992).

rise of confidence in institutions began in 1982, when the recession was still under way. At the end of his presidency, public-opinion experts tied the improvement in confidence throughout the 1980s to Reagan's leadership and performance, even after some slippage related to Iran-Contra.

Another rough measure that cynicism and feelings of political inefficacy subsided in the 1980s can be found in the turnaround, as small as it might have been, in voter turnout trends. Consistent with a pattern beginning after 1960, average voter turnout in presidential elections continued to fall in the 1980s. However, the rate of turnout decline slowed considerably in the 1980s compared to the 1970s.[87] In fact, in 1984 (the year Reagan sought reelection) voter turnout moved slightly upward, the first presidential election in which it had increased since 1960. Overall, the 1980s achieved a stabilization of average turnout lasting through the 1990s (see chart 3.1). National election studies also showed that the percentage of the electorate that claimed to be "not much interested" in the campaign fell slightly in the 1980s, while the percentage of the electorate that had high or very high knowledge of the candidates or parties, declared strong partisan identification, or cared "a great deal" which party won the presidency all rose, some substantially. Some other indicators showed a substantial improvement in 1984, followed by a drop in the George Bush–Michael Dukakis race of 1988.[88] In any event, most important indicators of political interest and participation stabilized or even improved for the first time since the early 1960s.

Furthermore, voting is only one form of participation, and in other respects political interest and activity among Americans during the 1980s grew substantially. At the end of the 1980s, "the number and variety of organized interests represented in Washington were at an all-time high."[89] Political action committees, the campaign arms of interest groups, quadrupled in number, to

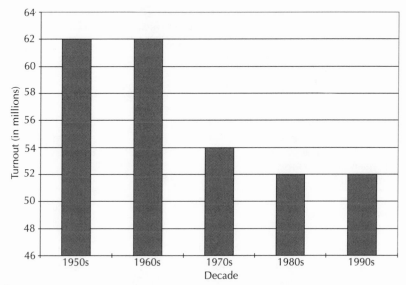

Chart 3.1
Average Presidential Election Turnout by Decade, 1950s–1990s

four thousand between 1976 and 1990. The membership of many of the most active interest groups—including the American Association of Retired Persons, the National Rifle Association, and Common Cause—grew considerably, according to surveys conducted by the respected *Encyclopedia of Associations*.[90] From another vantage point, of course, this development was problematic—it is not at all clear that the profusion and increased influence of narrowly focused interest groups is good for American politics—but it was, at any rate, indicative of greater participation.

Another possible measure of participation was the extent to which citizens organize initiative drives in the twenty-three states that permit them. As political scientist Daniel Smith has demonstrated, not every initiative represents a genuine upsurge of public interest or participation.[91] Yet many do. The 1980s saw a level of state initiative activity unparalleled since the early 1930s, after a low point in the 1950s and 1960s. In 1982, there were sixty-one citizen initiatives and referenda on state ballots, a fifty-year high; that record was surpassed again in the 1987–88 election cycle, when sixty-seven initiatives reached the ballot.[92]

Reagan and American Institutions: Evaluations

In several respects, the record of American institutions in the Reagan years was mixed. Popular confidence in the institutions of government and society was enhanced but not restored to the level that had existed before the long decline starting in the 1960s. Likewise, political parties experienced a renaissance that was important but incomplete. The presidency regained its authority but was tarnished by Iran-Contra. Voting turnout stabilized, even went up briefly in 1984, but did not show significant improvement.

Some important institutional tensions in American government were left to the future to resolve. The stronger presidency was achieved partly through increased use of executive orders to bypass Congress and through greater centralization of the parties. This made the presidency somewhat less subject to the traditional checks of the American system, both formal and informal. Conservatives who applauded Reagan's decisive use of executive orders came to rue the example he provided for Bill Clinton.

Nevertheless, on balance, crucial American political institutions and the more intangible political morale of the nation were undoubtedly stronger in 1989 than they were in 1980. A large part of that improvement was traceable to Reagan. In some cases, he quite deliberately sought to bring about that result. The revival of patriotism was a goal that Reagan carefully cultivated, as was the newfound strength of the presidency. The multifaceted rebuilding of the Republican Party was also an explicit goal of the president, who was, as David Broder conveyed, a "party's soldier."[93] In these cases, there was a direct causal link between Reagan's actions as chief executive and positive outcomes. In other respects, Reagan's impact was more indirect. His aim was to strengthen the Republican Party, not parties generally; yet Democrats had to copy Republican organizational and fund-raising techniques to remain competitive. The improvement of public confidence in governmental institutions, including the presidency, was welcomed by Reagan but was mostly traceable to things that he did for other reasons, or to circumstances to which he was connected only in an attenuated way. The end of the long slide in voter turnout was probably an incidental by-product of the other institutional improvements.

By whatever route, Reagan gave Americans a variety of reasons to believe that their institutions, undeniably crucial to their liberty, could work again. In 1987, a prominent group of public opinion analysts submitted that "Ronald Reagan's legacy should include a higher sense of national morale and confidence in government than when he took office."[94] For his part, Reagan declared in his 1989 farewell address to the nation that he viewed the restoration of the nation's morale as one of the "great triumphs" of his presidency.[95] That triumph was twofold, since the enhanced confidence of Americans was largely a consequence of a concrete improvement in the functioning of American institutions. In that sense, the Reagan years can accurately be considered a period of renewal.

Notes

1. Ronald Reagan, *An American Life: The Autobiography* (New York: Simon and Schuster, 1990), 219.

2. "Goodbye to the Gipper," *Newsweek*, January 9, 1989, 19.

3. Seymour Martin Lipset, "Feeling Better: Measuring the Nation's Confidence," *Public Opinion*, April–May 1985, 7. For just one example of this phenomenon, see *U.S. News & World Report*, December 30, 1985–January 6, 1986; this combined year-end issue featured a cover picture of the torch on the Statue of Liberty, with the headline "A Rekindled Spirit."

4. "Patriotism Is Back in Style," *U.S. News & World Report*, July 9, 1984, 58.

5. William Broyles Jr., "At Last, Loyalty Makes the Headlines," *U.S. News & World Report*, June 30, 1986, 13.

6. "Patriotism Is Back in Style," 58–59.

7. Meg Greenfield, "Patriotism and Disappointment," *Newsweek*, November 14, 1983, 124.

8. R. W. Apple Jr., "New Stirrings of Patriotism," *New York Times Magazine*, December 11, 1983, 43, 47.

9. Greenfield, "Patriotism and Disappointment."

10. Tami R. Davis and Sean M. Lynn-Jones, "Citty upon a Hill," *Foreign Policy* (Spring 1987), 20.

11. Davis and Lynn-Jones, "Citty upon a Hill."

12. Russell Baker, "Flagging Enthusiasm," *New York Times Magazine*, September 23, 1984, 14.

13. "'New Patriotism' Called Dangerous," *USA Today*, August 1985, 13.

14. Martin Marty, "Sailing through Waves of Patriotism," *Christian Century*, July 16–23, 1986, 641.

15. Sidney Blumenthal, "Reaganism and the Neokitsch Aesthetic," in *The Reagan Legacy*, ed. Sidney Blumenthal and Thomas Byrne Edsall (New York: Pantheon, 1988), 276–79; David Edestein, "Somewhere over the Rambo," *Rolling Stone*, December 19, 1985–January 2, 1986, 105.

16. Vladimir Simonov, "The 'New Patriotism,'" *World Press Review*, December 1985, 50.

17. Apple, "New Stirrings of Patriotism," 43.

18. Lewis H. Lapham, "The New Patriotism," *Harper's*, June 1984, 7.

19. Reagan, *An American Life*, 235.

20. John McLaughlin, "Military Love Affair," *National Review*, October 24, 1986, 24.

21. "America's Youth in Search of a Cause," *U.S. News & World Report*, April 16, 1984, 32.

22. See "Patriotism Is Back in Style," 59.

23. "America's Youth in Search of a Cause."

24. McLaughlin, "Military Love Affair," 24.

25. "Patriotism Is Back in Style," 59.

26. Davis and Lynn-Jones, "Citty upon a Hill," 31.

27. Davis and Lynn-Jones, "Citty upon a Hill," 29–30.

28. "The Nation's Mood," *New York Times Magazine*, December 11, 1983, 47.

29. "The Public Assesses the Reagan Record on Foreign Policy," *Public Opinion* (Summer 1986), 24; "U.S. Prefers War to 'Amerika,' G.W. Survey Finds," Office of News and Public Affairs, George Washington University, February 20, 1987.

30. "America at War," *Newsweek* Commemorative Edition, Spring–Summer 1991, 74.

31. "Psychic Shock for a Generation," *Newsweek*, February 18, 1991, 50.

32. Nancy Gibbs, "Land That They Love," *Time*, February 11, 1991, 53; "Psychic Shock for a Generation," 50.

33. Frederick Edwords, "The Religious Character of American Patriotism," *Humanist* (November–December 1987), 24, 31.

34. E. J. Dionne, *Why Americans Hate Politics* (New York: Touchstone, 1991), 79.

35. Richard Neustadt, *Presidential Power: The Politics of Leadership from FDR to Carter*, 3rd ed. (New York: Wiley, 1980), 208.

36. Sidney M. Milkis and Michael Nelson, *The American Presidency: Origins and Development, 1776–1990* (Washington, D.C.: Congressional Quarterly, 1990), 333.

37. Alexander Hamilton, *Federalist* 70.

38. Charles O. Jones, "Ronald Reagan and the U.S. Congress," in *The Reagan Legacy: Promise and Performance*, ed. Charles O. Jones (Chatham, N.J.: Chatham House, 1988), 56.

39. Michael Nelson, "Evaluating the Presidency," in *The Presidency and the Political System*, ed. Michael Nelson, 3rd ed. (Washington, D.C.: Congressional Quarterly, 1990), 9; Milkis and Nelson, *The American Presidency*, 337.

40. Tip O'Neill, *Man of the House* (New York: St. Martin's, 1987), 410, 413.

41. Arthur Miller, "Is Confidence Rebounding?" *Public Opinion* (June–July 1983), 20.

42. James Ceaser, "The Reagan Presidency and American Public Opinion," in *The Reagan Legacy*, ed. Jones, 196.

43. Peter M. Benda and Charles H. Levine, "Reagan and the Bureaucracy: The Bequest, the Promise, and the Legacy," in *The Reagan Legacy*, ed. Jones, 102. See also Donald Devine, *Reagan's Terrible Swift Sword* (Ottawa, Ill.: Jameson, 1991).

44. See Richard Nathan, *The Administrative Presidency* (New York: Wiley, 1983); Laurence E. Lynn Jr., "The Reagan Administration and the Renitent Bureaucracy," in *The Reagan Presidency and the Governing of America*, ed. Lester M. Salamon and Michael S. Lund (Washington, D.C.: Urban Institute, 1984), 339–70; Robert E. DiClerico, *The American President*, 4th ed. (Englewood Cliffs, N.J.: Prentice-Hall, 1995), 189–90.

45. Richard Nathan, "Institutional Change under Reagan," in *Perspectives on the Reagan Years*, ed. John L. Palmer (Washington, D.C.: Urban Institute, 1986), 130.

46. DiClerico, *The American President*, 191.

47. Elizabeth Sanders, "The Presidency and the Bureaucratic State," in *The Presidency and the Political System*, ed. Nelson, 410.

48. According to a *U.S. News & World Report* study published in early 1984, Reagan spent 24 percent of his time on vacation or at Camp David, compared with 24 percent for Lyndon Johnson, 28 percent for both Richard Nixon and Franklin Roosevelt, 29 percent for John Kennedy, and 33 percent for Dwight Eisenhower. See "When Presidents Take It Easy," March 19, 1984, 33.

49. Cited by Peggy Noonan, *What I Saw at the Revolution: A Political Life in the Reagan Era* (New York: Random House, 1990), 166.

50. Cited by I. M. Destler, "Reagan and the World: An 'Awesome Stubbornness,'" in *The Reagan Legacy*, ed. Jones, 244, 257.

51. John W. Sloan, *The Reagan Effect: Economics and Presidential Leadership* (Lawrence: University Press of Kansas, 1999), 186–93.

52. Lance Blakesly, *Presidential Leadership from Eisenhower to Clinton* (Chicago: Nelson Hall, 1995), 175–90.

53. Mike Feinsilber, "Reagan Just a Mediocre President, Historians Say," *Rocky Mountain News*, December 10, 1993, 52A.

54. Arthur M. Schlesinger Jr., "The Ultimate Approval Rating," *New York Times Magazine*, December 15, 1996, 46–51.

55. Richard Reeves, "The Ideological Election," *New York Times Magazine*, February 19, 1984, 29.

56. Nathan, "Institutional Change under Reagan," 122–23. See also Dom Bonafede, "Presidential Scholars Expect History to Treat the Reagan Presidency Kindly," *National Journal*, April 6, 1985, 743–47.

57. Paul Kengor, "Reagan among the Professors," *Policy Review* (December 1999–January 2000), 15–27. The author is particularly indebted to Prof. Kengor's discussion of Kernell, Neustadt, and Skowronek.

58. Marc Landy and Sidney M. Milkis, *Presidential Greatness* (Lawrence: University Press of Kansas, 2000), 219.

59. Richard Neustadt, *Presidential Power and the Modern Presidents: The Politics of Leadership from Roosevelt to Reagan* (New York: Free Press, 1990), 269–70.

60. Samuel Kernell, *Going Public: New Strategies of Presidential Leadership*, 2nd ed. (Washington, D.C.: Congressional Quarterly, 1993), 227–28.

61. Stephen Skowronek, *The Politics Presidents Make: Leadership from John Adams to George Bush* (Cambridge, Mass.: Belknap, 1993).

62. Aaron Wildavsky, *The Beleaguered Presidency* (New Brunswick, N.J.: Transaction, 1991), 213.

63. Wildavsky, *The Beleaguered Presidency*, 239.

64. Marc Lacey, "Clinton Ranks in the Middle, but Falls Last on Morality," *New York Times*, February 21, 2000, A11; "Presidential Timber: How Chief Executives Stack Up," *U.S. News & World Report*, November 27, 2000, 16. The second survey excluded two presidents, William Henry Harrison and James Garfield, because they each served less than one year in office.

65. David S. Broder, *The Party's Over: The Failure of Politics in America* (New York: Harper and Row, 1972).

66. Sidney M. Milkis, "The Presidency and Political Parties," in *The Presidency and the Political System*, ed. Nelson, 354.

67. James W. Ceaser, "Political Parties—Declining, Stabilizing, or Resurging?" in *The New American Political System*, ed. Anthony King, 2nd version (Washington, D.C.: American Enterprise Institute [hereafter AEI], 1990), 104.

68. Ceaser, "Political Parties," 106.

69. Ceaser, "Political Parties," 122.

70. Paul Allen Beck, "Incomplete Realignment: The Reagan Legacy for Parties and Elections," in *The Reagan Legacy*, ed. Jones, 157.

71. White House political director Mitch Daniels, cited by Milkis and Nelson, *The American Presidency*, 340.

72. Larry J. Sabato, *The Party's Just Begun: Shaping Political Parties for America's Future* (Glenview, Ill.: Scott Foresman, 1988), 60–61.

73. Milkis, "The Presidency and Political Parties," 366–67.

74. Sabato, *The Party's Just Begun*, 77.

75. Sabato, *The Party's Just Begun*, 77–81.

76. Paul S. Herrnson, "National Party Organizations and the Postreform Congress," in *The Postreform Congress*, ed. Roger H. Davidson (New York: St. Martin's, 1992), 48–70.

77. David S. Broder, "The Invalids Are Sitting Up," *Washington Post*, February 9, 1983, A19.

78. Ceaser, "Political Parties—Declining, Stabilizing, or Resurging?"

79. Lipset, "Feeling Better," 8.

80. Milkis and Nelson, *The American Presidency*, 333–43.

81. James W. Ceaser, "As Good as Their Words: Reagan's Rhetoric," *Public Opinion* (June–July 1984), 11.

82. In 1981, 77 percent agreed, and 23 percent disagreed; in 1986, 62 percent agreed, 38 percent disagreed. "Opinion Roundup," *Public Opinion* (March–April 1987), 25. Other surveys showed declining fear of big government throughout the decade (21–29).

83. Ruy A. Teixeira, *The Disappearing American Voter* (Washington, D.C.: Brookings Institution, 1992), 32.

84. Lipset, "Feeling Better," 7.

85. "State of the Nation," *Public Opinion* (February–March 1984), 21.

86. Destler, "Reagan and the World," 245–46.

87. Average turnout in presidential elections in the 1980s (52 percent) was lower than average turnout had been in the 1970s (54.4 percent), in the same way that turnout in the 1970s was much lower than it had been in the 1960s (61.9 percent). Turnout declined through the sixties from its high point of 62.8 percent in 1960 to 60.9 percent in 1968.

88. Figures from national election studies compiled and presented in Teixeira, *The Disappearing American Voter*, 41, 44.

89. Robert H. Salisbury, "The Paradox of Interest Groups in Washington: More Groups, Less Clout," in *The New American Political System*, ed. King, 203.

90. For examples, see Nancy Yakes and Denise Akey, eds., *Encyclopedia of Associations 1980*, 14th ed. (Detroit: Gale Research, 1980); Denise S. Akey and Katherine Gruber eds., *Encyclopedia of Associations 1985*, 19th ed. (Detroit: Gale Research, 1985); Deborah M. Burek, Karen E. Koek, and Annette Novallo eds., *Encyclopedia of Associations 1990*, 24th ed. (Detroit: Gale Research, 1990). Since membership and chapter figures in the *Encyclopedia of Associations* are self-reported, they cannot be considered authoritative; however, while self-interested overreporting may taint the numbers, it probably does not change the direction of real trends.

91. Daniel Smith, *Tax Crusaders* (New York: Routledge, 1998).

92. David D. Schmidt, *Citizen Lawmakers: The Ballot Initiative Revolution* (Philadelphia: Temple University Press, 1989), 24, 37, 214.

93. David S. Broder, "A Party's Soldier," *Washington Post*, October 20, 1985, C7.

94. Jack Citrin, Donald Green, and Beth Reingold, "The Soundness of Our Structure: Confidence in the Reagan Years," *Public Opinion* (November–December 1987), 60. Also Jack Citrin and Donald Philips Green, "Presidential Leadership and the Resurgence of Trust in Government," *British Journal of Political Science* 16, part 4 (October 1986).

95. "Farewell Address to the Nation, January 11, 1989," *Public Papers of the Presidents: Ronald Reagan 1988–89* (Washington, D.C.: Government Printing Office, 1991), 1719.

4

Reagan, Economic Freedom, and the Economic Recovery

T O BOTH THE CRITICS OF RONALD REAGAN and his defenders, the economic expansion of 1983–90 is the most tangible emblem of his presidency. To the critics, the recovery was part and parcel of the Decade of Greed, obtained at the expense of fairness and future prosperity. Indeed, some have claimed that the nation actually experienced not an economic boom at all but an "age of diminished expectations," even a "silent depression."[1] To economist James Tobin, "Reaganomics was a fraud from the beginning."[2] Anthony S. Campagna argued that Reagan's economic policies "left the economy in shambles" and "failed conservative tests, failed liberal tests, failed to achieve the goals it set for itself, and failed the American public that invested such hope and trust in it."[3] As candidate Bill Clinton said in a 1992 campaign speech to the Economic Club of Detroit, "The old economic ideas of the last two decades didn't produce growth, didn't create upward mobility, and most important, didn't prepare millions and millions of Americans to compete and win in the new world economy. . . . For the last twelve years, we have been in the grip of a failed economic theory."[4]

Reagan's supporters, on the other hand, credit his policies with bringing prosperity not only in the 1980s but beyond. Authors like Robert L. Bartley, who touted the recovery of the 1980s as "The Seven Fat Years,"[5] have put forward a very positive interpretation. Reagan himself declared in his 1990 autobiography that of his presidential accomplishments, "I'm probably proudest about the economy."[6] This is an important debate, and one in which Reagan's supporters have a stronger argument than his opponents. In certain respects, though, it obscures another issue that was at least as important as far as Reagan was concerned. One of the chief goals of Reagan's presidency, and indeed of his entire political career, was to strengthen economic freedom, on the basis of a conception that feared the political as well as economic consequences of growing governmental controls. In the 1980s, he accomplished that goal in a variety of ways. Most directly, economic policy emphasized limited government and nurtured a decentralized, entrepreneurial economy. Furthermore, because that policy worked better than many critics had thought possible, it helped end an economic crisis that might otherwise have led to a renewed assault on economic freedom. By helping overcome the crisis, Reagan's policy provided renewed legitimacy to free-market economics that endured long after his presidency ended. Indeed, largely because of that success, the market became the dominant paradigm at home and abroad.

The Economic Crisis of 1973–1982

An assessment of Reagan's economic policy must begin with a review of the circumstances under which he took office. Starting in roughly 1973, the American economy began a slide that culminated in the worst economic crisis since the Great Depression. On January 20, 1981, Ronald Reagan inherited an unemployment rate of 7.5 percent, higher than when Clinton defeated George Bush in 1992. In addition, inflation in 1980 had been recorded at an annual rate of 13.5 percent, leading to very high interest rates—mortgage rates at 15 percent and a prime interest rate of 21.5 percent. Productivity was dropping. Real family incomes had dropped considerably since 1973 and were to continue dropping through 1982. Yet income taxes were not adjusted for inflation, so "bracket creep" pushed more and more people—especially at the lower end of the income spectrum—into higher tax rates. Consequently, a family of four with an income of twenty-five thousand dollars in 1978 would have seen the tax rate on its last dollar of income rise from 19 percent in 1965 to 28 percent in 1978, if its income had exactly kept pace with inflation.[7] Bracket creep had also ensured that government's share of the economy would automatically grow due to inflation; the proportion of gross domestic product (GDP) taken by federal taxes rose from 17.2 percent in 1976 to 19.7 percent in 1981.

At the same time, the dominant economic paradigm of Keynesianism seemed incapable of explaining or remedying the problems. By the late 1970s, "stagflation"—high unemployment coinciding with high inflation—rendered highly problematic the Keynesian "Phillips curve," which postulated a mathematical tradeoff between the two. There was a sense, as Robert Bartley put it, that "the world stood on an economic precipice. . . . [W]e could believe that the world was stumbling toward an economic catastrophe on the order of the 1930s."[8] In 1982, economist Lester Thurow argued that "the engines of economic growth have shut down here and across the globe, and they are likely to stay that way for years to come."[9]

In the minds of many, the economic crisis was serious enough to call into question the viability of the free-market system itself. Throughout the late 1970s and early 1980s, scholars openly asked whether capitalism was in its death throes, while socialists were still claiming to represent the "wave of the future." *Time* magazine noted in 1975 that "as capitalism approaches the bicentennial [of Adam Smith's *Wealth of Nations*], it is beset by crisis. Increasingly, its supporters as well as its critics ask: Can capitalism survive?"[10] As late as 1982, economist Robert Heilbroner likewise asked in a piece in the *New York Times Magazine*, "Does Capitalism Have a Future?" His answer was Yes, but only through a reconstruction that ended with the public sector consuming 40–50 percent of the national economy; much greater government planning, including permanent controls on wages, prices, and dividends; an end to free trade; and adoption of a so-called state capitalism featuring massive government investment in (and control of) private industry.[11]

Reagan's Economic Policy

The crisis of the economy and of prevalent economic theory led to a reexamination of assumptions and policies, including the rapidly increasing federal spending, taxing, and regulating that had characterized the late 1960s and 1970s. There was a revival of classical economics, focusing on the money supply, microeconomic factors, and arguments for limited government. This revival took at least two major forms: the limited government monetarism of Milton Friedman, and an emergent supply-side doctrine, urging major cuts in marginal tax rates.

Friedman argued that the key to noninflationary growth was to maintain a stable money supply and otherwise allow the free market to operate with minimal governmental interference. Supply-side economists argued that an increase in supply made possible by greater productivity could relieve both inflation and unemployment. In keeping with this skepticism toward demand management, supply-siders emphasized "microeconomics"—the factors leading to employment, consumption, and investment decisions by individuals and businesses. This emphasis recognized the importance of incentives in a market economy and, likewise, the importance of avoiding government-imposed disincentives. Supply-siders considered marginal tax rates the key to the economy's incentive structure and believed that the reduction of those rates could loose a burst of entrepreneurial activity, especially if the government avoided other antigrowth policies, like excessive regulation.

In Congress, this idea took the form of the 1978 Steiger Amendment, cutting capital gains taxes, and the Kemp-Roth bill. Named after Rep. Jack Kemp (R-N.Y.) and Sen. William Roth (R-Del.), Kemp-Roth called for a three-year, 30 percent, across-the-board reduction in income tax rates; it was introduced in 1977 and passed the Senate in modified form in 1978. Reagan embraced the proposal in 1980. A newfound skepticism also arose regarding the ability of government to regulate large industries more efficiently than did the market; airline, trucking, railroad, banking, and oil deregulation were begun in this period.

Drawing heavily on varying threads of conservative economic thought, including monetarism and supply-side thinking, Reagan sought to establish a new direction for economic policy. Government would remain committed to establishing a floor beneath which people would not be allowed to fall (the "safety net"), but Reagan would otherwise seek to reduce the role of government in the economy. Observers like Anthony S. Campagna have often claimed that Reagan's economic program was based on "some untested ideas of a few arrogant individuals,"[12] but it was actually the product of the collaborative efforts of dozens of mainstream conservative economists, including Arthur F. Burns, Milton Friedman, Alan Greenspan, Paul McCracken, George Shultz, William Simon, and Murray Weidenbaum.[13] It also clearly reflected the long-held beliefs Reagan himself had expressed since his days on the speaking circuit in the 1950s.

Indeed, Reagan had been an economics major at Eureka College, where he had learned economics of "the old, classical variety, straight from the works of Adam Smith, Alfred Marshall, Irving Fisher, Eugene Boem-Barwek, David Ricardo, and Jean-Baptiste Say." In the view of economic adviser Martin Anderson, "The essence of the comprehensive economic program Reagan pursued in the 1980s [was] derived from the classical economic principles he learned almost sixty years ago as a young man."[14] His experience as an actor reaching the 91 percent marginal income-tax bracket also made him receptive to supply-side arguments. Reagan would later say, "I think my own experience with our tax laws in Hollywood probably taught me more about practical economic theory than I ever learned in a classroom or from an economist. . . . I began asking myself whether it was worth it to keep on taking work. . . . The same principle that affected my thinking applied to people in all tax brackets: The more government takes in taxes, the less incentive people have to work."[15] Finally, as a speaker, columnist, and public figure, Anderson said, Reagan "read and studied the writings of some of the best economists in the world, including the giants of the free-market economy—Ludwig von Mises, Friedrich Hayek, and Milton Friedman."[16]

Reagan's program ultimately consisted of four major pillars: reducing the rate of growth of federal spending, reducing tax rates, proceeding with deregulation, and attaining slow, stable growth in the money supply.[17] These four pillars, as well as other major themes like free trade, were held together by a unifying proposition—that, in the words of Reagan's 1981 Inaugural Address, "in this present crisis, government is not the solution to our problem; government is the problem."[18] In his view, high taxes, excessive regulation, and bloated government were stifling the creative vigor of the American economy, destroying jobs, and curtailing the production necessary to alleviate the pressure on prices. Overweening government was consequently undermining the American vision of a land of freedom and opportunity. As Reagan saw it, the growth of governmental influence over the economy ultimately endangered American liberty: "Throughout human history, taxes have been one of the foremost ways that governments intrude on the rights of citizens. . . . Our forefathers knew that if you bind up a man's economic life with taxes, tariffs, and regulations, you deprive him of some of his most basic civil rights."[19] Reagan also believed that the talk of the "limits to growth" permeating the Carter years was mistaken, that American economic growth could resume its pre-1973 vigor. In his view, "Freedom and incentives unleash the drive and entrepreneurial genius that are at the core of human progress. . . . There are no limits to growth and human progress when men and women are free to follow their dreams."[20]

Reagan would later write that economic policy was his administration's

> most immediate priority. . . . In 1981, no problem the country faced was more serious than the economic crisis—not even the need to modernize our armed forces—because without a recovery, we couldn't afford to do the things necessary to make the country strong again or make a serious effort to lessen the dangers of nuclear war. Nor could America regain confidence in itself and stand tall again. Nothing was possible unless we made the economy sound again.[21]

The centerpiece of the Reagan economic plan was the budget proposal he submitted to Congress in 1981. It consisted of income and other tax cuts and a package of domestic spending cuts totaling forty-two billion dollars for the next fiscal year. Congress ultimately passed thirty-eight billion in spending cuts and most of the tax package, including Kemp-Roth, revised to 25 percent over three years. At the same time, the top marginal rate was reduced from 70 percent to 50 percent; at the end of the three years, tax rates were to be indexed to inflation. The tax bill also contained an accelerated depreciation schedule for business investment and dozens of special-interest tax provisions. Democratic senator Henry Jackson declared the Reagan program "the greatest economic experiment since the New Deal."[22] Five years later, Congress passed the most substantial overhaul of the federal income tax code since it was established in 1913. The tax reform act reduced the number of brackets from fourteen to two, lowered the top rate from 50 percent to 28 percent, took four million working poor off of the tax rolls, and substantially reduced tax loopholes.

The Federal Reserve Board is independent of direct control of the president, but presidents make appointments to the board and retain an informal—but not insignificant—influence if they choose to apply public pressure. Reagan's position may have been based on a visceral conviction that inflation had to be stopped rather than on a detailed knowledge of the intricacies of monetary policy, but that conviction was solid and consequential. Reagan stood behind the "Fed's" tightening policy, despite the high economic and political costs of the recession of 1981–82, and "at two critical junctures in the spring of 1981 and the winter of 1982—had personally pressured the Fed to tighten its control of money."[23] At times when Federal Reserve Board chairman Paul Volcker was under severe criticism, even from some congressional Republicans and administration voices, "Reagan stuck by the Fed chairman when it counted."[24] Indeed, he reappointed Volcker in 1983 and then appointed noted inflation-fighter Alan Greenspan to replace him in 1987.

Aside from proceeding with the deregulation of several specific industries, the Reagan administration took steps to lighten the overall regulatory burden on business. Within ten days of Reagan's 1981 inauguration, he froze more than 170 pending regulations. More stringent cost-benefit standards were imposed for new regulations, and the administration enacted six thousand fewer rules in its first four years than had the Carter administration.[25] All new regulations had to receive "central clearance" from the Office of Management and Budget, a requirement that supporters and critics alike agreed was "a powerful obstacle to the entire regulatory process."[26] Altogether, the *Federal Register* shrank from 87,012 pages in 1980 to 53,376 pages in 1988. The regulatory philosophy of the Reagan administration did not abandon regulation as an instrument of policy—there were only twenty thousand pages of the *Federal Register* in 1970—but rather was guided by the proposition that in a free society the burden of proof should rest on those wishing to impose regulation on individuals and businesses. To the deregulation drive one might add a shift in antitrust policy in which the Reagan administration showed greater reluctance to interfere with mergers deemed "economically efficient."

Beyond his four-point program, Reagan established a free-market trade framework that endured largely intact throughout his presidency. That framework, announced in 1981 by the Council of Economic Advisers, included domestic deregulation for the sake of competitiveness, reliance on market forces rather than government to deal with dislocation produced by trade, and reduction of trade barriers.[27] Reagan achieved both the free-trade Caribbean

Basin Initiative and a broad free-trade agreement with Canada that established the framework for the North American Free Trade Agreement, as well as for other trade measures of the 1990s. His administration also opened a key new round of the General Agreement on Tariffs and Trade (GATT) talks in 1986 aimed at reducing worldwide agricultural subsidies. He often described a goal of a unified free-trade zone stretching from Canada to Chile, and he clearly understood the importance of high technology and global interdependence to America's economic future. As *Washington Post* correspondent David Broder pointed out at the time, "It is part of Reagan's insistence, in both public speeches and private meetings, that government policy must assist—and not resist—the great transition of the American manufacturing base from heavy industry to high technology. And it comes at a time when the Democratic Party and most of its leading presidential hopefuls are lashing themselves ever more tightly to the very protectionist measures Reagan has rejected."[28]

Two other policy decisions made in 1981 had important long-term effects in increasing investment by ordinary Americans. First, the tax-cut bill of 1981 established tax deductions for individual retirement accounts (or IRAs). In the first full year they were available (1982), twelve million taxpayers contributed $28.3 billion to IRAs, a figure that has grown dramatically since then.[29] Second, a decision by the Reagan administration, little noted at the time, established the principle that employees' income could be tax free if matched by employers and channeled into private retirement accounts. From a base of zero in 1981, the number of American workers with 401(k) plans grew to 7.5 million by 1984; by 1998, the figure had reached thirty-nine million, with investments totaling $1.54 trillion in assets. By the end of the 1990s, as a result of this "democratization of the stock market," 43 percent of American households held shares in corporate or equity mutual funds, and over half of all shareholders had incomes below fifty thousand dollars a year. Reagan policies were largely responsible for creating a massive class of small investors that had simply not existed before.[30]

Despite the partisan rancor that later overshadowed them, these shifts in policy, while championed by Reagan, reflected something of a brief bipartisan consensus in favor of government retrenchment.[31] Furthermore, the consistency of Reagan's economic policies should not be exaggerated. The tax cuts were partially counterbalanced by tax increases in 1982, 1984, and 1987; while decrying federal spending, Reagan vetoed few appropriations bills; administration policy toward international finance shifted from a pure market approach to greater reliance on currency intervention and International Monetary Fund bailouts. Yet even these inconsistencies often represented a tactical flexibility on Reagan's part that allowed him to meet other important objectives. Altogether, his policies reduced the economic power of government, reduced the dependence of citizens on the government, and promoted a more decentralized and entrepreneurial economy.

Economic Results

Economic conditions in the Reagan presidency must be divided into two distinct periods. In the first period, 1981–82, the United States suffered from its worst economic recession since the Great Depression. The Federal Reserve Board's anti-inflation policy, backed by Reagan, drove unemployment to a postwar high of 10.8 percent. The recession not only had roots in the economic crisis Reagan inherited but was, in many respects, a relatively straightforward continuation of that crisis. Technically, the downturns of 1979–80 and 1981–82 were two distinct recessions; however, the time separating them was so brief and the underlying causes so similar that it is reasonable to consider them a single, long recession. Indeed, Harvard economist James Tobin acknowledged as much when he alluded in a 1990 interview to a "recession such as the one we had in 1979–82."[32] Nevertheless, given Reagan's support for the Fed's policy, he must share some responsibility for the outcomes, bad as well as good.

After that recession ended in 1982, the U.S. economy entered a ninety-two-month period of sustained, noninflationary economic growth. This expansion was longer than any prior period of peacetime economic growth in the history of the United States, and it was to be eclipsed only by the new record set in the 1990s. The previous record since World War II had been fifty-eight months, and the average expansion had lasted only thirty-four months. Indeed, in the equivalent period of eight years prior to the end of 1982, the nation had experienced three recessions. Furthermore, the real growth in gross domestic product resumed its average pace from 1950 to 1973. Ultimately, the expansion added one-third to the real national economy—a total the equivalent of West Germany's entire economy in 1982. By 1986, news reports were claiming that "an American economy fundamentally different from the one that sapped the nation of its industrial strength and sense of confidence in the 1970s is springing to life today. . . . [A]fter years of a dizzying roller-coaster ride, the country is enjoying a sounder economy and could have a rising standard of living for years to come."[33]

Reagan was the only U.S. president from Harry Truman through George H. W. Bush to preside over the reduction of both unemployment and inflation. In the 1988 words of George Washington University economics professor Robert M. Dunn, "In the areas of unemployment and inflation, [Reagan's] has been the most successful administration since World War II."[34] Harvard economist Robert Barro likewise evaluated all presidents from Truman through the first Bush administration on four factors: change in inflation, change in unemployment, change in long-term interest rates, and shortfall versus the average 3 percent growth in the economy. Barro's conclusion was that on these criteria the most successful administrations from 1949 to 1992 were Reagan I and Reagan II.[35]

Inflation was brought under control by 1983 and continued downward to 3.5 percent in 1989. As a result of the taming of inflation, and thus of inflationary expectations, interest rates began a decline that continued into the 1990s. Unemployment too started a downward trend in 1983. By 1989, the unemployment rate had fallen to 5.3 percent. An instructive measure of this economic turnaround could be seen in contrasting responses to national election studies queries about what voters considered "the most important problems facing the country." In 1980, 43 percent cited inflation or unemployment (33 and 10 percent, respectively); by 1988, only 2 percent named inflation and 5 percent said unemployment.[36] Very few analysts in the late 1970s had dared to hope for this sort of simultaneous and substantial reduction of inflation and unemployment.

Furthermore, contrary to conventional wisdom, the bulk of the 19.3 million jobs created in the recovery were relatively high-paying jobs; "only 12 percent of the increase in employment occurred in the lowest-paid, low-skilled service occupations such as retailing and fast-food restaurants."[37] In fact, the areas of fastest job growth in the 1980s strongly correlated with relatively high median earnings (table 4.1).

Not only did the economy experience a strong recovery, but the "new economy" that began to take shape was more decentralized, more innovative, and more competitive than the one it replaced. Job growth was spurred not by the

TABLE 4.1
Job Creation, January 1982–December 1989

Job Category	Number (in millions)	Percent Increase	1989 Median Earnings
Managerial/ Professional	7.600	33.1%	$32,873
Production	2.194	19.0%	$25,831
Technical	6.630	21.8%	$20,905
Operators	1.364	8.2%	$19,886
Services	2.210	16.8%	$14,858
Farming	–0.116	-3.7%	$13,539
TOTAL	**19.892**	**20.3%**	**$23,333**

Source: Edwin S. Rubenstein, "More than 'McJobs,'" *The Right Data* (1994), 220.

Fortune 500 establishment but by a burst of entrepreneurship. The number of new businesses incorporated reached a record high of 635,000 in 1984, an increase of almost 20 percent in four years.[38] Studies showed that as many as four out of every five new jobs were created by smaller businesses.

What economics correspondent Daniel Akst called "a time of enormous, even radical change" became manifest in the rise of the microchip: "Personal computers became ubiquitous, ushering in the greatest revolution in information management since papyrus."[39] As Akst pointed out, fax machines, cellular phones, and even Nintendo video games had been unknown in 1980. Furthermore, the United States faced an increasingly interconnected and competitive global economy in the 1980s. The United States became the world's largest debtor nation; the trade balance went from a small surplus in 1980 to a record large deficit in 1988, leading many to fear that American economic prospects were in decline. In retrospect, the trade deficit obscured a variety of ways in which the competitive position of the nation was actually bolstered during the Reagan years. To start, the trade deficit itself was not primarily the result of a weak and noncompetitive export sector; while exports were stagnant for a few years in the early 1980s, from 1983 to 1989 they increased by 79 percent. Only the subsequent strength of the export sector prevented net job losses in the recession of 1990–91 from being much worse.

Perhaps most importantly, worker productivity—especially manufacturing productivity—rebounded in the 1980s, after the flat period from 1973 to 1982. Overall, real hourly output of all workers grew by only 3.7 percent from 1973 to 1982; between 1982 and 1988, it increased 13.5 percent. Productivity gains in the service sector were much weaker, but output per employee hour in manufacturing increased by more than 3.5 percent a year throughout the eighties. As a result, even though manufacturing employment fell as a proportion of the workforce, manufacturing production rose from its 20 percent share of the economy in 1982 to 23 percent in 1990. During the years of expansion, the growth of manufacturing output surpassed the overall growth of the economy by one-half. Indeed, manufacturing productivity "climbed at a record rate from 1979 to 1990."[40] By mid-decade, observers could note that industrial survivors "have emerged fitter, more cost-effective and more productive than ever. . . . In field after field, U.S. companies are discovering niches in which they can whip foreign competitors."[41] At the beginning of the 1990s, the *New York Times* reported that U.S. manufacturing productivity had reached a par with Japan's and Europe's, and had returned to the level of output achieved in the 1960s when American factories had "hummed at a feverish clip"; this "almost unbelievable productivity revival" had led to recovery by the United States of a larger share of global manufacturing than it had held in 1980.[42]

While it remains a matter of contention whether overall investment in the 1980s was a boon or a disappointment,[43] there is no question that entrepreneurial investment grew at a rapid pace. Between 1980 and 1987, venture capital investment, crucial for economic dynamism and job creation, increased by an astonishing 544 percent.[44] From just 1981 to 1983, the pool of venture capital nearly doubled.[45] Overall, the Dow-Jones industrial average, which had fallen by 70 percent in real terms during the long bear market from 1967 to 1982, roughly tripled through the remainder of the 1980s (despite a momentarily frightening 25 percent drop in October 1987), only to quintuple again in the 1990s.

Innovative financial instruments contributed to this outcome. Commentators at the time frequently criticized the "speculation" exemplified by high-yield "junk" bonds and corporate raiders like T. Boone Pickens and Carl Icahn, who shuffled money, sometimes destroyed companies, but did not create anything. While junk bonds did contribute heavily to leveraged buyouts, more than two-thirds of junk bond activity in the 1980s was used for traditional capital formation for new or expanding businesses. High-yield bonds allowed new and "nonrated" small businesses to gain access to capital markets, and they contributed substantially to the 17.3 million new jobs in such firms in the 1980s. They also funded pioneers like MCI Communications and Turner Broadcasting.[46] Many economists noted that even the corporate takeover craze did not lack economic rationale and benefit. Takeovers often functioned as a market mechanism to increase efficiency—with substantial payoffs in the 1990s.[47]

There is no doubt that the economy in the 1980s continued to experience problems, some of them serious, as many sectors of the economy underwent a painful restructuring. However, even many of the highly publicized problems of the 1980s appear, on closer examination, to have been less serious than previously thought. As we will see in chapter 5, the federal deficit—thought by many to have been the defining economic catastrophe of the 1980s—was much more complicated, both in cause and consequence. A strong argument was made by many economists that measurement errors accounted both for the apparent decline in the U.S. personal savings rate and for the apparent superiority of the Japanese savings rate.[48] Likewise, consumer credit, said to have exploded, remained stable by some measures.[49] As economist Richard McKenzie notes, while the rate of growth of personal debt in the 1980s was higher than in the 1970s, it was much lower than in the 1950s and 1960s.[50] Overall, while household liabilities increased by $1.3 trillion between 1981 and 1987, household assets grew by six trillion dollars.[51] Much of the gap that remained between the amount that was needed for investment and the amount available in savings was made up with foreign investment.

America's foreign-held debt, rather than representing a weight on the economy, was an important source of economic growth. It was also a result of American economic growth, at least one piece of evidence that America in the 1980s was "the world's premier investment opportunity."[52] At the end of the 1980s, corporate debt as a proportion of the economy was still substantially lower in the United States than in Germany, Japan, France, Britain, or Canada, and the U.S. position relative to those countries had in many cases (including Japan's) improved.[53]

The primary causes for the trade deficit were a strong U.S. economy and a strong dollar that made American exports relatively more expensive and foreign imports cheaper. Because the American economy after 1982 was healthier than the economies of most of the rest of the world, Americans were better able to buy foreign goods than foreigners were to buy American goods. This phenomenon was to repeat itself in the late 1990s, when the United States experienced a new record-high trade deficit for largely the same reason. In fact, as Robert L. Bartley points out, "The United States ran a trade deficit in nearly all of its first 100 years, and ran surpluses in the midst of the Great Depression. A trade deficit is typical of rapidly growing economies, which require a disproportionate share of the world's resources, and provide investment opportunities to balance the equation."[54]

The notion, widely disseminated in the 1980s, that Germany and Japan were on the verge of overwhelming the United States economically was never true. In the end, the American standard of living—the ultimate object of competitiveness—climbed by a fifth in the 1980s. In 1988, in terms adjusted not only for market exchange rates but for the real cost of the same basket of goods, the American standard of living was still first in the world, according to the Organization of Economic Cooperation and Development. On an index with America as one hundred, the closest country was Canada at 92.5; West Germany was tenth at 78.6, and Japan was twelfth at 71.5.[55]

In any event, the suggestion that Americans after 1982 were suffering through an "age of diminished expectations," let alone a "silent depression," is not consistent with the facts. The real alternative at the beginning of the 1980s was a continuation of the conditions of the late 1970s. Instead, the economy at the end of the decade was far stronger than at the beginning by virtually any measure, and that strength was solid, not illusory. A recession finally arrived in mid-1990, helped along by fears (and higher energy prices) associated with the Iraqi war, a widely reported "credit crunch" provoked by overeager bank regulators, a large tax increase, and the extreme aging of the expansion. When it came, critics claimed it was a "natural outcome of the excesses of the 1980s,"[56] but that interpretation is difficult to reconcile with the fact that the recession appeared a full fifty-eight months after the average postwar recovery would have ended. Moreover, the recession itself was, by historical standards, relatively short and mild, giving way by spring of 1991 to renewed, though sometimes sluggish, growth.

It is difficult to overstate the positive impact this economic turnaround had on American society and on the world. The "malaise" ended, and the United States entered a period of renewed self-confidence, as well as of virtually un-paralleled technological innovation. The expansion also meant that "the United States could no longer be accurately viewed as a declining super-power."[57] As the crisis ended and the new economy took hold, calls for a major expansion of state intervention became less frequent and less influential.

Economic Explanations

Even the best (or worst) conceived economic policy does not have unlimited impact on the economy, and no president or set of policies should ever be given the full credit (or blame) for the nation's economic performance. Ulti-mately, American workers, entrepreneurs, investors, and consumers hold the keys to the economy. New technologies have clearly driven much of the eco-nomic growth of the 1980s and 1990s. Demographic factors may have also been important. Some economists attribute the low productivity of the 1970s at least partly to a bulge in the working-age population; as those new workers gained experience, productivity subsequently rose again. Also, events not in the immediate control of U.S. policy makers—like the oil shocks of the 1970s, the Iraqi invasion of Kuwait in 1990, or the end of the Cold War—exerted a powerful economic influence, both positive and negative.

Nevertheless, the strong economic performance of the 1980s could be traced in large part to the economic policies of the Reagan administration. That those policies were held together by a free-market orientation con-tributed to movement in the direction of greater economic freedom. The sce-nario connecting Reagan and the recovery follows these lines:

First, the anti-inflationary monetary policy that was one of the four pillars of the Reagan administration's comprehensive economic policy was crucial. Broadly consistent with this goal—though deviating from Milton Friedman's money-supply targets, which proved practically impossible to calibrate—the Federal Reserve Board managed monetary policy in a way that reduced infla-tion substantially.

Another policy factor contributing to the downfall of inflation was the re-duction in the rate of growth of federal spending, a second pillar of the Rea-gan program. The 1980s saw the slowest real increase in federal spending since before World War II. Indeed, as we will see in chapter 5, the 1980s represented a key turning point in a long struggle to control federal outlays.

Deregulation, a third pillar of the program, helped reduce inflation in two ways. It "sharply increased competition and held down prices in areas such as trucking, airlines, and railroads"[58]—areas where price increases are quickly transmitted to the rest of the economy. It also generally reduced the cost of doing business, though it is difficult to quantify by exactly how much. Deregulation of the communications industry alone contributed to the burst of technological innovation that transformed the American economy in the 1980s and beyond. Most economists supported this deregulation at the time, and few have changed their minds. According to scholars Martha Derthick and Paul Quirk, deregulation of specific industries "pitted particularistic interests against diffuse, widely encompassing interests"—or, to perhaps put it another way, narrower interests, which opposed deregulation, against a broader public interest.[59]

For example, most studies show that consumers gained as the result of the competition fostered by airline deregulation. The Transportation Research Board issued a report in 1991 stating that market competition was considerably strengthened, services expanded, fares rose at a slower rate than industry costs, and accident rates declined.[60] Before deregulation, only 17 percent of fliers could choose among three or more airlines on a particular route; by 1991, 65 percent could do so. The Brookings Institution estimated that deregulation saved consumers over six billion dollars through 1993; overall, in real terms, fares declined by 40 percent from 1977 to 1993.[61]

Trucking and railroad deregulation had the effect of similarly shaking out those industries. Donald L. Barlett and James B. Steele claimed that trucking deregulation had "triggered price wars and cutthroat discounting."[62] This is another way of saying that it had the effect of reducing prices and providing greater service to the consumer, a conclusion confirmed by former chairmen of the Interstate Commerce Commission and another Brookings Institution study.[63]

Deregulation also occurred in oil in the late 1970s and early 1980s; indeed, one of Reagan's first actions as president was to end oil price controls. The effect was to increase domestic oil production substantially, contributing to the decline of OPEC and leading in 1986 to the lowest real cost of a gallon of gasoline in U.S. history. This decision alone may have added up to a percentage point to the U.S. GNP through the 1980s.[64]

The communications field also benefited. Telephone deregulation, which followed when a federal judge ordered the breakup of AT&T on antitrust grounds, led to a 47 percent decline in the real cost of an average long-distance telephone call.[65] From 1980 to 1992, the number of American households receiving cable television more than tripled, largely due to the competition spurred by deregulation.[66]

Overall, the White House estimated that time devoted by the public to paperwork was decreased by over six hundred million hours from 1981 through 1987 due to deregulation.[67] Even if this estimate is exaggerated, there can be little doubt that this process saved business—and hence indirectly workers and consumers—billions of dollars.[68]

Strong domestic pressures for protectionism produced a mixed record on trade; one of the administration's first foreign policy successes lay in persuading Japan to accept voluntary auto import quotas, an agreement that cost American consumers as much as a billion dollars per year.[69] Nevertheless, by blocking most of the protectionist agenda and by opening other trade avenues, Reagan fostered an economy in which international competitiveness—and hence, downward pressure on prices—took shape.

Administration policies concerning labor costs, while less openly declared, further tamed inflation. The minimum wage was allowed to decline substantially in real terms, thus holding down price pressures, especially in the increasingly important service sector. When Reagan fired the striking PATCO air traffic controllers in August 1981, he signaled those engaged in business-labor disputes that the administration would not look askance at the hiring of permanent replacement workers when the demands of labor became exorbitant. This new labor relations environment combined with the pressures of domestic deregulation and international competition to curtail substantially the power of labor unions in the economy. Clearly, "economic circumstances in the early 1980s severely threatened [labor's] economic and political power."[70] By 1988 it could be said that "the reduced power of organized labor now produces less inflationary wage settlements despite relatively tight labor markets."[71]

Not least, the tax cuts had substantial positive effects on the economy. By some estimates, increased consumption, driven largely by the tax cuts, accounted for over two-thirds of the growth of the economy from 1982 to 1990.[72] At the same time, while the supply-side hope for an increased personal savings rate was not satisfied, entrepreneurial investment and manufacturing productivity did increase. In the view of some economists, this increase in work effort, spurred by the increased incentives offered by lower taxes, contributed to the easing of inflation by increasing supply at the same time demand was being driven down by monetary and other policies. Along these lines, Lawrence Lindsey argued that by adding at least 0.5 percent per year to real GNP growth, the tax cuts had helped relieve inflationary pressures. Lindsey further claimed that the tax cuts had contributed to a strong dollar, lower interest rates, and less consumer borrowing, consequently reducing the velocity of money through the economy—and hence inflation.[73] Indexing of the income tax, starting in 1984, provided an extra incentive for federal policy makers to keep inflation under control, since inflation would no longer automatically produce disproportionately rising revenues due to bracket creep. Finally, deregulation and free trade increased supply as well—indeed, the combination of the two were largely responsible for the profusion of new products and whole new industries throughout the 1980s and 1990s—and the declining real minimum wage not only held down costs but increased entry-level employment opportunities.

In this scenario, what Reagan did not do was at least as important as what he did do: He avoided or prevented numerous policies that might have posed serious dangers for the economy in the future. Despite strong calls for a "national industrial policy" from political figures and commentators who feared Japanese and German competition, including several credible members of the 1984 and 1988 Democratic presidential fields, government mostly resisted the temptation to try to pick economic winners and losers. Such a policy was considered dangerous by economists of all stripes, including liberals like Charles Schultze, who called it "absolute nonsense," and Alfred Kahn, who predicted it would lead to "bureaucratization of the entire economy and ensconcement of exploitation and mediocrity."[74] Despite demands for action to remedy the male-female earnings gap, the administration also rejected the call for "comparable worth." Comparable-worth legislation would have replaced the free-market system of supply and demand for setting wages with a system of committees attempting to score jobs on an arbitrary numerical scale. While a few state and local governments adopted comparable worth for public employees, the idea faded as people began to recognize the radical (and potentially destructive) nature of the reform, and as women continued to close the pay gap without it.[75] Aside from the catastrophic health care program, which was repealed after less than a year, Reagan blocked the creation of new government programs, including entitlements that would have imposed further "uncontrollable" costs on future taxpayers. Many liberal economists conceded this success, even as they deplored it. Anthony S. Campagna, for instance, remarked that Reagan sent the "liberal establishment scurrying to protect its programs" and consequently prevented "them from initiating new ones."[76] Many other proposals that would have slowed growth or endangered future competitiveness were defeated or mitigated, such as plant-closing notification requirements (trimmed from ninety days to sixty days) and the anti-free-trade Gephardt Amendment (withdrawn under the threat of presidential veto).

Simply halting the seemingly inexorable growth of federal intervention in the economy—one of Reagan's chief goals—was a notable accomplishment. If federal spending, taxing, and regulation had been allowed to grow as fast in the 1980s as they had in the 1970s, by 1990 spending would have consumed 25.3 percent of GDP (instead of 22), taxes would have taken 22.3 percent of GDP (instead of 18.2), and there would have been almost 153,000 pages of federal regulations (instead of fewer than fifty-four thousand pages).[77] If these trends had continued to the year 2000, government would have attained a size and power increasingly incompatible with a free-market economy (see table 4.2).

Of course, it cannot be said with certainty that the trends would have continued unbroken except for Reagan, but the potential dangers to economic growth and productivity of such an all-encompassing welfare state have since become clear in Western Europe. As the *New York Times* reported, the high taxes and employer mandates of the European "nanny state" smother innovation, flexibility, and growth, leading to levels of unemployment in most European social democracies that are chronically much higher than unemployment rates in the United States. In short, high taxes and employer mandates "may be shutting Europe out of business in an increasingly competitive global economy."[78] Some thirty-three million new jobs were created in the United States between 1980 and 1998; in that same time, net job creation in the European Community was stagnant. This economic sluggishness has led to a continuing reevaluation in Europe of many of the mechanisms of state control and influence that Reagan resisted, mostly successfully, in the 1980s.

In contrast, the strongest opponents of the Reagan economic program appeared to be consistently confounded throughout the 1980s; they predicted everything from hyperinflation to a surge in interest rates to full-scale depression, none of which happened. Symptomatic of this confusion, many Keynesians who had long endorsed budget deficits urged rigorous action to end them, then criticized proposals to cut spending. Consequently, critics of Reagan's policies have had difficulty formulating a persuasive counterexplanation for the noninflationary growth of that decade. Three essential lines of argument have developed, some more plausible than others.

The first approach is simply to ignore the recovery of the 1980s altogether. Among some economists and many politicians, the economic expansion has

TABLE 4.2
Size of U.S. Government, 2000: Actual Outcome versus
Outcome If 1970s Growth Had Continued

	2000 actual	2000 at 1970s rate
Federal spending (as % of GDP)	18.2	28.8
Federal revenue (as % of GDP)	20.6	25.2
Federal Register (pages of regulation)	72,356 (1998)	219,972

Source: *Historical Tables, Budget of the United States Government, Fiscal Year 2002* (Washington: GPO, 2001), table 1.3; Norman J. Ornstein, Thomas E. Mann, and Michael J. Malbin, *Vital Statistics on Congress 1999–2000* (Washington, D.C.: AEI, 2000), 160. Calculations by author.

been sent into the memory hole, like a Soviet space program accident. Bill Clinton's 1992 presidential campaign, which was emulated by Al Gore in 2000, exemplified this approach. Economists published books like Wallace Peterson's *Silent Depression*, which collapsed the clearly distinct periods of 1973–82 and 1983–90 and then condemned the entire era. A more temperate variation was taken up by MIT economist Paul Krugman, who argued in early 2000 that "nothing extraordinary happened to the U.S. economy during the Reagan years."[79] In a sense, this was true—aside from the longevity of the expansion, which was itself extraordinary, the economy after 1982 was not much different from the economy from 1950 to 1973. Yet it was the very return of the economy to its pre-1973 patterns that was so notable, given the problems of the intervening years.

The second line of argument acknowledges the recovery, but its explanation for the noninflationary expansion is ultimately reduced to "luck." Ronald Reagan and America in the 1980s, according to these analysts, were simply lucky. There was no oil shock and no major war. In fact, the lack of an exogenous shock certainly did not hurt, though inflation at the levels seen in 1980 could easily have become self-perpetuating even after the initial shocks that had set it in motion were no longer a factor (the so-called wage-price spiral). In any event, Reagan inherited an economy in the worst overall condition it had experienced since the Great Depression, saw that economy continue to sink in his first two years in office to the worst level of unemployment since the Depression, and in 1987 presided over the largest one-day stock market decline in the history of the United States. It would, of course, have been bad luck if there *had* been an oil shock or war, but it can hardly be considered good luck that there was not, unless one wishes to assume that the normal state of affairs consists of every possible bad thing happening simultaneously. Altogether, as political scientist John W. Sloan declared, the luck explanation is a "particularly weak argument."[80]

The third line of argument is significantly more plausible than the first two. Many Keynesians argue that a "one-two punch" righted the economy in the 1980s. The Federal Reserve Board extinguished inflation with tight money in the early 1980s, then the tax cuts and defense spending increases produced a demand-driven recovery, starting in 1983.[81] In this view, the tax cuts had a purely demand-side effect, stimulating consumption and employment. As evidence, Keynesians point to the fact that the tax cuts did not produce the rising savings rate that supply-siders had promised, at least not as conventionally measured (though they have tended to cite only the productivity and investment statistics that bolstered their case).[82] While plausible, this explanation almost certainly is incomplete. Most importantly, the decline in inflation and the increase in employment in the 1980s were not purely sequential events but overlapped significantly: Inflation continued falling and remained low long after the recession ended in 1982. In any event, the demand-side "one-two punch" theory recognizes the reality of the recovery and the centrality to the recovery of both tight money and the tax cuts, albeit in a manner disputed by tax cut proponents. To the extent that this interpretation has merit, the recovery of 1983–90 may not have vindicated supply-side theory, but it was nevertheless a vindication of the actual policies of the Reagan administration and the Federal Reserve Board.

Some Keynesians, like Robert Eisner, bridge the gap between the two explanations of demand-driven growth and shock-free price stability. In this view, growth occurred because of the demand stimulus of the deficit, while inflation was controlled because there was no war or oil shock. This interpretation of inflation essentially ignores the effects of monetary policy, and it still does not explain why the same demand increase that produced employment growth would not also produce inflation, even without an oil shock.[83]

Many who adhere to some form of this third position, while conceding the positive effect of some Reagan policies, argue that alternative policies could have produced as good an economy, perhaps even one without the recession of 1981–82. This argument may or may not be correct—it is impossible to know without replicating the 1980s with a different set of policies—but it is completely speculative. Ultimately, it is difficult to escape from the conclusion that the framework of Keynesianism cannot fully explain how the tax cuts could produce an entirely demand-side recovery in an already inflationary environment without making inflation much worse. Indeed, Keynesian economists warned against the tax cuts in 1981 precisely on the grounds that they would be grossly inflationary. In the words of one such economist, a former chairman of the Council of Economic Advisers,

> What I am ready to predict and to promise is that the effect of the president's program will not be—as he so confidently predicted—to cut the present inflation rate more than in half.
>
> Whatever effects it would have on the inflation rate surely would work in the opposite direction—unless there is a great deal to the supply-side argument. . . .
>
> The administration's projection is that inflation in the consumer price index will decline from 11.1% in 1981 to 4.2% in 1986—that, I think, would truly be a miracle.[84]

In 1986, the actual inflation rate was 1.1 percent.

The Recovery and Free-Market Economics

What made the economy of the 1980s politically significant was that the economic successes coincided with, and were probably largely produced by, free-market policies. The recovery cast serious doubt on the wisdom of placing control of the economy in the hands of government. At the start of the 1980s, government wage and price controls and fuel rationing were considered serious policy proposals to contain inflation, and respected economists like Robert Heilbroner suggested that capitalism could be saved only by an unprecedented expansion in the size and role of the federal government. By the end of the decade, such notions sounded hopelessly anachronistic. Altogether, the conjunction of Reagan's program and the economic recovery seemed to revalidate, as Reagan hoped, the principles of individual initiative, economic freedom, and limited government. Similarly, the expansion of the 1980s ended the "zero growth" talk that had permeated the Carter administration, arguably reducing both pressures for redistributionism and government's currency as the agent of redistribution.[85]

This outcome may help to explain why large portions of the political class, as well as many on the intellectual Left whose primary goal was to reallocate the fruits of the economy in conformity with their conception of social justice, were disturbed by the economic policies of the Reagan administration. As former budget director David Stockman noted about many of the critics, in *The Triumph of Politics*,

> They wanted nothing to do with this uncongenial supply-side notion that the betterment of the common man did not depend exclusively upon their own largesse; that the politically brokered redistributions of Washington were the problem, not the solution. Nor could they abide the proposition that social progress might come about as the result of the invisible exertions of workers and entrepreneurs down in the anthill of a $3 trillion economy.[86]

As Anthony S. Campagna complained in his 1994 critique of Reaganomics, "The economy was allowed to operate without constraints or guidance."[87]

The simultaneous recovery of the American economy and of free-market economics had effects well beyond American shores. The economic performance of the United States came to be known abroad as the "American miracle," and the success of the U.S. economy led to a worldwide reappraisal of the benefits of free-market economics. Through the decade, major tax cuts were enacted by Great Britain, Canada, France, Germany, Denmark, Italy, and Japan; even Sweden, long noted for its high taxes and generous welfare state, began reducing its top tax rate from 80 percent to 51 percent. Deregulation and privatization efforts were also enacted to some extent in most European democracies. This occurred both under conservative governments like Margaret Thatcher's and Helmut Kohl's, and under socialist governments like France's and Sweden's. The developed world was soon followed by much of the largely socialist developing world, which made major strides toward market-based reforms. The industrializing countries of East Asia, such as Singapore, South Korea, Indonesia, Malaysia, and Thailand, also cut their tax rates. Even Leninist states like the Soviet Union and China began moving away from rigid control over their economies. An enormous change occurred in the 1980s in the way the world looked at economics. That change was driven by a variety of factors, but not least was the example of the American economy. By the end of the 1980s, the question of whether capitalism would survive was no longer being asked, at home or abroad.

The renewed strength of free-market economics endured throughout the 1990s as well, around the world and in the United States. Despite much talk of a reversal of course at the onset of the Clinton administration, limited government remained a key direction of economic policy. While taxes were raised significantly in 1990 and 1993, marginal tax rates never came close to resuming their pre-1981 levels (the top rate in 1980 was 70 percent and only 39.6 percent in 2000). A new tax cut was passed in 1997, and effective tax rates continued falling for most taxpayers through the 1990s.[88] Federal executive-branch civilian employment fell by nearly one-fifth as a proportion of the population.[89] By 2000, federal spending had fallen to 18.2 percent of GDP. The minimum wage was raised twice, but Congress declined to enact the most elaborate proposals for government intervention in the economy, such as President Clinton's stimulus spending package, energy tax, and health care reform proposals. The *Federal Register* of government regulations grew again, starting in the first Bush administration, but industry deregulation was never reversed, additional deregulation of communications and agriculture was enacted, and the *Federal Register* never regained its 1980 peak.

Where Reagan appointed Alan Greenspan as chairman of the Federal Reserve Board, Clinton reappointed him, endorsing the board's preeminent (and conservative) goal of controlling inflation. Where Reagan envisioned NAFTA, Clinton consummated it. Where Reagan championed technology and small investors, Clinton adopted similar themes and allowed Congress to cut capital-gains taxes. Clinton also adopted the Reagan emphasis on economic growth, in preference to the Carter-era talk of inevitable limits and zero-sum economics. Bill Clinton's greatest economic legacy might well be that while trimming at the edges, he fundamentally (though often reluctantly) consolidated the structure and legitimacy of the free-market economics that had characterized the 1980s.

As America entered the year 2000, numerous commentators across the political spectrum noted how substantially economics had become divorced from politics and governmental direction over the previous two decades. Pointing to the undeniable importance of technology to the boom, Paul Krugman declared it possible that "as far as the economy is concerned we don't need to elect a great man as president; all we need is someone who won't do too much damage."[90] To commentator George Will, most voters grasp that "politics today is only marginally related" to prosperity or social betterment.[91] It is difficult to imagine a domestic development more pleasing to Reagan than that, or one of greater import.

Liberty, Equality, and the Costs of Prosperity

While Reagan largely succeeded in his goal of strengthening economic freedom in American life, the question remains whether economic freedom was pursued at the expense of other important values. Many commentators have held that the costs of the recovery mitigated or even outweighed the benefits, and that the costs were unavoidably linked to the benefits. Foremost, it is argued that while the economy grew, only the top incomes benefited, while the income and well-being of the rest of society stagnated or declined. Frances Fox Piven and Richard Cloward argued in 1982 that "the Reagan administration and its big-business allies declared a new class war on the unemployed, the unemployable, and the working poor."[92] This "rich got richer and poor got poorer" argument was put forward prominently in books such as Kevin Phillips's *The Politics of Rich and Poor* and Donald L. Barlett and James B. Steele's *America: What Went Wrong?*[93] "During the 1980s," Bill Clinton echoed in 1992, "the rich got richer while the forgotten middle class—the people who work hard and play by the rules—took it on the chin."[94] Some scholarly assessments make the more nuanced argument that while "the policies of the Reagan administration were not the origin of the growing inequality[,] . . . they contributed to the trend. More importantly, Reagan's policies did nothing to inhibit inequality, and his administration attempted to delegitimize any governmental endeavors to promote equality."[95] In one form or another, this argument is, indeed, the unifying theme behind much of the criticism of the Reagan years. According to the critics, income inequality grew as the middle class shrank and tottered on the edge of poverty; economic mobility was sharply curtailed; the poor, women, and minorities got poorer; poverty itself worsened; and deregulation benefited big business but only at a heavy cost to other values like public health and safety. At the heart of these concerns lay the tension between economic freedom and economic growth on one hand—values to which Reagan's economic policy deliberately tilted—and equality of economic outcome on the other. Together, these charges represent perhaps the most challenging counterinterpretation of the Reagan economic program.

The Rise of Inequality

At the center of the egalitarian critique of the 1980s are two distinct questions. The first is whether income inequality grew, and the second is whether the poor and middle class got "poorer." The answers, as it turns out, are yes and no, respectively.

Inequality between income groupings clearly did grow in the 1980s. The number of millionaires ballooned, and at the end of the 1980s the top fifth of households was farther ahead of the rest of the nation than it had been at the beginning of the decade. Disparities in the shares of wealth held by each quintile also grew. This trend of increased inequality started around 1970; it was partially (perhaps one-fifth) the result of policy but primarily the result of the rise of single-parent families, the aging of the American population, mass immigration, and structural changes in the American and global economy, particularly the increased importance of technology and thus of advanced training and education.[96] As economist Marvin Kosters pointed out, "In 1980, college graduates on average earned about 30 percent more than high school graduates; by 1988, they earned about 60 percent more."[97] This trend continued unabated throughout most of the 1990s, though there is some evidence that it slowed at the end of the decade.

There is a debate over the trend of real wages in the 1980s. By the conventional measurement, average real weekly wages declined in both the 1970s and the 1980s, though at a much slower rate from 1982 to 1989 (3.4 percent) than from 1973 to 1982 (9.2 percent).[98] However, wages in manufacturing jobs actually increased substantially in the 1980s, surpassing wages in West Germany to become the highest in the world.[99] Furthermore, the conventional measurement of weekly wages was flawed, for several reasons. When adjusted for these factors, real employee compensation per man-hour rose in the 1980s, though not as quickly as in previous decades.[100]

More to the point, increased inequality in the 1980s did not occur because the annual household incomes of the poor and middle class stagnated or declined. In fact, household incomes grew substantially in every quintile, though incomes in the top fifth grew faster than incomes below. Incongruously, the argument that middle- and lower-income Americans were hurt by Reagan's economic policies is often based on income figures starting in the mid 1970s. For example, the income trends Kevin Phillips cited in *The Politics of Rich and Poor* start in 1977. Other prominent analysts, including Wallace Peterson in *Silent Depression*, use figures starting in 1973. Real incomes did drop substantially between 1973 and 1982, due to the effects of stagnant productivity, high inflation, and the recessions of 1974–75, 1979–80, and 1981–82. In particular, 1980 was the worst year for family income since World War II.

From 1982 through 1989, however, real household incomes increased substantially in *all* quintiles, and median family income increased 12.5 percent (see table 4.3). Some of that income gain was due to the increase in two-earner families; on the other hand, per family income went farther in the 1980s than an equal income would have gone in the 1970s, because of declining average family size.[101] Claims that incomes were "stagnant" from 1973 or 1977 to 1989 are hence technically true but highly misleading.

If one were to draw a straight line from the mid-1970s to 1989, it would indeed be flat; if one were to fill in the data between 1973 or 1977 and 1989, the line would form a pronounced V (see chart 4.1 and chart 4.2). All income groups benefited from the economic expansion of the 1980s, though by 1989 some had only just recovered from the damage suffered between 1973 and 1982. Furthermore, when examining yearly expenditures (or consumption)—what one might consider a household's "permanent income"—distribution by quintiles was much more equal than distribution of yearly income. As Richard McKenzie showed, that distribution remained basically unchanged in the 1960s, 1970s, and 1980s.[102]

Mobility and the Middle Class

Perhaps the greatest shortcoming of the quintile system of measuring income is that it does not show movement by individuals or families into and out of different quintiles.[103] Studies that tracked individuals showed that upward economic mobility remained high in the 1980s. A Treasury Department study of income mobility from 1979 to 1987 demonstrated that 86 percent of those in the bottom fifth in 1979, and 60 percent in the next fifth, had moved into a

TABLE 4.3
Average Household Income by Quintile, 1990 Dollars

	Lowest Fifth	Second Fifth	Third Fifth	Fourth Fifth	Highest Fifth
1977	7,193	17,715	29,298	42,911	76,522
1980	6,836	17,015	28,077	41,364	73,752
1989	7,372	18,341	30,488	46,177	90,150
Change, 1980–89					
Dollars	$536	$1,326	$2,411	$4,813	$16,398
Percentage	7.8%	7.8%	8.6%	11.6%	22.2%

Source: Bureau of the Census, *Money Income of Households, Families, and Persons*, 1990, 202. Calculations by author.

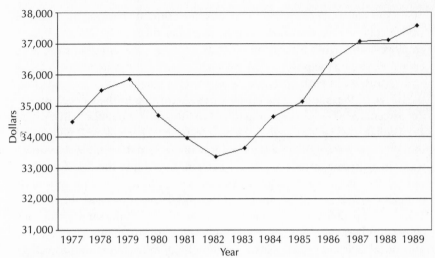

Chart 4.1
Average Real Family Income, Middle Quintile (1991 Dollars), 1977–1989

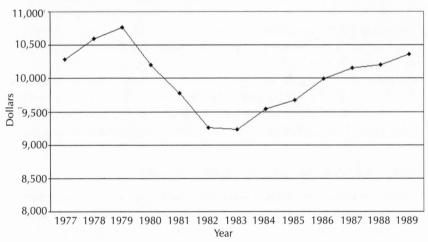

Chart 4.2
Average Real Family Income, Bottom Quintile (1991 Dollars), 1977–1989

higher quintile by 1988. Indeed, a larger share of those in the bottom quintile in 1979 were in the top quintile in 1988 than were still in the bottom quintile.[104] A separate longitudinal study done by economist Isabel Sawhill for the Urban Institute showed that individuals who started in the lowest fifth increased their average family income by 77 percent in real terms from 1977 to 1986, while those who started in the top fifth saw their incomes rise only 5 percent.[105]

These sorts of studies have come under some criticism, because they have in-cluded college students whose income rose after they graduated and became employed—though it is far from obvious why such cases should be excluded, or that excluding them would fundamentally change the conclusion.

It is this income growth among all sectors that produced the oft-noted shrinkage of the middle class in the 1980s. According to the Census Bureau, the percentage of families earning fifteen to fifty thousand dollars (in constant 1990 dollars) fell by 5 percent in the decade, from 58 percent to 53 percent. Al-though there was some movement of individuals from the middle class down-ward, in aggregate terms the entire 5 percent moved into the *over*-fifty-thou-sand-dollar category, which grew from 25 percent to nearly 31 percent of the population. In short, the shrinking of the middle class "was essentially a con-sequence of people moving up in the distribution."[106] At the same time, home ownership became more affordable, by several measurements.[107] These facts are crucial, because high levels of social mobility mitigate the negative effects of the economic inequality captured in any snapshot of income quintiles: if most Americans will move up in the income distribution over the course of their lives, then greater separation between quintiles actually means that they will end up at a higher level of economic well-being than if the income distri-bution was more compressed.

As Herbert Stein, a former chairman of the Council of Economic Advisers, ar-gued in 1992, the middle class was "being fed an interpretation of the record that describes them as being the victims of one or two decades of neglect." While this interpretation was "useful for politicians and other policy activists," it was un-true. To the contrary, Stein contended, "the standard of living of Americans has been, and continues to be, higher than for any previous generation."[108]

Women and Minorities in the Economy of the 1980s

Some analysts have contended that economic trends of the 1980s "fell hard-est on women, blacks, and other minority groups."[109] However, women fared quite well in income and jobs in the 1980s, and the black and Hispanic mid-dle classes grew considerably. For example:

- The real income of a median black family fell 11 percent from 1977 to 1982, then went up 17 percent from 1982 to 1989.[110] The number of black households earning fifty thousand dollars or more grew by 40 percent in the 1980s.[111]
- In those same years of recovery, Hispanic family income grew by 11 per-cent, leading commentator Roger E. Hernandez to argue that "Hispanics made impressive progress in nearly every measure of economic well-

being" during the 1980s.[112] In fact, according to Census Bureau figures, median household income for both blacks and Hispanics grew much faster in the economic expansion from 1982 to 1989 than in the boom from 1991 through 1998.

- The number of black-owned businesses rose by 38 percent in the first five years of the recovery of the 1980s, during which time the number of Hispanic businesses grew by 81 percent.[113]
- During the 1980s, blacks and Hispanics accounted for a disproportionate share of all new jobs generated, and black unemployment actually fell at a faster rate than white unemployment.[114]
- While college enrollment by whites increased by 6 percent from 1980 to 1990, black college enrollment increased by 29 percent, and Hispanic enrollment increased by 45 percent.[115]
- The yearly earnings gap between men and women, though an imperfect indicator of women's economic progress, climbed from sixty cents for every dollar of men's earnings in 1980 to seventy-one cents by the end of the decade.[116] Women's employment and median earnings grew faster than men's, and the largest gains were registered by minority women.[117]

Altogether, economics correspondent Sylvia Nasar declared in 1987 that "the average American has never had it so good. By almost any measure of health and wealth, if not wisdom, we are demonstrably better off now than in the palmy 50's and 60's. And that goes for just about any group you would care to name: the middle class, the poor, baby-boomers, old people, black people, women."[118] Kevin Phillips, who was highly critical of Reaganomics, nevertheless concluded that "the Reagan economy was a triumph of outsider access— a cavalcade of inventors, leveragers, speculators, packagers, performers, and promoters, ethnically spiced by Vietnamese-American shrimp wholesalers, Korean greengrocers and Asian high-tech entrepreneurs."[119]

Poverty

In the late 1970s through 1982, poverty increased to a peak of 15.2 percent as a result of stagflation. Beginning with the economic recovery of 1983, the poverty rate declined every year for the remainder of the decade, steadily descending to 12.8 percent in 1989. Thus, the poverty rate fell in six of Reagan's eight years in office. These declines were consistent across races. Infant mortality rates, while remaining higher than in most other industrial democracies, also fell throughout the 1980s.[120]

The annual snapshot of the poverty rate, like the quintile figures, does not register the movement of individuals in and out of poverty. Longitudinal studies show that between one-third and one-half of those under the poverty line one year will be above the line the next year, and there was probably no more than a 3 percent core of persistent poverty in the 1980s, essentially unchanged from the late 1960s and early 1970s. According to sociologist Christopher Jencks, per family consumption expenditures—for a variety of reasons, a better measure than income of the economic health of the poor—increased by 13 percent over inflation from 1980 to 1989 among poor families.[121]

Though the poverty rate was lower in 1989 than in 1980, it was higher than it had been at its low point in 1978. This continuing level of poverty stemmed in large measure from an increase in illegitimacy rates throughout the 1980s. Black married couples saw their poverty rate drop from 15.5 percent in 1980 to 12.5 percent in 1989, lower than the national average. However, this improvement was overshadowed by the growth of black single-parent families, which consistently had poverty rates in excess of 50 percent throughout the decade. White single-parent families, which also grew in number, had poverty rates of 30 percent or more. As one commentator observed, divorce was "the single most common reason that middle-class people slip into poverty."[122] Any causal link between Reagan's economic policies and these social problems was highly attenuated, at best.

For some time, homeless-advocate Mitch Snyder insisted that there were approximately three million homeless in America. This figure intuitively seemed incredible, and indeed it was.[123] By the late 1980s, most studies had put the figure at about three hundred thousand nationwide, and no reputable study had put the number above six hundred thousand. Snyder ultimately conceded that his estimate was meaningless. The media, however, uncritically adopted the three million figure and continued using it long after it was debunked.[124] Indeed, the issue of homelessness was consistently misreported; the Center for Media and Public Affairs reported that in 103 network news stories on the homeless run over a typical thirty-month period in the 1980s, only 12 percent of the homeless who were interviewed were unemployed and only 3 percent used drugs or alcohol, a substantial inversion of reality. Most estimates put the actual proportion of homeless who were mentally ill or had drug or alcohol abuse problems at upward of 70 percent, while 56 percent had spent five days or more in jail.[125]

If the number of homeless actually did increase in the 1980s—and it may well have—it was not because of cuts in federal housing programs. Federal expenditures for housing actually increased by 58 percent from 1980 to 1990, the number of subsidized units rose from 3.3 million in 1981 to 4.3 million in 1990, and the number of persons served grew from 8.2 million to 10.8 million.[126] Nor can unemployment and poverty be blamed, since both declined for most of the decade. Instead, the cumulative impact of several other factors produces a more plausible explanation. Rent control and other regulations gradually reduced the supply of low-cost rental apartments in many major metropolitan areas like New York and San Francisco, which were (and are) especially hard hit by homelessness.[127] Urban renewal projects over the previous quarter-century also destroyed large numbers of "flop houses." Deinstitutionalization of mental patients, often mandated by the courts, sent into the streets thousands of people ill equipped to live on their own. In addition, the 1972 Supreme Court decision *Papachristou v. City of Jacksonville* made it far more difficult for cities to evict vagrants from public areas.

Though Congress blocked most action, the Reagan administration made a strong argument for using market mechanisms to combat poverty through low-tax "enterprise zones," tenant control of public housing, and rental and education vouchers. Modest but significant welfare reforms were made in 1981 and 1988. At the behest of the administration, federal antipoverty spending priorities shifted throughout the 1980s in ways that were not only more cost-effective but more beneficial to the poor. From 1981 to 1989, real spending on Aid to Families with Dependent Children—the cornerstone of federal welfare—declined by 1 percent, while dollars devoted to the Earned Income Tax Credit—a program providing refundable tax credits to the working poor—more than doubled in real terms.[128] This shift in many respects served as the unspoken model for the welfare policy of the Clinton era. At least partially spurred by Reagan, a bipartisan consensus ultimately emerged that welfare was broken and needed to be fixed—a consensus represented by Bill Clinton's 1992 promise to "end welfare as we know it." Clearly, the political and economic sea change of the 1980s was largely responsible for the increased agitation for welfare reform in the 1990s culminating in the welfare reform provisions of 1996. While this antipoverty strategy was, and is, highly controversial in some quarters, it was an active strategy that contrasts sharply with the picture of negligence that is painted by some of Reagan's critics.

The Costs of Deregulation

Exemplifying the critics of deregulation, Donald L. Barlett and James B. Steele declared that the deregulation of specific industries like airlines, railroads, trucking, financial institutions, and telecommunications "has been costly to workers and consumers alike."[129] Two authors of a 1993 public policy text likewise attacked deregulation more generally, claiming that "our willingness . . . to compromise job safety and the environment through deregulation made the economy look better than it was during much of the 1980s."[130]

However, as we have already seen, most deregulation of industries worked to the advantage of the consumer. Without question, the best example of deregulation gone awry was the savings and loan fiasco, but that story is a complicated one. The industry was already insolvent prior to deregulation, its liabilities exceeding its assets by $110 billion in 1980—due largely to overregulation that stifled the flexibility that had been necessary for survival in the inflationary 1970s.[131] The deregulation of 1982 was a reasonable response to this situation, but it was coupled with a Carter-era decision to increase per deposit federal insurance from forty thousand dollars to a hundred thousand. As a result, there was neither effective regulation nor market discipline. The scope and cost of the debacle was hence less the result of deregulation per se than of initial overregulation followed by the simultaneous reduction of regulation and market risk.[132] While there were some notable convictions, a variety of analysts have concluded that fraud played no role at all in an estimated two-thirds of the 650 S&L collapses. Economist Catherine England placed "the losses caused by outright fraud (as opposed to second-guessing poor judgments) at only 3 to 10 percent of the total losses. In short, the lion's share of the two hundred billion dollars lost (before interest) in the S&L disaster did not come from private greed run amok."[133] Costly misjudgments were made by figures ranging from savings and loan operators to regulators, to members of Congress, to the president of the United States and his advisers, but the S&L disaster was not representative of deregulation generally.

Furthermore, there is little evidence that the Reagan administration sacrificed the environment or public safety in its pursuit of regulatory relief. At the end of the 1980s, most concrete measures of the national environment showed continued improvement. Between 1978 and 1987, recorded levels of sulphur dioxide fell 35 percent; airborne lead fell 88 percent; carbon monoxide fell 32 percent; dust, soot, and particulate matter fell 21 percent; and ground-level ozone fell 16 percent. Oil spills declined from fourteen million gallons yearly in the 1970s to nine million gallons yearly in the Reagan years; reforestation increased from two million acres annually to three million acres; wilderness preserves were increased from eighty million acres to ninety-one million acres; soil erosion declined; and the Great Lakes were made demonstrably cleaner.[134] Taking a longer view, according to the National Wildlife Federation's twentieth Environmental Quality Index, issued in 1988, "The nation's water quality has vastly improved. . . . [T]he air in our cities is visibly cleaner than it was two decades ago. . . . [W]e have made steady progress against ills recognized in 1968." From 1968 through 1988, visible particulates in the air declined by 25 percent, while lead, sulphur dioxide, and nitrogen dioxide levels were "dramatically reduced." In the view of the National Wildlife Federation, the problems that remained were the result less of neglect than of scientific discoveries of previously unknown environmental dangers.[135]

Despite declining budgets and staff for the Consumer Product Safety Commission, consumer safety continued improving. For example, the CPSC reported that consumer product–related electrocutions declined by one-third from 1983 to 1990, and nonfire carbon-monoxide poisoning deaths associated with consumer products fell by one-fifth between 1981 and 1990.[136] The Occupational Safety and Health Administration faced budget cuts and reduced its volume of new rules; however, the number of annual OSHA inspections from 1981 to 1989 was slightly *higher* than the number of inspections recorded in 1980, before the Reagan administration. After a sharp drop from 1980 to 1982, OSHA also produced a steadily increasing number of citations for serious violations through the rest of the 1980s, until the citations given in 1989 surpassed the number from 1980.[137] Altogether, rates of occupational illnesses and injuries were unchanged or slightly lower in 1989 compared with 1980, and average yearly rates of total occupational injuries and illnesses were actually lower from 1981 to 1989 (8.1 per hundred full-time workers) than they were from 1973 to 1980 (9.6 per hundred workers).[138]

Reagan and the Economy of the 1990s

One sign of the continuing economic influence of Reagan and his program is the debate over whether he was largely responsible for the boom of the 1990s. Predictably, conservative economists like James Glassman, Lawrence Kudlow, and Stephen Moore said, "It's Reagan's Economy, Stupid!" Kudlow and Moore argued in early 2000 that "Reagan's supply side economic ideas . . . unleashed a great wave of entrepreneurial-technological innovation that transformed and restructured the economy, resulting in a long boom prosperity that continues to throw off economic benefits to this day."[139] Equally predictably, economists on the Left have denied such claims. Martin N. Baily, chairman of President Clinton's Council of Economic Advisers, argued in response that the recovery of the 1990s was fundamentally different (and superior) to that of the 1980s.[140] Paul Krugman has not only disputed the connection between the 1980s and 1990s but accused proponents of that view of intellectual dishonesty. Krugman pointed out that when the economy was slow in the early 1990s, many of the same people who declared the late 1990s to vindicate Reagan were insisting that Reagan's policies be considered terminated in 1989.[141] Krugman was justified in drawing attention to the opportunism and shifting perspectives of his opponents (and, perhaps, of human nature generally— many Keynesians, after all, have to grapple with their own record of shifting interpretations in the 1980s). Such an exercise does not, however, draw us any closer to the truth of the matter.

An increasing number of people without obvious partisan or ideological stakes in this debate now side with Reagan. Professor John W. Sloan argued in *The Reagan Effect,* a scrupulously balanced academic treatment, that "Reagan's tax cuts for both individuals and corporations stimulated the prosperity that, except for a short, mild recession in 1990–91, has continued into the 1990s. . . . By focusing on the economy, the Reagan administration, with the help of Paul Volcker, increased the capacity of our economic system to provide long-term growth with low inflation and to compete successfully in international markets."[142] Interestingly, Sloan had begun his research with a predisposition to view Reagan as a political success but an economic failure. To noted liberal historian Robert Dallek, who is highly critical of Reagan in many other areas, Reagan's economic policies deserve "significant credit" for the "buoyant American economy of the 1980s and 1990s."[143] In early 2000, *Fortune* magazine correspondent Anna Bernasek traced the boom of the 1990s to three interrelated long-term factors: deregulation, globalization, and financial innovation.[144] Each of these was an important feature of the economic policy of the 1980s. Robert D. McTeeter Jr., president of the Federal Reserve Bank of Dallas, similarly credited technology plus deregulation, free trade and international competition, the collapse of communism, efficient and innovative U.S. capital markets, the switch from federal deficits to surpluses, and the successful war against inflation—again, a series of explanations mostly traceable to policies of the 1980s.[145] Numerous leaders of Silicon Valley also give a large share of credit to Reagan. As recounted by Dinesh D'Souza, who interviewed a group of computer executives in the mid-1990s,

> The entrepreneurs also credited Reagan's policies of limited government, deregulation, and open markets with creating an atmosphere in which the revolution could flourish. Michael Dell, who founded Dell Computers in the mid-1980s, argues that Reagan did this in part by championing the entrepreneur as an American hero who defies limits to the imagination and creates new things. "Reagan was the inspirational leader of the technological revolution," remarks T. J. Rodgers, founder and chief executive of Cypress Semiconductors. Other entrepreneurs who got their start in the 1980s echo Rodgers's judgment that without Reagan the technological surge of the past two decades "would not have happened this way, and this fast."[146]

On behalf of this argument, it can be said that the prosperity of the 1990s appeared to be a straightforward extension of the prosperity of the 1980s. The back-to-back expansions of 1983–90 and 1991 forward meant that the United States had experienced prosperity for at least part of every year from 1983 through 2001, slipping into recession for roughly 4 percent of that period (by historical comparison, the U.S. economy has been in recession for one-third of its existence). The business cycle seems to have become longer and more stable since 1983. Without the recovery of the 1980s, which overcame the worst economic crisis since the Great Depression, the expansion of the 1990s would not have been possible. As Moore and Kudlow demonstrated, an examination of key economic indicators like inflation, stock prices, interest rates, and manufacturing productivity clearly points to the early 1980s, not the 1990s, as the decisive turning point.

The strong economy of the 1990s was built on essentially the same foundation as the strong economy of the 1980s: entrepreneurial innovation, increased international competitiveness, the rise and dispersion of new technologies, and the growth of the small-investor class. As well, what many considered to be the economic vices of the 1980s continued seamlessly through the 1990s: growing income inequality, large trade deficits, and declining personal savings rates. For these reasons alone, economic historians may well come to view the last two decades of the twentieth century as parts of the same basic phenomenon: the Twenty-Year Boom.

It may be surprising to discover that the much-touted (and in most respects genuinely impressive) economic boom of the 1990s was actually inferior to the 1980s recovery in some important respects. The economic expansion of the 1990s surpassed the record peacetime length of the 1980s expansion, setting a new record in January 1999, and the stock market recorded new highs. However, average rates of GDP growth, household median income growth, job creation, export growth, and poverty in the expansion of the 1980s were all superior to those in the expansion of the 1990s (see table 4.4).

While unemployment and inflation fell lower in the 1990s than in the 1980s, the recovery of the 1980s started from a much worse position and showed greater improvement (see table 4.5). Further, according to Census Bureau data, income shifts in the 1990s actually were what they were incorrectly

TABLE 4.4
The Recovery of the 1980s versus the Recovery of the 1990s

	1983–89	1992–99
Avg. real GDP growth	+4.3%	+3.6%
Avg. real productivity growth	+2.0%	+2.0%
Total employment increase	+19.4%	+13.4%
Avg. inflation	3.7%	2.5%
Avg. unemployment	6.9%	5.6%
Avg. poverty rate	13.8%	14.0%
Total export growth	+79.4%	+52.2%
Total household median income	+11.2%	+9.2%

Source: *Economic Report of the President to Congress 2000* (Washington, D.C.: GPO, February 2000), tables B-4, B-31, B-33, B-40, B-48, B-61, B-101. U.S. Census Web site, Historical Income Tables, table H-6. Employment increase is for 1982–90 and 1991–99; poverty rates and household median income for 1990s only include 1992–98.

TABLE 4.5
Improvement of Key Economic Indicators, 1980s and 1990s

	1980s			1990s		
	Worst	1989	Change	Worst	1999	Change
Inflation	13.3 (1979)	4.6	-8.7	6.1 (1990)	2.7	-3.4
Unemployment	9.7 (1982)	5.3	-4.4	7.5 (1992)	4.2	-3.3
GDP	(1.9) (1982)	3.5	5.4	(.2) (1991)	4.0	4.2

Source: *Economic Report of the President to Congress 2000,* tables B-4, B-40, I.

alleged to have been in the 1980s. In the 1980s, there was a general shift of household incomes upward, as the percentage of households shrank in each income grouping except the top; in the 1990s, both the top and the bottom grew at the expense of the middle.[147] By one academic analysis reviewing eighteen different economic indicators, Bill Clinton's first-term economy was rated only seventh out of ten postwar presidencies,[148] and it is possible that much of the economic sluggishness of the early 1990s was attributable to the marginal changes that occurred in the Bush and Clinton administrations in terms of tax, spending, and regulatory policy.[149] Only from 1996 forward was the recovery on truly solid ground, a turning point that coincided with a new Congress that cut spending, cut taxes, and encouraged the Clinton administration to regulate with greater caution.

In one sense, these facts might be said to vindicate Reagan both in the observance and in the breach. At the very least, given that the fundamental direction of economic policy changed relatively little in the 1990s, concerns that Reagan's policies would lead to long-term disaster seem misplaced. At the same time, however, if the economic expansion of the 1990s seemed to demonstrate that Reagan's direction of greater economic freedom had been well conceived, it also challenged supporters of that course by showing that within certain limits, marginally bigger or smaller government can both coincide with a large measure of prosperity. Even if taxes and regulation cannot go above a certain point without sacrificing economic health, there was room at the end of the 1980s for them to go higher than they were without restoring the economic conditions of the late 1970s. In any event, the very debate over whether Reagan shared responsibility for the prosperity of the 1990s was itself a demonstration of the staying power of the economic ideas he turned into policy in 1981.

Reagan and Economic Freedom: Evaluations

Though it is not possible to prove incontrovertibly, it is probable that Reagan's economic policies contributed heavily to the economic expansions of the

1980s and 1990s. Without doubt, he directly and indirectly strengthened the economic component of the architectural structure of American freedom. Directly, he promoted and secured the adoption of economic policies that were designed to restrict the power and scope of the central government. The apparent success of those policies ended an economic crisis that could easily have led to a significant expansion of the power and scope of the central government, had it continued. Those policies also promoted the rise of the "new economy," the decentralization and entrepreneurialism of which made future departures in the direction of democratic socialism even more problematic. The renewed legitimacy of free-market economics made possible by Reagan's success defined America's, and much of the world's, economic policy for at least two decades.

Many of Reagan's critics argue that economic liberty was pursued so single-mindedly that other valid economic goals and values, particularly economic equality, were slighted. In one sense, they are right. The equalization of incomes was not a high Reagan administration priority; in fact, the administration clearly considered policies aimed explicitly at that goal as part of the economic and political problem to be overcome. However, not much evidence supports the conclusion that economic equality itself suffered significantly from this neglect. Income inequality grew, mostly as the result of nonpolicy factors, but so did real household incomes in all quintiles; poverty rates declined six of eight years; the middle class shrank, but mostly because people moved up in the income distribution; women and minorities posted significant economic gains. Nor is there any consensus on what level of economic equality is optimum in a democracy, or under what circumstances (if any) equality of condition should take precedence over the competing values of freedom, opportunity, or equality under the law.

Notes

1. See Wallace Peterson, *Silent Depression* (New York: W. W. Norton, 1994); Robert Kuttner similarly wrote of "fifteen years of invisible depression," in his "Is There a Democratic Economics?" *The American Prospect* (Winter 1992), 25; Paul Krugman, *The Age of Diminished Expectations* (Washington, D.C.: Washington Post, 1990).

2. James Tobin, "Reaganomics in Retrospect," in *The Reagan Revolution*, ed. B. B. Kymlicka and Jean V. Matthews (Chicago: Dorsey, 1988), 103.

3. Anthony S. Campagna, *The Economy in the Reagan Years: The Economic Consequences of the Reagan Administrations* (Westport, Conn.: Greenwood, 1994), 213, 215.

4. "Remarks by Governor Bill Clinton," Economic Club of Detroit, Detroit, Michigan, August 21, 1992, 2, 5.

5. Robert L. Bartley, *The Seven Fat Years . . . and How to Do It Again* (New York: Free Press, 1992).

6. Ronald Reagan, *An American Life: The Autobiography* (New York: Simon and Schuster, 1990), 333.

7. James Ring Adams, *Secrets of the Tax Revolt* (New York: Harcourt Brace Jovanovich, 1984), 7.

8. Bartley, *The Seven Fat Years*, 163–64.

9. Lester Thurow, "The Great Stagnation," *New York Times Magazine*, October 17, 1982, 32–36.

10. "Can Capitalism Survive?" *Time*, July 14, 1975, 52.

11. Robert Heilbroner, "Does Capitalism Have a Future?" *New York Times Magazine*, August 5, 1982, 20.

12. Campagna, *The Economy in the Reagan Years*, 209.

13. Martin Anderson, *Revolution* (New York: Harcourt Brace Jovanovich, 1988), 158. See more generally 140–74.

14. Anderson, *Revolution*, 171–72.

15. Reagan, *An American Life*, 231–32.

16. Anderson, *Revolution*, 164.

17. For a more in-depth examination of the fundamental elements of the Reagan economic policy and the development of supply-side economics, see Bartley, *The Seven Fat Years*; William A. Niskanen, *Reaganomics: An Insider's View of the Policies and the People* (New York: Oxford University Press, 1988); Paul Craig Roberts, *The Supply-Side Revolution* (Cambridge, Mass.: Harvard University Press, 1984); Anderson, *Revolution*; Lawrence Lindsey, *The Growth Experiment* (New York: Basic, 1990).

18. "Inaugural Address, January 20, 1981," *Public Papers of the Presidents: Ronald Reagan 1981* (Washington, D.C.: Government Printing Office [hereafter GPO], 1982), 1.

19. "Radio Address to the Nation on Independence Day and the Centennial of the Statue of Liberty, July 5, 1986," *Public Papers of the Presidents: Ronald Reagan 1986* (Washington, D.C.: GPO, 1988), 925.

20. "Inaugural Address, January 21, 1985," *Public Papers of the Presidents: Ronald Reagan 1985* (Washington, D.C.: GPO, 1988).

21. Reagan, *An American Life*, 230, 333.

22. "Tax Cuts: How You Will Be Better Off," *U.S. News & World Report*, August 10, 1981, 20.

23. See William Greider, *Secrets of the Temple: How the Federal Reserve Runs the Country* (New York: Touchstone, 1987), 542. See also Lou Cannon, *President Reagan: The Role of a Lifetime* (New York: Simon and Schuster, 1991), 268–74.

24. Cannon, *President Reagan*, 277.

25. "Rolling Back Regulation," *Time*, July 6, 1987, 51; Elizabeth Sanders, "The Presidency and the Bureaucratic State," in *The Presidency and the Political System*, ed. Michael Nelson, 3rd ed. (Washington, D.C.: Congressional Quarterly, 1990), 419.

26. Campagna, *The Economy in the Reagan Years*, 210.

27. Campagna, *The Economy in the Reagan Years*, 57.

28. David S. Broder, "The Words Do Mean Something," *Washington Post*, January 30, 1983, C7.

29. Lindsey, *The Growth Experiment*, 118–20.

30. See Richard Nadler, "Special(k)," *National Review*, April 19, 1999, 52–54.

31. President Carter and Sen. Edward Kennedy contributed heavily to the initial round of deregulation in the late 1970s. Carter had initially appointed Paul Volcker as chairman of the Federal Reserve Board. Prominent Democratic senators like Sam Nunn and Lloyd Bentsen supported both individual and business tax cuts; the Democratic-controlled Con-

gressional Joint Economic Committee released numerous reports in 1979–80 with a supply-side orientation. When the 1981 tax-cut bill finally passed, it did so by large margins: 238–195 in a House controlled by Democrats, and eighty-nine to eleven in a Senate narrowly controlled by Republicans. Likewise, the critical moment in the 1985–86 tax-reform debate came when the Senate Finance Committee approved a radical tax overhaul by a twenty-to-zero vote; on the floor, final passage of tax reform came by a vote of 292–136 in the House and seventy-four to twenty-three in the Senate.

32. "The Competition of Ideas," *The American Enterprise* (January–February 1990), 77–78.

33. "Brave New Economy," *U.S. News & World Report*, March 31, 1986, 42.

34. Robert M. Dunn Jr., "Don't Knock Reaganomics," *Washington Post*, July 24, 1988, C5. Three years earlier Dunn had written a highly unflattering critique of supply-side tax theory, entitled "Bye-Bye, Supply Side," *Washington Post*, July 30, 1985.

35. Robert J. Barro, "A Gentleman's B- for Bush on Economics," *Wall Street Journal*, September 30, 1992, A16.

36. Paul R. Abramson, John H. Aldrich, and David W. Rohde, *Change and Continuity in the 1988 Elections*, rev. ed. (Washington, D.C.: Congressional Quarterly, 1991), 157.

37. Ed Rubenstein, "More than McJobs," *National Review*, August 31, 1992, 31.

38. "The Spirit of Independence," *Inc.*, July 1988, 47.

39. Daniel Akst, "The Real 1980s," *Los Angeles Times Magazine*, November 13, 1994, 26.

40. Sylvia Nasar, "American Revival in Manufacturing Seen in U.S. Report," *New York Times*, February 5, 1991, 1. Also see Lois M. Plunkert, "The 1990s: A Decade of Job Growth and Industry Shifts," *Monthly Labor Review* 113, no. 9, 3; Council of Economic Advisers, *Economic Report of the President 1991* (Washington, D.C.: GPO, 1991), table B-13.

41. "Brave New Economy," 42.

42. Nasar, "American Revival in Manufacturing Seen in U.S. Report."

43. Average gross investment as a proportion of the economy actually fell slightly from 1981 to 1991 compared with 1974–81. John W. Sloan, *The Reagan Effect: Economics and Presidential Leadership* (Lawrence: University of Kansas, 1999), 236. However, real gross business fixed investment grew one-fifth faster from 1981 to 1985 than it had from 1977 to 1981, and in the first two years of the recovery, investment spending grew twice as fast as the average rate immediately following a recession. Paul Craig Roberts, "Debt, Lies, and Inflation," *National Review*, August 31, 1992, 34. See also Niskanen, *Reaganomics*, 232–35; Lindsey, *The Growth Experiment*, 155.

44. See Kevin Phillips, *The Politics of Rich and Poor* (New York: Random House, 1990), 71.

45. Dinesh D'Souza, "How Reagan Reelected Clinton," *Forbes*, November 3, 1997, 122.

46. Bartley, *The Seven Fat Years*, 144, from Glenn Yago, *How High-Yield Securities Restructured Corporate America* (New York: Oxford University Press, 1991); Akst, "The Real 1980s," 37, Benjamin Zycher, "Debt, Lies, and Reaganomics," *National Review*, December 14, 1992, 43.

47. See Robert J. Samuelson, "The Irony of Capitalism," *Newsweek*, January 9, 1989, 44; John Pound, Kenneth Lehn, and Gregg Jarrell, "Are Takeovers Hostile to Economic Performance?" *Regulation* (September–October 1986), 25–30, 55–56.

48. See Fred Block and Robert Heilbroner, "The Myth of a Savings Shortage," *The American Prospect* (Spring 1992), 101–106; Fumio Hayashi, "Is Japan's Saving Rate High?" *Quarterly Review*, Federal Reserve Bank of Minneapolis (Spring 1989), 3–9. See also Niskanen, *Reaganomics*, 254–55. Block and Heilbroner, for example, contended that the Commerce Department's savings measurement was flawed; "When we take that error into account, the much touted decline in the savings rate disappears" (102).

49. As a proportion of after-tax personal income, consumer credit grew by about two-fifths from 1980 to 1990 (Sloan, *The Reagan Effect*, 236) but remained stable at about 25 percent when measured as a proportion of ready cash (like currency, checking and savings, and money market accounts). See Lindsey, *The Growth Experiment*, 122. For a slightly different measure with a similar conclusion, see Herbert Stein and Murray Foss, *An Illustrated Guide to the American Economy* (Washington, D.C.: American Enterprise Institute [hereafter AEI], 1992), 156–57.

50. Richard McKenzie, *What Went Right in the 1980s* (San Francisco: Pacific Research Institute for Public Policy, 1994), 175.

51. Lindsey, *The Growth Experiment*, 121.

52. Lindsey, *The Growth Experiment*, 125.

53. Roberts, "Debt, Lies, and Inflation," 32.

54. Bartley, *The Seven Fat Years*, 54; see also 197–217.

55. See *The Economist Book of Vital World Statistics*, American ed. (New York: Economist Books/Times Books/Random House), 1990.

56. Campagna, *The Economy in the Reagan Years*, 210.

57. Sloan, *The Reagan Effect*, 229.

58. Dunn, "Don't Knock Reaganomics."

59. Martha Derthick and Paul J. Quirk, *The Politics of Deregulation* (Washington, D.C.: Brookings Institution, 1985), 14.

60. See Transportation Research Board, *Winds of Change: Domestic Air Transport since Deregulation* (Washington D.C.: National Research Council, 1991).

61. "Kahn Tells Airlines: Sit Tight, Cut Costs," *Aviation Week and Space Technology*, August 16, 1993, 41. See also Alfred E. Kahn, "Change, Challenge and Competition," *Regulation*, no. 2 (1993), 57.

62. Donald L. Barlett and James B. Steele, *America: What Went Wrong?* (Kansas City, Mo.: Andrews and McMeel, 1992), 112.

63. Barlett and Steele, *America: What Went Wrong?* 112.

64. See David R. Henderson, *The Truth about the 1980s* (Palo Alto, Calif.: Hoover Institution, 1994), 12–13; "The Reagan Record: Five Years of Continuous Economic Growth," White House Office of Public Affairs, November 1987, 12.

65. See Henderson, *The Truth about the 1980s*, 17.

66. In 1980, before cable television deregulation, only eighteen million households were on cable television and the average family received fewer than twenty channels; by 1992, there were fifty-five million cable subscribers receiving an average of more than thirty-five channels. Robert W. Crandall, "Relaxing the Regulatory Stranglehold on Communications," *Regulation* (Summer 1992), 32.

67. "The Reagan Record: Five Years of Continuous Economic Growth," 16.

68. Edward F. Denison estimated in 1979 that the burden of environmental and worker safety regulations alone had reduced GNP by up to 0.3 percent in the mid-1970s. Denison, *Accounting for Slower Economic Growth* (Washington, D.C.: Brookings Institution, 1979), 69–73.

69. William E. Pemberton, *Exit with Honor: The Life and Presidency of Ronald Reagan* (New York: M. E. Sharpe, 1998), 211.

70. Marvin H. Kosters and Murray N. Ross, "A Shrinking Middle Class?" *The Public Interest* (Winter 1988), 6–7.

71. Dunn, "Don't Knock Reaganomics."

72. Sloan, *The Reagan Effect*, 236.

73. Lindsey, *The Growth Experiment*, chap. 7.

74. Quoted in Steven E. Rhoads, *The Economist's View of the World* (New York: Cambridge University Press, 1985), 73–74.

75. See Steven E. Rhoads, *Incomparable Worth: Pay Equity Meets the Market* (New York: Cambridge University Press, 1993); June O'Neill, "An Argument against Comparable Worth," *Comparable Worth*, U.S. Commission on Civil Rights (June 1984), 177–86.

76. Campagna, *The Economy in the Reagan Years*, 46–47.

77. These calculations apply the percentage rate of increase in federal spending and federal revenue from 1971 to 1981, and the absolute increase in number of pages in the *Federal Register* from 1970 to 1980.

78. Roger Cohen, "Europe's Recession Prompts New Look at Welfare Costs," *New York Times*, August 9, 1993, A1, A8.

79. Paul Krugman, "The Dishonest Truth," *New York Times*, February 23, 2000, A21.

80. Sloan, *The Reagan Effect*, 30.

81. For example, see Robert Kuttner, *The End of Laissez-Faire* (New York: Knopf, 1991), 84–85.

82. For this interpretation, see for example Dunn, "Bye-Bye, Supply Side," and James Tobin, "Current Controversy in Macroeconomics: The Four Schools," *Harvard Graduate Society Newsletter*, 1990.

83. Robert Eisner, *How Real Is the Federal Deficit?* (New York: Free Press, 1986).

84. Gardner Ackley, in congressional testimony on March 4, 1981. Cited in Richard W. Rahn, "A Settling of Accounts," *The Wall Street Journal*, October 12, 1987.

85. Economist Frank S. Levy argues that the reverse is true, that people are more tolerant of redistributionism in a prosperous climate, and he points to the onset of the Great Society in the midst of the expansion of the 1960s. It is instructive, however, to note the differing levels of public support for and legitimacy of the Great Society and the New Deal. The latter, undertaken in the depths of the Depression, commanded great public loyalty at the time and retained its legitimacy thereafter; the popular backlash against the former contributed no small amount to the collapse of the Democratic presidential majority.

86. David Stockman, *The Triumph of Politics* (New York: Avon, 1987), 249.

87. Campagna, *The Economy in the Reagan Years*, 210.

88. *Statistical Abstract of the United States 1998*, prepared by the Chief of the Bureau of Statistics (Washington, D.C.: GPO, 1998), table 557.

89. From 1989 to 1998, this figure declined from 12.4 per thousand to 10.1 per thousand. *Budget of the United States Government Fiscal Year 1999, Historical Tables* (Washington, D.C.: Office of Management and Budget, 2000), 280.

90. Paul Krugman, "Dynamo and Microchip," *New York Times*, February 20, 2000, IV 13.

91. George F. Will, "Greenspan Tweaks . . . ," *Washington Post*, February 20, 2000, B7.

92. Frances Fox Piven and Richard A. Cloward, *The New Class War* (New York: Pantheon, 1982), 1.

93. Phillips, *The Politics of Rich and Poor*; Barlett and Steele, *America: What Went Wrong?*

94. Bill Clinton, *Putting People First: A National Economic Strategy for America* (n.p.: 1992).

95. Sloan, *The Reagan Effect*, 262.

96. See Herbert Stein and Murray Foss, *An Illustrated Guide to the American Economy* (Washington, D.C.: AEI, 1992), 108; Mickey Kaus, *The End of Equality* (New York: Basic, 1992), 29. Phillips presents a theory of the effects of policy on wealth distribution in the 1980s (*The Politics of Rich and Poor*, chap. 4) but brushes over the fact that the trend predated those policies by a decade.

97. Marvin H. Kosters, "The Rise in Income Inequality," *The American Enterprise* (November–December 1992), 32. At least one study actually attributed the stalling of the

trend of black-white wage convergence to the growth of the black-white "education gap," largely in the inner city. Kevin Murphy, "The Education Gap Rap," *The American Enterprise* (March–April 1990), 62–63.

98. Peterson, *Silent Depression*, 35–37.

99. "Will the U.S. Stay Number One?" *U.S. News & World Report*, February 2, 1987, 22.

100. Stein and Foss, *An Illustrated Guide to the American Economy*, 100–105; McKenzie, *What Went Right in the 1980s*, 84–87. The standard measurement of wages does not include annual salaries, year-end or production bonuses, or fringe benefits, though fringe benefits grew faster than wages in the 1970s and 1980s; it declined in the 1980s partly because workers voluntarily worked shorter workweeks (hourly wages were better than weekly wages and showed virtually no change through the 1980s); and the consumer price index probably overstated the actual rate of inflation, thus reducing the apparent real value of wages too much. Even conventional measures of hourly wages captured less than half of total wages and salaries in 1989.

101. Herbert Stein, "The Middle-Class Blues," *The American Enterprise* (March–April 1992), 8.

102. McKenzie, *What Went Right in the 1980s*, 157–60.

103. It is also important to remember that the quintile system, based on declared, taxable income, cannot take into account growth in taxable income resulting from an increased willingness to take compensation in the form of income rather than "perks" and benefits. These sorts of choices are most available to individuals at the higher end of the socioeconomic ladder, and the lower tax rates on income probably drew more compensation into that form than before. See Lindsey, *The Growth Experiment*, 88–89; Kosters, "The Rise in Income Inequality," 32.

104. Kosters, "The Rise in Income Inequality," 33. Of those in the bottom quintile in 1979, 14.2 percent were still in the bottom quintile in 1988; 14.7 percent were in the top quintile. These figures are consistent with several other longer-term longitudinal income studies. See *By Our Own Bootstraps: Economic Opportunity & The Dynamics of Income Distribution* (Dallas: Federal Reserve Bank of Dallas, 1995).

105. "The Poor Aren't Poorer," *U.S. News & World Report*, July 25, 1994, 36.

106. Kosters, "The Rise in Income Inequality," 36. Also see Kosters and Ross, "A Shrinking Middle Class?" 3–27; Marvin Cetron and Owen Davies, *American Renaissance* (New York: St. Martin's, 1989), 11–15.

107. In 1981, annual principal and interest payments on the median house took 36.3 percent of the median income; by 1988, that figure had dropped to 22 percent. After nearly a decade of declining affordability in the 1970s, the National Board of Realtors "Affordability Index" reached a low of 68.9 in 1981; by 1988, the index was at 122 (a score of 100 represented the level of housing affordability in 1968). National Association of Realtors, cited in Ed Rubenstein, "The Fading American Dream?" *National Review*, August 31, 1992, 50.

108. Stein, "The Middle-Class Blues," 9.

109. Pemberton, *Exit with Honor*, 208.

110. *Statistical Abstract of the United States 1992*, prepared by the Chief of the Bureau of Statistics (Washington, D.C.: GPO, 1992), table 696; calculations by author.

111. Clifford D. May, "In the Post-Greed Era: A Varoom at the Top," *Rocky Mountain News*, July 18, 1993, 3A.

112. Roger E. Hernandez, "Hispanics Gained in Reagan Years," *Rocky Mountain News*, July 15, 1994, 35A.

113. Census Bureau, "Poverty in the U.S.: 1990, August 1991"; cited by Ed Rubenstein, "Race and Poverty," *National Review,* August 31, 1992, 42; "Hispanic-Owned Businesses Are Growing," *The 1992 Information Please Almanac* (Boston: Information Please LLC, 1992), 42.

114. "The Reagan Record: Five Years of Continuous Economic Growth," 10; Cetron and Davies, *American Renaissance,* 14; Linda Chavez, *Out of the Barrio* (New York: Basic, 1991), 111.

115. *Statistical Abstract of the United States 1992;* calculations by author.

116. Rhoads, *Incomparable Worth,* 6.

117. Niskanen, *Reaganomics,* 264.

118. Sylvia Nasar, "Do We Live as Well as We Used To?" *Fortune,* September 14, 1987, 32.

119. Phillips, *The Politics of Rich and Poor,* 68.

120. William J. Bennett, *The Index of Leading Cultural Indicators* (Washington, D.C.: Heritage Foundation and Empower America, 1993), vol. 1, 8.

121. "The Poor Aren't Poorer," 36.

122. Cetron and Davies, *American Renaissance,* 15–17; *Poverty in the U.S.: 1990* (Washington, D.C.: Bureau of the Census, August 1991).

123. Three million would have represented about 1.2 percent of the population of the United States. Assuming (against all probability) that New York City had only its proportionate share of homeless and no more, that city of eight million would have had ninety-six thousand homeless people, a group larger than the Union army at Gettysburg. There was no evidence of ninety-six thousand homeless people in New York, let alone the disproportionate number that would have been more likely.

124. For example, *U.S. News & World Report* was repeating the three million estimate as late as 1993 (60th Anniversary Report, October 25, 1993, 61).

125. See Myron Magnet, *The Dream and the Nightmare* (New York: Morrow, 1993), 81–82.

126. John F. Cogan and Timothy J. Muris, "The Great Budget Shell Game," *The American Enterprise* (November–December 1990), 38. Expenditures or appropriations for housing programs should not be confused with authorizations. "Authorization" refers to the legal authority to spend money on a given project, usually including a dollar limit and often spread out over multiple years, especially on capital projects like new housing. In the 1980s, budget authority for housing was cut, but this decline reflected a reduction in future long-term commitments. Because of previous authorizations, actual spending continued to rise substantially.

127. See Cetron and Davies, *American Renaissance,* 17–19.

128. McKenzie, *What Went Right in the 1980s,* 268–71.

129. Barlett and Steele, *America: What Went Wrong?* 105. This attack on deregulation frequently betrayed a lack of understanding of basic economics. For example, Barlett and Steele demonstrated their point about the negative consequences of airline deregulation by comparing the price of an airline ticket from Philadelphia to Pittsburgh before and after deregulation: eighty-six dollars in 1978, $460 in 1992. There are at least three major flaws with their analysis. First, no adjustment was made for inflation. Second, and more importantly, the ticket prices quoted were for same-day purchases; there are now typically substantial discounts for advance purchases. Finally, and most importantly, deregulation had no direct impact on the Philadelphia to Pittsburgh flight, since federal airline regulation before 1978 only affected *interstate* flights. Philadelphia and Pittsburgh are in the same state.

130. Lawrence G. Brewster and Michael E. Brown, *The Public Agenda: Issues in American Politics,* 3rd ed. (New York: St. Martin's, 1994), 53.

131. Catherine England, "Lessons from the Savings and Loan Debacle," _Regulation_ (Summer 1992), 37.

132. England, "Lessons from the Savings and Loan Debacle," 36–43.

133. See Steve Lohr, "Little of $100 Billion Loss Can Be Retrieved," _New York Times_, February 20, 1992, D7; England, "Lessons from the Savings and Loan Debacle," 40; Bert Ely, "The Savings and Loan Crisis," in _Fortune Encyclopedia of Economics_, ed. David R. Henderson (New York: Warner, 1993).

134. Edwin S. Rubenstein, _The Right Data_ (New York: National Review, 1994), 180, 286.

135. "20th Environmental Quality Index," _National Wildlife_ (February–March 1988), 38–39.

136. See Consumer Product Safety Commission, "1993 National Estimates of Electrocutions Associated with Consumer Products," report issued September 10, 1996; "Non-Fire Carbon Monoxide Deaths and Injuries Associated with the Use of Consumer Products Annual Estimates," report issued December 10, 1997; both Consumer Product Safety Commission Website, www.cpsc.gov/.

137. See Charleston C. K. Wang, _OSHA Compliance and Management Handbook_ (Park Ridge, N.J.: Noyes, 1993); "OSHA Enforcement Policy," Hearings before a Subcommittee of the Committee on Government Operations, U.S. House of Representatives, 98th Congress, November 9–10, 1983, 346; "Stepping into the Middle of OSHA's Muddle," _Business Week_, August 2, 1993, 53.

138. See Occupational Safety and Health Administration Website, www.osha.gov/.

139. Lawrence Kudlow and Stephen Moore, "It's the Reagan Economy, Stupid," www.clubforgrowth.org, February 2000. See also James F. Glassman, "It's Reagan's Economy, Stupid," _Rising Tide_ (Fall 1997); Paul Craig Roberts, "Coasting on the Reagan Boom," _Washington Times National Weekly Edition_, March 13–19, 2000, 32.

140. Martin N. Baily, "Boom vs. Boom: '90s Beat the '80s," _Wall Street Journal_, February 25, 2000, A18.

141. Krugman, "The Dishonest Truth," A21.

142. Sloan, _The Reagan Effect_, 244, 269.

143. Robert Dallek, _Ronald Reagan: The Politics of Symbolism with a New Preface_ (Cambridge, Mass.: Harvard University Press, 1999), xiii.

144. Anna Bernasek, "What's Really behind the Boom," _Fortune_, January 24, 2000, 26–27.

145. Robert C. McTeeter Jr., "Out on a New-Paradigm Limb," _The New Paradigm: Federal Reserve Bank of Dallas 1999 Annual Report_ (Dallas: Federal Reserve Bank of Dallas, 1999), 1.

146. Dinesh D'Souza, _Ronald Reagan: How an Ordinary Man Became an Extraordinary Leader_ (New York: Free Press, 1997), 125.

147. _Statistical Abstract of the United States 1998_, table 738. For further analysis of this trend, see Clay Chandler, "A Market Tide That Isn't Lifting Everybody," _Washington Post National Weekly Edition_, April 13, 1998, 18; Stephanie Salter, "There's No Boom in World of Have-Nots," _Rocky Mountain News_, May 26, 1998, 31A; Molly Ivins, "Prosperity Bypasses the Masses," _Rocky Mountain News_, May 5, 1999, 53A.

148. Richard J. Carroll, "Clinton's Economy in a Historical Context, or Why Media Coverage on Economic Issues is Suspect," _Presidential Studies Quarterly_ 26 (Summer 1996), 828–34.

149. Robert Genetski and Associates of Chicago estimated that the Clean Air Act of 1990 and the Americans with Disabilities Act of 1991 imposed mandates on business that were

equivalent to an additional seventy-billion-dollar tax. Overall, the number of major rules costing more than a hundred million grew by 40 percent at the beginning of the George H. W. Bush administration. Bill Clinton's 1993 tax increase was estimated by some economists to have reduced annual GNP growth by half of a percentage point. C. Boyden Gray, "Lessons," *Regulation* no. 3 (1993), 31; Cited in "Bush vs. Bush vs. Clinton," *National Review*, November 19, 1992, 32; Ed Rubenstein, "The Re-regulation President," *National Review*, September 14, 1992, 16.

5

Reagan and the Rise and Fall of the Federal Deficit

WHILE THE 1980S SAW A RESTORATION of noninflationary economic growth that continued, with brief interruption, through the 1990s, one feature of Ronald Reagan's economic policy remains a source of severe criticism. The annual federal deficit grew, in nominal dollars, from seventy-four billion dollars in 1980 to a peak of $221 billion in 1986. By 1989, it had fallen to $152 billion, but it was still twice the size of the deficit at the beginning of the decade in nominal (noninflation-adjusted) dollars. All in all, the federal debt tripled, from roughly a trillion dollars to about three trillion, and interest payments on that debt more than doubled, to $184 billion annually. Conventional wisdom holds that defense spending increases and tax cuts weighted toward the wealthy, supported by Reagan, combined to produce this hemorrhage of red ink. Indeed, some analysts have ascribed the deficit to either the deceit or the stupidity of the Reagan administration. Reagan himself acknowledged that the deficit was "one of my biggest disappointments as President."[1]

Indeed, no president had overseen a larger overall expansion of the national debt since Franklin Roosevelt. Under Reagan, the debt increased by 214 percent; Roosevelt nearly tripled the national debt in the 1930s and then nearly quintupled it again in the 1940s. Roosevelt, of course, had a reasonable explanation, faced as he was with the combination of a grave economic crisis and a worldwide struggle against totalitarianism. Reagan was faced with a similar combination, if on a lesser scale.

Ultimately, neither Roosevelt nor Reagan, despite promising balanced budgets in 1932 and 1980, made balancing the budget their first priority. Reagan acknowledged in 1981, "I did not come here to balance the budget—not at the expense of my tax cutting program and my defense program."[2] Rather, both men understood the federal budget as the means to an end (or more precisely, a broad array of ends). Reagan made reasonably clear throughout the 1980s the ends to which he considered the budget a means. For him, federal budget policy, as a subset of his broader economic program, was an instrument in the effort to maintain American freedom, which he saw as endangered abroad by aggressive Leninism and at home by a creeping democratic socialism akin to Alexis de Tocqueville's "democratic despotism." The common strand holding together the disparate elements of the Reagan budgets, like his economic plan in general, was the goal of strengthening liberty.

Within this scheme, the defense buildup was a measure aimed at protecting Western democracies from their foreign enemies. Discretionary spending cuts and limits on the growth of "entitlement" spending were meant to reduce the social-engineering role of the federal government, to restore the role of the states in the federal system, and to limit government's claim on the private resources of civil society. Tax cuts returned to civil society and to individuals' resources, and the power that comes with those resources. Tax indexation meant that the federal government's share of the national economy could no longer automatically increase with inflation. Tax reform—reducing the number of rates, reducing the level of the top rate, and eliminating scores of deductions—delegitimized the open redistribution of income by government and restricted the ability of government to direct society through targeted tax breaks. Indeed, both the policies and rhetoric of the Reagan administration promoted, as even critics acknowledged, a general "taxaphobia" in public attitudes, a reaction that was itself a powerful brake on the future growth of government.[3] Reagan himself described the tax cuts and tax reform as "the first important steps back to economic liberty";[4] he explained in his autobiography, "I have always thought of government as a kind of organism with an insatiable appetite for money, whose natural state is to grow forever unless you do something to starve it. By cutting taxes, I not only wanted to stimulate the economy but to curb the growth of government and reduce its intrusion into the economic life of the country."[5]

Many Americans had lauded the growth of the federal government as an instrument of what they considered to be social justice; Reagan's budget policies, however, tapped into the perception of many others that American democracy since the New Deal had undergone a troubling transformation from a limited government of enumerated powers to an increasingly unlimited one in which the needs of government, or of the organized interests patronizing government, seemed to take precedence over the needs and the freedom of the unorganized many. Reagan's budgets sought to reverse, or at least halt, this trend. As two academic analysts contended in 1988, the "iron triangles" of vested interests, congressional subcommittees, and executive agencies that had long guaranteed the automatic growth of government programs were "severely wounded during the Reagan era."[6] Thus, while Reagan's budgets had an economic purpose (to reduce government involvement in the economy while promoting investment and rewarding work) and economic consequences (among other things, contributing to the economic expansion), their primary significance was political, even social. Reagan's budgets were documents in which freedom, as he conceived it, was the preeminent and guiding principle.

Nevertheless, the growth of the federal deficit in the 1980s called into question the long-term viability of Reagan's program in a variety of ways. Commentators on the Left and Right consistently declared the deficit to have been Reagan's darkest, if not most important, legacy. Former Speaker of the House Tip O'Neill, echoing a plethora of critics, predicted in 1989 that Reagan's "increasing the deficit will be a disaster. Within 10 years, West Germany will be the richest nation in the world and Japan will be the strongest economic power. We're losing the economic leadership in the 20th century because of Reaganomics."[7] A decade later, however, it was difficult to detect any long-term damage to the American economy resulting from those deficits. Indeed, the net public-sector borrowing requirement (federal, state, and local) in the United States during the 1980s as a proportion of the economy was not significantly different from that of the other G-7 countries, our most important allies and trading partners. Furthermore, the accumulated federal debt was no greater proportion of the American economy in 1990 than it had been in 1960, and the upward trend in this measurement began in 1974, not 1981.[8]

Two more specific negative consequences of the deficits frequently hypothesized by analysts have also been called into question by subsequent events. First, it was argued that the deficits had the effect of driving up interest rates by reducing national savings. Yet experience since 1980 has shown that interest rates fluctuate without any clear connection to the size or direction of the deficit. Rather, they are most sensitive to such factors as inflation, inflationary expectations, and the perceived need of the Federal Reserve Board either to stimulate or slow the economy. Second, this assumed but empirically tenuous connection between the deficit and interest rates led some economists to fear that the budget deficit hampered American competitiveness and contributed to a poor balance of trade, by creating an artificially high dollar on foreign markets. This argument, too, was difficult to sustain given the experience at the turn of the twenty-first century, when new record-high trade deficits coexisted with federal surpluses.

On the other hand, there were sound economic, political, and even ethical reasons to be concerned about the rapid rise of the deficit and about the potential for large deficits to extend indefinitely into the future. As the total federal debt rose, interest payments alone drove up federal spending and imposed an increasing burden on the economy. From a standpoint of limited government, there was reason to fear the long-term political consequences of allowing Americans to enjoy government programs at less than full cost. The perpetuation of large deficits left Reagan open to charges of severe mismanagement, and in so doing threatened to call into question the validity of his entire program. Ethically, a wide range of voices expressed concern that voters were shifting onto future generations the costs of their own profligacy. In the end, most Americans (including Reagan himself) were inclined to see the deficit, if not controlled, as a long-term threat to economic well-being.

Thus, while it is clear that the pursuit of freedom animated Reagan's budgets, it was an open question at the end of the 1980s whether the gains for economic freedom in the short term would outweigh the costs of the deficit, both economic and political, over time. In assessing Reagan's impact, it is therefore crucial to determine the answer to two questions. First, to what extent was the conventional wisdom regarding the source of the deficits correct? In other words, to what extent were the deficits actually a result of Reagan's tax cuts, defense increases, and incompetence or deceit? Second, to what extent, if any, can the end of the deficits in the 1990s be traced to Reagan-era fiscal policies? In other words, was Reagan just lucky that deficits ended before they could inflict the damage some had predicted, or did he play a part in producing that outcome?

The budget politics of the 1990s were often framed as an antipode to the Reagan record. When President Bill Clinton proposed his deficit-reduction package in February 1993, *U.S. News & World Report* hailed him for "clarity, courage, and authority. . . . Clinton has proposed in his first 100 days that the consequences of Ronald Reagan's first 100 days be reversed. It's about time."[9] When that package squeaked through Congress later in the year, *Time* magazine exulted that it "brought to an end a bankrupt period in American history. . . . It is the beginning, however modest, of a return to the economic orthodoxy of balanced budgets."[10]

However, the 1980s, though unique for the size of the deficits at that time, were not unique in another important sense. In real terms, every administration since Eisenhower's had a higher average annual deficit than the one before. In the Eisenhower years, the cumulative deficits were ninety-two billion dollars (in constant 1987 dollars) over eight years. In the Kennedy-Johnson administrations, combined deficits were $220 billion in eight years. In the Nixon-Ford administrations, there were $463 billion of deficit in eight years. Jimmy Carter accumulated $363 billion in four years. Ronald Reagan's administration saw an additional $1.445 trillion in deficits over eight years.

George H. W. Bush piled on $805 billion in four years.[11] Even Bill Clinton's initial budget package anticipated adding $1.045 trillion in deficits in real dollars through his first term, a total that would have set a new record had other factors not intervened to change the outcome dramatically. Thus, from the 1950s through the early 1990s, every administration ran larger annual deficits than the one before. The Reagan years were hence part of a pattern reaching back thirty years or more (see chart 5.1).

This retrospective look strongly implies that the budget deficits of the 1980s cannot be easily explained by the usual short-term suspects, Reagan's tax cuts and defense spending increases. As the following examination of federal revenue, defense spending, and nondefense spending in the 1980s will show, whether Reagan's policies were responsible for the deficits depends on which measures one wishes to consult. Additionally, Reagan should not be summarily dismissed as fiscally irresponsible. As we will see, his budget policies actually set the stage for some relimitation of government in the 1990s. If budget balancing orthodoxy was reestablished in the 1990s, it was after an absence not of twelve years but of sixty, and that restoration owed more to Reagan than most commentators acknowledged.

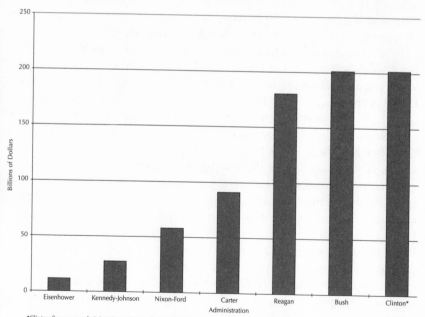

*Clinton figures are administration estimates for FY 1994–98 contained in FY 1994 budget.

Chart 5.1

Average Annual Deficit by Administration, Eisenhower through Clinton (Projections) in Real (1987) Dollars

Bumbling into the Deficit?

The accusation that the Reagan administration either bumbled or deceived its way into triple-digit deficits has a long pedigree. As early as November 1981, Reagan budget director David Stockman confided in an interview with William Greider that, in his view, the administration had won its 1981 tax and budget votes with "cooked numbers" based on a "rosy scenario" of unreasonably optimistic economic forecasts. After leaving the White House, Stockman expanded on this theme, revealing that some portion of the defense buildup had been approved based on a misunderstanding of the numbers involved, and arguing that the whole process leading to the 1981 tax and spending plans had been shrouded in confusion.[12] A variety of commentators have repeated the charge since then. Furthermore, some economists have maintained that Reagan's program was based on the improbable presumption that the tax cuts would not result in any loss of prospective revenue.

As Martin Anderson, Norman Ture, and others have pointed out, the Reagan economic plan did not postulate that prospective revenue would be higher because of the tax cuts than it would be without them. Rather, the plan expected that some of the prospective revenue loss (the Reagan plan of 1980 estimated 17 percent) would be recouped by economic growth and that overall receipts would continue rising, though not as quickly.[13]

Furthermore, the Reagan proposal was drafted and submitted during the brief window between the recessions of 1979–80 and 1981–82, at a time when outside economic forecasters, including the Congressional Budget Office, were predicting a strong recovery from the first downturn and a looming budget surplus. The administration's economic estimates in 1981 and 1982 were slightly more optimistic than those of private economists or the CBO, but there was a far greater disparity between *all* forecasts and what actually happened. At the time the Reagan plan passed Congress, *Blue Chip Economic Indicators* was heralding "economic exuberance" for 1982, and CBO was predicting a small surplus by 1983, growing to a $209 billion surplus by 1986.[14] In the view of one analyst, "Such projections, not reliance on extreme economic assumptions, explain how the Reagan administration could propose a tax cut and defense-spending increase, yet still expect to avoid massive deficits. . . . [T]he problem of large deficits was not created by malevolence or even overoptimism. A major source of the problem was a deep recession, the severity and, at first, even the existence of which were unforeseen."[15]

Given the sense of crisis that had enveloped the economy and Reagan's own rhetoric about the urgency of his program, his administration should have been more cautious. It was, however, far from alone in its overoptimism.

The Case of Tax Cuts

If one discounts deception and incompetence as factors, the Reagan tax cuts of the 1980s are to many critics the chief causal factor behind persistently high federal deficits in the 1980s and early 1990s. Starting with Walter Mondale's acceptance speech at the Democratic National Convention in 1984, it became an article of faith among many that the deficit could not be reduced without massive tax increases to counteract the effects of those tax cuts. Even David Stockman came around to this point of view. By Stockman's calculation, revenue foregone due to the tax cuts amounted to $1.8 trillion from 1982 to 1990.[16] As noted above, even Reagan administration officials who defend the tax cuts concede that revenue was lower with the tax cuts than it would have been without.

Yet there are at least two major shortcomings of this analysis. It is based not on actual revenue but on estimates of how much the government might have collected had the tax cuts not been in effect (what is called "baseline budgeting"). Further, these estimates of revenue loss utilize what is known as "static analysis." In other words, they apply the higher, pre-tax-cut tax rate to the post-tax-cut economy, as if people's behavior or economic conditions had not changed as a result of the tax cut itself. The shortcomings of static analysis could be seen operating in 1990, when a new 10 percent tax (the "luxury tax") was assigned to yachts, luxury automobiles, airplanes, and furs. In estimating the revenue to be gained from this tax, Congress assumed that as many people were going to buy yachts after the tax increase as before. Instead, the U.S. yacht market dropped precipitously, so the Treasury Department brought in only a small percentage of what it had expected from the tax; at the same time, as many as thirty thousand boat workers lost their jobs from January 1991 through mid-1993, so the government not only lost income-tax receipts from them but had to pay them unemployment benefits.[17] Overall, the luxury tax probably cost the government more than it raised. In 1993, it was repealed.

If one examines the Reagan tax cuts from a perspective less dependent on bureaucratic conventions like baseline budgeting and static analysis— conventions that contain a built-in bias favoring higher taxes and higher spending—a different picture emerges. There are at least three alternative ways of measuring the fiscal effects of the tax cuts (and of spending), metrics that are arguably more solid than any comparison to the essentially imaginary and highly fluid baseline. One commonly used measurement examines the share of the national economy represented by federal revenue or spending. This measurement takes the form of a proportion of gross domestic product (GDP). It is useful for weighing the overall burden on the economy of taxes or spending, and it can help to illuminate shifting national priorities. A second measurement examines actual revenue or spending, in either nominal or inflation-adjusted ("real") dollars. Since deficits represent the gap between dollars spent and dollars raised, this measure is the most straightforward. (Note that it is possible for revenues and spending to go up in real dollars but down as a proportion of GDP, if they grow more slowly than the economy.) Finally, either or both of these measures can be applied across time, in a historical sequence aimed at understanding long-term trends. Because the deficit was a long-term phenomenon, growing larger in each administration from Eisenhower through Bush, this approach might be the most illuminating. These measures deliver a mixed verdict for the tax cuts.

As a proportion of GDP, federal taxation in 1980 took 18.9 percent of gross domestic product; in 1989, it took nearly as much (18.3 percent). Looking at the 1980–89 period as a whole, federal revenue averaged 18.2 percent of GDP.[18] By this standard, the tax cuts did contribute modestly to the deficit.

However, of the years from 1980 through 1990, federal revenue declined in real terms from one year to the next only twice, in fiscal year 1982 and fiscal year 1983. A third year, 1990, showed basically no change in revenue. What these three years had in common was not real tax cuts (the fiscal year 1982 and 1983 installments of the tax cuts were largely offset by inflation, and there was no tax cut at all in 1990) but recession or the lingering aftereffects of recession (see table 5.1). Indeed, according to a 1989 estimate by the Office of Management and Budget, the recession of 1980–82 by itself was responsible for nearly 40 percent of the accumulated deficits of the 1980s.[19] Consequently, the greatest fiscal mistake of the 1980s may have been the decision to delay and spread out the tax cut, which in its original form might have mitigated the recession.

TABLE 5.1
Federal Revenue 1980–1990, in Billions of Dollars

	Nominal	Real (1987 Dollars)
1980	$517.1	$728.1
1981	$599.3	$766.6
1982	$617.8	$738.2
1983	$600.6	$684.3
1984	$666.5	$730.4
1985	$734.1	$776.6
1986	$769.1	$790.0
1987	$854.1	$854.1
1988	$909.0	$877.3
1989	$990.7	$916.2
1990	$1031.3	$914.0
Change	$514.2	$185.9
	+99.4%	+25.5%

For most of the 1980s, however, the economy grew enough to produce rising revenues. One study showed that up to 50 percent of the revenue deemed "lost" by static analysis had actually been recovered due to economic growth (a figure three times greater than the Reagan planning document had projected).[20] Overall, federal revenue grew by $474 billion from 1980 to 1989, nearly doubling in nominal terms, and rising by 27 percent even after adjustment for inflation.[21]

Furthermore, as table 5.2 demonstrates, the rate of real-dollar revenue growth in the 1980s was actually slightly greater than that experienced in the 1970s, though it was smaller than in the 1950s or 1960s. Taking federal revenue as a proportion of GDP, the 18.2 percent average of the 1980s was significantly higher than the 17.7 percent average from 1950 to 1979 (see chart 5.2). In 1960, when the federal government was running a budget surplus, federal taxation took 17.8 percent of GDP. From then until 1990—when the deficit reached $220 billion—real revenue increased by 144 percent.[22] Looking only at income-tax revenue, income tax as a proportion of GNP never fell below 8.05 percent under Reagan, but it had been 7.94 percent as recently as 1976; the individual income tax reductions "never even restored tax rates to the lower level of only a few years before."[23]

Thus, taking the long view, it is easy to argue that the Reagan tax cuts did not cause the deficits of the 1980s. The *New York Times* acknowledged as much in December 1992, when correspondent David E. Rosenbaum wrote that this idea was a "popular misconception": "The fact is, the large deficit resulted because the government vastly increased what it spent each year, while tax revenues changed little."[24]

A complementary critique, that the Reagan tax policies were regressive, is also inconsistent with the record. The 1981 personal income tax cuts reduced marginal rates by 25 percent across the board for all taxpayers, and they included indexation, which protected lower- and middle-class taxpayers much more than higher-income ones (bracket creep is not a concern for taxpayers

TABLE 5.2
Real Growth in Federal Revenues by Decade, 1950–2000

	Revenue
1950–59	+40.0%
1960–69	+53.9%
1970–79	+25.7%
1980–89	+27.0%

Source: *Budget of the United States Government Fiscal Year 2001, Historical Tables,* table 1.3. Calculations by author.

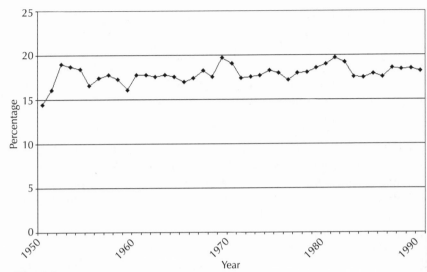

Chart 5.2
Revenue as Percentage of GDP, 1950–1990

already in the top bracket).[25] In the words of a *New York Times* editorialist, indexing was "one of the fairest pieces of tax law in many a year."[26] The 1986 tax reform reduced the top rate from 50 percent to 28 percent but also lowered the rate for most Americans, eliminated numerous tax loopholes utilized primarily by the wealthy, and freed four million of the working poor from paying any federal income tax.

Critics have tended to overlook the salutary effects of these policies for most Americans and to focus instead on the reduction of the top rate. Robert Reich, for example, claimed on the basis of the reduction in the top rate that "the progressive income tax was substantially ended" with tax reform in 1986.[27] The overall effects on revenue distribution, however, were not what one would expect given the hyperbole surrounding the issue. Indeed, the overall structure of federal tax returns became more, not less, progressive in the eighties, arguably at least partly because of the very changes in the tax code decried by the critics.

From 1980 to 1990, not only did the effective federal income tax rate—the actual percentage of income paid in income tax—decline for the average taxpayer in each income quintile, but that decline was steepest among the poor and middle class. According to data compiled by the Congressional Budget Office, the average taxpayer in the highest quintile saw the smallest cut in his effective tax rate from 1980 to 1990, only two-fifths to one-half as large as the cut received by the other quintiles.[28] Furthermore, after tax reform passed in 1986, the effective tax rate on the richest actually went up a bit.[29] Taking a longer-term view, the effective tax rate on the top 1 percent of taxpayers rose by more than half between 1966 and 1990.[30]

From 1981 to 1988, the share of federal income tax revenue paid by the bottom 50 percent of taxpayers fell, while the share paid by the top 5 percent and by the top 1 percent of taxpayers rose considerably (see table 5.3). The ratio of the average tax payment in the top 1 percent versus the average payment in the bottom 50 percent also doubled from 1980 to 1988.[31] Altogether, a disproportionate share of the revenue increase in the 1980s came from the higher brackets; by 1985, revenue raised from taxpayers with adjusted gross incomes over two hundred thousand dollars had increased 25 percent more than the amount that had been projected before the tax cuts took effect.[32]

Although the 1981 and 1986 reductions in the top rate were controversial, many critics came tacitly to acknowledge that the reductions were well founded. Bill Clinton, who touted tax increases on the affluent, proposed increasing the top rate only from 31 to 39.6 percent, far from the 70 percent it had been when Reagan took office. The *Washington Post*, defending Clinton's 1993 proposed energy tax, contrasted it with the alternative of raising the top rate even more: "Unfortunately," said *Post* editorial writers, "high tax rates give great incentives to people with money to hire accountants and lawyers to avoid the IRS. The higher rates go, the less efficient the collection system becomes. That was one powerful reason for the tax cuts of the 1980s."[33]

By one estimate, the average middle-class taxpayer saved two thousand dollars a year in income tax because of Kemp-Roth.[34] To whatever degree the middle class was hurt by tax policy in the 1980s, it was as the result not of income tax cuts but of other direct or hidden tax increases, such as excise tax increases in 1982, 1984, and 1987, and the failure of the per-child deduction to keep pace with inflation. Reagan accepted those latter policies reluctantly, as

TABLE 5.3
Percentage of Income Taxes Paid by Income Group, 1981–1988

	Top 1%	Top 5%	51st–95th Percentile	Bottom 50%	Burden Ratio*
1981	18%	35%	57%	8%	118:1
1988	28%	46%	49%	6%	240:1

*Burden ratio: tax dollars paid by the average family in the top 1% for every $1 paid by the average family in the bottom 50%.
Source: Richard McKenzie, *What Went Right in the 1980s* (San Francisco: Pacific Research Institute for Public Policy, 1994), 277.

part of compromises with Democrats and moderate Republicans in Congress. The chief factor, however, was the steep 1977 multiyear FICA payroll-tax increase, which was accelerated as part of the 1983 Social Security bailout. The payroll tax is strictly proportional up to a threshold income and regressive thereafter. In all cases, it exempts investment income. By 1990, almost three-quarters of all Americans were paying more in Social Security tax than in individual income tax, if one counted their employers' contributions.[35] While the proportion of household income taken by federal income tax fell from 15.3 percent in 1980 to 12.4 percent in 1990, the share taken by payroll taxes grew from 4.6 percent to 6.0 percent.[36] Thus, it was pre-Reagan payroll tax policies that had the most regressive revenue effects during the 1980s and beyond; if the tax cuts contributed to the deficit, it was not at the expense of middle- and lower-income Americans.

The Case of Defense Spending

The defense buildup of the early 1980s is second only to the tax cuts as an object of blame among many commentators. To critics, defense spending combined with the tax cuts to drive the deficit up. Independent presidential candidate John Anderson anticipated this line of argument when he said in the 1980 presidential campaign that the idea of cutting taxes, increasing defense spending, and balancing the budget at the same time required "blue smoke and mirrors."

A crucial, though oft-forgotten, point about the defense buildup of the 1980s is how necessary it was thought to be, across the political spectrum, when it was launched—a point we will explore in greater depth in chapter 7. The defense buildup was not forced onto the nation by Reagan but was a policy that responded to a real threat and was supported (indeed, in 1979–80, insisted upon) by a broad majority of the American people.[37] In any event, by applying the three measures, we can see that the contribution of defense spending to the deficit has been generally overstated.

In terms of proportion of the economy, the defense buildup did contribute to the deficit. Starting at 4.9 percent of GDP in 1980, the defense budget averaged 5.8 percent of GDP from 1980 to 1989 and was consuming 6.2 percent of GDP at its peak. By the time of the 1990 budget deal, it was down to 5.2 percent, not much higher than in 1980.[38] In terms of real dollar spending, there is also no question that defense increases drove up the deficit in the early 1980s. This is especially the case when defense expenditures are viewed in isolation. Between 1980 and 1985, defense spending rose $119 billion in nominal terms; in real terms, it increased by 35 percent in that half-decade. Given that the total deficit increased by $138 billion in nominal terms during this same period, it is possible to argue (as indeed some have argued) that the defense buildup alone mathematically accounts for almost the entire growth of the deficit in the early 1980s. However, given a federal budget that had grown to nearly one trillion dollars by 1985, this sort of argument could be used to prove the same thing about virtually any combination of spending programs. In reality, the defense budget does not exist in isolation but rather as one component of an overall spending plan; it must be viewed within the context of that overall plan. From this perspective, even in the half-decade when the defense buildup was proceeding at full speed, nondefense spending grew by far more, from $443 billion to $693 billion (a nominal increase of $250 billion). Once interest payments are subtracted from nondefense spending, the increase from 1980 to 1985 was still $146 billion, 23 percent *more* than the defense spending increase.[39]

From 1985 on, defense spending increases slowed tremendously. From 1985 to its peak in 1987, defense spending grew slightly in real dollars before beginning a descent that left the 1990 defense budget slightly smaller than it had been in 1985. All in all, defense spending increases accounted for only $163 billion of the $564 billion nominal increase in annual federal spending (excluding interest) from 1980 to 1990, or less than 30 percent.[40] Reagan's defenders argue that it is not appropriate to blame defense spending for the deficit when more than 70 percent of the total federal budget, and more than 70 percent of the growth of the budget from 1980 to 1990, was spent on programs less central to the core function of the national government.

Furthermore, from a historical perspective, the defense buildup, like the post-tax-cut revenue stream, cannot be assigned primary blame for the federal deficit in the 1980s. Throughout the 1950s and early 1960s, when the federal government regularly ran either budget surpluses or small deficits, defense spending accounted for around 10 percent of GDP (see chart 5.3). From 1950 to 1979, defense averaged 8.3 percent of GDP—yet, to repeat, in the 1980s it averaged only 5.8 percent and never exceeded 6.2 percent of GDP. In the 1980s, defense spending never reached 29 percent of the federal budget and was less than a quarter by 1990; yet in the 1950s and early 1960s, it had regularly been 45–50 percent of all federal spending.[41]

Thus, by only one of the three alternative measures (proportion of GDP from 1980 to the end of the decade) were either tax cuts or defense spending responsible for the increased deficits of the 1980s. Taking the long view, the primary force driving the rise of the deficit in the 1980s was neither tax cuts (since taxes were lower in the balanced-budget Eisenhower era than in the 1980s) nor defense spending increases (since defense spending was higher under Eisenhower).

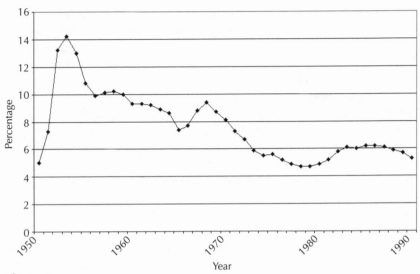

Chart 5.3
Defense Spending as Percentage of GDP, 1950–1990

The Case of Domestic Spending

Domestic spending presents a mirror image of defense and the tax cuts. As a proportion of the economy, so-called mandatory spending programs, or "entitlements," excluding interest, rose slightly, starting at 10.3 percent of GDP in 1980 and averaging 10.4 percent through the decade (though it fell back to 9.8 percent of GDP in 1988 and 1989). "Discretionary domestic spending" was tightly limited, falling from 4.7 percent of GDP in 1980 to 3.1 percent of GDP in 1989, approaching pre–Great Society levels.[42] Total nondefense spending as a proportion of GDP (total outlays minus defense and interest) actually fell, from 14.8 percent to 12.5 percent. These figures reveal a shift in national priorities toward defense and away from domestic spending, as well as a shift within domestic spending toward entitlements and away from discretionary and general government outlays. When one examines either actual dollar spending or trends over time, however, domestic spending emerges as the primary cause of rising deficits.

As a category, discretionary domestic spending was cut by 14 percent in real terms from 1980 to 1989, and some of the entitlement or mandatory-spending programs, like Food Stamps and Aid to Families with Dependent Children, were also cut (Food Stamps declined 6 percent and AFDC 1 percent from 1981 to 1989, in real terms).[43] However, this spending restraint had the effect only of slowing, not halting, the overall increase of domestic spending.

As already illustrated, nondefense programs accounted for nearly three-fourths of the increase in spending during the 1980s. Federal outlays from 1981 to 1989 exceeded the president's spending requests in eight of nine years, by an average of $28.9 billion, all for domestic programs.[44] In real dollars, from 1980 to 1989 the federal employee retirement program grew 21 percent; Social Security, mandatory agriculture spending, and Supplemental Security Income each grew 31 percent; Medicaid grew 61 percent; housing assistance grew 66 percent; Medicare grew 74 percent; and the earned income tax credit grew by 105 percent. The nominal increase from 1980 in annual spending in Social Security, Medicare, and Medicaid alone accounted for $186 billion in 1989; counting all direct-transfer programs to individuals, the increase was $223 billion.[45]

Domestic spending accounts for an even higher percentage of the overall increase in spending over time, driven by a thirtyfold increase in the number of domestic federal programs since the end of World War II.[46] From 1965 to 1990, there was a total reversal of government spending priorities. In 1965, the federal government spent 40 percent on defense and 28 percent on entitlements; in 1990, it spent 24 percent on defense and 46 percent on entitlements. There were two components to this spending explosion: social insurance programs like Social Security and Medicare, and Great Society antipoverty programs. In constant dollars, for instance, Social Security grew ninefold from 1954 to 1986. Spending on poverty programs, taken together, grew 713 percent from 1962 to 1980, then experienced another real increase of 18 percent through the 1980s.[47] Overall, direct federal payments to individuals grew from an average of 3.3 percent of GDP in the 1950s to 4.6 percent in the 1960s, to 7.6 percent in the 1970s, to 9.2 percent in the 1980s.[48] That increase in transfer payments from the 1970s to the 1980s was twice the size of the increase in average defense spending. The trends driving the deficit over time seem clear: revenue remained stable as a proportion of GDP, except for the bracket-creep-induced bulge in the late 1970s, while entitlement spending grew, gradually at first but then rapidly after 1974 (see chart 5.4).

A broad range of observers agree that the 1960s were a crucial turning point in the explosion of the deficit. From the Right, British historian Paul Johnson argued that "the big change in principle" regarding the federal budget came under Presidents Kennedy and Johnson, who decided that deficits would be deliberately created even in times of prosperity. To this historian, the JFK-LBJ years produced a "momentous change in the fundamental purpose and cost of American central government."[49] On the Left, Frances Fox Piven and Richard Cloward conceded that "the great expansion and

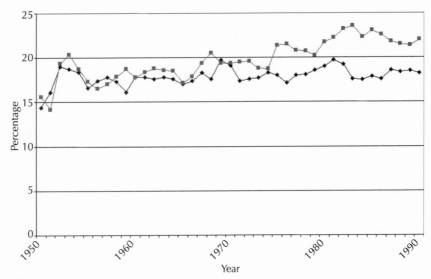

Chart 5.4
Annual Outlays and Revenues as Percentage of GDP, 1950–1990

elaboration of income-maintenance programs did not occur until the 1960s and 1970s."[50] In between, liberal commentator Mickey Kaus pointed to the 1960s as the decade when "a set of powerful new pro-dole ideas had come to the fore within the Democratic Party's policy elite."[51] Social critic Lawrence Mead likewise indicted the Great Society as driven by assumptions that helped lead to the explosion of the deficit: "In the Great Society conception the public responsibility was potentially unlimited."[52] Social scientists Joseph White and Aaron Wildavsky contended that the deficit in the 1980s represented the final landfall of a "fiscal tidal wave" generated by programmatic commitments made prior to 1973.[53] In 1990, the *Washington Post*—which in the 1980s seldom missed an opportunity to blame the federal deficit on Reagan—declared, "The current deficits have their roots in the mid-1960s."[54]

In this view, the combination of programs and culture launched in the New Deal and significantly expanded in the 1960s represented a fiscal time bomb. In the beginning, the costs remained manageable, and the political benefits for the architects of the programs were enormous. Over time, however, the programs exploded with costs that the nation was unable to afford but that proved politically very difficult to control. Consequently, if one insists on assigning blame for the deficits of the 1980s and early 1990s somewhere, it is not unreasonable to start with previous policy makers, Franklin Roosevelt and Lyndon Johnson chief among them, who were responsible for designing the American entitlement state.

The 1980s as a Fiscal Turning Point

Altogether, a very good argument can be made that the tax cuts and defense spending increases are largely exonerated as causes for the deficit, and that domestic spending was to blame. Such an interpretation entirely depends, however, on replacing the assumption of the built-in growth of government inherent in baseline budgeting with an assumption that actual dollars spent and trends over time are more accurate and philosophically acceptable measures. Such an assumption—and, of course, the opposite assumption—is largely a normative rather than a technical matter and depends on one's view of how much government growth there *should* be. Hence, it is impossible simply to blame Reagan's tax cuts and defense buildup for the deficit; there is no single "correct" answer to that question.

Even if one locates most of the responsibility for the deficits of the Reagan era in prior political decisions, this is not to say that more could not or should not have been done by policy makers in the 1980s. Defense spending could probably have been increased at a somewhat slower rate from 1981 to 1985 without compromising national safety. After Reagan's budget victories in 1981 and 1982, little comprehensive effort was made by the White House to cut domestic spending seriously, largely because even sporadic proposals to do so were considered "dead on arrival" in Congress. A 1981 Reagan plan to slow the growth of Social Security, an initiative that would have saved an estimated fifty billion dollars over 1982–86 alone, died in Congress and became a damaging campaign issue in the elections of 1982. Reagan was never willing to take a chance on trimming Social Security spending again, even when Senate Republicans were able to corral the votes. Also in late 1981, Congress ignored the president's request, made when deficit projections had been revised upward, for an additional sixteen billion dollars in supplemental cuts for fiscal year 1982. If those cuts had been enacted, perhaps two hundred billion dollars or more would have been saved through the decade.[55] Instead, throughout the 1980s, numerous cuts made in 1981–82 were restored by Congress, over presidential objections.[56] Those objections were not often translated into vetoes, partly due to presidential unwillingness to confront Congress and partly because Congress governed throughout much of the 1980s with omnibus continuing resolutions that forced the president either to approve or veto all federal spending at once. At least from Reagan's perspective, Congress after 1982 held the defense buildup and tax relief hostage to higher domestic spending.

Yet contrary to suggestions that Reagan promoted complacent indifference to the deficit, the record suggests that more effort was made to deal with it in the 1980s than at any time in the previous two or three decades, and that these efforts set the stage for the budget balancing of the 1990s. Foremost, Reagan promoted a new and more limited conception of the role of government, one that was, if not as dramatic as his supporters claimed or desired, nevertheless real enough. The 1981–82 domestic spending "cuts" (reductions in baseline increases) were the largest in U.S. history—thirty-eight billion dollars in fiscal year 1982, $140 billion in 1982–84. The 1981 budget battle also represented the first presidential use of budget reconciliation procedures to force spending cuts, though the procedures had been available since 1974. Those almost certainly required more political courage and more social sacrifice than any spending reductions accomplished thereafter until 1996. One contemporary news account claimed that "Americans of all ages and all walks of life will feel the pinch of the far-reaching budget cuts. . . . Sacrifices—large and small—will be asked of virtually everyone."[57] Senator Pete Domenici (R-N.M.) called it "the single most heroic effort in controlling spending in the nation's history."[58] Overall, by one estimate, five hundred billion dollars in domestic spending savings were achieved from 1981 to 1989, in comparison to the 1980 baseline.[59]

In 1984, the President's Private Sector Survey on Cost Control (or Grace Commission) produced 2,478 recommendations for revising government practices, proposals that it claimed could save $424 billion in three years.[60] While the General Accounting Office disputed the potential savings, it agreed that at least ninety-eight billion dollars could be saved. Reagan later contended that his administration carried out about one-third of the commission's proposals, and the Bush White House reported that total savings approximated a hundred billion dollars from 1985 to 1991. Citizens Against Government Waste, a group formed by Peter Grace to monitor implementation of the Grace Commission report, estimated in 1994 that in the previous decade up to 65 percent of the commission's recommendations had been implemented, saving $250 billion from 1986 to 1992.[61] The 1980s also saw movement toward privatization of some federal government services. In some respects, the Grace Commission and the privatization initiatives prepared the ground for the Clinton administration's "reinventing government" campaign.

The move to add a balanced-budget amendment to the U.S. Constitution also gained strength. Throughout the 1980s, Reagan was a strong advocate of the balanced-budget amendment. By 1986, thirty-two of the necessary thirty-four states had called for a convention to propose such an amendment. Though the drive for a convention stalled, Ross Perot took up the cause in the 1992 presidential election, when he mobilized twenty million voters. In 1994, the House of Representatives and Senate both came within a handful of votes of approving the amendment; in 1995, the House actually did approve a balanced-budget amendment with more than the requisite two-thirds vote, while the Senate came only one vote short. Much of the deficit-reduction maneuvering of the early 1990s can be explained by a desire to alleviate the political pressure generated by this effort.

Reagan's refusal after 1982 to accept a large tax increase was probably crucial to later deficit reduction. For one thing, by declining to risk long-term economic health for a short-term deficit fix, he made less likely a relapse into revenue-killing economic stagnation. For another, as economist June O'Neill pointed out, "By accommodating higher levels of spending with tax increases, pressure to restrain spending growth (and therefore help control future deficits) would have been diminished."[62] By foreclosing the option of large infusions of new revenue, Reagan forced Congress and future presidents to address more seriously the spending side of the budget equation and made nearly impossible the creation of large new programs. Most notably, the $212 billion deficit of fiscal year 1985 drove Congress to adopt the first Gramm-Rudman-Hollings Deficit Reduction Act, ultimately with Reagan's support. GRH I set deficit-reduction targets leading to a balanced budget by 1990; failure to meet the targets triggered automatic spending cuts, divided evenly between defense and domestic programs. The legislation had to be rewritten two years later as the result of a Supreme Court ruling that one of its provisions violated separation of powers. GRH II maintained the same essential structure as GRH I, though revising the targets with the goal of achieving a balanced budget in 1993.

In one sense, GRH was a clear failure. The targets were never reached in any year. The automatic spending cut mechanism was inadequate to the task, in no small part because it was both too finely tuned and too indiscriminate. GRH II ultimately exempted programs totaling 70 percent of federal spending, including most entitlements, from sequestration but required the remainder to be cut across the board. Congress also found it convenient to move paydays back and forth across fiscal years, add supplemental appropriations after the "final" deficit calculations, and operate on the basis of excessively optimistic economic forecasts.

In another sense, though, GRH was a breakthrough. While the deficit targets were never reached, the deficit assumed a downward path for the rest of the decade. After rising slightly to $221 billion in 1986, the deficit fell to just below $150 billion in 1987 and stayed at that level until 1990. Indeed, by 1989, the federal deficit had been brought down to virtually the same level it had been in 1980 as a proportion of GDP.[63] This sentence is worth repeating: *By 1989, the federal deficit had been brought down to virtually the same level it had been in 1980 as a proportion of GDP.* It was the first time since Eisenhower that the upward momentum of the deficit had been broken. Under the pressure of GRH, the annual growth of federal spending slowed to an average of 1.4 percent over inflation in the period 1986–89, the lowest rate in decades. As a result, federal spending as a proportion of GDP fell almost two full percentage points, from 22.9 percent in 1985 to 21.2 percent in 1989. Even entitlement spending growth was curbed, under the incentive of avoiding deep automatic cuts in other programs; by 1988 and 1989, entitlements accounted for only 9.8 percent of GDP, in comparison to 10.3 percent in 1980.[64] Democrats like Sen. Daniel Patrick Moynihan concurred that the new fiscal climate required trading off one program against another. Detailing the program cuts that would have to be made to secure a proposed Medicaid expansion, he complained, "In order to go forward, you have to go back."[65]

Structurally, GRH served as a model for future deficit-reduction plans. Sequestration was replaced in the 1990s with rules that specified spending caps rather than deficit targets, but the principle was similar. GRH also set a precedent followed by the budget plans of the 1990s in requiring for the first time that no new spending could be proposed without proposing a way to pay for it, either through a tax increase or reduced spending elsewhere. This measure had enormous budgetary and political impact.[66] Above all, GRH helped restrain not only spending on existing programs but the creation of new entitlement programs. The only major new program created in the entire decade was the catastrophic-medical-care insurance program, which passed Congress in 1988. Because of GRH's "pay as you go" requirement, the measure was funded by a new tax on the program's beneficiaries, the elderly. An outcry raised by the American Association of Retired Persons forced its repeal in 1989. By changing the political equation in such a way that the establishment of new programs became less politically feasible, GRH helped ensure that additional future uncontrollable costs were avoided.

GRH was not only a crucial first step toward the deficit-reduction efforts of the next decade but actually a more serious effort at deficit reduction than anything that would be done by Congress in the first half of the 1990s. Indeed, GRH was superseded by new legislation not because it was too weak on the deficit but because many policy makers thought it was too strong. The 1990 budget agreement was prompted by the specter of automatic budget cuts from a GRH sequester that would have gone into effect had a new budget arrangement not been devised. Neither Congress nor President Bush was willing to allow those cuts to occur. Instead, an entirely new, and in important respects weaker, regimen was instituted. From 1990 to 1992, entitlement spending grew eight times faster than it had under GRH, and discretionary domestic spending five times faster.[67] As *Congressional Quarterly* put it in mid-1992, "The $300 billion to $400 billion deficit projected for fiscal 1992 may be politically embarrassing, but thanks to the 1990 budget summit agreement, nobody has to do anything about it."[68]

This 1990 plan was itself superseded by the 1993 Clinton budget plan, in which the structural spending restraints from the 1990 agreement were weakened and in which many of the spending "cuts" were either veiled tax increases or came in defense, and after the next presidential election. As *Time* magazine conceded, the 1993 budget plan "was in some ways actually *less* bold than the one passed in 1990 and signed by President Bush."[69] In contrast to both GRH and the 1990 agreement, there were no impediments to the creation of numerous new entitlement programs. Within a few years, several had been proposed, including the relatively minor Americorps national-service plan (which passed) and the much more expensive universal-health-care coverage (which failed). The demise of the 1990 agreement was anticipated and preceded by at least a year of preparatory maneuvering by congressional Democrats, who objected that the rules required them to use all defense savings for deficit reduction rather than for domestic spending programs. (Incidentally, this objection demonstrated that lower defense spending in the 1980s might have simply meant more domestic spending, not a lower deficit.) Thus, while GRH was flawed, it was at least as effective in deficit control than any fiscal plan of the early 1990s.

Altogether, the 1980s constituted the first decade since the advent of the New Deal in which the dominant ethos, represented by Reagan, considered the deficit to be an economic and moral problem rather than a tool of economic policy to be manipulated for the purposes of aggregate-demand management. Even in the late 1970s, Congress had publicly entertained the question of whether deficits were too small and ought to be deliberately enlarged.[70] In the 1980s, such debates did not occur. Indeed, many of those who became the most vociferous deficit critics of the period (such as Walter Mondale and Tip O'Neill) had been noted for their lack of fiscal restraint prior to 1981. The political economy of the 1980s forced the Democratic Party to the center on the question of budget deficits, requiring first a commitment to deficit reduction (Mondale, Dukakis, and Clinton 1992) and then a commitment to an actual balanced budget (Clinton 1996 and Gore 2000) as the price of political relevance. As Paul Allen Beck, a scholar of political parties, remarked in 1988, "Who would have thought, before the 1980s, that today many liberal Democrats would be decrying the nation's unprecedented budget deficit or that a bipartisan consensus would emerge around the proposition that the deficit should be reduced?"[71]

In retrospect, then, the mid-1980s were a key turning point in the struggle against the deficit. Overall, the gap between growth of spending and growth of revenues narrowed considerably compared with the 1970s, and the 1980s saw the slowest growth of spending of any of the four decades starting in 1950 (see table 5.4). In the half-decade from 1985 to 1989, spending growth slowed to a rate only one-third as fast as revenue growth. In terms both of real dollars and proportion of the economy, the federal deficit assumed a downward path from 1985 until a surplus was reached in 1998, a trend broken only briefly by a spike tied to the recession of 1990–91 and one-time savings and loan bailout costs (see chart 5.5). The efforts of the 1980s carried into, and fiscally defined, the 1990s.

TABLE 5.4
Real Growth in Federal Spending and Revenues by Decade, 1950–2000

	Revenue	Outlays
1950–59	40.0%	50.8%
1960–69	53.9%	51.7%
1970–79	25.7%	34.7%
1980–89	27.0%	28.2%
1985–89	19.9%	7.3%
1990–99	43.4%	10.0%

Source: *Budget of the United States Government Fiscal Year 2001, Historical Tables,* table 1.3. Calculations by author.

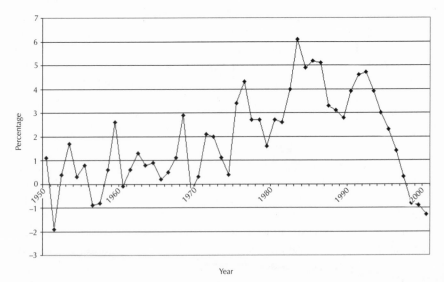

Chart 5.5
Annual Deficit as Percentage of GDP, 1950–2000

The Surprising Surpluses

Given the unconventional nature of this argument—that, despite record deficits, the seeds were sown in the 1980s for the surpluses of the 1990s—a closer look must be taken at those surpluses. As many analysts have observed, official surplus projections are highly contingent and possibly unrealistic.[72] The following analysis makes no claims about the duration or size of federal budget surpluses in the future. That such surpluses did appear in the late 1990s, however, is a fact that calls for explanation. Two key converging factors produced the decline of the deficit after 1992 and the onset of federal surpluses in 1998.

First, overall federal spending was restrained. While the budget plans of 1990 and 1993 were a deliberate escape from the fiscal restraints imposed by GRH, the spending limits of 1990 and 1993 were still stronger than anything before GRH. A bipartisan coalition of deficit hawks in Congress battled for control of the fiscal agenda in 1993, forcing President Clinton to scale back many of his spending proposals in exchange for passage of his budget, and they asserted even greater influence almost immediately after.[73] The political shock of the midterm elections of 1994 and the aggressiveness of the 104th Congress decisively forced the budget debate back in a more serious direction in the mid-1990s. As George Hager of *Congressional Quarterly* and Eric Pianin of the *Washington Post* argued in 1997, congressional Republicans in 1995–96 "moved the budget debate farther in a year than it had come in two decades. The question was no longer *whether* to balance the budget but *how*, and even liberal Democrats felt obliged to produce plans to do it."[74]

As a proportion of GDP, spending fell from 21.8 percent in 1990 to 18.7 percent in 1999; the decade 1990–99 saw the slowest real growth of federal spending of any decade since before the Great Depression.[75] Defense spending fell absolutely and as a proportion of the economy. From 5.2 percent of GDP in 1990, defense declined to 3.1 percent in 1998, the year of the first surplus.[76] These defense cuts were made possible only by America's victory in the Cold War, which—as we will see in chapter 7—was arguably the most profound policy success of the Reagan administration.

After a burst of growth from 1989 to 1992, some elements of domestic spending were also further reined in. Discretionary domestic spending fell from the decade's high of 3.5 percent of GDP in 1993 to 3.1 percent in 1999, mostly due to the assault waged against it by the 104th Congress in 1995–96.[77] While entitlements grew, their growth was slowed by congressional action and by the highly significant, though largely overlooked, fact that no new entitlements were created in the 1980s to burden the 1990s with a fresh explosion of "uncontrollable" costs. Administrative action was also taken, without fanfare, to ensure de facto limitations on the growth of entitlements tied to cost-of-living adjustments.[78] Overall, from 1993 to 1998, the 103rd, 104th, and 105th Congresses spent $452 billion less than Clinton's original budget plan had called for (see table 5.5).[79]

Second, federal revenue expanded four times faster than spending; as a percentage of GDP, it rose from 18 percent in 1990 to 20 percent in 1999.[80] The most important reason for this was the resumption and acceleration of economic growth. The argument that declining deficits led to a strong economy in the 1990s is mostly backward: It was the strong economy that provided the revenue growth that ended the deficit. In early 2000, Secretary of the Treasury Lawrence Summers pointed out that increased federal revenue in the 1990s was driven largely by rising capital-gains collections (mostly in stocks) and by the taxes levied on corporate profits—both products of the economic expansion.[81] According to Congressional Budget Office estimates, 40 percent of the unanticipated rise of individual income tax revenues was attributable to the movement of many more individuals into higher tax brackets and the growth in income of those already within high tax brackets. Another 30 percent was due to the growth of taxable capital gains, while 10 percent was produced by a rise in retirement income from sources like 401(k) plans. The final 20 percent was owed to an increase in the share of GDP represented by taxable income.[82]

A 1990 analysis by economist Lawrence Lindsey can help to illuminate this outcome. The former Reagan Treasury Department official laid out what at the time seemed to be the far-fetched scenario of a federal surplus by 1994, achieved with no tax increases at all and moderate spending restraint. Lindsey pointed out that despite the indexing of personal income tax rates to inflation, some parts of the income tax (like cutoffs for certain deductions) were not indexed, so there was still a slight tendency of inflation to produce higher real revenue. More importantly, because of income-tax progressivity, real income growth (which is generally a product of a growing economy) causes federal revenue to take a gradually increasing share of the economy. By Lindsey's calculations, every 1 percent of real GDP growth produces a 1.3–1.4 percent real

TABLE 5.5
Actual Spending and Revenue 1993–98 versus 1993 Projections in Billions of Dollars

	Revenue	Outlays
1993 Projection	8,145	9,653
Actual	8,516	9,201
Difference	+371	−452

Source: "Budget Totals," *Budget of the United States Government Fiscal Year 1994*, 2; *Budget of the United States Government Fiscal Year 2001, Historical Tables*, table 1.3. Calculations by author.

growth of individual income tax revenue and a 1.4 percent real growth of corporate income tax revenue. Consequently, had the recession of 1990–91 not intervened, federal revenue would have risen to about $1.4 trillion by 1994 without any tax increase at all; in reality, revenue only reached $1.2 trillion, despite the tax increases of 1990 and 1993. Lindsey predicted the possibility of annual surpluses exceeding three hundred billion dollars by 1999.[83] One need not accept every detail of Lindsey's scenario to appreciate that as early as 1990 it was possible not only to imagine but to demonstrate mathematically that a significant surplus could exist by 1999—indeed, a larger one than actually existed—based on the cumulative revenue effects of economic growth alone.

The raising of tax rates in 1990 and 1993 is also seen by some as decisive to the growth of federal revenue in the 1990s. The tax increase of 1990, however, is not a very plausible explanation for the decline of the deficit in the 1990s, since the deficit doubled from $150 billion in 1989 to $290 billion in 1992. Indeed, the two years immediately following the Bush tax increase both saw real revenue lower that it had been in 1990; even three years later, real revenue was only 1.5 percent higher than it had been before the tax increase.[84] The tax increase of 1993 may have contributed to deficit reduction, but more modestly than is often supposed. For one thing, the capital-gains tax rate—identified by President Clinton's treasury secretary and CBO analysts as largely responsible for producing new revenue in the 1990s—was not raised in 1993, and was actually cut in 1997. Altogether, President Clinton touted his tax increase as a means of reducing the deficit to a *low point* of $212 billion in 1996, after which it was predicted to begin rising again. It is difficult to believe that the same tax increase that promised a $250 billion deficit in 1998 would actually produce a small surplus instead, all by itself. To the contrary, the argument that the deficit could not be conquered without tax increases was dealt a serious blow by Congress in 1995, when a plan backed by the congressional majority showed it was possible to eliminate the still-formidable deficit not only without a tax increase but with a major tax cut included. A stripped-down version of this budget became the cornerstone of the 1997 balanced-budget agreement. Annual real revenue growth after the 1997 tax cut (1998–2000) was only a little bit slower than annual revenue growth immediately after the 1993 tax increase (1994–97)—5.6 percent versus 5.9 percent—and the largest single year of revenue growth in the entire period came the year after the tax cut.

Unlike the aftermath of the 1990 tax increase, revenues did not fall after passage of the 1993 bill. Clinton won his tax hike at a fortuitous time—toward the beginning of an economic upswing, not in the middle of a recession. From 1993 to 1998, federal revenue outpaced the administration's own 1993 projections by $371 billion. Yet even if every dollar of unanticipated revenue was the result of the tax increase rather than of the independent effects of economic growth—an implausible scenario repudiated by the administration itself—this figure is still considerably outweighed by the unwillingness of both Democratic and Republican-controlled Congresses to fulfill the president's spending requests.

Thus, to the extent that President Clinton claimed credit for the end of the deficit, his claim was not a particularly strong one. It is not insignificant that he ultimately adopted balanced budgets as his own signature issue, though in doing so he often seemed to be engaged in an attempt to make a virtue of political necessity. Clinton was a bystander at the end of the Cold War, and he was connected to the strong economy largely to the extent that he failed to overturn the basic economic direction set by Reagan. He cut defense spending more and cut taxes less than his opponents in Congress wanted to, but the deficit-cutting effects of these decisions were more than balanced out by the fact that he also insisted on spending more on domestic programs than his opponents wanted, and that they forced him to spend less on those programs than he would have preferred. He was the first president since Lyndon Johnson to pressure Congress consistently to spend more than it planned, rather than less. After 1998, he did nothing to inhibit, and many things to encourage, a fresh burst of spending that threatened to extinguish the surplus if not controlled. Thus, the evidence suggests that without Clinton, there would still have been a surplus—perhaps a larger one, and perhaps one built on somewhat lower levels of both spending and taxing. On the other hand, without the extended economic expansion, the spending restraint legacy of Gramm-Rudman-Hollings, the Reagan-reinforced skepticism of new government programs like universal health care, and the end of the Cold War, the surpluses of the late 1990s would not have occurred.

Reagan and the Federal Budget: An Evaluation

Because revenue grew more slowly, and defense spending more quickly, than the economy, their proportions of GDP changed enough in the 1980s to produce, by that measurement, a larger deficit. Beyond that fact, which is rarely explained in as narrow or qualified a manner as the truth requires, almost all of the common fiscal criticisms of the 1980s fall wide of the mark. The Reagan years were not uniquely prone to deficits; they were part of a pattern of rising deficits with their roots in the New Deal and the Great Society. The tax cuts limited the growth of federal revenue, but revenue still increased by 27 percent over inflation—more than in the 1970s—and remained at or above the historical standard of GDP. The tax cuts did not produce a regressive tax structure; the wealthy bore a higher percentage of the national tax burden after the tax cuts than before. The defense buildup contributed to the deficit in the early part of the decade, but its contribution was secondary compared with that of other programs; defense spending essentially stopped growing after 1985, accounted for only 30 percent of increased programmatic spending from 1980 to 1990, remained below the historical standard of GDP, and was in any event arguably a necessary precondition for national safety in a dangerous time. Also, a serious effort was made to restrain the deficit, including discretionary domestic-spending restraint throughout the 1980s and the adoption of Gramm-Rudman-Hollings in the latter part of the decade. The most balanced explanation is that the deficit went up in the early 1980s because of a combination of defense spending increases, even greater domestic spending increases in entitlements, and above all, the recession of 1981–82. From the mid-eighties on, it went down as revenues from the booming economy caught up with and surpassed newly restricted spending. The deficits that remained almost entirely represented increases in nondefense programs and increased interest payments.

It is not difficult to speculate that many of the criticisms of Reagan's budgets and of the deficit—especially those coming from unexpected sources like Tip O'Neill, Walter Mondale, and Keynesian economists—were based on political rather than economic calculations. It is not hard to imagine, for example, that the tax cuts were attacked so vehemently by many not because they were unambiguously responsible for the deficit but because they violated a central tenet of the egalitarian Left: that policy must have not merely incidental "progressive" effects but proclaim as a positive goal the deliberate redistribution of income from the affluent to the less affluent. The tax cuts also advanced two assumptions that threatened the moral foundations of welfare-state liberalism: that citizens are entitled to keep what they earn as a matter of moral justice, and that the private sector rather than government is the primary engine of prosperity and progress in a free society. Defense spending was likewise an inviting target for advocates of activist domestic government because, among other things, they believed (rightly or wrongly) that it was crowding out the domestic spending and social experimentation that they preferred. These concerns were fundamentally political rather than economic in nature, though the deficit provided a more broadly acceptable rationale under which these critics could advance their positions.

The actual fiscal significance of the 1980s was that although the federal budgets of the 1980s were not balanced, the fiscal climate produced by Reagan's policies reestablished fiscal restraint as a bipartisan consensus, though each party had its own version of what that restraint should mean in practice. Reagan should not be considered merely fortunate that deficits ended before they could undo the benefits of his economic program. In many respects, he positively contributed to that fortune. As well, his frequent assertion that economic growth was the most important single factor in long-term deficit reduction, much belittled at the time, was shown in the 1990s to have contained more than a small amount of truth.

The budgets of the 1980s also provide important lessons for policy makers. If the deficits of the 1980s were a consequence not primarily of tax cuts but of the lagging costs of expensive programs established or expanded in the flush 1960s, the prudent response to future surpluses becomes more clear. Proposals counting on projected surpluses to fund new spending programs, and claims that such a course is less risky than cutting taxes, must be received with skepticism. Furthermore, if economic growth is the key to fiscal health, surrendering some portion of the surplus in order to cut taxes might actually be necessary to safeguard the economy, and hence the rest of the surplus.

The common criticisms of the deficits of the Reagan era, despite their many flaws, have hardened into a virtually unquestioned dogma among much of the media, many politicians, and large numbers of ordinary citizens. So far the result, aside from unfairly portraying Reagan and other policy makers of the 1980s, has been the enactment of two large tax increases of questionable economic value. Despite the Bush tax cut victory of 2001, if the dogma remains uncorrected, it may be only a matter of time before it exacts an even higher cost from the economic well-being and freedom of Americans.

Notes

1. Ronald Reagan, *An American Life: The Autobiography* (New York: Simon and Schuster, 1990), 335.

2. "Goodbye Balanced Budget," *Newsweek*, November 16, 1981, 32. See also Reagan, *An American Life*, 235, where he writes about how he was often asked on the 1980 campaign trail what he would do if faced with "a choice between national security and the deficit?" His consistent answer: "I'd have to come down on the side of national defense."

3. Anthony S. Campagna, *The Economy in the Reagan Years: The Economic Consequences of the Reagan Administrations* (Westport, Conn.: Greenwood, 1994), 213.

4. "Remarks at a White House Briefing for the American Legislative Exchange Council, December 12, 1986," *Public Papers of the Presidents: Ronald Reagan 1986* (Washington, D.C.: Government Printing Office [hereafter GPO], 1988), 1624.

5. Reagan, *An American Life*, 232.

6. Paul E. Peterson and Mark Rom, "Lower Taxes, More Spending, and Budget Deficits," in *The Reagan Legacy: Promise and Performance*, ed. Charles O. Jones (Chatham, N.J.: Chatham House, 1988), 230.

7. "The Long Shadow of the Deficit," *Newsweek*, January 9, 1989, 21.

8. See Robert L. Bartley, *The Seven Fat Years . . . and How to Do It Again* (New York: Free Press, 1992), 180–82.

9. Mortimer B. Zuckerman, "Doing What Is Necessary," *U.S. News & World Report*, March 1, 1993, 72.

10. Nancy Gibbs, "The Low Road to Revolution," *Time*, August 16, 1993, 20.

11. *Budget of the United States Government, Fiscal Year 1994, Historical Tables* (Washington, D.C.: Office of Management and Budget, 1993), table 1.3, 17.

12. David Stockman, *The Triumph of Politics* (New York: Avon, 1987).

13. See Norman B. Ture, "To Cut and to Please," *National Review*, August 31, 1992, 36; Martin Anderson, "When the Losers Write the History," *National Review*, August 31, 1992, 61; Martin Anderson, *Revolution* (New York: Harcourt, Brace, Jovanovich, 1988), 151–57.

14. Timothy J. Muris, "Ronald Reagan and the Rise of Large Deficits: What Really Happened in 1981," *The Independent Review* 4, no. 3 (Winter 2000), 365–76.

15. Muris, "Ronald Reagan and the Rise of Large Deficits," 371, 375.

16. Stockman, *The Triumph of Politics*, 290.

17. Graham Button, "Topping Out," *Forbes*, June 21, 1993, 12.

18. *Budget of the United States Government Fiscal Year 2001, Historical Tables* (Washington, D.C.: Office of Management and Budget, 2000), table 1.3.

19. Edwin S. Rubenstein, *The Right Data* (New York: National Review, 1994), 76.

20. Lawrence B. Lindsey, "Taxpayer Behavior and the Distribution of the 1982 Tax Cut," Working Paper 1760, Cambridge, Mass.: National Bureau of Economic Research, Inc., October 1985, 35.

21. *Budget of the United States Government Fiscal Year 2001, Historical Tables*, table 1.3.

22. *Budget of the United States Government Fiscal Year 2001, Historical Tables*, table 1.3.

23. C. Eugene Steuerle, *The Tax Decade* (Washington, D.C.: Urban Institute, 1992), 43.

24. David E. Rosenbaum, "A New Heave in Tax Policy," *New York Times*, December 8, 1992, D1.

25. C. Eugene Steuerle argues that indexation was by far the most important of the 1981 tax changes; Steuerle, *The Tax Decade*, 43.

26. "Truth in Taxing," *New York Times*, March 10, 1983, 26.

27. Robert Reich, *The Resurgent Liberal* (New York: Times Books, 1989), 243.

28. Cited by Rubenstein, *The Right Data*, 328. See also Richard McKenzie, *What Went Right in the 1980s* (San Francisco: Pacific Research Institute for Public Policy, 1994), 278.

29. Mickey Kaus, *The End of Equality* (New York: Basic, 1992), chap. 5, n 9.

30. In 1990, that rate was 27 percent; in 1966, it had only been 16.4 percent. Kaus, *The End of Equality*, 60–61.

31. McKenzie, *What Went Right in the 1980s*, 277.

32. Anderson, *Revolution*, 152.

33. "Reviving the Energy Tax," *Washington Post*, July 6, 1993, A14.

34. Richard K. Armey, "Economic Revisionism," *Common Sense* (Winter 1994), 48.

35. David E. Rosenbaum, "Prof. Moynihan Wakes the Class with Truth about Taxes," *New York Times*, January 24, 1990, Sec. 4, 4.

36. *Statistical Abstract of the United States 1998*, prepared by the Chief of the Bureau of Statistics (Washington, D.C.: GPO, 1998), table 742.

37. Daniel Yankelovich and Larry Kaagan, "Assertive America," in *The Reagan Foreign Policy*, ed. William G. Hyland (New York: New American Library, 1987), 1–18.

38. *Budget of the United States Government Fiscal Year 2001, Historical Tables*, table 8.4.

39. See *Budget of the United States Government Fiscal Year 2001, Historical Tables*, tables 6.1 and 8.3. Because of consistently high deficits, interest payments on the national debt more than doubled from 1980 to 1990, by which time they accounted for 14 percent of

federal spending. To a certain extent, this problem is self-perpetuating, as interest payments have to be made on that portion of the debt produced by earlier interest payments. However, without the increase in substantive defense and domestic spending programs, the initial surge in the deficit and hence in interest would not have occurred.

40. *Budget of the United States Government Fiscal Year 2001, Historical Tables*, table 8.3

41. *Budget of the United States Government Fiscal Year 2001, Historical Tables*, table 6.1.

42. *Budget of the United States Government Fiscal Year 2001, Historical Tables*, table 8.4 See also McKenzie, *What Went Right in the 1980s*, 299–300; William E. Pemberton, *Exit with Honor: The Life and Presidency of Ronald Reagan* (Armonk, N.Y.: M. E. Sharpe, 1998), 208.

43. *Budget of the United States Government Fiscal Year 2001, Historical Tables*, table 8.2. See also McKenzie, *What Went Right in the 1980s*, 268–69.

44. Even taking into account the one year when actual spending was less than the president's request, the difference between the president's requests and actual spending accounted for $220.3 billion from 1981 through 1989.

45. *Budget of the United States Government Fiscal Year 1998, Historical Tables* (Washington, D.C.: Office of Management and Budget, 1997), table 8.6.

46. Susan Dentzer, "How to Reinvent Washington & Co.," *U.S. News & World Report*, September 13, 1993, 68.

47. Stockman, *The Triumph of Politics*, 443–44; "The Real Reagan Record," *National Review*, August 31, 1992, 38.

48. *Budget of the United States Government Fiscal Year 2001, Historical Tables*, table 6.1.

49. Paul Johnson, *Modern Times: From the Twenties to the Nineties*, rev. ed. (New York: HarperCollins, 1991), 638–40.

50. Frances Fox Piven and Richard A. Cloward, *The New Class War* (New York: Pantheon, 1982), 14.

51. Kaus, *The End of Equality*, 113–15.

52. Lawrence M. Mead, *Beyond Entitlement* (New York: Free Press, 1986), 59; more generally, chapter 3.

53. Joseph White and Aaron Wildavsky, *The Deficit and the Public Interest: The Search for Responsible Budgeting in the 1980s* (Berkeley: University of California Press, 1989), 341.

54. "The Numbers behind the Budget: Growing Deficits," *Washington Post*, August 29, 1990, A23.

55. Stockman, *The Triumph of Politics*, 196–209; Reagan, *An American Life*, 337.

56. See John F. Cogan and Timothy J. Muris, "The Great Budget Shell Game," *The American Enterprise* (November–December 1990), 34–41.

57. "Those Budget Cuts: Who'll Be Hit Hardest," *U.S. News & World Report*, August 10, 1981, 45.

58. "Those Budget Cuts," 45.

59. Bill Archer, "Who's the Fairest of Them All?" *Policy Review* (Summer 1991), 67.

60. For the full report of the commission, see J. Peter Grace, *War on Waste: President's Private Sector Survey on Cost Control* (New York: Macmillan, 1984).

61. Reagan, *An American Life*, 341; Ronald Grover, "Whatever Happened to the Grace Commission?" *Business Week*, June 16, 1986, 71; Citizens Against Government Waste statement, Washington, D.C., February 22, 1994. The Citizens Against Government Waste estimate is probably too optimistic, but it is nevertheless clear that savings have totaled in the tens of billions, at a minimum.

62. June E. O'Neill, "The Story of the Surplus," *Policy Review* (June–July 2000), 8.

63. In 1980, the deficit was 2.7 percent of GDP; in 1990, 2.8 percent. See *Budget of the Government of the United States Fiscal Year 2001, Historical Tables,* table 1.3.

64. *Budget of the Government of the United States Fiscal Year 2001, Historical Tables,* table 8.4.

65. William Schneider, "The Political Legacy of the Reagan Years," in *The Reagan Legacy,* ed. Sidney Blumenthal and Thomas Byrne Edsall (New York: Pantheon, 1988), 51–52.

66. See Aaron Wildavsky, *The New Politics of the Budgetary Process,* 2nd ed. (New York: HarperCollins, 1992), 265–71.

67. Daniel J. Mitchell, "Bush's Rasputin," *National Review,* December 28, 1992, 30.

68. George Hager, "What the Budget Rules Say," *CQ Weekly Report,* May 2, 1992, 1143.

69. Gibbs, "The Low Road to Revolution," 23.

70. Dennis S. Ippolito, *Congressional Spending* (Ithaca, N.Y.: Cornell University Press, 1981), 107, 182–84.

71. Paul Allen Beck, "Incomplete Realignment: The Reagan Legacy for Parties and Elections," in *The Reagan Legacy,* ed. Jones, 161. See also James D. Savage, *Balanced Budgets and American Politics* (Ithaca, N.Y.: Cornell University Press, 1988).

72. Robert D. Reischauer, "The Phantom Surplus," *New York Times,* January 28, 2000, A23.

73. See Robert Woodward, *The Agenda: Inside the Clinton White House* (New York: Simon and Schuster, 1994).

74. George Hager and Eric Pianin, *Mirage: Why Neither Democrats nor Republicans Can Balance the Budget, End the Deficit, and Satisfy the Public* (New York: Times Books, 1997), 7.

75. *Budget of the United States Government Fiscal Year 2001, Historical Tables,* table 1.3.

76. *Budget of the United States Government Fiscal Year 2001, Historical Tables,* table 8.4.

77. *Budget of the United States Government Fiscal Year 2001, Historical Tables,* table 8.4.

78. For years, many economists argued that the common measurement of inflation, the consumer price index (CPI), overstated the actual cost of living for a variety of technical reasons. Consequently, a perennial favorite of would-be budget cutters was a proposal either to delay or scale back cost-of-living allowances (COLAs) based on the CPI for programs like Social Security and veterans benefits. In the winter of 1997, as budget negotiations between Congress and the president reached their climax, discussions centered around whether to adopt such a proposal. It was nixed as part of the balanced-budget agreement by House Minority Leader Richard Gephardt, who did not want the Democratic Party on record as endorsing it. However, shortly thereafter the Bureau of Labor Statistics, the administrative unit responsible for compiling the CPI, quietly adopted a revised CPI formula that had the effect of lowering inflation estimates, and hence COLAs.

79. *Budget of the United States Government Fiscal Year 1994, Budget Summary; Budget of the United States Government Fiscal Year 2001, Historical Tables,* table 1.3.

80. *Budget of the United States Government Fiscal Year 2001, Historical Tables,* table 1.3.

81. Curt Anderson, "Despite Cuts, Overall Tax Intake Highest since World War II," *Denver Rocky Mountain News,* April 9, 2000, 60A.

82. O'Neill, "The Story of the Surplus," 11–13.

83. Lindsey, *The Growth Experiment,* 171–79.

84. *Budget of the United States Government Fiscal Year 2001, Historical Tables,* table 1.3.

6

Reagan and the
(Partial) Recovery of Society

WHEN RONALD REAGAN TOOK OFFICE in 1981, America was in the midst of a quiet social crisis easily as consequential as the economic crisis. As in other realms of policy, the Reagan administration adopted a strategy informed by a framework of ordered liberty. Without fanfare—indeed, at times almost imperceptibly—the Reagan years saw the stabilization or improvement of many crucial indicators of social health that had sharply deteriorated in the 1960s and 1970s.

The signs of social deterioration were easily observed. Crime rates soared by 215 percent from 1960 to 1980, while violent crime grew even faster, by 271 percent.[1] Likewise, starting in the 1960s, the widespread use of drugs grew tremendously, Scholastic Aptitude Test (SAT) scores began a long decline, and popular culture began what many perceived to be a full-scale process of vulgarization and coarsening. As David Frum documented in *How We Got Here: The 70s: The Decade That Brought You Modern Life (for Better or Worse)*, these trends broadened and continued through the 1970s.

More broadly, there was cause to be increasingly concerned about the condition of important social institutions. The family—arguably the most fundamental social institution—was in evident decline. The illegitimacy rate more than tripled from 1960 to 1980, and divorce rates more than doubled in the same time. Indeed, by 1970 anthropologist Margaret Mead was asking, "Can the family survive?"[2] Other analysts have lamented what they view as a decline of American civic participation since the 1960s. Robert Putnam, for example, wrote in 1995 a celebrated essay entitled "Bowling Alone," in which he argued that membership in groups had declined by one-quarter since 1967.[3] Voluntarism and charitable giving also declined in the 1960s and 1970s. Declining church membership and religiosity led some observers to predict the gradual decline of religion into irrelevance.

A variety of theories have been offered by commentators trying to explain what Francis Fukuyama called "The great disruption." Some theories—that the deterioration of social indicators was the consequence of growing poverty or, conversely, greater wealth—fail the test of plausibility. As Fukuyama pointed out, the start of that deterioration coincided with the most affluent decade in prior American history and continued through many economic ups and downs. If it was reversed, it was also reversed in a period of unparalleled affluence.[4] Many conservatives—including, it is fair to say, Reagan and those influencing social policy in his administration—attributed it to a combination of changes in the law and cultural changes.[5] Analysts like Charles Murray suggested that government policies, especially regarding welfare and criminal justice, contributed to the breakdown. Others pointed to cultural shifts regarding social mores as the decisive factor. Gertrude Himmelfarb, for example, referred to the "demoralization of society," in which "virtues," grounded in truth and supported by social constraint, were replaced by "values," or fundamentally subjective personal preferences.[6] More specifically, traditional virtues of self-restraint, individual responsibility, and respect for lawful authority, as well as supporting institutions like religion and the family, came under sustained attack from the counterculture. By the 1970s, this ethos had become mainstream, abetted by educators, entertainers, and journalists who shared the counterculture's basic assumptions of radical individualism and hostility to social constraints.

Reagan and the Social Crisis

In Reagan's view, there was an important social component of the architecture of freedom that depended on basic social health, a strong civil society, and the character and responsibility of individual citizens. Reagan and his administration were clearly affected by at least four influences in their views of social problems and remedies.

For Reagan, the first of these was the American Founders, whose views on religion and citizen character Reagan often quoted. There can be little doubt that a significant majority of the Founders considered religion—properly channeled—to be a crucial bulwark of social and political well-being. George Washington, for example, said in his Farewell Address that "of all the dispositions and habits which lead to political prosperity, religion and morality are indispensable supports. . . . [R]eason and experience both forbid us to expect that national morality can prevail in exclusion of religious principle."[7] Indeed, it was the common understanding of the founding generation that "virtue and morality are necessary for free, republican government; religion is necessary for virtue and morality; religion is, therefore, necessary for republican government."[8] Aside from this general notion, common to most of the Founders, the antifederalist and Jeffersonian traditions, from which Reagan often drew, particularly emphasized "republican virtue," a sturdy character of independence and self-reliance combined with community duty. In this line of thinking, excessive dependence or servility among citizens corrupted them and society. Overall, the Founders can be considered the primary source of Reagan's concept of ordered liberty.

A second obvious source of influence on the administration was the social analysis offered by Alexis de Tocqueville in *Democracy in America*. Tocqueville argued at length that the health of civil society is essential to the maintenance of political liberty. It is the social infrastructure of democracy, the "customs and manners," that make it possible for a free people to sustain a free society. Two elements of Tocqueville's analysis particularly corresponded to Reagan's. First, Tocqueville emphasized the importance of civic associations, and civil society more generally. In his view, the equality and individualism of democracy tend to produce social fragmentation, even atomization, unless supplemented by the attachment of individuals to each other through free associations. Associations thus serve an important function as mediating institutions between the state and the individual, without which the individual would be isolated, unhappy, and exposed to the full force (or seduction) of the state.[9] On a smaller scale, families constituted an indispensable mediating structure.

Second, like the Founders, Tocqueville argued that the health of American society and the safety of its liberty rested on a foundation of religion. This was because religion provided the voluntary constraints necessary to prevent both moral anarchy and political tyranny; it provided a means for people to grasp the imperatives of "self interest rightly understood."[10] Individualism might be prevented from degenerating into selfishness, and transcendent limits could be placed on the action of government. For Tocqueville, religion also served as a crucial nexus in civil society, connecting people to private organizations, helping them practice self-government on a small scale, and even contributing to the maintenance of the family. Altogether, Tocqueville offered the opinion that

while the law permits the Americans to do what they please, religion prevents them from conceiving, and forbids them to commit, what is rash or unjust. Religion in America takes no direct part in the government of society, but it must be regarded as the first of their political institutions; for if it does not impart a taste for freedom, it facilitates the use of it.[11]

The third source of influence was found in the newly organized force of conservative Christians, who made a biblically based argument featuring the importance of moral standards. In this view, the decline of Judeo-Christian morality was responsible for a large proportion of the social ills found in 1980. This line of thinking identified religion, family, and an ethos of individual responsibility, grounded in the biblical understanding of the human soul, as the most pivotal foundations of social health and political liberty. The congruence of this argument with Reagan's own religious convictions undoubtedly increased its resonance for him.

The final source of influence on the social policies of the Reagan administration came in the form of the ideas of conservative intellectuals like Murray and Himmelfarb. This process actually began in the 1970s, with the prominence of individuals like Norman Podhoretz, Irving Kristol, Nathan Glazer, and Ben Wattenberg. In the 1980s, these neoconservative thinkers tended to focus largely on questions of culture, or on the interplay between law and culture, and tended to emphasize themes of responsibility, self-restraint, and the establishment and maintenance of community norms.

For example, social scientist James Q. Wilson concluded in his 1983 book *Thinking about Crime* that while demographic factors (like a relatively youthful population) contributed to the post-1960 burst of crime, the central fact defining the contemporary period has been the "collapse of the Victorian popular culture and of the moral legitimacy of the institutions embodying it," with all of the attendant negative consequences.[12] Wilson ultimately popularized the "broken windows" interpretation of crime, which held that smaller manifestations of disorder (like buildings with broken windows) create a climate that is open to more violent and more widespread disorder.

Others focused on the nexus between family breakdown, government policy, culture, and inner-city poverty. Murray provoked a storm of controversy when his 1984 book *Losing Ground: American Social Policy 1950–1980* argued that government programs had become counterproductive by subsidizing illegitimacy, single-parent families, and poor working habits, and more generally by creating an ethos of irresponsibility among program recipients.[13] Lawrence Mead likewise argued, in *The End of Entitlement*, that government had inadvertently created a culture of entitlement that was preventing the poor from either reaching for their full potential or facing the consequences of their own misjudgments.[14] These works powerfully influenced the debate over family breakdown and welfare reform in the 1980s and 1990s.

In a sense, George Gilder initiated this line of argument in his 1981 book *Wealth and Poverty*. Fundamentally a moral defense of capitalism, *Wealth and Poverty* proposed that capitalism (and by inference, limited government) promotes a series of crucial human virtues like patience, prudence, self-discipline, an orientation toward the future, and service. Gilder was arguing that economic and political freedom contribute to a culture of virtue; implicitly, too much government could produce a culture of vice.[15]

Culture itself was the key concern of writers like Himmelfarb, who probed the breakdown of moral norms in American society. Authors like Midge Decter and Richard John Neuhaus (*The Naked Public Square: Religion and Democracy in America*) likewise addressed issues of morality, religion, and culture. What held this conservative intellectual thought together, like sinews of an organism, was journals like *Commentary*, *The Public Interest*, and *The National Interest*, which gained increasing influence through the 1980s.[16] Aside from dismissing these concerns about social disorder as a kind of incipient authoritarianism, liberals had little to say in this conversation. As William Pemberton argued in his 1998 biography of Ronald Reagan, *Exit with Honor*, starting in the 1970s "liberal intellectuals abandoned to conservatives serious discussion of issues concerning crime, family and community problems, need for welfare reform, and the relationship between individual responsibility and rights."[17] As a result, conservatives arguably dominated the intellectual direction of the 1980s.

It is impossible to say in what proportions or by what means Reagan himself or others in his administration imbibed these influences—influences that were themselves largely overlapping. Conservative Christians looked to both the Bible and the Founders; the conservative intellectuals frequently drew on Tocqueville. Altogether, the four strands shared certain assumptions, which Reagan voiced regularly. One was that liberty is not the same as social or legal license; liberty is not only compatible with but depends upon a certain minimum level of social and legal structure. Another was that the arrangement of social structure and social mores helps to produce both the character of citizens and the social outcomes that will either uphold or undermine a free political order. Social institutions could be as important to the architecture of freedom as were political institutions. In particular, civil society (broadly understood to include community participation, the family, and religion) and an ethos of individual responsibility and self-control are essential to liberty, and they can and should be encouraged in law and in culture. In many cases, this may require less active government, though in some cases more active government. Accordingly, the Reagan administration promoted changes in the law where it thought necessary and acted on the assumption that "public officials, as opinion leaders, influence the direction of cultural change, and they should do so."[18]

This framework was highly controversial. The libertarian-minded objected to what they saw as a contradiction between limited government and a more active government in some social realms. To an even greater degree, Reagan's framework came under criticism provoked by its nonconformity with social concepts that had become dominant in the intellectual world in the years prior to 1980, including behavioralism, secularism, feminist interpretations of the family, and a variety of forms of collectivism. In many respects, it represented a frontal assault on the counterculture ethos of the 1960s, a fact that was well understood—and resented—by adherents of that ethos.

Nevertheless, Reagan's approach was not without credible defenders. Regarding the family, Barbara Dafoe Whitehead argued in 1993, "Over the past 2-1/2 decades Americans have been conducting a vast natural experiment in family life. The results are becoming clear": The breakdown of the American family was responsible for a large proportion of the social miseries suffered by Americans since 1960.[19] In the words of Rutgers sociologist David Popenoe, "In three decades of work as a social scientist, I know of few other bodies of data in which the evidence is so decisively on one side of the issue; on the whole, for children, two parent families are preferable."[20]

Reagan's emphasis on religion, if not his particular policies, also received support, after the fact, from some unexpected sources. In widely reported 1993 remarks, Hillary Clinton extolled the importance of the spiritual to human happiness, while the thesis of Yale legal scholar Stephen Carter's 1993 book *The Culture of Disbelief*—that the tendency of American elites to relegate religion to the status of irrelevance is bad for America—drew sympathetic comment from President Clinton himself. During the 2000 campaign, Democratic vice-presidential candidate Joseph Lieberman quoted Washington's maxim about the importance of religion to national morality.

A large body of sociological evidence confirms that religiosity is positively correlated with individual and social well-being. While researchers are not unanimous, studies too numerous to dismiss have indicated that the strength of an individual's religious affiliation and church-going is significantly connected to lower drug use, lower rates of juvenile delinquency and adult crime, lower teenage pregnancy and illegitimacy rates, lower divorce rates and greater marital happiness, successful recovery from alcohol or drug addiction, fewer psychological disturbances such as chronic depression, successful efforts to move out of poverty, longevity itself, and, with qualifications, lower levels of racial prejudice.[21] Sociologist Gunther Lewy, himself an agnostic, concluded in his 1996 book *Why America Needs Religion* that "there exists a significant relationship between religiousness and the observance of certain moral and social norms."[22]

In any case, Reagan's social framework was much better received outside of the academy and the media. Indeed, it corresponded with a noticeable change in public sensibilities that began to take shape in the late 1970s. By the 1980s, the values of the counterculture were being critically reexamined in mainstream society. National surveys uniformly indicated a major shift of values on crime and drugs, favoring a less permissive approach.[23] There were also some signs that the promiscuity of the 1960s and 1970s was giving way to more moderate behavior, partly as a result of the shift in values and partly in response to the grim danger of AIDS that arose in the mid-1980s. Researchers reported that among high-achievement high school students, approval of premarital sex and legalized abortion, as well as actual sexual activity, had fallen by anywhere from one-quarter to one-third since the mid-1970s. In the early 1970s, 68 percent of eighteen-to-twenty-four-year-olds described extramarital sex as wrong; a decade later, that figure had risen to 85 percent.[24] Some authors perceived a more general resurgence of "traditionalism."[25]

It remains an open question what accounted for this shift, but it is not difficult to offer a theory. By 1980, Americans no longer had to "Imagine," as the quintessential song of the 1960s asked them to, a world devoid of religion, patriotism, and the restraints of bourgeois responsibility. For two decades they had been able to observe it directly, and an increasing number decided they did not like many of the apparent consequences. The generation that came of age in the 1960s matured. In the face of the realities of job, home, and family, perspectives changed; those who had called for "free love" twenty years before were understandably less sanguine when confronted with their daughters' prom dates. Those who came from before the 1960s, as well as many of those who came after, staged a partial counterrevolution against the social excesses of that era. Consequently, throughout society, the predominant civic discourse changed dramatically on topics including crime, drugs, the family, rigorous educational standards, and religion itself.

Reagan's connection with this cultural shift was complex. He both promoted it and benefited from it, both harnessed it and reflected it. It is not easy to disentangle Reagan's policies and the social outcomes of the 1980s from the broader cultural shift that almost certainly contributed to both. However, by whatever link of causation, we can see that policy addressed many social problems from a new perspective and that substantive outcomes were largely consistent with Reagan's goals.

Reagan's Social Policy

In several specific areas, Reagan supported changes in the law that took a less permissive approach. In terms of crime, Reagan complained that in the years prior to 1980 "the scales of justice had become seriously unbalanced, making it difficult to arrest criminals and harder and harder to convict them."[26] In response, his administration supported stricter sentencing guidelines, the appointment of tough "law and order" judges, construction of additional prison space, curbs on criminal appeals, and expanded use of capital punishment at the federal and state levels. As a result of that drive, the median prison sentence for all serious crimes increased by 54 percent from 1974 to 1988, though it still did not regain the level of 1964.[27] From 1980 to 1990, the number of prisoners in state and federal prisons increased from 305,000 to 713,000, because a higher proportion of criminals were being incarcerated than in the previous two decades. In 1980, barely two hundred out of every thousand arrests for serious crime led to imprisonment; by 1990, that figure had increased to over 350, more than in 1960, when the long decline began.[28]

The drug culture that took root in the 1960s and 1970s was also confronted in the 1980s, as both Ronald and Nancy Reagan declared a "war on drugs." Budgets for drug enforcement activities increased dramatically (from one billion dollars yearly in 1980 to thirteen billion by 1993), sentences for drug dealing were lengthened, federal officials began confiscating the property of drug traffickers, and a public-relations campaign, with the First Lady at the head and with the theme "Just Say No," was directed at students. State and local arrests for drug offenses increased from 560,000 in 1981 to nearly 1.4 million in 1989.[29]

Other forms of substance abuse were also targeted. The 1980s saw a major public campaign against drunk driving. Harsher sentences were established for drunk-driving offenses and increased priority was given to police roadblocks and other means of enforcing the law. These measures resulted in an increase in arrests for driving under the influence from 1.3 million in 1979 to 1.8 million in 1990.[30] The minimum drinking age was also increased nationwide to twenty-one, prodded by the threat of a federal highway funds cutoff—one of the few times that the Reagan administration flatly ignored the imperatives of federalism.

Where the shaping of culture was at issue, Reagan unreservedly embraced religion, indicating in speeches that renewal of America's "spiritual strength" was an important social goal. He was a frequent speaker at religious meetings; he delivered the famed "evil empire" speech at the 1983 meeting of the National Association of Evangelicals. Virtually no major Reagan address in eight years failed to mention God or the place of God in American life. By one estimate, nearly 10 percent of Reagan's speeches were devoted primarily to religious themes, twice the number under Jimmy Carter. In eight years, he gave eighty-one funeral orations, thirty-six speeches to religious audiences, and another seventy-four speeches with religious themes to more general audiences.[31] The essence of his argument was "that religion and morality, that faith in something higher, are prerequisites for freedom."[32] Reagan also saw religion as necessary for the correction of the social problems America had developed;

it was not a coincidence that, when he was first inaugurated, the Bible on which he placed his hand was opened to 2 Chronicles 7:14: "If my people, which are called by my name, shall humble themselves, and pray, and seek my face, and turn from their wicked ways; then will I hear from heaven, and will forgive their sin, and will heal their land."[33]

Concretely, Reagan supported school prayer and tuition tax credits for parochial schools, measures that failed legislatively but put the presidential stamp of approval on the concerns of millions of religious Americans. More broadly, Reagan consistently advocated a more traditional "accommodationist" notion of church-state relations, in contradistinction to the relatively recent absolutist interpretation of the First Amendment's nonestablishment clause. Reagan so thoroughly identified America with a special Providential purpose—the vision of a "shining city on a hill" had strong religious overtones—that at times he seemed almost to imply that it was unpatriotic to fail to acknowledge or celebrate that purpose. Naturally, many citizens (especially, but not exclusively, the less religious) resented this rhetorical device, but it seemed to remain powerful for many more. In the view of Reagan speechwriter William Ker Muir Jr., Reagan deliberately sought to cultivate America's churches as "moral institutions" playing an important role in civil society; his rhetoric "galvanized" his religious audiences, even becoming the focus for discussion in religious journals.[34]

Likewise, the Reagan administration both legitimized and empowered the intellectual movement advocating greater individual responsibility and a turn away from moral, social, and legal permissiveness. The administration often translated these intellectual critiques into public rhetoric, and sometimes into public policy. Indeed, at the center of Reagan's attempt to influence culture lay his effective use of the presidential "bully pulpit." For example, the "Just Say No" antidrug campaign, though widely ridiculed, almost certainly contributed to changing the bounds of the acceptable in American society. Reagan's consistently voiced antiabortion position, while bearing little fruit in the legal realm, sought as well to affect the way Americans thought about the issue.

Often, power and rhetoric worked together. While Jimmy Carter had introduced the subject of family to national prominence with his 1980 National Conference on Families, Reagan was the first president to make family a consistent part of the nation's public dialogue. The political groundwork for the debate over family was laid when Reagan, receiving the Republican presidential nomination in 1980, built his acceptance speech around the five themes of "family, work, neighborhood, peace, and freedom." Family came first, as Reagan called on Americans to make a commitment to "teach our children the values and the virtues handed down to us by our families. . . . Work and family are at the center of our lives; the foundation of our dignity as a free people."[35] This rhetorical theme was a consistent one throughout the Reagan administration, and it was continued by the George H. W. Bush administration.

As with religion, Reagan saw family, which he called a "divine institution," as necessary not only for social health but for national freedom. As he put it in 1986, "Family life and the life of freedom are interdependent. Children learn the most important lessons they will ever receive about their inherent dignity as individuals. . . . Totalitarian societies see in the family a natural enemy, a bulwark of basic loyalties and inherited ideals that places allegiance in relationships that precede the claims of the state."[36] In Reagan's view, "in recent decades, the American family has come under virtual attack," mostly from encroaching government. That development was particularly disturbing because "all those aspects of civilized life that we most deeply cherish— freedom, the rule of law, economic prosperity and opportunity . . . depend upon the strength and integrity of the family."[37]

Seeking ways of translating these themes into policies, Reagan appointed a White House Working Group on the Family, which produced a report in December 1986 offering several guidelines for administrative action. The report argued that the rights and responsibilities of families were superior to those of government, that government should first and foremost avoid doing further harm to families, and that local government and civil society were the best places for families to seek assistance. More specifically, the report urged more difficult divorce, restrictions on abortion, and limits to government-subsidized day care outside of the home (none of which became law at the time). In 1987, Reagan issued Executive Order 12606, requiring executive departments and agencies to identify and justify proposed policy changes that might negatively affect families (the Family Impact Statement).

> The order included criteria in the form of seven questions to which department or agency heads were required to respond in writing. For example, does this action by government strengthen or erode the stability of the family? Does this action strengthen or erode the authority and rights of parents? Can this activity be carried out by a lower level of government or by the family itself? And what message does this policy send to young people concerning the relationship among their behavior, their personal responsibility, and the norms of American society?[38]

In 1988, the Reagan administration reached an accord with Congress on the Family Support Act, the first major welfare reform in twenty years. Among other things, the act strengthened child-support collection mechanisms, provided assistance for welfare recipients making the transition to work, required that welfare cover two-parent (and not just one-parent) families, and allowed states to require minors with a child to live with relatives until their eighteenth birthday. The central message of the act was that "even poor parents must take responsibility for the financial support of dependent children and themselves."[39] Altogether, the Reagan administration pursued a variety of strategies to promote stronger families and reduce some of the dysfunctions that had become increasingly common since the 1960s. Most important, perhaps, was simply the high degree of sustained emphasis placed on the issue.

At the time, such appeals drew a mixture of ridicule and anger from Reagan's opponents. Barbara Ehrenreich, for example, called the discussion of family "from some angles the most perverse . . . of the new era's new values." In the 1980s, for Ehrenreich, "the winning political faction has . . . brought [family] out, along with flag and faith, to silence any voices they found obscene, offensive, disturbing, or merely different."[40] Feminist writers like Susan Faludi concluded that the emphasis on family was little more than part of an antifeminist backlash against the recent gains of women.[41] This reaction was still evident in 1992, when Vice President Dan Quayle became the object of scorn by numerous commentators for suggesting in a major speech that Hollywood had an obligation to avoid glamorizing unwed mothering.

It is clear in retrospect, however, that tectonic plates were shifting beneath the surface. By the end of 1993, President Clinton's domestic adviser William Galston was saying, "If people don't do right because they believe that it's right, we cannot solve any of our problems. Our most important line of defense is the family."[42] Clinton himself declared, "We've got to bring down the number of children who are born out of wedlock[;] . . . we're going to have to demand that people take more responsibility for the consequences of their actions."[43] Persistent attention to this issue, combined with substantial empirical evidence supporting Reagan's position, ultimately resulted in something resembling a bipartisan consensus.

Education was another social issue on which political power and culture-influencing rhetoric interacted. This process began in earnest when Reagan's National Commission on Excellence in Education published its 1983 report *A Nation at Risk*, widely heralded as a national "wake-up call" on education. "If a foreign country had done to us what we have done to ourselves," the commissioners reported, "we would consider it an act of war."[44] Spurred by both the report itself and a subsequent administration campaign, the United States experienced a "tidalwave of school reform movement which promises to renew American education."[45] Within eighteen months, thirty-five states had approved tougher high school graduation requirements, twenty-four states were examining some sort of master-teacher or merit-pay program, twenty-one states had launched initiatives to improve textbooks and instructional material, eighteen states had mandated greater instructional time, eight states had lengthened the school day, and seven states had lengthened the school year. School innovation was also more generally encouraged by the Reagan administration through the replacement of dozens of categorical grants with block grants, which increased the discretion available to state and local administrators in the use of federal funds.

Enthusiasm for school reform continued through the decade. At the intellectual level, books such as E. D. Hirsch's *Cultural Literacy* and Allan Bloom's *The Closing of the American Mind* opened highly charged debates over the kind of substantive standards that ought to guide the educational process. School choice, as represented by programs that would give parents vouchers that could be spent at schools of their choice, was an idea backed by the Reagan administration. Home schooling, touted by the Working Group on Families, became a serious option in many states for parents who were dissatisfied with their alternatives. Corporations also began potentially far-reaching programs to sponsor particular schools. These reforms were driven largely from the grassroots, and a key idea holding them together was a bottom-up, or decentralized, approach. Vouchers, for example, were tried on a major scale for the first time in Milwaukee, when Polly Williams, a black state legislator and former welfare mother of four, pushed through in the late 1980s an experimental voucher plan. This attention to education issues continued into the 1990s.

One of the most significant social developments of the 1980s lay in the revitalization of civil society and the development of a broadly based "civil society movement," which grew in strength throughout the 1990s. This phenomenon was undergirded by the Reagan administration both in rhetoric and in law. Many contemporary news reports about the growth of charitable giving and voluntarism during the Reagan years (discussed below) attributed it to a popular reaction against the "excesses of the 1980s." Yet it was fully consistent with the tone set by Reagan in his 1980 nomination acceptance speech when he said, "Let us pledge to restore, in our time, the American spirit of voluntary service, of cooperation, of private and community initiative; a spirit that flows like a deep and mighty river through the history of our nation."[46] George H. W. Bush inherited this theme from Reagan, calling for "a thousand points of light" and "the age of the offered hand."

Despite the skepticism of some who feared abandonment of the disadvantaged, Reagan argued that his emphasis on voluntarism was not simply the result of a desire to reduce federal expenditures. He repeatedly explained that he viewed the spirit of community self-responsibility as necessary to a healthy free society, essential to the independence and dignity of individuals, and more practically effective than solutions imposed from Washington. Above all, it was in keeping with the essential spirit of America, as Reagan saw it. In his autobiography, *An American Life*, Reagan related his hope that history would look back on the 1980s as having brought, among other things, "a resurgence of the American spirit of generosity that touched off an unprecedented outpouring of good deeds."[47] Reagan described this vision in a 1984 address in which he argued that "America is more than just government on one hand and helpless individuals on the other."[48] As Dinesh D'Souza put it, "Reagan believed that as citizens of a free society we should demand less of the state and more of ourselves."[49]

To Reagan, "What federalism is to the public sector, voluntarism and private initiative are to the private sector. The country is bursting with ideas and creativity, but a government run by central decree has no way to respond.... Voluntarism is an essential part of our plan to give the government back to the people."[50] By Reagan's reckoning, "A strong, cooperative community spirit is the heart and soul of our democracy," but that spirit in recent years "has been weakened by the growth of big government," which tended to "preempt those mitigating institutions like family, neighborhood, church, and schools ... that act as both a buffer and a bridge between the individual and the naked power of the state."[51]

The administration actively promoted the revival of civil society in a variety of ways. In his first thirty-two months in office, Reagan featured the subject of private-sector initiatives in more than eighty-four speeches and other communications.[52] Shortly after assuming office, Reagan created the White House Office of Private Sector Initiatives, with its task to "revitalize the great American spirit of neighbor helping neighbor."[53] In October 1981, he named a Task Force on Private Sector Initiatives, comprising thirty-five members representing business, the nonprofit sector, religious leaders, government officials, and minorities. While limited in effectiveness by an ambiguous charge and a divided membership, the task force nevertheless succeeded in "serving as an information broker, engendering networks, and promoting new approaches particularly at the state and local levels of government for solving community problems."[54] It developed and operated a data bank for private-sector initiatives. It also organized meetings of "religious organizations, trade associations, community-based organizations, and community colleges[,] ... governors' aides, corporate chief executives, congressional aides, and numerous other groups."[55] The task force and Reagan encouraged states and local governments to establish their own task forces, leading to commitments to do so by forty states and some cities, including San Francisco and Houston. Finally, the task force put a new emphasis on corporate philanthropy, an area that had not received much attention from previous administrations.

After the President's Task Force on Private Sector Initiatives disbanded in December 1982, the permanent Office of Private Sector Initiatives continued implementing much of the task force's program. It maintained the data bank, coordinated numerous local programs focusing on particular private-sector initiative issues like business education and day care, and continued publicly promoting the idea of private-sector initiatives. The office provided organizational support for an awards program to recognize outstanding volunteers, as well as a "Presidential Citation for Private Sector Initiatives." It also aided the president in promoting national volunteer initiatives like Adopt-a-School and an adult literacy program. Outside of the Office for Private Sector Initiatives, numerous executive departments and agencies, including the Department of Housing and Urban Development, the Economic Development Administration, and the Small Business Administration, began on their own to advocate strenuously such initiatives.[56] While previous administrations had supported public sector/private sector partnerships through a variety of programs, the Reagan administration was more highly committed, more innovative in its approach, and took greater care to emphasize the "private" and distinct nature of the private sector. Amid all of the attention paid to Reagan's tax and spending changes, John B. Olsen offered the opinion in 1984 that this emphasis on private-sector activity "may prove to be the most significant policy initiative of the Reagan administration."[57]

While these active strategies to promote greater private-sector responsibility were important, they were disappointing to some advocates of a stronger "independent sector," who hoped for more radical action.[58] They were also probably less important than the administration's outwardly passive strategy. Reagan's call to "demand more of ourselves" was logically connected to political attempts to reinvigorate the idea and practice of limited government, which both requires strong civil society and leaves open the space that civil society needs in order to develop strength. In this sense, Reagan attempted to contribute to America's social regeneration not only by what he did but by what he did not do: By not insisting that the federal government attempt to solve every social problem in America, he deliberately left open space that a free society could use to renew itself. As Reagan argued, "In this era of big government, we sometimes forget that many of our proudest achievements as a nation came not through government, but through private citizens, individuals whose genius and generosity flourished in this climate of freedom."[59] Tocqueville described the importance of that "open space" when he concluded that under the sway of democracy, "the grandeur is not in what the public administration does, but in what is done without it or outside of it"; democracy allows "an all-pervading and restless activity, a super-abundant force, and an energy which is inseparable from it and which may, however unfavorable circumstances may be, produce wonders."[60]

While the 1980s did not produce social wonders by anyone's reckoning, they did produce improvement—modest, but hardly insignificant—across a wide range of indicators. This was true of both the critical institutions of civil society broadly understood and some of the secondary indicators that had deteriorated since 1960, like crime, drugs, and educational performance.

Social Outcomes in the 1980s: The Social Institutions of Civil Society

Civil Society: Civic Associations

In the 1980s, there were some signs that this aspect of civil society was actually becoming somewhat stronger. Robert Putnam's evidence for the 1980s (as opposed to the whole period from 1967 to 1993) was mixed. Many fraternal organizations were down, but professional associations were up; labor unions were down, but the Parent-Teacher Association (PTA) grew by 40 percent from 1982 to 1995, after falling by nearly 60 percent from 1964 to 1982.[61] According to the *Encyclopedia of Associations*, which has been surveying organizations for forty years, thirteen of twenty-two representative service organizations gained members in the 1980s, eight lost members, and one reported no change. In aggregate, these twenty-two organizations reported a net gain of 4,889,878 members from 1980 to 1990 (see table 6.1), an increase of 16 percent.[62] This growth rate in percentage terms was twice as great as the increase reported in the 1970s.[63]

This is not to say that Putnam's concerns were without foundation. Some of the most venerable associations in America, like the Elks and Freemasons, lost members in the 1980s and continued shrinking at an accelerated rate in the 1990s. Setting aside youth organizations changes the picture somewhat, too. Growth in nonyouth organizations was slower in the 1980s than in the 1970s, and by the end of the 1990s the aggregate membership of these groups had actually fallen slightly. Nevertheless, if the self-reported membership figures are to be believed, the overall picture in the 1980s regarding these service organizations was solid in absolute terms and was brighter than in the 1970s by some standards. According to some researchers, in the early 1990s somewhere between two-thirds and 90 percent of Americans still belonged to at least one organization, and the average American belonged to four organizations.[64]

Civil Society: Community Participation

At the same time, the Reagan years saw a significant increase in charitable giving and voluntarism by the American people—a form of civic engagement

TABLE 6.1
Service Organizations, Percentage Change by Decades, 1961–1999

Organization	1961–70	1970–80	1980–90	1990–99
Assn of Jr. Leagues	+15%	+45%	+38%	+8%
Civitan Intl.	+6%	+53%	+4%	0
Elks	+16%	+13%	–9%	–13%
Freemasons	+5%	+12%	–11%	–23%
Jaycees	–8%	+27%	–37%	–52%
Kiwanis	+6%	+8%	+6%	+3%
Knights/Columbus	+6%	+10%	+12%	+6%
Lions	+53%	+35%	+11%	+3%
Optimist	+33%	+25%	+28%	–6%
Rotary	+30%	+29%	+25%	+15%
Ruritan	+23%	+5%	0	+1%
Salvation Army	+29%	+22%	+10%	+4%
Sertoma	+25%	+25%	–3%	–12%
Soroptimist	+16%	+20%	+39%	+16%
Women's Clubs	–6%	–25%	–33%	–33%
Boy Scouts	+24%	–28%	+6%	+13%
Boys Clubs	+60%	+34%	+20%	+56%
Girl Scouts	+10%	–18%	–1%	+15%
Camp Fire	+20%	+25%	–40%	+33%
Key Club	+10%	–6%	+40%	+60%
YMCA	+54%	+56%	+55%	–4%
YWCA	+20%	+2%	–21%	0
Net % Change	**+24%**	**+8%**	**+16%**	**+3%**

Sources: *Encyclopedia of Associations 1961; Encyclopedia of Associations 1970; Encyclopedia of Associations 1980; Encyclopedia of Associations 1990; Encyclopedia of Associations 1999.* Calculations by author.

not easily captured in the membership statistics of national associations. Indeed, America in the 1980s seemed to experience a reinvigoration of that aspect of civil society that manifests itself in community efforts at local problem solving. As unofficial Reagan biographer Lou Cannon said, "On Main Street, the 1980s were more often than not a 'we decade.'"[65]

Contributions to charity increased by all possible measures: total contributions (up 56 percent in real terms through the decade), per capita contributions, and contributions as percentage of gross national product. The increase in charitable giving took place in both individual giving and corporate giving. Those increases were at rates half again higher than growth rates from 1955 to 1980, and they were considerably higher than growth rates that could have been statistically predicted on the basis of past experience given equivalent economic conditions. Charitable giving in the 1980s also increased faster than debt and faster than expenditures for numerous luxury items, such as jewelry and watches, health clubs, beauty parlors, and eating out. All in all, one study of charitable giving in the Reagan years proclaimed, "No matter how the record of giving is measured, the 1980s were in fact a decade of renewed charity and generosity."[66] This generosity was more remarkable when one realizes that the tax advantage of charitable giving declined significantly after income tax rates were cut starting in 1981, a change that had led a respected national think tank to publish a study predicting an absolute decline in charitable giving.[67]

The expansion in charitable giving that actually occurred reversed the trends of the previous two decades. In the words of Marvin Cetron and Owen Davies, during the 1960s and early 1970s "traditional charities seemed somehow obsolete; the only way to make changes that mattered was to storm the barricades in Washington until the government fell to its knees."[68] Perhaps as a result of this attitude, "total giving as a percentage of national income began a marked decline in the 1970s," before turning around in the late 1970s and growing significantly in the 1980s.[69] There were also some spectacular charity drives that utilized new approaches. The "all-star intercontinental rock extravaganza" raised seventy million dollars for Ethiopian famine relief (Live Aid) and nine million dollars for family farmers in the Midwest (Farm Aid).[70] "Hands Across America," a charity venture for the homeless and hungry, raised twenty million dollars when an estimated 5.4 million Americans attempted to create a transcontinental human chain in 1986.[71]

Similarly, voluntarism made a comeback in the 1980s. Cetron and Davies noted in 1989 that "one triumph of the Reagan administration was to make voluntarism fashionable again. . . . [D]espite accusations that today's yuppies are self-centered and even downright selfish, many young professionals are already making time to do volunteer work in many fields."[72] Habitat for Humanity, which built its first home for the poor in 1979, had fourteen U.S. affiliates in 1981; by 1990, there were five hundred Habitat affiliates in the United States.[73] In 1979, about three hundred companies had programs to encourage workers to participate in community service projects; by 1988 the number had grown to six hundred. By the late 1980s, at least two hundred companies were sending workers into the community on company time, volunteering fifty million hours of labor, worth five hundred million dollars. Overall, in 1987 an estimated eighty million adults volunteered 19.5 billion hours at a value of about $150 billion.[74] By way of comparison, that same year the Food Stamp program cost $12.4 billion, and all federal, state, and local-public assistance programs combined cost $110.7 billion.[75] In the half-decade following 1984, the number of Americans claiming to be involved in charity or volunteer work in Gallup Polls rose from 34 percent to 50 percent. On balance, it could be said at the end of the 1980s that "More Americans than ever before are giving their time and energy to others."[76]

Community involvement took other organized forms, as well. For example, Kimi Gray and her fellow residents won a fight for tenant control and operation of the Kenilworth-Parkside public housing project in Washington, D.C. Within a few years, Kenilworth-Parkside was a model housing project, cleaner and safer than the bulk of inner-city projects. Though the example was not perfectly replicable elsewhere—substantial federal resources were funneled to Kenilworth—the success of that experiment led numerous other projects to seek greater autonomy, and Kenilworth was a metaphor for greater bottom-up self-help in a variety of spheres.[77]

Americans also participated in increasing numbers in their own defense against crime. Neighborhood-watch committees expanded significantly in the 1980s, as did the "Crime Stopper" program. Likewise, the Guardian Angels, a volunteer anticrime group, started in 1979 and grew enormously in the eighties. By the mid-1980s, sixty thousand arrests were attributable to Crime Stoppers.[78] *U.S. News & World Report* observed that "more people are taking a part in the battle against criminals. . . . We've come out of the 'I don't want to get involved' syndrome. . . . Private citizens and law enforcers are enthusiastic about the rise of community anticrime spirit."[79] Ten million Americans were participating in some twenty thousand neighborhood-watch committees, and the National Crime Prevention Council estimated that nineteen to twenty million Americans were "actively involved in some form of community crime prevention."[80] At times there was a fine line between vigorous self-defense and vigilantism—in the most famous case, Bernard Goetz shot and wounded four reprobates who threatened him on a New York subway—but the crucial fact was that citizens in the 1980s organized their own large-scale resistance to crime rather than simply surrendering or leaving solutions to higher authorities.

The national campaign against drunk driving and for a federal twenty-one-year-old drinking age was led by Mothers Against Drunk Driving, an organization created in 1980 by women whose children had been killed or injured by drunk drivers. At the end of the decade MADD claimed one million members in four hundred local chapters. A companion group, Students Against Driving Drunk (SADD), was formed in 1981 and grew tremendously throughout the decade. SADD had 175 local chapters, many in high schools, in 1985; by 1990, the number of local chapters had exploded to 20,100.[81]

The increase in voluntarism also occurred on college campuses. In 1988, observers noted that this campus voluntarism "springs from grassroots sources (students are driving the movement) and . . . represents a renewed belief that ordinary citizens can solve the problems of society. . . . [C]ampus-based community service has moved to center stage for students and educators."[82] Between 1981 and 1988, the number of states actively encouraging youth-volunteer efforts went from two to forty; by decade's end, more than two hundred school districts and a quarter of all colleges included volunteer service in their curricula.[83] By some estimates, the core of campus volunteers rose by 400 percent just from 1984 to 1988.[84] A volunteer coordinator at Harvard explained, "In the 1970s, students were more involved with rhetoric; now they want to do things."[85]

Civil Society: Families

In one very important respect, family trends during the 1980s continued deteriorating. The illegitimacy rate, which had been 5 percent in 1960, rose from 18 percent of all births in 1980 to 28 percent in 1990. This increase was evident among both whites and blacks, doubling among whites (from 11 percent to 21 percent) and going up by one-fifth among blacks (from 55 percent to 65 percent). Overall, the proportion of families headed by single parents continued growing, from 21 percent in 1980 to 27 percent in 1990.[86]

In many other important respects, however, the condition of American families improved in the 1980s. The divorce rate peaked and then went down for the first time in three decades. The number of children affected by divorce also dropped throughout the 1980s (see table 6.2). While demographic shifts may have played a role, these declines were at least partially the result of a gradual reestablishment of a view of marriage as a lifetime commitment, to be taken seriously. Contemporary news accounts reported that "marriage is back in style after two decades during which men and women dabbled at alternative lifestyles."[87]

After rapid growth post–*Roe v. Wade*, the abortion rate in America also stabilized and then gradually fell throughout the 1980s. Among teenagers, one of the proximate causes of increased illegitimacy rates was the combination of increased pregnancy rates with stabilized abortion rates; by 1990, for the first time since *Roe*, almost as many pregnant teenagers carried their children to term as had abortions.[88]

TABLE 6.2
Divorce Rate and Children Affected by Divorce, 1960–1990

	Divorce Rate*	Children Affected by Divorce
1960	9.2	463,000
1970	14.9	870,000
1980	22.6	1,174,000
1990	20.7	1,005,000

*Divorces per 1,000 married women.
Source: National Center for Health Statistics; Census Bureau. Cited by William J. Bennett, *Index of Leading Cultural Indicators*, vol. 1 (1993), 14–15.

Civil Society: Religion

In the 1980s two social observers noted "a dramatic return to faith by formerly irreligious Americans. . . . The generation that once embraced the illicit joys of sex, drugs, and rock and roll is finding its way into church, and many of today's college students are joining them."[89] Overall church membership stabilized as a percentage and in absolute terms rose from 135 million to 148 million. Church attendance—not necessarily, of course, synonymous with membership—also went up. The percentage of the electorate reporting that it "never" attended church fell from 23.3 percent in 1980 to 21.1 percent in 1988, and the proportion reporting that it "regularly" or "often" attended rose from 48 percent to 50.4 percent, reversing a significant downward trend that had started in the early 1960s.[90] Religious organizations on college campuses drew increasing numbers of students.[91] Among older baby-boomers, religious participation increased from 34 percent in the 1970s to 43 percent in the early 1980s.[92] Christian television and radio stations grew exponentially in number, and Christian schools became "the fastest growing sector of private education."[93]

Moreover, the overall stabilization of church membership masked an important trend. The religious revival of the 1980s clearly drew most of its energy from the theologically conservative churches. Those denominations most inclined to accommodate themselves to the negative social trends of recent decades continued losing membership. The denominations least likely to make such accommodations, and most likely to insist on stricter standards of moral behavior, grew substantially, not least among educated suburbanites.[94]

Many secular citizens as well as members of the more liberal churches viewed this development with dismay. They were particularly disconcerted by the increasing forays of some (though hardly all) of the conservative churches into politics, though the tactic was borrowed from the liberal churches active in the civil rights and anti–Vietnam War movements. Looking to medieval Europe or modern-day Iran, some even feared the onslaught of a theocracy. The primary social significance of the growth of the conservative churches, however, lay in the fact that increasing numbers of Americans were consciously choosing to reject the amorality and hedonism that seemed to have become ascendant in American society since the mid-1960s.

Polls throughout the 1980s consistently showed the American people placing a higher priority on religion and expressing a belief that religion was becoming more important in society. A 1986 Gallup poll showed that 48 percent believed that religious influence in America was gaining, up from only 14 percent in 1969 and 36 percent in 1977. A total of 51 percent said that they were more interested in spiritual matters than they had been five years before. Among the young, more college students went to church, and more students evinced a belief that religion should be an important part of life. George Gallup declared this shift to be "a very dramatic trend": the number of people aged eighteen to twenty-nine taking part in religious education doubled to 35 percent from 1980 to 1984, and from 1979 to 1984 the proportion saying that religion was important grew from 39 percent to 50 percent.[95] Contemporary accounts held that "people are growing bolder about standing up for their beliefs—and the place of the spiritual in American life."[96] In short, a major newsmagazine declared in 1987 that "religion in America is back. . . . The God-is-dead philosophy is itself dead."[97] It was symbolic of the times that in the 1980s two ministers—Jesse Jackson on the Left and Pat Robertson on the Right—launched presidential campaigns and scored some campaign successes.

This revival was clearly incomplete. It could not be said at the end of the 1980s that American society and culture had returned wholeheartedly to its Judeo-Christian roots, and even many Christian analysts questioned the depth of commitment of many self-identified Christians in America.[98] The antics of televangelists like Jim Bakker and Jimmy Swaggart were often distracting. It was also almost certainly true that the social, political, and conceptual gap between the religiously committed and wholly secularized elements of American society widened during the 1980s.[99] Nevertheless, if Reagan was right about the importance of religion to the health of society, the 1980s contained more good news than had any recent decade.

Other Social Outcomes in the 1980s

Crime

In the 1980s, violent crime resumed rising after a dip in mid-decade, and juvenile violent crime arrest rates increased. However, in other respects the crime situation improved markedly, especially in contrast to the previous two decades. The total crime rate actually declined by 2 percent from 1980 to 1990, the first decline in three decades. The murder rate declined by 8 percent, and overall violent crime, while continuing to increase, rose at a much slower rate than in the 1960s or 1970s: it increased 126 percent in the 1960s and 64 percent in the 1970s, but only 22 percent in the 1980s.[100] Indeed, both total crime and violent crime rates actually fell substantially from 1980 to 1985, though both moved up again at the end of the decade (see table 6.3).

Substance Abuse

The influx of illegal drugs into the United States continued in the 1980s,[101] and crack cocaine became widely available in American cities in the latter half of the decade. Nevertheless, most evidence pointed to an improvement in the

TABLE 6.3
Crime Rate Changes, 1960–1990

	Total Crime Rate	Violent Crime Rate
1960–1970	+111%	+126%
1970–1980	+49%	+64%
1980–1990	−2%	+22%

Source: Federal Bureau of Investigation, cited by Bennett, *Index*, vol. 1, 3. Calculations by author.

drug problem throughout the 1980s. Former drug control director William Bennett was able to say at the end of the 1980s that "overall drug use is at its lowest levels since the government started collecting information on drug usage in the 1970s."[102] Rates of marijuana use, cocaine use, and the use of hallucinogens among high school students dropped considerably throughout the decade. The proportion of high school seniors, for example, who said that they had used marijuana fell from 60 percent in 1981 to 41 percent in 1990. Similarly, cocaine use fell from 17 percent to 9 percent of the population, and use of hallucinogens fell from 13 percent to 9 percent.[103]

There were numerous other indications that drug use was on the decline. For instance, from 1979 to 1990 the percentage of persons aged twelve to seventeen reporting that they had used illicit drugs in their lifetime fell from 34 percent to 23 percent, and the number reporting use in the past year fell from 26 percent to 16 percent. Similarly, among those aged eighteen to twenty-five, lifetime drug use fell from 70 percent to 56 percent. Among persons twenty-six and older, those using drugs in the past year went up slightly in the early 1980s before falling back in 1990 to near the same level as in 1979, about 10 percent.[104] On a different front, per capita adult liquor consumption declined throughout the 1980s, and highway fatalities, including fatalities caused by drunk driving, also dropped steadily.[105]

Regarding both drugs and alcohol, the boundaries of socially acceptable behavior moved toward greater self-restraint. By the mid-1980s, even entertainment-industry attitudes toward substance abuse shifted demonstrably, as most drug users and dealers in movies "suddenly became villains and losers" after more than a decade of idealization. Designated drivers were also increasingly written into the plots of movies and television sitcoms; from 1987 to 1990 more than a hundred television episodes included a designated driver.[106]

Education

While American students continued to show poorly in standardized tests compared to students from other industrial democracies, the educational decline of the previous two decades was arrested. The sharp decline of SAT scores from 1960 to 1980 was halted, and scores crept upward for the first time in three decades (see table 6.4). High school dropout rates, after remaining steady in the 1970s, fell considerably in the 1980s.[107] Despite rising college costs, a significantly larger percentage of young Americans had four years or more of college; in 1980, 20 percent of men and 13 percent of women over the age of twenty-five fell into that category, while by 1990 it was 24 percent of men and 18 percent of women.[108]

Reagan and Society: Evaluations

Two observations can be made without much difficulty about society and social policy in the 1980s. First, Reagan faced, diagnosed, and attempted to mitigate a significant social deterioration rooted in the 1960s. His diagnosis traced the social crisis to the confluence of counterculture mores and Great Society governance. In this view, the counterculture had deliberately undermined respect for "bourgeois" virtues like self-restraint, moral responsibility, duty to the community, and respect for the law—virtues underpinned by family, religion, and patriotism, which also came under assault. Simultaneously, the law had subsidized one-parent families, made divorce easier to obtain, mandated abortion on demand, increasingly drove religion from the public square, and eased criminal penalties. More generally, the strength of civil society had been undermined by a centralizing government that had appropriated a variety of functions previously left to state and local governments, private groups, communities, and families. Reagan's prescription was to confront the two cardinal errors of the 1960s. If law and culture were largely responsible for Fukuyama's great disruption, a decidedly different vision of law and culture—rooted in the overlapping principles of the Founders, Tocqueville, conservative Christianity, and neoconservativism—would be promoted instead.

Second, despite the continuation of some negative social trends, if the state of American society in the Reagan years had to be reduced to a single

TABLE 6.4
SAT Scores, 1960–1990

Year	Average Combined SAT Score
1960	975
1970	948
1980	890
1990	900

Source: The College Board, cited by Bennett, *Index*, vol. 1, 30.

sentence, it would be that most things stopped getting worse and many actually started getting better. The social component of the architecture of freedom was strengthened. Indeed, the 1980s offered the first tentative signs since the onset of the great disruption that it was still possible for Americans to reinvigorate the Tocquevillian "customs and manners" that undergirded their freedom and social happiness. Compared directly to administration goals, actual social outcomes in the 1980s were a failure in regard to illegitimacy rates but at least a qualified success regarding civic organizations, civic participation, religion, divorce and abortion rates, crime, drug usage, and educational indicators like SAT scores and high school dropout rates. Whatever the reason, America seemed to turn a social corner. In ways as diverse as a major drop in crime, a stabilization of the teen pregnancy rate, continued falling rates of divorce and abortion, a growing religious revival, and the onset of the civil society movement, America in the 1990s continued in the direction established in the Reagan years.

Beyond these two observations, analysis is complicated by several factors. First, many analysts detected a certain ambivalence in Reagan himself toward the social agenda his administration embraced. On particularly divisive issues like abortion and school prayer, Reagan often used the bully pulpit but rarely expended political capital on legislation, even when he seemed to have capital to spare. This record led some of his socially conservative supporters to feel taken for granted, if not betrayed. At a minimum, he clearly considered the economic and national security crises more pressing and devoted significantly more energy to their resolution. Furthermore, his own background arguably made it politically, or even emotionally, difficult for Reagan to participate in the sort of full-scale legislative press many social conservatives expected. He himself was divorced with few apparent regrets, and as governor of California he had signed what was at the time one of the most liberal abortion laws in the country (though he later said he had not anticipated that the law would lead to abortion on demand). Some analysts postulated that he was uncomfortable with the certitude shown by some of his social allies.[109] In any event, though he was always able to illuminate looming dangers, Reagan was more comfortable with a rhetoric of optimism than with the rhetoric of pessimism, or even despair, that was often heard from those allies and that may have been a necessary precondition for a more serious frontal assault on some of the social problems facing the nation.

Second, the issues themselves formed a complicated mixture. Reagan's position—limited government as part of the solution, more active government (for instance, in the war on drugs) as another part—provoked charges of inconsistency. From one perspective, Reagan's policy was more consistently libertarian on the economy than on social issues. However, it is easy to miss a subtle point. In a sense, Reagan applied the same standard of ordered liberty to both the economy and social issues: The maximum degree of liberty consistent with an orderly society was to be preferred. The difference came in his diagnosis of what had gone wrong in each sphere. It might be said that Reagan perceived the economic crisis to have derived, relatively simply, from too little liberty but the social crisis to have derived from both too little liberty and too much license. In any event, it was much harder to summarize Reagan's social policy than his economic policy, and those looking for a thread of coherence had to look a bit deeper.

Not least, analysis of the two obvious social facts of the 1980s is complicated because it is even more difficult to establish causation with social policy than with economic policy. Social trends produced by the individual choices of tens of millions of people can never simply be laid at the doorstep of a president or an administration. To attempt to do so would betray an unfounded belief in the easy malleability of human beings and the capacity of government and politics to engineer human societies. Ultimately, the partial recovery of American society in the 1980s came about because a large number of Americans were increasingly concerned about what their country was becoming and were resolved to change it. The incomplete social recovery of the 1980s was driven from the bottom up, by neighborhood-watch committees and Crime Stoppers, by MADD and SADD, by Kimi Gray and Polly Williams, by thousands of Optimist Clubs and school partnerships and churches, and by millions of volunteers for and contributors to charitable causes.

Nevertheless, if law matters in the shaping of society—not only by what it allows but by what it teaches—then so does government. If culture establishes the direction of society by communicating what is acceptable and what is not, then politics—which is in no small measure about communication—necessarily contributes to culture. What presidential administrations cannot control, they can either promote and encourage or inhibit and undermine. In the area of social health, the test of statesmanship in the 1980s was whether the president would promote, encourage, and even rally the sentiment for change, despite the unpopularity of such a course among the media and academic elites who largely controlled the day-to-day interpretation of events. It can be said that Reagan passed this test. What he could do to contribute to the social recovery, he mostly did. What he could have done to harm, he mostly avoided. What he could not do, he left to the American people to work out in a greater measure of freedom. Reagan provided moral leadership on behalf of a simple yet seemingly effective formula: a rediscovery of old virtues and a government strong enough to ensure justice but humble enough to give free civil society its due.

On some dimensions, that is the most that can be said. Reagan owed at least as much to the religious revival as it owed to him, though he clearly encouraged and legitimized it. On other dimensions, however, a much clearer link can be established between policy and outcome. For instance, the administration's preference for incarceration and order was largely responsible for the brighter outlook on crime in the 1980s and beyond. By one estimate, the tripling of the prison population from 1975 to 1989 prevented at least 390,000 murders, rapes, robberies, and aggravated assaults in 1989 alone.[110] The importance of Reagan's antidrug emphasis can at least be strongly inferred: almost as soon as that emphasis was given up by the Clinton administration, drug use began growing again. To the extent that progress was made on education in the 1980s, the process of change was set in motion by Reagan's reform commission, advanced by key administration officials like education secretary William Bennett, made possible by federal respect for state and local innovation, legitimized by a cultural change in the intellectual terms of debate, and brought to fruition by the activity of civil society.

In a broader sense, a strong case can be made that Reagan's policies—both active and passive, both legal and rhetorical—contributed to the strengthening of civil society, and that the strengthening of civil society contributed to the progress America made on its more specific problems in the 1980s and beyond. The relimiting of government was central to that process. In his discussion of the "great disruption," Francis Fukuyama attributed part of the recent social recovery to a natural process of spontaneous self-organization.[111] That spontaneity, however, depends for its success on the willingness of those with political power to permit it to operate. Yet the dominant ethos of the welfare state from Theodore Roosevelt or Woodrow Wilson until Reagan was to distrust social spontaneity, preferring instead the organized planning of experts. If Fukuyama is right, Americans were fortunate that Reagan broke the mold by preferring freedom and spontaneity over planning and supposed expertise. The revival of civil society in the 1980s was at once crucial for strengthening the social infrastructure of democracy and made possible by the renewed attention given to principles of liberty and limited government in the political realm.

Furthermore, Reagan's preference for spontaneity and strong civil society has subsequently become a new norm, or at least has come to compete effectively with the old norm. In the 1980s, the tendency of liberals to consider idealism to be synonymous with support for big government was pronounced. During the 1988 presidential campaign, Michael Dukakis assured a debate audience that he did not know what George Bush meant by his call for a "thousand points of light." Only weeks later, Harvard president Derek Bok dismissed the evidence of burgeoning community service by declaring, "I don't see the beginning yet of a real upturn in idealism. What I see is a heartening upturn in community service, which indicates there is a spirit that could be challenged by government. We need some important successes by government that show what it can do."[112]

This ill-concealed skepticism of (if not contempt for) the institutions of independent civil society did not survive the 1980s. The three successive Reagan-Bush victories and the subsequent social mobilization of voluntarism combined to shift fundamentally the center of gravity on this question.

Instead, the 1990s saw the development of a new intellectual movement, spanning the political spectrum, dedicated to the restoration of American civil society. As Don E. Eberly describes it, this civil society movement "reflects a search for a new citizenship that is less self-centered, more civil, and civically engaged. It is an attempt to draw Americans together again at a time of isolation and fragmentation, to restore community institutions, to transcend political differences in order to become neighbors again, to recover the spirit of volunteerism, and more."[113] By the middle 1990s, organizations like the National Commission on Civic Renewal, the Communitarian Network, the Points of Light Foundation, the Alliance for National Renewal, and the Civic Practices Network worked to strengthen civic engagement. Furthermore, Eberly points out, "The social landscape is coming alive with new movements to recover character, ethics, sexual responsibility, fatherhood, marriage, and a less corrupt popular culture."[114]

Reflecting the influence of this new movement, the 1990s saw the active encouragement of voluntarism exemplified by the volunteer summit headed by Colin Powell and George H. W. Bush. After dipping at the beginning of the decade, charitable contributions resumed their upward trend, and surveys of college freshmen showed a continuing surge of interest in community voluntarism, surpassing even that of the 1980s. By 1997, more than 70 percent said they had performed volunteer work within the previous year.[115] In 2000, the two leading presidential contenders, Al Gore and George W. Bush, made commitment to strengthening and utilizing faith-based community organizations an important part of their public appeals.

That the social improvements of the 1980s were uneven—and that they failed to restore society to the level of health it had enjoyed in 1960—shows that it cannot be said with certainty whether the 1980s represented a permanent turning of the cultural tide. Some social commentators, like Gertrude Himmelfarb, have argued that the revival of moral traditionalism has led both to an improvement of some social indices and to greater division in society, between a dominant culture of permissiveness and a resurgent dissident culture opposing it.[116] And many of Reagan's strongest critics are hardly apt to accept an interpretation that credits either his diagnosis of or his prescription for the social harms he inherited. To accede that point would require surrendering the myth of the benign sixties, the assumption of the progressive nature of secularism, Marxist and feminist shibboleths regarding the family, and a variety of other beliefs tightly held by many intellectuals. Nevertheless, it bears noting that no comprehensive alternative explanation for the improvement in social indices in the 1980s has been offered by any of Reagan's critics.

Notes

1. William J. Bennett, *The Index of Leading Cultural Indicators* (Washington, D.C.: Heritage Foundation and Empower America, March 1993), vol. 1, 2.

2. "The U.S. Family: Help!" *Time*, December 28, 1970, 34.

3. Robert D. Putnam, "Bowling Alone: America's Declining Social Capital," *Journal of Democracy* (January 1995), 65–78.

4. Francis Fukuyama, *The Great Disruption: Human Nature and the Reconstitution of Social Order* (New York: Free Press, 1999), 64–70.

5. Fukuyama himself credited both law and culture (which he called the "most plausible" of the four common theories) but made an additional claim: that the great disruption was driven by the economic transition from an industrial economy to an information economy. Such an account may help to explain why social disruption crossed national boundaries; far from being confined to the United States, phenomena like higher crime, family breakdown, and drug abuse were common to one degree or another in most Western industrial societies starting in the 1960s. It falls short, however, in explaining why the breakdown began in earnest before the information revolution was under way on a mass scale, or why it has seemingly stabilized at the very time when the economic revolution is reaching full throttle.

6. Gertrude Himmelfarb, *The Demoralization of Society: From Victorian Virtues to Modern Values* (New York: Knopf, 1995).

7. John G. West Jr., "George Washington and the Religious Impulse," in *Patriot Sage: George Washington and the American Political Tradition,* ed. Gary Gregg II and Matthew Spalding (Wilmington, Del.: Intercollegiate Studies Insitute [hereafter ISI], 1999), 267.

8. James H. Hutson, *Religion and the Founding of the American Republic* (Washington, D.C.: Library of Congress, 1998), 81.

9. Alexis de Tocqueville, *Democracy in America* (New York: Vintage, 1945), vol. 1, chap. 11; vol. 2, book 4, chap. 7.

10. Tocqueville, *Democracy in America,* vol. 1, 310–26; vol. 2, 133–35.

11. Tocqueville, *Democracy in America,* vol. 1, 316.

12. James Q. Wilson, *Thinking about Crime,* rev. ed. (New York: Basic, 1983), 237. See chapter 12 in general. Amplifying this theme a decade later, Wilson argued that there is no complete explanation for the post-1960 increase in crime "that does not assign an important role to a profound cultural shift in the strength of either social constraints or internal conscience or both." James Q. Wilson, *The Moral Sense* (New York: Free Press, 1993), 9.

13. Charles Murray, *Losing Ground: American Social Policy 1950–1980* (New York: Basic, 1984).

14. Lawrence Mead, *Beyond Entitlement: The Social Obligations of Citizenship* (New York: Free Press, 1986).

15. George Gilder, *Wealth and Poverty* (New York: Basic, 1981).

16. For further discussion of this phenomenon, see George H. Nash, *The Conservative Intellectual Movement in America since 1945* (Wilmington, Del.: ISI, 1996), 329–37.

17. William E. Pemberton, *Exit with Honor: The Life and Presidency of Ronald Reagan* (Armonk, N.Y.: M. E. Sharpe, 1998), 58.

18. Steven K. Wisensale, "Family Policy during the Reagan Years: The Private Side of the Conservative Agenda," in *Ronald Reagan's America*, ed. Eric J. Schmertz, Natalie Datlof, and Alexej Ugrinsky (Westport, Conn.: Greenwood, 1997), vol. 1, p. 281.

19. For example, Whitehead showed that divorce scars children emotionally for years. Families headed by a single parent, whether divorced or never married, are far more likely to live in poverty than their two-parent counterparts. Children who grow up in single-parent homes are significantly more likely to take drugs, commit crimes, drop out of school, commit suicide, and become single parents themselves than children who grow up in two-parent homes. Over 70 percent of juveniles in state reform institutions come from homes without both parents. Barbara Defoe Whitehead, "Dan Quayle Was Right," *The Atlantic Monthly*, April 1993.

20. David Popenoe, "The Controversial Truth: Two-Parent Families Are Better," *New York Times*, December 26, 1992, I 21.

21. For summaries of the voluminous evidence on this score, see Gunther Lewy, *Why America Needs Religion* (Grand Rapids, Mich.: Eerdmans, 1996), esp. 87–115; Patrick F. Fagan, "Why Religion Matters: The Impact of Religious Practice on Social Stability," *Heritage Foundation Backgrounder*, no. 1064, January 25, 1996. See also Bill Scanlon, "If Longevity Is Your Goal, Go to Church," *Rocky Mountain News*, May 19, 1999, 5A; Martha Sawyer Allen, "Survey: Church a Blessing for Teens," *Rocky Mountain News*, February 19, 1994, 8D. Studies of prejudice have indicated that the most religious have levels of prejudice that are lower than those of the nonreligious; marginally religious people, who attend church infrequently and have not internalized religious doctrines, are more prejudiced than either the highly religious or the nonreligious.

22. Lewy, *Why America Needs Religion*, 114.

23. William G. Mayer, *The Changing American Mind* (Ann Arbor: University of Michigan Press, 1992); John J. DiIulio Jr., "New Crime Policies for America," in *The New Promise of American Life*, ed. Lamar Alexander and Chester E. Finn Jr. (Indianapolis: Hudson Institute, 1995), 264–65.

24. George Barna and William Paul McKay, *Vital Signs: Emerging Social Trends and the Future of American Christianity* (Westchester, Ill.: Crossway, 1984), 22–23; Nathan Glazer, "The 'Social Agenda,'" in *Perspectives on the Reagan Years*, ed. John L. Palmer (Washington, D.C.: Urban Institute, 1986), 20–21, and more generally, 15–22.

25. Burton Yale Pines, *Back to Basics: The Traditionalist Movement That Is Sweeping Grass-Roots America* (New York: William Morrow, 1982).

26. "Radio Address to the Nation on the Federal Judiciary, June 21, 1986," *Public Papers of the President: Ronald Reagan 1986* (Washington, D.C.: Government Printing Office [hereafter GPO], 1988), 818.

27. Bennett, *Index*, 3.

28. See Ben Wattenberg, "GOP's Faith in Punishment May Not Have Been in Vain," *Rocky Mountain News*, August 30, 1993, 35A; "Breakdown of the Justice System," *U.S. News & World Report*, January 17, 1994, 27.

29. Geraldine Woods, *Drug Abuse in Society* (Santa Barbara, Calif.: ABC-CLIO, 1993), 101.

30. *Sourcebook of Criminal Justice Statistics 1981* (Washington, D.C.: Department of Justice, 1981), 338; *Sourcebook of Criminal Justice Statistics 1991* (Washington, D.C.: Department of Justice, 1991), 432.

31. William Ker Muir Jr., *The Bully Pulpit: The Presidential Leadership of Ronald Reagan* (San Francisco: ICS, 1992), 129.

32. "Address before the 43rd Session of the United Nations General Assembly, September 26, 1988," *Public Papers of the Presidents: Ronald Reagan 1988* (Washington, D.C.: GPO, 1991), 1225.

33. Ronald Reagan, *An American Life: The Autobiography* (New York: Simon and Schuster, 1990), 226.

34. Muir, *The Bully Pulpit*, 141.

35. "Acceptance Speech by Governor Ronald Reagan," Republican National Convention, Detroit, Michigan, July 17, 1980.

36. "Proclamation 5576—National Family Week, 1986, November 21, 1986," *Public Papers of the Presidents: Ronald Reagan 1986* (Washington, D.C.: GPO, 1988), 1578.

37. "Radio Address to the Nation on Family Values, December 20, 1986," *Public Papers of the Presidents: Ronald Reagan 1986* (Washington, D.C.: GPO, 1988), 1137–38.

38. Wisensale, "Family Policy during the Reagan Years," 282.

39. Wisensale, "Family Policy during the Reagan Years," 283–84.

40. Barbara Ehrenreich, *The Worst Years of Our Lives: Irreverent Notes from a Decade of Greed* (New York: Pantheon, 1990), 3–4.

41. Susan Faludi, *Backlash: The Undeclared War against American Women* (New York: Crown, 1991).

42. Lars-Erik Nelson, "Family Values Are Now a Liberal Cause," *Denver Post*, November 7, 1993, 4D.

43. "Exchange with Reporters, December 3, 1993," *Presidential Papers of the Presidents: Bill Clinton 1993* (Washington, D.C.: GPO, 1994), 2103.

44. United States National Commission on Excellence in Education, *A Nation at Risk: The Imperative for Educational Reform: A Report to the Nation and the Secretary of Education, United States Department of Education* (Washington, D.C.: GPO, 1983).

45. United States Department of Education, *The Nation Responds: Recent Efforts to Improve Education* (Washington, D.C.: GPO, 1984).

46. "Acceptance Speech by Governor Reagan," 1.

47. See Reagan, *An American Life*, 342.

48. "Remarks at the Annual Convention of the National Religious Broadcasters," January 30, 1984, *Public Papers of the Presidents: Ronald Reagan 1984* (Washington, D.C.: GPO, 1986), 121.

49. Dinesh D'Souza, *Ronald Reagan: How an Ordinary Man Became an Extraordinary Leader* (New York: Free Press, 1997), 118.

50. "Remarks at the Annual Meeting of the National Alliance of Business, October 5, 1981," *Public Papers of the Presidents: Ronald Reagan 1981* (Washington, D.C.: GPO, 1982), 883, 886.

51. "Remarks and a Question and Answer Session at a White House Reception for Participants in the Youth Volunteer Conference, November 12, 1982," *Public Papers of the Presidents: Ronald Reagan 1982* (Washington, D.C.: GPO, 1983), 1460; "Remarks at a Luncheon Meeting with Members of the President's Task Force on Private Sector Initiatives, December 2, 1981," *Public Papers of the Presidents: Ronald Reagan 1981* (Washington, D.C.: GPO, 1982), 1109; Muir, *The Bully Pulpit*, 59–60.

52. Muir, *The Bully Pulpit*, 58.

53. Reagan, *An American Life*, 342.

54. Renée A. Berger, "Private Sector Initiatives in the Reagan Era: New Actors Rework an Old Theme," in *The Reagan Presidency and the Governing of America*, ed. Lester M. Salamon and Michael S. Lund (Washington, D.C.: Urban Institute, 1984), 201.

55. Berger, "Private Sector Initiatives in the Reagan Era," 201.

56. Berger, "Private Sector Initiatives in the Reagan Era," 206–209.

57. John B. Olsen, "Assessing an Unfinished but Promising Experiment," in *The Reagan Presidency*, ed. Salamon and Lund, 218.

58. See Richard C. Cornuelle, *Reclaiming the American Dream: The Role of Private Individuals and Voluntary Associations* (New Brunswick, N.J.: Transaction, 1993), 197.

59. "Radio Address to the Nation on Independence Day and the Centennial of the Statue of Liberty, July 5, 1986," *Public Papers of the Presidents: Ronald Reagan 1986* (Washington, D.C.: GPO, 1988), 925.

60. Tocqueville, *Democracy in America*, vol. 1, chap. 14, 261–62.

61. Putnam, "Bowling Alone."

62. See Nancy Yakes and Denise Akey, eds., *Encyclopedia of Associations 1980*, 14th ed. (Detroit: Gale Research, 1980); Deborah M. Burek, Karen E. Koek, and Annette Novallo eds., *Encyclopedia of Associations 1990*, 24th ed. (Detroit: Gale Research, 1990).

63. See *Encyclopedia of Associations*, 3rd ed. (Detroit: Gale Research, 1961); Margaret Fisk, ed., *Encyclopedia of Associations*, 6th ed. (Detroit: Gale Research, 1970); Yakes and Akey, *Encyclopedia of Associations*; Burek, Koek, and Novallo, *Enclyclopedia of Associations*; Christine Maurer and Tara E. Sheets, eds., *Encyclopedia of Associations*, 34th ed. (Detroit: Gale Research, 1999).

64. Don E. Eberly, *America's Promise: Civil Society and the Renewal of American Culture* (Lanham, Md.: Rowman & Littlefield, 1998), 84–85; Thomas Hargrove and Guido H. Stempel III, "America Losing the Volunteer Spirit," *Rocky Mountain News*, December 28, 1993, 20A.

65. Lou Cannon, *President Reagan: The Role of a Lifetime* (New York: Simon and Schuster, 1991), 831.

66. Richard B. McKenzie, "Decade of Greed?" *National Review*, August 31, 1992, 52–54; also, Richard B. McKenzie, *What Went Right in the 1980s* (San Francisco: Pacific Research Institute for Public Policy, 1994), chap. 3.

67. Lester M. Salamon and Alan J. Abramson, *The Federal Government and the Nonprofit Sector: The Impact of the 1981 Tax Act on Charitable Giving* (Washington D.C.: Urban Institute, 1981).

68. Marvin Cetron and Owen Davies, *American Renaissance* (New York: St. Martin's, 1989), 94.

69. McKenzie, "Decade of Greed?"

70. See Michael Barone, "1983: Falling Walls, Rising Dreams," *U.S. News & World Report*, October 25, 1993, 61.

71. "Hands across America Organizers Estimate Turnout at 5,442,960," *Washington Post*, May 30, 1986, A2.

72. Cetron and Davies, *American Renaissance*, 94.

73. Habitat for Humanity International Website, historical information, www.habitat.org/.

74. See "The New Volunteerism," *Newsweek*, February 8, 1988, 42–43; "Special Report: The New Volunteers," *Newsweek*, July 10, 1989, 36–66.

75. "Social Welfare Expenditures under Public Programs," *The 1992 Information Please Almanac* (Boston: Information Please LLC, 1992), 64.

76. "Special Report: The New Volunteers"; "The New Volunteerism."

77. For numerous other examples, see "Special Report: The New Volunteers," 36–66.

78. "Street Crime: People Fight Back," *U.S. News & World Report*, April 15, 1985, 42.

79. "Street Crime: People Fight Back," 42, 46.

80. After experiencing a crime wave in 1986, a Richmond, Virginia, neighborhood organized an anticrime patrol and information network. Within a year, crime had fallen from three murders, two rapes, and 134 burglaries to no murders, no rapes, and twenty burglaries. A New Orleans housing project similarly established patrols and successfully enforced a "drug free zone." "Fighting Crime: Talk or Action?" *U.S. News & World Report*, April 21, 1986, 74; "Street Crime: People Fight Back," 42; "Special Report: The New Volunteers," 36–66.

81. See Denise S. Akey and Katherine Gruber, eds., *Encyclopedia of Associations 1985*, 19th ed. (Detroit: Gale Research, 1985); Burek, Koek, and Novallo, eds., *Encyclopedia of Associations 1990*.

82. Kathryn T. Theus, "Campus-Based Community Service," *Change* (September–October 1988), 27.

83. Theus, "Campus-Based Community Service," 30; "Special Report: The New Volunteers."

84. Theus, "Campus-Based Community Service," 33.

85. "America's Youth in Search of a Cause," *U.S. News & World Report*, April 16, 1984, 32.

86. Bennett, *Index*, 9, 15.

87. "Marriage: It's Back in Style!" *U.S. News & World Report*, June 20, 1983, 44.

88. See Bennett, *Index*, 17.

89. Cetron and Davies, *American Renaissance*, 296–97. See also Martin Marty, "What People Seek—and Find—in Belief," *U.S. News & World Report*, December 29, 1986–January 5, 1987, 43.

90. National Election Surveys, reported in Ruy A. Texeira, *The Disappearing American Voter* (Washington, D.C.: Brookings Institution, 1992), 38.

91. "America's Youth in Search of a Cause," 32.

92. "Americans Return to Church and Temple," *U.S. News & World Report*, January 5, 1987, 40.

93. Susan D. Rose, "Gender, Education, and the New Christian Right," *Society* (January–February 1989), 60.

94. This growth of the conservative and evangelical churches had already begun in the late 1970s; see "Back to that Oldtime Religion," *Time*, December 26, 1977, 52–59.

95. "A Revival of Religion on Campus," *U.S. News & World Report*, January 9, 1984, 44.

96. "A Search for the Sacred," *U.S. News & World Report*, April 4, 1983, 35. See also "Americans Return to Church and Temple," 40; Ronald Schiller, "How Religious Are We?" *Reader's Digest*, May 1986, 102–104.

97. "Americans Return to Church and Temple," 40.

98. See Barna and McKay, *Vital Signs*; Richard John Neuhaus, "So Little Change, So Much Difference," *National Review*, March 24, 1989, 20; Kenneth L. Woodward, "The Rites of Americans," *Newsweek*, November 29, 1993, 80–82.

99. See Stephen L. Carter, *The Culture of Disbelief: How American Law and Politics Trivialize Religious Devotion* (New York: Basic, 1993).

100. Bennett, *Index*, 2; calculations by author.

101. It was estimated that the 55,897 kilograms of cocaine interdicted in 1988 represented only 10 percent of the cocaine coming into the country. See Harrison Rainie, "His Moment Arrives," *U.S. News & World Report*, January 30, 1989, 22.

102. "Rethinking Drugs," *The National Journal*, February 2, 1991.

103. Bennett, *Index*, 19.

104. See Woods, *Drug Abuse in Society*, 86–89.

105. "A Sobering Decision," *U.S. News & World Report*, April 7, 1986, 79.

106. Michael Medved, *Hollywood vs. America* (New York: HarperCollins, 1993), 337–38.

107. See Bennett, *Index*, 30–31.

108. Judith Waldrop and Thomas Exter, "Legacy of the 1980s," *American Demographics* (March 1991).

109. Sidney M. Milkis and Marc Landy, *Presidential Greatness* (Lawrence: University of Kansas Press, 2000), 224.

110. DiIulio, "New Crime Policies for America," 272. See also Michael K. Block and Steven J. Twist, "Lessons from the Eighties: Incarceration Works," *Commonsense* (Spring 1994), 73–83.

111. Fukuyama, *The Great Disruption*, 275, 279.

112. "Idealism's Rebirth," *U.S. News & World Report*, October 24, 1988, 40.

113. See Eberly, *America's Promise*, 5. More generally, esp. 19–33.

114. Eberly, *America's Promise*, 28.

115. Rene Sanches, "Survey of College Freshmen Finds Rise in Volunteerism," *Washington Post*, January 13, 1997, 1.

116. Gertrude Himmelfarb, *One Nation, Two Cultures: A Moral Divide* (New York: Knopf, 1999).

7

Reagan and the Cold War

"American policy in the 1980s was a catalyst for the collapse of the Soviet Union."

Former KGB general Oleg Kalugin

IN 1980, THE SOVIET UNION posed a serious threat to the United States, America's allies, and the principle of self-government around the world. In 1990, the Berlin Wall was gone, the Warsaw Pact had disintegrated in all but name, and the Soviet Union was only months away from ceasing to exist as a nation. The United States had won what had been, for all practical purposes, the third world war.

Far from being either accidental or inevitable, this foreign policy triumph was the result of a coherent strategic vision forged and implemented by Ronald Reagan against much opposition and great odds. In the words of historian Stephen E. Ambrose, "Not in half a century had a President handed over to his successor an American foreign policy in better shape."[1]

The Foreign Policy Crisis of 1980

On Christmas Day 1979, the armed forces of the Soviet Union began the invasion of Afghanistan, to prop up against growing popular resistance Soviet clients who had taken power in 1978. The invasion of Afghanistan represented the first extensive use of Soviet forces outside Eastern Europe. While the invasion of Afghanistan was hence a departure in one sense, it was also the logical next step in an escalating ladder of Soviet aggressiveness over the previous twenty years: from Soviet arms and advisers in places like Vietnam, to massive Soviet-supported intervention by Soviet proxies in places like Angola and Ethiopia, to direct Soviet invasion. By New Year's Day 1980, the international wreckage caused by recent Soviet advances was visible virtually everywhere. In Southeast Asia, South Vietnam, Cambodia, and Laos had fallen into the Soviet orbit; in southern Africa, Angola and Mozambique had fallen, with the aid of tens of thousands of Cuban troops; in the Horn of Africa, it was Ethiopia and South Yemen, again with the help of Cuba; in the Caribbean, Nicaragua and Grenada; and finally, pointed—as observers were prone to put it—like a dagger at the heart of the Persian Gulf, Afghanistan. In all, from the communist victory in Vietnam until 1980, the Soviet empire absorbed ten countries: an average of one every six months. In addition, communists almost took over Portugal in 1975, Cuban-supported forces based in Angola attacked Zaire's mineral-rich Shaba Province in 1978, and Soviet-backed South Yemen attacked North Yemen, if unsuccessfully, in 1979. By mid-1979, commentators were calling this sequence of events "America in Retreat."[2]

This burst of Soviet adventurism, fed by America's failure in Vietnam,[3] was undergirded by an enormous military buildup. Starting in the mid-1960s, the Soviets had undertaken a sustained buildup in strategic nuclear weapons, centered on heavy, first-strike intercontinental ballistic missiles (ICBMs) like the SS-9, SS-18, and SS-19. This buildup was particularly ominous when coupled with what was known about Soviet war doctrine: at its heart lay a massive, surprise assault on Western war-making capacity. In the words of a high-ranking Soviet defector writing under the pseudonym "Viktor Suvorov," all Soviet military manuals "advocated, most insistently, the delivery of a massive preemptive attack on the enemy. . . . The best protection for rockets in a war is to use them immediately."[4] (The Soviet minister of defense later told Jack Matlock Jr., U.S. ambassador to the Soviet Union, "Until Chernobyl, I was convinced we could fight a nuclear war and prevail.")[5] In 1977, the Soviets began a major buildup of theater nuclear forces in Europe. Throughout the 1970s, the USSR was engaged in an unprecedented expansion of conventional forces, expanding its armed forces by four hundred thousand men from 1970 to 1980, a period when the United States was cutting manpower by 1.4 million. The Soviets poured immense resources into new tanks, artillery, and tactical aircraft. Power projection was emphasized, through more airborne forces and long-range airlift capacity. The Soviet navy expanded and began to move aggressively into areas once ceded to Western navies. In strategic defense, the Soviets upgraded their air defense, antiballistic missile, and civil defense systems, and devoted large sums to missile-defense research projects.

All this occurred while the United States was reducing its defense budget, showing reluctance to intervene in new foreign crises, and eagerly seeking arms control agreements. The bipartisan consensus in favor of anticommunist containment—a consensus that had served as the basis for American policy since 1947—had been lost in the jungles of Vietnam. In its place, the United States had sought the "detente" of the 1970s, which Americans supposed to mean reciprocity, mutual restraint, and increasing cooperation. To the Soviets, detente, or what they preferred to call "peaceful coexistence," was clearly a tactical maneuver to seek unilateral advantage. In the words of Soviet spokesman Leonid Ilichev,

> Peaceful coexistence not only does not exclude the class struggle but is itself a form of the class struggle, between victorious socialism and decrepit capitalism on the world scene, a sharp and irreconcilable struggle, the final outcome of which will be the triumph of communism throughout the entire world.[6]

By the beginning of the 1980s, "Soviet leaders stated with growing confidence that the correlation of forces had shifted in their favor."[7] Military trends favored the Soviets. Strategically, they were encircling the oil-rich Persian Gulf, mineral-rich southern Africa, and the sea-lanes passing through the Horn of Africa, the South China Sea, and the Caribbean. They were gaining diplomatically, as their military and strategic gains magnified the effects of America's post-Vietnam neo-isolationism. NATO was divided and lacked effective leadership. Further, if the Soviet economy remained weak, the American economy was in the throes of what Marxist analysts were tempted to consider the death rattle of capitalism. To the Soviets, in short, "detente" was a means of soothing the West while they worked to tip the correlation of forces irrevocably in their favor.

Americans took some time to perceive this disparity of purposes, but public opinion at length began favoring a firmer line toward the Soviets, a trend that accelerated through 1979 and 1980.[8] Defense spending finally stopped its downward slide in 1978. Jimmy Carter used a veiled threat of intervention, for the first time in his presidency, when he deployed an aircraft carrier offshore to halt the South Yemeni and Cuban offensive against North Yemen. The second Strategic Arms Limitations Talks accord (SALT II), signed in July 1979, was in trouble in the Senate even before Afghanistan; in Europe, Carter and the allies decided in December 1979 to deploy a counter to Soviet intermediate-range SS-20 missiles. In October 1979, Carter faced a public outcry when it was discovered that a Soviet combat brigade was stationed on Cuba and had been since 1962. In November 1979, the Iranian hostage crisis began, a crisis emblematic to many Americans of the weakness into which their country had been allowed to fall; the nation's response to the hostage crisis foreshadowed the patriotic fervor of the 1980s. Then in December, the Soviets drove the final nail into the coffin of detente when they took Kabul. Newsmagazines carried covers with cartoons of doves crushed by Soviet tanks.[9] Carter admitted, "The action of the Soviets has made a more dramatic change in my opinion of what the Soviets' ultimate goals are than anything they've done in the previous time that I've been office."[10] Ultimately, the Soviet invasion of Afghanistan set in motion a political, diplomatic, and military reaction on the part of the United States and the West that was to end a decade later in the collapse of the Soviet empire.

In 1980 there was, for a brief moment, as broad a foreign policy consensus as had existed in America at any time since before 1968: unhappily, but without hesitation, the United States must rejoin the Cold War. Carter's new policy reflected that consensus, as well as his transformation from the days of the 1977 Notre Dame speech when he had scorned the "inordinate fear of communism" that, he said, had preoccupied postwar American foreign policy. In response to the invasion of Afghanistan, Carter withdrew SALT II from Senate consideration and proposed reinstatement of Selective Service registration, a major increase in defense spending, a grain embargo on the Soviets, and a boycott of the Moscow Summer Olympics. In his January 1980 State of the Union Address, Carter declared that Afghanistan represented "the greatest threat to peace since World War II," and he announced a strategic policy that came to be known as the Carter Doctrine, promising to repel any outside attempt to control the Persian Gulf "by any means necessary, including military force." The more assertive post-Afghanistan Carter, however, was only a transitional figure, serving as a bridge between the accommodationist pre-Afghanistan Carter and Ronald Reagan.

The Restoration of Containment and Deterrence

To Reagan, the struggle with Soviet totalitarianism was the central issue of our time, a struggle for which the United States must fully mobilize its resources. The fundamental nature of the Soviet regime—not a series of misunderstandings between morally equivalent superpowers—was the source of conflict. As Reagan understood, the Soviet Union he faced as he took office "was guided by a policy of immoral and unbridled expansion" and "Lenin's secular religion of expansionism and world domination."[11] Consequently, Reagan believed, as he put it in his 1985 inaugural address, that "every victory for human freedom will be a victory for world peace."[12] Perceiving the numerous parallels between the USSR and National Socialist Germany—ranging from total state control over society to concentration camps, to the mass murder of tens of millions of human beings, to official ideologies calling for world domination[13]—Reagan took a view of foreign relations governed by the "Munich paradigm" rather than the "Vietnam paradigm." In other words, while he sought to avoid another foreign policy disaster such as Vietnam, he was more afraid of appeasement than of assertiveness, and he viewed Vietnam as a "noble cause" that had gone awry because of political timidity. Above all, while Reagan offered peace—with greater sincerity than domestic skeptics at the time credited—he made it clear that America would pay a high price rather than accede to Soviet domination of the world. In his first inaugural address, Reagan declared, "Peace is the highest aspiration of the American people. We will negotiate for it, sacrifice for it; we will not surrender for it now or ever."[14] At the same time, Reagan believed that "communism was doomed. . . . [A]ny totalitarian society that deprived its people of liberty and freedom of choice was ultimately doomed." In the long run, the Soviet leadership, in Reagan's view, "could not survive against the inherent drive of all men and women to be free."[15]

The first task facing Reagan was to prevent further erosion of America's position in the world and to restore the vigor of the policy of containment and the military strength needed to deter further Soviet expansionism. A month before taking office, Reagan was warned by France's intelligence director, Alexandre de Marenches, that in the absence of significant American stiffening even France and other close allies might begin to waver between East and West.[16] This task, though vital, was defensive and reactive in character. Its purpose was to prevent war due to Soviet miscalculation and to lay the groundwork for a more proactive policy in the future. There were three major components of this defensive track: the military buildup, the reestablishment of containment, and the solidification of America's alliances.

Defense Buildup

Reagan had been a strong advocate of U.S. military superiority since he entered the national political arena in 1964. By the time he took office in January 1981, a majority of Americans agreed that the Soviet buildup and recent expansionism required a major American response. After Vietnam, the defense budget had been cut substantially; if one does not count short-term war expenditures, defense spending had actually been declining since the mid-1960s. By 1980, U.S. armed forces recruiting quotas were going unfilled, readiness was so low that one report referred to a "hollow army," an estimated half of the navy's aircraft carriers were not combat ready at any given time, and morale was shaky. As far as U.S. intelligence could tell, Soviet military expenditures had surpassed American expenditures in 1971 and by 1979 were outstripping those of the United States by 70 percent.[17] The failed Iranian rescue mission of April 1980 served as a metaphor for these broader failures.

By the time Jimmy Carter left office, he had planned 5 percent a year real growth in defense spending for the next half-decade. Reagan expanded on this proposal, and U.S. defense spending increased from $134 billion in 1980 to $253 billion in 1985 before leveling off. Overall, defense spending increased by 43 percent in real terms from 1981 to 1989. As Secretary of Defense Caspar Weinberger described it, "Our policy was simple to state and very difficult to achieve; it was to regain, as quickly as possible, sufficient military strength to convince our friends to stay closely allied with us and to convince the Soviets they could not win any war they might start against us or our allies."[18]

This defense buildup contained numerous components. The strategic modernization program consisted of plans to build MX land-based nuclear missiles to complement the aging Minuteman and obsolete Titan force; B-1B bombers to complement the twenty-year-old B-52s; and D-5 Trident II submarine-launched ballistic missiles to replace the nation's aging Polaris and Poseidon fleet. This strategic buildup was meant to achieve three objectives: 1) maintain the reality and perception of strategic balance by keeping pace with the rapid Soviet strategic modernization of the 1970s, 2) make possible a counterforce strategy, that is, one aimed at Soviet military forces rather than the civilian population, and 3) restore American negotiating leverage.

The program quickly came under attack from a resurgent anti–nuclear weapons movement. These forces argued that the nuclear balance was unimportant and that the buildup—far from improving American leverage—would provoke the Soviets into hostility that would make arms control more difficult and war more likely. At its peak before 1984, the "nuclear freeze" movement claimed millions of sympathizers. In one week in April 1982—dubbed by its organizers "Ground Zero Week"—over a million Americans in over six hundred cities and 350 college campuses participated in a variety of antinuclear activities, followed by an antinuclear demonstration in New York on June 12, 1982, that drew five hundred thousand people.[19] By July 1982, nuclear freeze supporters had collected 2,365,000 petition signatures for nonbinding state and local referenda, "probably the largest for any petition in U.S. history."[20] Another 885,000 petition signatures sent to Congress contributed to the passage of a nonbinding nuclear freeze resolution in the House in 1983,[21] and in 1984 the freeze was written into the Democratic national platform. The Reagan administration nevertheless convinced a majority of Congress to press ahead with most of the strategic modernization program.

In conventional forces the administration increased the number of men and divisions under arms, the number of tactical fighter wings, and the number of ships in the navy (with the goal of a six-hundred-ship fleet), added ten thousand tanks, and built up special-operations forces. Military pay and benefits were expanded in a successful effort to fill manpower quotas with high-quality recruits.

This conventional buildup was meant to counter the growing Soviet preponderance of power in Central Europe, as well as to provide means for more effective use of force in the third world. In both conventional and strategic arms, the buildup was not only quantitative but, more importantly, qualitative, putting to full use the technological superiority of the United States.[22]

Finally, tied to the conventional buildup was the effort to improve readiness and mobility. Training budgets were increased and more realistic training exercises developed. Because recruitment no longer lagged, units were again at full strength; the number of combat-ready units in 1983 had increased by 32 percent from the 1980 low. Replacement parts were once again easily available. Sealift and airlift capability was strengthened. The Rapid Deployment Force became a reality, and a shortfall of four hundred thousand men in the reserves was almost filled. In short, by the mid-1980s, the U.S. armed forces were no longer "hollow" but at full strength, in a high state of readiness, with high morale, and well trained. In 1983, news analysts declared, "Rarely in peacetime have U.S. military forces been better prepared to defend the nation.... [F]ew experts doubt that the U.S. armed forces have stepped back from the brink of the disaster they faced not long ago."[23]

Restoring Containment

From the declaration of the Truman Doctrine in 1947 until 1968, there had been a bipartisan consensus in favor of preserving the security of the West by containing Soviet expansionism. This policy had led to U.S. intervention in places as diverse as Turkey and Greece, Korea, Lebanon, the Dominican Republic, and Vietnam. By the end of the Vietnam War, however, the bipartisan nature of the policy had frayed, as the dominant left wing of the Democratic Party opted out. Additionally, public opinion had made enforcement of containment in the 1970s politically impossible.

Thus, in the 1980s it was as difficult as it was imperative for the United States to reestablish the credibility of containment. The Carter Doctrine in the Persian Gulf was a first step, but it was Reagan who faced the most crucial test of this new firmness, in Central America. As early as 1961, Soviet premier Nikita Khrushchev declared that Soviet victory in the Cold War would come through Soviet alliances with "wars of national liberation" in the third world, by which means the Soviets could encircle and isolate the West. The Soviet gains of the 1970s had all come in this manner. Upon taking office, Reagan found himself confronted with another Soviet third-world thrust, in a part of the world that he believed could not be ignored.

In 1979, two revolutions occurred in Central America. The first was in Nicaragua, where Anastazio Somoza was overthrown by the Sandinista

National Liberation Front, a Marxist-Leninist group aligned with Cuba. The Sandinistas, while proclaiming democracy and accepting tens of millions of dollars in U.S. aid, imported Cuban military advisers, doubled the size of the armed forces, began repressing business, labor, political parties, and the church, and announced a goal of spreading "revolution without frontiers." The second revolution of 1979 was in El Salvador, where Gen. Carlos Humberto Romero was overthrown by reformist junior officers who began land and banking reforms, promised elections, and brought back as president the democrat Jose Napoleon Duarte. El Salvador was quickly engulfed in civil war. The political center came under assault by the extreme Left in the form of the communist Faribundo Marti National Liberation Front (FMLN), with several thousand guerrillas in the field, and by the extreme Right in the form of large landowners and their allies in the army, who terrorized Salvadorans with "death squads." The FMLN had been cobbled together by Fidel Castro in 1980, was headquartered in Sandinista Managua, and received tons of weapons from the Soviet bloc funneled through Nicaragua. Any lingering doubts about Sandinista involvement in the Salvadoran war were ended when an arms cache in Managua exploded in May 1993, exposing a weapons pipeline to El Salvador and elsewhere that had continued in existence even after the Sandinistas were driven from power. The battle in Central America in the 1980s was over which version of revolution would prevail.

Days before Reagan's inauguration, the FMLN launched a "final offensive" and called on Salvadorans to support their bid for power. The offensive failed, but El Salvador became a feature of America's foreign policy debate for the rest of the decade. In the face of the "final offensive," Jimmy Carter had resumed military aid to the Salvadoran government. Reagan promptly expanded that aid and sent fifty-five military advisers to train the Salvadoran forces. Critics of the policy charged throughout that it would lead to "another Vietnam" and that the Salvadoran government was unworthy of support. Reagan believed that modest and indirect action immediately could prevent any need for direct U.S. intervention and pointed to the substantial improvements occurring under the Salvadoran government, including a marked decline in death-squad killings, as well as free elections in 1982, 1984, and 1985.[24] In any event, Reagan argued, the stakes were too high to let El Salvador fall.

The Soviets throughout the 1980s explicitly referred to Central America and the Caribbean as America's "strategic rear." In their view, if the United States could be challenged near its own borders, it would be hampered in responding effectively to a Soviet thrust in Europe or the Middle East. Resupply and lines of communication would be threatened, and the United States would have to expend precious military resources to secure them. Thus, Soviet control of Central America—or, ultimately, Mexico—could tilt the strategic balance so heavily against the United States that its allies elsewhere would find neutralism increasingly attractive. In short, some strategic analysts argued that "Soviet goals ... include nothing less than an elaborate encampment designed to effect 'hemispheric denial' via a flanking movement" as "part of a broader design of global hegemony."[25] For his part, the Soviet chief of the General Staff, Marshal Nikolai Ogarkov, boasted that "over two decades ago there was only Cuba in Latin America, today there are Nicaragua, Grenada, and a serious battle is going on in El Salvador."[26]

Despite consistent congressional challenges and the objections of a well-organized political movement—the pro-FMLN Committee in Solidarity with the People of El Salvador (CISPES) claimed to have three hundred local chapters by 1985—the administration succeeded in gaining acceptance of its policy of arming the pro-Western Salvadoran government while urging it to continue reforms. As late as 1983, there was doubt as to whether the Salvadoran government would survive. *Newsweek* speculated that the army might collapse by Christmas.[27] Now it is clear that 1983 marked the high point of the FMLN's fortunes; at that point, El Salvador turned the corner. Nor were smaller Sandinista-backed insurgencies and terrorist groups in Guatemala, Honduras, and Costa Rica successful. While numerous local factors, grievances, and forces were clearly at work, Central America was the foremost test of containment in the 1980s, and the United States passed. In the election of 1984, Reagan was able to boast that his had been the first administration since World War II that had not given up an inch of territory to the communists. When the FMLN finally agreed in 1992 to lay down its arms, the *Washington Post* editorialized that "the United States did what it had to do to help a small, vulnerable, friendly neighbor fend off a foreign-assisted revolutionary assault. . . . American constancy was crucial."[28]

Strengthening America's Alliances

Part of maintaining the global equilibrium of the 1980s was the maintenance of a solid relationship with mainland China. While not a formal ally of the United States, China opposed Soviet expansionism and tied down forty-five Soviet divisions in Siberia in 1981, a number that would grow to fifty-seven by 1987. Throughout the 1980s, the Reagan administration—contrary to its earliest inclinations, which were to tilt to Taiwan—strengthened its economic, diplomatic, and military ties with China. Starting in 1983, the administration liberalized trade in "dual-use" technology. That fall, Defense Secretary Weinberger made a crucial visit to China to establish military ties, followed by an exchange of visits between Reagan and Chinese premier Deng Xiaoping the next year. Military sales to China and joint naval exercises

became part of the U.S.-China relationship.[29] American failure to have secured this cooperation, or worse yet successful Soviet entreaties to China,
would have seriously complicated the task of containing Soviet power.

Traditional alliances with Japan and Europe were also strengthened. Reagan
maintained good relations with Japan despite intense domestic pressure to engage in a trade war, and he quietly persuaded Japan to increase its defense efforts and to take responsibility for defending crucial sea-lanes out to a thousand miles.[30] Most importantly, NATO, the cornerstone alliance of America's
postwar security, was preserved amid crisis. By 1980, many of America's closest European allies had doubted American strength and constancy of purpose.
Only a few years before, Jimmy Carter had succumbed to the pressure of the
antinuclear movement and canceled the neutron bomb, a weapon designed to
counter Soviet tank superiority in Europe, after numerous European leaders
had risked their futures by publicly endorsing its deployment. In the early
1980s, the United States and Europe faced a similar test but of far greater consequence. Failure to navigate it could have destroyed the alliance.

In 1977, the Soviets began deployment of the SS-20, a triple-warhead, mo-
bile, intermediate-range ballistic missile aimed at Western Europe. By 1981,
they had deployed 250 (of which 175 were aimed at Europe) and were field-
ing an average of one per week. No Western provocation had encouraged the
SS-20 buildup. These weapons were both military and political/psychological
in nature; they seemed aimed above all against the will of Western Europe to
maintain its independence and its alliance with America.[31] By 1979, the allies
had agreed that if negotiations did not produce results by 1983, nuclear Pershing II and cruise missiles would be deployed to counter the SS-20s.

Starting in 1980, however, an antinuclear movement like the one that had
stopped the neutron bomb reemerged in Europe, bringing enormous pressure
to bear on European governments.[32] Instead of reversing course as Carter had
done, Reagan remained steady. The Soviets finally came to the table in the fall
of 1981, but no progress was made—undoubtedly because they held out hope
that the peace movement would stop the deployment, eliminating the need to
make concessions. As the NATO deployment deadline of November 1983 approached, the pressure to retreat grew, but the United States and the allies held
firm. Elections were held in 1983 in six NATO nations, including such vital
countries as Great Britain, the Federal Republic of Germany, and Italy. In each
country, Euromissile deployment was a key issue, dividing the contending
parties. If antideployment parties had won in the six, or simply in Britain and
Germany, the NATO position on deployment would have collapsed. German
chancellor Helmut Kohl later argued that failure to deploy the missiles would
have had "devastating consequences. . . . [I]t could have resulted in the breakdown of NATO."[33] By the end of 1983, however, prodeployment parties had

won in every one of the six countries holding elections. The deployment proceeded on schedule, and NATO was preserved.

Predictions made in 1981 that Reagan would destroy the alliance unless he changed his policies proved untrue.[34] In the words of Margaret Thatcher, "President Reagan strengthened not only America's defenses, but also the will of America's allies."[35] For this feat, former Japanese prime minister Yasuhiro Nakasone declared that Reagan was the "Great Architect. . . . He [had] put the tumble-down house called the Free World back in shape again, shoring up the pillars and tightening the bolts."[36]

The United States Goes on the Offensive

The restoration of America's military strength, its commitment to containment, and the vigor of its alliances were crucial to halting the Soviet momentum of the 1970s and to reducing the prospect of war due to Soviet miscalculation. Nevertheless, the United States had only achieved the restoration of the strategic balance and the stalemate of the Cold War. A fundamental problem still faced the West: as long as containment was the sole objective of policy, the West would be on the permanent defensive. This problem was exacerbated by the relatively short attention span and impatience of the democratic public, which ensured that periods of firmness would alternate with periods of lethargy, like the 1970s. Hence, some strategic analysts feared that "a policy that was strictly defensive and that had to endure in perpetuity was indeed doomed to failure."[37]

Reagan's great strategic innovation was the combination of containment with an attempt to break the stalemate of the Cold War by a complementary policy of offense. The idea of an offensive in the Cold War was not new. Douglas MacArthur had called for taking the offensive in Korea but had been fired; Dwight Eisenhower had promised a policy of "liberation," or "roll-back," in his 1952 campaign, but implementation had proved too risky; Barry Goldwater had argued that "victory over communism must be the dominant, proximate goal of American policy,"[38] but he had lost the 1964 election soundly.

Only in the 1980s did the political will and the geopolitical opportunities exist for a comprehensive offensive policy. Even before taking office, Reagan shared his vision of a strategic offensive with Richard V. Allen, who later became his first national security adviser. "My idea of American policy toward the Soviet Union," Reagan told Allen, "is simple. It is this: 'we win and they lose.'"[39] Believing the evidence showed increasing strains on the Soviet empire, Reagan "wondered how we as a nation could use these cracks in the Soviet system to accelerate the process of collapse."[40] The intellectual framework for this policy was established in 1982 and early 1983 with three secret "national security decision directives" and a secret Defense Department five-year planning directive. NSDD-32 proclaimed that it was U.S. policy to "neutralize" Soviet control of Eastern Europe by supporting underground movements and psychological operations against the communist regimes; NSDD-66 outlined a strategy of economic warfare against the Soviet regime; and NSDD-75 declared roll-back of Soviet influence around the world, and ultimately a change in the Soviet system itself, to be a key U.S. policy objective. The Defense Department guidance led to a "national security decision memorandum" focusing defense policy on exploiting Soviet economic vulnerabilities.[41] By 1983 the United States was taking the strategic offensive for the first time in the Cold War, radically changing the complexion of the East-West struggle. As intelligence analyst Herbert E. Meyer said in 1993, "Ronald Reagan was the first Western leader whose objective was to win. . . . [Reagan] made one of the greatest decisions in geostrategic history, and he made it work."[42]

The Ideological Counteroffensive

At the height of detente, Gerald Ford's White House refused to entertain Aleksandr Solzhenitsyn, the Russian exile and author of *The Gulag Archipelago,* for fear of offending the Kremlin. When Reagan entered the White House, this approach ended, and an ideological counteroffensive was launched. According to Fitzhugh Green, "No longer would the U.S. stand mute in the face of communist vilification. No longer would the nation compete shyly in the idea marts of the world."[43]

To cite a few notable examples: In his first press conference as president, Reagan (quoting Lenin) accused the Soviets of willingness to "commit any crime, to lie, to cheat" in order to advance world communism.[44] At his Notre Dame speech a few months later, he predicted that "the years ahead are great ones for this country, for the cause of freedom. . . . The West won't contain communism. It will transcend communism. It will dismiss it as some bizarre chapter in human history whose last pages are even now being written."[45] In London in June 1982, Reagan elaborated on this theme, calling for a "crusade for freedom" and telling Parliament that it was Marxism-Leninism that would end up "on the ash heap of history."[46] In March 1983, Reagan told a convention of evangelicals that the Soviet Union was an "evil empire" and "the focus of evil in the modern world."[47]

An effort was also made to strengthen the United States Information Agency (USIA), Voice of America, and Radio Free Europe; new outlets were also created, like Radio Marti and TV Marti (directed at Cuba), and "Worldnet," a USIA satellite television network. As Reagan himself declared in his 1982 State of the Union Address, "We've promised the world a season of truth—the truth of our great civilized ideas: individual liberty, representative government, the rule of law under God."[48]

The first and most overarching objective of this ideological and rhetorical counteroffensive was to illuminate the nature of the Soviet regime in stark terms of good and evil. The Soviet dictatorship was denied legitimacy, and those in the West who had to carry the burden of fighting the Cold War were reminded of its moral purpose. A secondary object was to strengthen and encourage the latent resistance of those behind the Iron Curtain. Thus, the ideological attack served as the moral foundation for the more tangible elements of the strategic counteroffensive. Soviet-studies scholar Seweryn Bialer recounted, after three trips to the Soviet Union in 1983–84, that "President Reagan's rhetoric has badly shaken the self-esteem and patriotic pride of the Soviet political elites . . . [who are] stunned and humiliated."[49]

At the time, this offensive was treated by much of the Western press and intelligentsia as a mixture of embarrassment and menace to peace. Historian Henry Steele Commager called the evil empire speech "the worst presidential speech in American history."[50] Columnist Anthony Lewis called it "illegitimate," "outrageous," "primitive," "simplistic," and "terribly dangerous."[51] These criticisms, however, were hampered by the inability of the critics to specify which portion of the "evil empire" formulation was actually open to dispute. Were they arguing that the Soviet Union was not imperial? That "evil" was so narrow in meaning that it did not include tens of millions of deaths, the Gulag, and the depths of the Lubyanka prison? Or simply that such moral clarity appeared insufficiently sophisticated? It was never entirely clear.

In the view of liberal Cold War historian John Lewis Gaddis, intellectuals "worried that if we talked too explicitly about these kinds of things, we might wind up sounding like John Foster Dulles, or, for a more recent generation, Ronald Reagan." Yet, "now that they are free to speak—and act—the people of the former Soviet Union appear to have associated themselves more closely with President Reagan's famous indictment of that state as an 'evil empire' than with more balanced academic assessments."[52] Ambassador Jack Matlock Jr., a career diplomat, agreed that the evil empire speech "did much to undermine the legitimacy of the Soviet empire."[53] Lech Walesa would say that the speech played an important role in the breakdown of communist control in Eastern Europe. Soviet officials themselves later admitted that it had led them to consider the possibility that "the motherland was indeed evil."[54] In 1992, Russian foreign minister Andrei Kozyrev further vindicated the "evil empire" speech: the Soviet Union, Kozyrev said, *had* been an evil empire, one that was "despotic and repressive, trampling upon the freedom and the very existence of human beings," guided by a state ideology of communism that had been "the main breeding ground for the Cold War."[55]

Economic Warfare

The American strategic offensive against Soviet power was also held to-gether by an understanding of Soviet economic weakness and a determination to exploit that weakness. NSDD-66 in 1982, which outlined this policy, repre-sented, in the words of its principal author, "a secret declaration of economic war on the Soviet Union."[56] As Peter Schweizer outlined in his 1994 book *Vic-tory*, numerous policies flowed from this economic warfare. The technologi-cal emphasis of the military buildup (discussed above) and the threat of the Strategic Defense Initiative (discussed below) were part of the war. Economic sanctions imposed in response to Polish martial law gave the United States im-portant leverage that it used to help Solidarity survive. An attempt to stop a Soviet natural gas pipeline to Western Europe was not completely successful, but it did result in two years' delay and a reduction of the scale of the project by half, costing the Soviets tens of billions of dollars in lost revenue. COCOM, the Coordinating Committee for Multilateral Export Controls, became much more aggressive in stopping Western technology transfers to the USSR. The CIA even devised elaborate disinformation programs to feed the Soviets faulty technology.

Perhaps the most sensitive element of the economic war was a long-term diplomatic strategy to drive down world energy prices. Most importantly, a close security relationship forged by the Reagan administration with Saudi Arabia gave the United States greater influence over Saudi production deci-sions. That influence was used to encourage the Saudis to increase production, which they did on a large scale in 1985. The consequent reduction in oil prices not only helped the American economy but contributed to the administra-tion's strategy for undermining the Soviet economy, which was highly reliant on hard currency earnings from oil sales. In the words of Soviet foreign min-istry official Yevgenny Novikov, "The drop in oil prices was devastating, just devastating. It was a catastrophic event. Tens of billions were wiped away."[57] At the same time, the American economic recovery of the 1980s cast doubts on the Soviets' confident predictions of capitalist collapse; indeed, special na-tional intelligence estimates prepared in 1984 indicated the Soviet leadership was "psychologically shaken" by the recovery and more generally by the re-newed American assertiveness.[58]

The Strategic Defense Initiative

Alongside the strengthening of deterrence through the strategic modern-ization program, Reagan announced in March 1983 that the United States would use its technological capabilities to develop a ballistic missile defense system that could end the standoff of "mutually assured destruction" (MAD). This research program became the Strategic Defense Initiative (SDI), also known as "Star Wars." Though it did not come close to producing a functioning ballistic missile defense during the 1980s, SDI fundamentally altered the strategic context in favor of the United States.

The Soviets had long been working on missile defense and were devoting to such programs "a far greater investment of plant space, capital, and manpower" than was the United States.[59] They also had maintained and upgraded outside of Moscow the one antiballistic-missile site permitted by the revised ABM Treaty. Overall, from 1976 to 1986 the Soviets spent an estimated twenty billion dollars a year on strategic defense, equal to the sum they spent on strategic offense.[60] Thus, to a certain extent, SDI was driven by a desire to prevent the Soviets from beating the United States to an effective ballistic missile defense system, an event that would have been catastrophic.[61] However, other factors weighed more heavily in the decision to launch SDI. The growing vulnerability of U.S. land-based ICBMs made some form of defense attractive. The credibility of "extended deterrence"—the threat that the United States would use its nuclear weapons to prevent Soviet conquest of Western Europe—had also been called into question as the American homeland became increasingly vulnerable. Reduction of that vulnerability through missile defense could strengthen extended deterrence. Crucially, Reagan believed it was ethically superior to rely primarily on defense than on the threat of retaliation—"Is it not better," Reagan asked, "to save lives than to avenge them?" Finally, technological breakthroughs since 1972 made missile defense seem increasingly plausible.

There has been a debate since March of 1983 about whether these technologies were promising enough to justify expenditures in excess of five billion dollars a year on SDI. Skeptics warned of possible Soviet countermeasures, pointed out correctly that no system would be 100 percent effective, and estimated the cost of future deployment to be exorbitant. Supporters pointed to advances in the computer, sensing, and optics fields, to progress made in tests, to calculations estimating that the marginal cost of bolstering the system would be less than the cost to the Soviets of trying to overcome it, and to numerous historical precedents of supposedly impossible scientific feats being achieved. In the early 1990s, supporters also cited the apparent success of the Patriot missile defense system in the war with Iraq; while the success rate of the Patriot may have been initially overstated, it was also true that Patriot had lacked state-of-the-art technology.

Until it is deployed, no definitive judgment can be made about the feasibility of ballistic missile defense. Yet the political consequences of the Strategic Defense Initiative were considerable. First, it contributed to the dispersion of the antinuclear movement, and hence contributed to saving the strategic modernization program. Antinuclear activists later conceded that SDI, by promising a technological means of transforming deterrence, had reduced their public appeal.[62]

Second, it threw the Soviet leadership into a state of despair. It now appears that the Politburo had a higher opinion of American technological prowess than did many Western critics of SDI and believed that the United States could indeed develop a successful ballistic missile defense system. As Anatoly Dobrynin, the Soviet ambassador to the United States, later remarked, the Soviet leadership "was convinced that the great technical potential of the U.S. had scored again."[63] The Soviets well understood the ramifications: hundreds of billions of rubles' worth of investment in heavy ICBMs would have been wasted, the United States would have achieved strategic superiority, and the Soviets would have been forced into a crash program to attempt to replicate the American defense and to negate it with countermeasures. Because of the economic and technological weaknesses of the Soviet system, there was no guarantee that such a crash program could be made to work at a cost that would not destroy the system, or indeed that it could be made to work at all. Instead of playing catch-up in the Soviet game of offensive buildup, the Americans were threatening to change the game entirely, so as to utilize their relative strengths against the Soviets.[64]

This realization led to two consequences in the Soviet Union. The Soviet leadership, which became obsessed with SDI, launched a propaganda campaign accusing the United States of threatening to militarize space. When propaganda showed no sign of working, the Soviets attempted to use arms control as a tool. Reagan refused to put SDI on the table, however, leading four well-known national security analysts to argue that he had to choose between SDI and arms control: "Unless it [SDI] is radically constrained during the next four years it will bring vast new costs and dangers to our country and to mankind."[65] McGeorge Bundy, one of the four, elaborated that "Reagan's bogus dream now blocks agreement and threatens to unleash a new and unlimited offensive-defensive competition."[66] The apex of the Soviet campaign to eliminate SDI at the bargaining table was reached at the Reykjavik summit in October 1986, where Gorbachev offered an (unverifiable) elimination of all nuclear weapons for surrender of SDI. After considering this option seriously (too seriously, it turned out, for the taste of his advisers and the allies), Reagan rejected it. In the end, the United States would get arms control anyway.

Aside from the failed strategy of trying to induce elimination of the program, the Soviets were also prodded by SDI into seeking greater modernization of their own society—which could only be achieved by liberalization. There were a number of factors (both external and internal) leading the Soviets in this direction, but the threat of having to compete with SDI seems to have been quite important. It led to greater toleration of reform by the military, which saw economic reform as essential to that competition.[67] Indeed, former Soviet officials have indicated that in many respects *perestroika* (restructuring) was a military initiative, aimed at redressing the military implications of Soviet technological weakness. Gorbachev's two foreign ministers, Eduard Shevardnadze and Aleksandr Bessmertnykh, have both attested to the catalytic impact of SDI on Soviet internal reform.[68] In the view of former CIA director Robert Gates, SDI was a symbol to the Soviet leadership of "the broad resurgence of the West," one that persuaded the leadership that major internal change was needed. [69] For his part, Reagan concluded that "if I had to choose the single most important reason, on the United States' side, for the historic breakthroughs that were to occur during the next five years in the quest for peace and a better relationship with the Soviet Union, I would say it was the Strategic Defense Initiative, along with the overall modernization of our military forces."[70] In the end, it is difficult to escape the conclusion that SDI played a prominent role in the successful termination of the Cold War.

The Reagan Doctrine and Roll-Back

In the same way that in SDI it had established a strategically bolder complement to deterrence, the Reagan administration developed an offensive complement to the policy of containment. By 1985, this departure had become known as the "Reagan Doctrine," a term coined by columnist Charles Krauthammer. Though it evolved gradually and informally, there can be no doubt that the Reagan Doctrine was largely the product of Reagan's own "convictions and aims."[71] It was a policy of attempting to "roll back" the periphery of the Soviet empire by assisting anticommunist guerrillas in many of the countries that had recently fallen. The American offensive also reached Eastern Europe and ultimately Soviet soil itself, in secret operations that were not revealed until 1994. The Reagan Doctrine sought actively to exploit the economic weakness of the Soviet Union as well as its imperial weaknesses of ethnic division and overextension.

Reagan inherited from Jimmy Carter, and then vastly expanded, a program of covert military assistance to the Afghan mujahedeen. This program had deep support in Congress, and it grew to approximately five hundred million dollars a year. By the end of 1981, Reagan had also authorized a major covert operation aimed at assisting armed opponents of the Sandinista regime in Nicaragua. The Nicaraguan resistance grew rapidly in number from five hundred to twelve thousand by 1983, when Congress openly approved twenty-four million dollars in funding for the first time. The administration made defeat of the Sandinistas one of its key foreign policy objectives, and while Congress repeatedly changed its collective mind on support for "Contra" aid, at least some form of aid was provided, with brief interludes, from 1981 on. After a one-year cutoff in 1984, when Congress became angered at CIA involvement in a harbor-mining operation, twenty-seven million dollars in "nonlethal" assistance was restored in 1985. In 1986 Congress passed a hundred-million-dollar military and humanitarian aid package, and nonmilitary aid continued even after the Iran-Contra revelations.

While the Afghan operation was the largest and the Nicaraguan operation the most controversial, they were not the only ones. Within a few days in July 1985, Congress authorized five million dollars in covert assistance to the noncommunist resistance in Cambodia and repealed the 1976 Clark Amendment, which had prohibited assistance to the pro-Western UNITA forces fighting the Cuban-backed government of Angola. By 1986, the administration gained approval of twenty-seven million dollars in aid for UNITA, a figure that climbed to about fifty million by the end of the decade. Ethiopia's communist government, also supported by thousands of Cuban troops, was long considered a target, though only minimal operations were undertaken against it. In Mozambique, the administration did not assist the guerrillas but rather tried to wean the Mozambiquean regime away from Moscow, partly with the threat of supporting rebels in that country.[72] In all these cases, the United States was supporting, or considered supporting, established rebel forces engaged in long-term guerrilla warfare against Soviet-imposed or Soviet-sponsored regimes dating from the late 1970s.

This policy was first openly announced in Reagan's 1985 State of the Union Address, when the president said:

> We cannot play innocents abroad in a world that's not innocent; nor can we be passive when freedom is under siege. . . . [W]e must not break faith with those who are risking their lives—on every continent, from Afghanistan to Nicaragua—to defy Soviet-supported aggression and secure rights which have been ours from birth. . . . Support for freedom fighters is self-defense.[73]

Two weeks later, Secretary of State George Shultz amplified this theme, naming Afghanistan, Cambodia, Ethiopia, Angola, and Nicaragua as communist dictatorships facing internal revolt and saying that America had a "moral duty" to help such insurgents. In the words of Shultz, the Soviet empire was "weakening under the strain of its own internal problems and external entanglements. . . . When the United States supports those resisting totalitarianism, we do so not only out of our historical sympathy for democracy and freedom but also, in many cases, in the interests of our national security."[74]

The Reagan Doctrine was pursued with three sets of objectives in mind. In the short term, aid to resistance forces could blunt Soviet advances by forcing the Soviets and their allies onto the defensive and could deter future Soviet adventurism by making clear that it would incur heavy resistance. The most notable example of the former was in Nicaragua, where aid to the Contras served to relieve the pressure on El Salvador. Afghanistan, where Soviet forces directly bore the cost of resistance, was the best example of the latter. At this level, the Reagan Doctrine was "a challenge indicating Soviet gains in the third world would not be considered permanent by the U.S."[75] In the medium term, the key objective was actually to prevail in one or more of the countries. Such a victory would, one State Department official argued, "demonstrate to communist and noncommunist nations alike that communism is not, as the Soviets propagate, the 'wave of the future,' and that communist rule, once installed, is reversible."[76] Finally, the long-term objective was to use a series of such successes (or the pressure resulting from the effort) to break the global strategic deadlock and achieve a secure peace by ultimately prevailing over the Soviet empire. This was the vision that had been outlined in January 1983 in NSDD-75. As Reagan said in 1987, "Our goal has been to break the deadlock of the past, to seek a forward strategy—a forward strategy for world peace, a forward strategy for world freedom. . . . [T]he forces of freedom grow steadily in strength, and they put ever greater pressure on the forces of totalitarianism"[77]

The Reagan Doctrine was the source of great controversy in the United States and abroad. Some analysts pointed out that the policy could not be implemented without impinging on traditional notions of state sovereignty and international law; the administration retorted that international law loses all meaning when it can be used by those who are its enemies as an instrument with which to defeat those who are its friends.[78] Other criticisms focused on the real or perceived shortcomings of the guerrillas the administration was aiding, pointing to alleged human rights abuses or unsavory connections in Angola, Nicaragua, and Cambodia. Finally, some feared that the Reagan Doctrine would prove to be either too little or too much. If inadequate support was given to the rebels, the policy would fail and lead only to more bloodshed; if enough support was given genuinely to threaten the targeted regimes, the policy might provoke a dangerous confrontation with the Soviet Union, or at the very least "greater unwillingness within the Soviet hierarchy to compromise."[79]

In the final analysis, however, the Reagan Doctrine has to be judged a success. In Afghanistan, the *mujahedeen* inflicted tens of thousands of casualties on the Soviet armed forces with U.S.-supplied materiel. There were two key policy decisions in Afghanistan. One was the decision made by Reagan in 1986, over the objections of many advisers, to supply the hand-held Stinger anti-aircraft missile to the resistance. The decision "tipped the balance in the last great superpower face-off of the cold war"; according to an army report, the Stinger decisively "changed the nature of combat" in Afghanistan, by curtailing Soviet close air support.[80] The second key decision was even riskier but raised the price to the Soviets beyond their willingness to pay. It consisted of secretly aiding *mujahedeen* military and political operations across the Soviet border. In the view of CIA director William Casey, Soviet Central Asia was the "soft underbelly" of the USSR. In 1986, Afghan guerrillas started directly attacking that soft underbelly. By 1988, the Kremlin had agreed to withdraw its troops from Afghanistan.[81] The war between the *mujahedeen* and the Soviets' clients dragged on for a few years, but on April 30, 1992, the *mujahedeen* retook Kabul. Ironically, that victory came seventeen years to the day after the fall of Saigon set into motion the Soviet juggernaut of the late 1970s.

Similarly, the pressure put on in Angola by UNITA forced the Cubans to the negotiating table. In October 1987, UNITA forces defeated Angolan and Cuban communist forces in the largest battle of that civil war, aided significantly by U.S.-supplied anti-aircraft and antitank weapons.[82] By 1991 the last Cuban soldier had left Angola, and the Marxist regime was left to its own devices, finally agreeing to elections. In Cambodia, the resistance forced the Vietnamese government to withdraw its troops in a UN-brokered plan that also led to elections. Despite the fits and starts of the Contra aid program, El Salvador was saved, and the Sandinistas were forced as the price of peace to agree to free elections held in 1990, in which they lost to the democratic opposition in a landslide. Uncertainties and difficulties have subsequently plagued all four countries: the Sandinistas did not fully give up power despite losing the election, the Angolan war rekindled after UNITA claimed election fraud, and peace remained elusive among the factions of Cambodia and Afghanistan. But the Reagan Doctrine did not and could not promise to establish unending peace within the affected countries; it aimed to drive the communists from power, roll back the boundaries of the Soviet empire, and provide those countries with an opportunity to determine their own future. It accomplished those goals.

According to Robert Huber, the effects on the Soviet Union of the assertive new U.S. policy in the third world were substantial: "Over the course of the early 1980s Soviet foreign policy specialists had become increasingly doubtful that political upheavals in the developing world served Soviet foreign policy interests. Instead, arguments about the likelihood of military confrontation with the United States as a result of such upheavals were occurring more frequently, while rising costs strained an increasingly burdened Soviet economy."[83] Other observers noted as early as 1986 that "the Kremlin under Mikhail Gorbachev is finding it more and more difficult and expensive to hold on to gains already made in the third world. . . . [S]ix major rebellions against pro-Soviet governments in Afghanistan, Ethiopia, Nicaragua, Angola, Mozambique, and Cambodia have punched holes in the Soviet assertion that it is riding a tide of history running against the Western world."[84]

Aside from the publicly pronounced third-world counteroffensive and the secret attacks on Soviet Central Asia, the U.S. offensive reached into the heart of the Soviet empire in Europe. Poland was the most crucial Soviet client in Eastern Europe, and the Solidarity labor movement threatened the communist hold. When the communists declared martial law in Poland in 1982, Solidarity was hanging by a thread. Through an intricate supply network, the United States government, working with the Catholic Church and the AFL-CIO, covertly supplied Solidarity with money, communications equipment, and other assistance necessary to help it survive underground. Indeed, in the 1990s it became apparent that Reagan and Pope John Paul II had formed a quiet alliance, the foremost aim of which was to "bring down communism in Europe."[85] Largely because of American support, which reached eight million dollars a year, Solidarity did survive. Ultimately, Solidarity was able to bring the communists down, and in 1989 Poland was to become the first Soviet satellite to break free.[86]

Once the American counteroffensive began to succeed, most notably with the Soviet withdrawal from Afghanistan and the victory of Solidarity in Poland—once it became clear that indigenous forces could reverse occupation by the Soviet army itself—Soviet subjects were emboldened, and the Soviet imperial position began to disintegrate. Casey had predicted that "when we win one, the whole house of cards will come tumbling down. It will set off a chain reaction throughout the empire."[87] His prediction proved correct.

Direct Military Action

The United States used military power in the 1980s in ways ranging from numerous blows exchanged with Libya to the reflagging of Kuwaiti oil tankers at the end of the decade. However, despite attempts by his political opponents to paint Reagan as a trigger-happy cowboy, he was actually relatively cautious about the direct use of military force. That caution was reinforced by the insistence of Secretary Weinberger that American forces not be deployed in the absence of clear goals, public and congressional support, and an "exit strategy." By one calculation, Reagan committed the U.S. armed forces to ten overseas missions in eight years, compared with twenty by George H. W. Bush in four years and over sixty by Bill Clinton in eight years.[88] When he struck, he tended to strike for maximum effect. By far the most important direct offensive military action under Reagan was the invasion of Grenada on October 25, 1983.

Grenada was a small island in the eastern Caribbean that had fallen in March 1979 under the control of the communist New Jewel Movement, headed by Maurice Bishop. After moving steadily into a political and military partnership with Cuba and the Soviet Union, Grenada had begun construction of a ten-thousand-foot runway that it insisted was destined for tourist purposes but that many military analysts considered a strategic threat. This danger was highlighted by the fact that even though the runway could accommodate 747s, the island had only had four hundred hotel beds and no apparent plans for more.[89] Grenada threatened to serve as the third point of a strategic triangle—consisting of itself, Cuba, and Nicaragua—enveloping the Caribbean, through which would flow half of U.S. reinforcements to NATO in time of war. Reagan argued in a televised address in March 1983 that "the Soviet-Cuban militarization of Grenada can only be seen as power projection into the region."[90]

On October 13, 1983, Bishop was overthrown by even more hard-line elements of the New Jewel Movement, who accused him of "bourgeois deviationism." On October 19, Bishop and several of his political allies were executed; troops fired into a crowd of his supporters, killing scores of people. The new Revolutionary Military Council declared a ninety-six-hour shoot-to-kill curfew. Two concerns soon coalesced for the United States: approximately a thousand American medical students on the island seemed endangered by the turn of events, and the Organization of East Caribbean States now requested an American invasion to depose the new regime.

On Saturday, October 22, Reagan gave the approval for an invasion. The next day, he was awakened to news that the Marine barracks in Beirut, Lebanon, had been attacked by terrorists, killing over 240 Marines. Reagan was urged by numerous advisers to cancel the Grenada invasion. Reagan, however, reportedly replied, "If it was right yesterday, it is right today," and ordered the invasion to proceed.[91] On the morning of October 25, the invasion began; within a few days, armed resistance, more from 1,100 well-armed Cuban "construction workers" than the Grenadian army, had been overcome.[92]

Aside from British prime minister Margaret Thatcher, who protested American intervention in a Commonwealth country, criticism of the operation was strongest among Democratic presidential candidates and members of Congress. Some, like Walter Mondale, George McGovern, and Congressman Ted Weiss, likened the eviction of communism from Grenada to Soviet intervention in Afghanistan and Poland or the Japanese attack on Pearl Harbor. Typical comments on the floor of the U.S. House referred to the invasion as "insane . . . dangerous . . . shocking . . . a shoot-first, ask-questions-later foreign policy . . . utterly irresponsible . . . illegal, immoral, and a wasteful expenditure of human lives . . . against the law . . . an impeachable offense."[93]

Nevertheless, the invasion of Grenada ultimately brought into American living rooms four sets of pictures. The first showed warehouses full of Soviet-made weapons, enough to arm a division and far in excess of what Grenada by itself could use. The second was of American spokesmen revealing reams of captured documents detailing the close relationship between Grenada and the Soviet/Cuban axis; among the documents was an agreement signed secretly in Moscow in May 1980 granting the Soviets landing rights at the new airport for Tu-95 Bear-D long-range reconnaissance aircraft.[94] The third picture showed American medical students kissing the ground upon their safe return to the United States, relieving any doubts that they had considered themselves in danger. The final picture showed "openly joyful" Grenadians welcoming U.S. troops as liberators.[95] Polls later indicated that up to two-thirds of Americans and nine out of every ten Grenadians had supported the invasion; when Reagan visited the island a year later, over one-half of the population of Grenada turned out to greet him.

Although Grenada was a small island with a small population, its importance was enormous. The invasion of Grenada represented the first time that a communist country was liberated by U.S. troops and the first major use of force by the United States since Vietnam. Cuban forces were defeated in battle, and the Brezhnev Doctrine, proclaiming the irreversibility of communist advances, was punctured. The danger of Soviet air or naval operations based in Grenada was eliminated, as was the more pressing danger of Cuban-backed subversion emanating from the island. The strategic and psychological balance in the Caribbean was altered favorably: As Latin America scholar Margaret Daly Hayes argued in 1988, "The propaganda impact of the Grenada operation was tremendous. . . . [A]nyone who questioned whether the Administration was a paper tiger had an answer."[96] For his part, Secretary Shultz perceived an immediate "rippling effect in faraway places."[97] Fidel Castro appeared in a televised interview clearly haggard, the Sandinistas prepared for what they thought was imminent invasion, and Suriname promptly ejected its contingent of a hundred Cuban advisers. Even Syria suddenly feared U.S. retaliation for terrorist attacks. For the first time in recent memory, it seemed riskier to be America's enemy than America's friend. Indeed, in retrospect, Grenada might well have been the pivot point of the Cold War. In any event, never again would the Soviet empire control as much territory as it did before U.S. Army Rangers parachuted onto the Point Salinas airfield.

The Campaign for Democracy

Reagan's human rights policy was heavily influenced by Jeane Kirkpatrick, whose 1979 piece "Dictatorships and Double Standards" argued that Jimmy

Carter had actually harmed both the cause of human rights and the strategic interest of the United States by his failure to recognize the distinction between totalitarianism and mere authoritarianism. In this view, Marxism-Leninism was the preeminent enemy of freedom in the world, and tactical alliances with pro-Western but authoritarian regimes were often necessary to prevent the victory of the greater evil of communism. At the same time, the United States could use quieter diplomatic prodding to improve those regimes.[98]

The influence of Kirkpatrick's ideas on Reagan foreign policy was easy to see, though Reagan added a more dynamic effort to promote freedom in non-communist countries. The international offensive against the Soviet Union undertaken by the United States in the 1980s was accompanied by a broader attempt to expand democracy worldwide. Reagan announced this "campaign for democracy" in his Parliament address of 1982. The campaign took form in the 1983 creation of the National Endowment for Democracy, which received USIA grants but remained an independent foundation. The NED in turn provided funding to the Free Trade Union Institute (affiliated with the AFL-CIO), the National Chamber Foundation (affiliated with the U.S. Chamber of Commerce), the Republican and Democratic Party International Affairs divisions, and other private organizations. Over the years, the NED assisted with poll-watching in several emerging democracies, assisted free labor union movements (including Solidarity when it was still banned in Poland), and trained third-world political figures in the techniques of democracy. Despite its fairly small budget through the 1980s (twenty to forty million dollars a year), the NED was an important part of the overall administration policy for the global advancement of democracy.

The Reagan administration also more directly encouraged the movement of authoritarian regimes to democracy throughout the 1980s. Even some long-time American allies like Ferdinand Marcos of the Philippines, and "Baby Doc" Duvalier of Haiti, were ushered out by their subjects with political help from the United States. Reagan's willingness to provide that help illustrated that his commitment to democracy was not simply rhetorical. Overall, by 1990 observers were noting that "a tide of democratic change is sweeping the world."[99] In 1981, there were fifty-four democracies in the world; in 1992, there were ninety-nine, with thirty-five more countries undertaking democratic transitions.[100] As the *New York Times* editorialized in December 1989, "The cause of human rights came triumphantly of age in the liberating 1980s."[101] Consequently, it can be argued that Reagan's human-rights record was, on balance, more impressive than that of Jimmy Carter. The Reagan administration also promoted economic freedom, arguing that capitalism was best for international economic development. Talk of a redistributionist "new international economic order," commonly heard in the 1970s, was muted. As the American economy expanded, driven by tax cuts and deregulation, the free-market model gained adherents around the world.

The policy of promoting democracy and economic liberalism was grounded both in Reagan's philosophy and in the promise of strategic benefit, as the Soviet empire could be isolated by a growing trend toward democratic capitalism in the rest of the world. The democracy initiative thus had the effect of changing the global "correlation of forces" not through a direct anti-Soviet counterattack but through a growth in democratic power gained in nonaligned and U.S.-allied countries.

The Role of Diplomacy

The Reagan administration adopted what was in several respects a new, more hardheaded approach to arms control. While declaring itself committed to arms control, the administration saw it primarily as the means to the end of enhanced national security. Arms control that failed to secure that end was considered worse than no arms control at all. Furthermore, since the administration saw the Cold War not as an unfortunate misunderstanding between morally equivalent superpowers but as a conflict between totalitarianism and freedom, the arms race was considered a symptom, rather than the central problem, of international relations. The real problem, in this view, was Leninism and Soviet aggression. Thus, effectively prosecuting the Cold War through containment, deterrence, and roll-back was more important than signing treaties with the Soviet regime. The corollary to this view was that good arms control—that is, arms control that secured the national interest of the United States and its allies—could be attained only from a position of strength.

The administration also accused the Soviets of violating existing arms control agreements, thus dampening public expectations and raising questions about their trustworthiness as negotiating partners. The most notable of these accusations was that a large radar at Krasnoyarsk in Siberia was an illegal ABM radar. In addition, the administration submitted that the Soviets were violating SALT II by encrypting test data and developing two new ICBMs when they were permitted only one, violating chemical weapons treaties, and exceeding the maximum yield permitted in underground nuclear tests.[102] Some critics perceived paranoia, until Soviet foreign minister Shevardnadze announced in 1989 that the Krasnoyarsk radar was in fact a "clear violation" of the ABM Treaty and was going to be dismantled.[103] Following the collapse of the Soviet Union, evidence surfaced confirming other Soviet treaty violations, including prohibited stockpiling of biological weapons. In any case, the American change in attitude toward arms control enhanced the diplomatic leverage of the United States.

Second, Reagan took the political initiative in arms control, by replacing the goal of nuclear arms limitation with one of reductions. It is clear from many sources that Reagan adopted this position out of a sincere desire to rid the world gradually of nuclear weapons, but it also put the Soviets on the diplomatic defensive. In Europe, the allied position was that the West would deploy no missiles if the Soviets eliminated all SS-20s; after the Euromissile deployment began in 1983, the West offered to trade elimination of all Pershing II and cruise missiles for that of all SS-20s. Critics at the time argued that this negotiating strategy was doomed to failure. Arms control expert William Hyland said that the zero option was a "clever tactic" but "puts the U.S. on a negotiating slope that will end in disaster."[104] To Sen. Edward Kennedy, it was "voodoo arms control."[105] Instead of retreating, however, Reagan and NATO deployed the missiles, negotiated from a position of strength, and in 1987 won Soviet acceptance of a treaty on intermediate nuclear forces in Europe, on basically the same terms as the West had offered in 1981.

On strategic weapons, Reagan repeated the call for substantial reductions. Again, many claimed that this negotiating stance was nothing but a public relations ploy to make the Soviets look bad by presenting an offer they would not accept, and in any case that the U.S. nuclear buildup would guarantee failure in the negotiations. *Time* correspondent Strobe Talbott (later an assistant secretary of state in the Clinton administration) called the Reagan strategy a "deadly gambit" and assured his readers that it would probably bring disaster. After years of on-and-off negotiation, the first Strategic Arms Reduction Treaty (START I) would be signed in 1991. This overall change in arms control approach put the diplomatic and political initiative in the hands of the West. Events at the end of the 1980s and beginning of the 1990s indicated that Reagan had been right about the arms race—as frightening as it was, the arms race was the symptom, not the cause, of U.S.-Soviet conflict. When the Soviet regime first mellowed and then disintegrated, the arms race ended.

More important than the treaties themselves, the United States and the West avoided the mistake of allowing the Soviets to reduce the stress building on their system through superficial arms control rather than fundamental internal reform. To Ambassador Matlock, "The obvious fact that the Soviet Union could not win the arms race and therefore would have to find a way to end it was Gorbachev's most powerful weapon in dealing with his hard-line critics."[106] Perhaps most decisively, Reagan refused, as noted above, to put SDI on the negotiating table. In the words of Kenneth Adelman, director of the Arms Control and Disarmament Agency under Reagan, at the Reykjavik summit "Reagan would not budge, when the pressure to do so was most staggering."[107] Matlock's analysis was that "after the Reykjavic Summit, [the Soviets] concluded they were going to have to take the rest of the agenda" of the administration, including Soviet disengagement from third world conflicts, respect for human rights, and an end to the Iron Curtain.[108] For his part, former U.S. national security adviser Zbigniew Brzezinski, not typically a supporter of Reagan, contended that America won the Cold War at the Reykjavik summit in 1986, when Gorbachev failed to dislodge Reagan from his position on SDI. His view was shared by Margaret Thatcher.[109]

The United States, having driven the Soviets to the brink of fundamental change, had to negotiate what were in effect the terms of Soviet surrender in the Cold War. This task was far from easy; to be too accommodating was to risk easing the pressure too early, while retaining a hard line for too long risked rebuffing a genuine effort at rapprochement. If Reagan's strategic plan to undermine Soviet power could be executed only over vehement objections from the Left, it was also true that the diplomacy required to close the Cold War could only be undertaken despite the natural suspicion and skepticism of the Right. From 1986 to 1988, when this diplomatic denouement was reaching its decisive stage, the Reagan administration had to contend with the objections of conservatives who were unable to believe that victory was actually at hand. Reagan, denounced as a warmonger from one side, was attacked for naivete by the other.

Nevertheless, he proceeded with summit meetings, negotiations, and an increasingly warm relationship with Mikhail Gorbachev. Indeed, as scholar Beth Fischer argued, far from simply responding to Gorbachev's initiatives, Reagan took the initiative in reaching out even before Gorbachev's ascension to power.[110] Reagan himself put great stock in personal diplomacy. Though Fischer probably placed too much emphasis on diplomatic atmospherics and not enough on the policy of anti-Soviet pressure, which remained fundamentally intact until the late 1980s, she made the important point that Reagan was the primary diplomatic actor in the winding-down of the Cold War. In retrospect, it took an uncanny ability on Reagan's part to see through the fog of events, seize the moment, and "close the deal." For this diplomatic acumen he later received commendation from John Lewis Gaddis, who praised Reagan's combination of toughness and flexibility. Writing in 1992, Gaddis argued that "it took more than luck to recognize what was happening, and to capitalize on it to the extent that the Reagan administration did." To Gaddis, along with Gorbachev, "Ronald Reagan deserves a great deal of the credit" for the negotiated end of the Cold War.[111]

Reagan's Foreign Policy: Evaluations

Altogether, the policies that Reagan developed to meet the international dangers the United States faced at the beginning of the 1980s were innovative and highly effective. His approach to foreign policy represented a blend of Jeffersonianism and Hamiltonianism, idealism and hard-headedness. His policy was grounded in fundamental American principles yet did not neglect the potential role of force when dealing with unsavory and aggressive adversaries. It avoided the counterproductive moralism that had undermined the Carter policy, without abandoning the ultimate goal of expanding the sphere of freedom. It restored a sense of national purpose that gave meaning to America's role in the world. And, presuming the long-term futility of a purely defensive posture toward the Soviets, Reagan sought to end the deadlock of the Cold War by taking the initiative and capitalizing on Western strengths and communist weaknesses in order to prevail.

There were, of course, failures. The peacekeeping mission in Beirut, while driven by legitimate strategic concerns over Syrian and Soviet influence in the Middle East, was ill conceived, ill executed, and ultimately disastrous. The Iran-Contra episode was a miscue of sizable proportion, a failure running the gamut from questions of policy (sending arms to Iran) to political judgment (linking two already controversial policies), to legality (possible violations of the Boland Amendments), to constitutional accountability (centered around allegations of a freestanding "secret government" running covert operations).

Nevertheless, claims of critics like I. M. Destler that the "overall balance" of Reagan's foreign policy "appears negative"[112] were dubious even when they were made (in 1988) and are now untenable. To the contrary, it is clear that the foreign policy failures of the 1980s were far outweighed by the successes. The central fact is that the Cold War was won. At the beginning of the 1980s, the outcome of that struggle had been in doubt. Indeed, it is not unreasonable to say that in 1979–80 the West was losing. Even America's friends were on the verge of wavering, and the danger of war had grown considerably. At the end of the American counteroffensive, the Soviet empire landed on the "ash heap of history" that Reagan had predicted in 1982, sooner than even the most hopeful would have dared to guess. By the early 1990s, the United States found itself in a position of security among nations unparalleled in its history. It was the world's sole superpower. Reagan's preeminent goal of safeguarding American freedom from its totalitarian adversaries abroad—the first prerequisite of national liberty—was met.

There is, of course, no way of knowing with certainty what would have happened in the absence of Reagan's policies. However, it can be said with certainty that most of the claims and predictions of Reagan's critics throughout the 1980s were unambiguously wrong. The arms buildup did not produce Armageddon or even arms control deadlock. The forceful application of containment in Central America did not produce another Vietnam. SDI did not accelerate the arms race, and Reagan's refusal to negotiate it away did not bring disaster. The Reagan Doctrine led to neither general war nor humiliation, but did drive the Soviets out of the third world. The ideological offensive did not destroy NATO or prevent Soviet reform. Sending Stinger missiles to Afghanistan did not lead to a Soviet attack on Pakistan. The Soviets did violate the ABM Treaty, the New Jewel Movement did promise the Soviets military use of the new airport on Grenada, the Sandinistas did arm the FMLN, and the Nicaraguan people did dispose of the Sandinistas as soon as they had an opportunity. Communism rather than great-power rivalry had been the primary source of conflict; as soon as Leninism collapsed, relations between the United States and Russia warmed. In the aftermath of that collapse, Leninism was declared by its own former subjects to have produced indeed an "evil empire." The simple principles that guided Reagan's foreign policy—peace through strength, "trust but verify," tyranny is evil and evil must not be allowed to triumph—held up far better over time than the rationalizations and moral equivocation that were offered as an alternative throughout the 1980s.

Many conservatives—though not Reagan—also made the mistake of underestimating the capacity of the Soviet leadership to change, or of other communist dictators to be dislodged by basically peaceful means. Most probably expected that when the Soviet empire fell, it would fall more in the bloody style of Ceaucescu's Romania, which in the event was the exception. Nevertheless, the opponents of Reagan's policy of anticommunist assertiveness were far guiltier of gross misjudgment.

There can be no doubt that Gorbachev's internal reforms and "new thinking" on foreign policy were largely responsible for the easing of Cold War tensions and for the ultimate collapse of the Soviet state. However, it is largely forgotten that in the first few years of his rule, Gorbachev's foreign policy was anything but accommodating. While proclaiming peace, he undertook a major propaganda offensive with the design of driving a wedge between the United States and Europe by talk of the "common European home." He also authorized a major new phase of the Soviet strategic nuclear buildup, escalated the wars in Afghanistan and Angola, and expanded aid to Vietnam, Cuba, Libya, and Nicaragua. Gorbachev made it clear that in his view *perestroika* was an attempt to improve the efficiency and vigor of Soviet society; his aim was to reform the communist state to make it more effective. Only in the late 1980s, when it became clear that his charm offensive and summit meetings were insufficient to relieve the growing pressure on the Soviet empire, did a new Gorbachev appear, agreeing to the "zero option," pulling troops out of Afghanistan, and ultimately allowing the satellites to collapse.

Thus, while it cannot be proven incontrovertibly that Reagan's policies were decisive in turning the tide of the Cold War, there is very good reason to believe they were. Eduard Shevardnadze discusses how these American initiatives created gloom for the Soviet leadership, where only a few years before there had been overwhelming confidence. To Shevardnadze, SDI, economic sanctions, elements of the ideological offensive, the Euromissile deployments, and accusations of Soviet treaty violations combined to create for the Soviets a "Gordian knot. . . . No matter where we turned, we came up against the fact that we would achieve nothing without normalization of Soviet-American relations. We did some hard thinking, at times sinking into despair over the impasse."[113] This Gordian knot led above all to a reexamination of the Leninist doctrine "that ideological struggle between the two social and political systems is inevitable," an assumption that had always been an obstacle to the normalization of relations.[114] Others emphasize the domestic implications in the USSR of American pressure, arguing that it drove experiments with reform. Former Soviet parliament member Ilya Zaslavsky says simply, "Ronald Reagan was the father of *perestroika.*"[115]

As early as 1981, a prescient Soviet arms negotiator already had a sense of what lay in store; he was quoted as saying, "Oh, you Americans! You are going to win the Cold War. You are going to make us spend and spend to keep up and our lousy standard of living will go down and down and in the end you will win."[116] As Genrikh Trofimenko, former head of the Department for the Study of the U.S. Foreign Policy at the former Soviet Institute of the USA and Canada, said in 1993, "Ninety-nine percent of Russian people believe that you won the Cold War because of your President's insistence on SDI."[117] This analysis is shared by many in the former satellite countries. In launching a drive to rename one of Warsaw's central squares "Reagan Square," Solidarity chief Marian Krazlewski declared in 1999 that "Reagan was the main author of the victory of the Free World over the Evil Empire."[118] Gorbachev himself denies the catalytic impact of assertive U.S. policy—though he does credit Reagan's diplomacy—but his denial fails to explain his own changed behavior after 1985–87, and it is in any case to be expected from a man who undoubtedly does not want to lend credence to the possibility that he was not really the "Man of the Decade" as *Time* magazine declared.[119] Ambassador Matlock, who was an eyewitness to the unraveling of Soviet power, argued that

> the Cold War ended because, in the mid-1980s, we had the coincidence of (1) a Western policy that combined strength and firmness with a willingness to negotiate fairly and (2) a Soviet leadership that finally realized that the country could not go on as it had. . . . The scenario was written in Washington and it is doubtful that it could have been written in Moscow, even by a leader as ingenious as Mikhail Gorbachev.[120]

While Matlock distinguished between the end of the Cold War (for which the United States was primarily responsible), the end of communism (for which Gorbachev was mostly responsible), and the end of the Soviet Union (for which a variety of Soviet actors were responsible), he allowed that America and the West "helped create the conditions" that made the last two possible as well as the first.[121]

This outcome had not been inevitable, for two reasons. First, the United States could have responded to the Soviet challenge of the 1970s by retreating in the 1980s, adopting a passive policy of isolationism, appeasement, and accommodation to the new realities. Indeed, there was a considerable chorus of Western voices urging just that, though usually covered with some rhetorical fig leaf. Every important policy and decision in the restoration of American assertiveness was made by human beings who could have chosen other options; every one of those policies was decried, often loudly, by powerful segments of American and Western opinion. It is not at all difficult to imagine another president not launching SDI, not deploying Euromissiles, not invading Grenada, not aiding El Salvador, not supporting anticommunist guerrillas, not calling the Soviet Union an evil empire, and not launching an economic war against that empire; indeed, the presidential campaigns of the 1980s were filled with such men.[122]

Second, it was not inevitable that internal Soviet difficulties would drive reforms rather than another, more dangerous, response. Declining empires have often tried to revive their fortunes by striking out. This possibility was discussed by veteran correspondent Harrison Salisbury at the death of Leonid Brezhnev in 1982: "What should concern Americans is that a new regime with less caution in foreign policy, conscious that the Soviet Union faces intractable domestic problems, may turn to adventures abroad to distract attention from internal failures."[123] The restoration of American strength channeled the Soviet response into reform by foreclosing the option of further aggression.

Many in the West have sidestepped these conclusions, arguing that the Soviets were never really a threat, because their economy was actually much smaller than had been estimated. Successive American administrations, according to this view, exaggerated the Soviet threat, leading to a "crackpot realism" based on a misunderstanding of true Soviet strength.[124] Yet while they are related, economic strength and military threat are not the same thing. As Kenneth Adelman observed, history is replete with examples of impoverished garrison states conquering their prosperous but unprepared or enervated foes.[125] A nation's power can be defined not simply as its resources but as its resources multiplied by its will. American preponderance of resources unaccompanied by the will to use them vigorously could not have averted failure. In any event, it was the proponents of assertiveness in the 1980s who understood Soviet economic weakness and the opponents of assertiveness who overestimated

Soviet economic strength. Reagan himself argued in his 1982 Westminster speech that

> We are witnessing today a great revolutionary crisis—a crisis where the demands of the economic order are colliding directly with those of the political order. But the crisis is happening not in the free, non-Marxist west, but in the home of Marxism-Leninism, the Soviet Union. . . . What we see here is a political structure that no longer corresponds to its economic base, a society where productive forces are hampered by political ones.[126]

Margaret Thatcher recounted a private conversation with Reagan in 1983 in which Reagan intimated to her that if the Soviets

> saw that the United States had the will and the determination to build up its defences as far as necessary, the Soviet attitude might change because they knew they could not keep up the pace. He believed that the Russians were now close to the limit in their expenditure on defence: their internal economic difficulties were such that they could not substantially increase the proportion of their resources devoted to the military.[127]

It was Reagan's opponents, who had greater faith in central planning, who considered such talk foolish. John Kenneth Galbraith, for example, held in 1984 that "the Soviet economy has made great national progress in recent years."[128] Paul Samuelson argued that the Soviets had proved that "a centrally planned economy can function and prosper."[129] Columnist Mary McGrory openly ridiculed Reagan's analysis of Soviet weakness, virtually guffawing in 1982 that "he says they're on the verge of economic collapse."[130] Reagan understood far better than his critics the vulnerability of the Soviet Union. Yet he also believed—historically, one can only say correctly—that this weakness did not obviate the enormous dangers emanating from the intersection of the massive Soviet arsenal and Marxist-Leninist ideology.

It is ironic that the same voices that in the 1980s held it futile to seek the roll-back of Soviet power, that counseled Reagan to give up his dangerous and hopeless dreams of victory in the Cold War, now proclaim that the collapse of Soviet power at the end of the 1980s had been preordained and proves that the Soviets were never really a threat. This argument would not be terribly different from isolationists arguing in 1946 that the Allied victory in World War II proved that the Axis powers had never really been a threat. Other ironies are no less notable. Strobe Talbott, who could hardly have been more mistaken about the effect of the arms buildup, declares, "The doves in the Great Debate of the past forty years were right all along."[131] Liberals who had dismissed containment as simplistic for the last twenty years of the Cold War now "wistfully recall how the Soviet threat brilliantly illuminated the foreign-policy landscape."[132] American academics even proclaim that the United States and USSR were equally losers of the Cold War, despite the fact that their own country survived and the other did not.[133]

Those who hold that Soviet power collapsed entirely on its own must contend with the fact that most of the empires of history have collapsed only when pushed from the outside.[134] Rome fell to barbarians, Byzantium to Mohammedans, the Incas and Aztecs to conquistadors, the Spanish to Admiral George Dewey; the kaisers, the tsars, the Ottomans, and the Habsburgs to the pressures of World War I; and the British and French empires to the costs of World War II. Each empire had its own internal weaknesses, to be sure, yet without external pressures imperial power had been sufficient to maintain itself for centuries. No convincing reason has been offered to believe that the Soviet empire, almost alone among the great empires of history, fell without influence from the outside.

To the contrary, as Jean-Francois Revel argued, "Translating communism's economic disaster into political disaster required translators."[135] There were many translators, including American scientists, allies like Thatcher and Kohl, third-world anticommunist guerrillas, Pope John Paul II, Polish shipyard workers, and those in the Soviet Union itself who struggled for human dignity even in the depths of the Gulag. Yet it was the United States, under Reagan's leadership, that rallied the West in the 1980s and apprehended to the fullest extent the very real weaknesses of the Soviet empire—the economic and social stagnation, the technology gap, the potential for political resistance, the nationalities problem, the imperial overreach, and the spiritual vacuity inherent in Communist ideology—and that possessed the resources and the political fortitude to exploit them systematically on a global scale. Above all, it was Reagan who had confidence that freedom was stronger than tyranny, that it could and would prevail if it acted on its strength. After the victory was won, Reagan contended that "democracy triumphed in the Cold War because it was a battle of values—between one system that gave preeminence to the state and another that gave preeminence to the individual and freedom."[136] For that confidence—and that victory—he deserves no small measure of credit, and of gratitude.

Notes

1. Stephen E. Ambrose, "Reagan's Foreign Policy: An Overview," in *President Reagan and the World*, ed. Eric J. Schmertz, Nancy Datlof, and Alexej Ugrinsky (Westport, Conn.: Greenwood, 1997), 10.

2. Ben J. Wattenberg, "It's Time to Stop America's Retreat," *New York Times Magazine*, July 22, 1979, 14–16.

3. See Bruce D. Porter, *The USSR in Third World Conflicts* (Cambridge: Cambridge University Press, 1984), 244.

4. Viktor Suvorov, *Inside the Soviet Army* (New York: Macmillan, 1982), 161–62.

5. Jack F. Matlock Jr., "Discussant," in *President Reagan and the World*, ed. Schmertz, Datlof, and Ugrinsky, 122.

6. Quoted in Gerald L. Steibel, *Detente: Dilemma or Disaster?* (New York: National Strategy Information Center, 1969), 26.

7. Paul H. Nitze, "Strategy in the Decade of the 1980s," *Foreign Affairs* (Fall 1980), 86.

8. Daniel Yankelovich and Larry Kaagan, "Assertive America," in *The Reagan Foreign Policy*, ed. William G. Hyland (New York: New American Library, 1987), 1–18.

9. *U.S. News & World Report*, January 14, 1980.

10. "Biggest Shock Yet," *U.S. News & World Report*, January 14, 1980, 20.

11. Ronald Reagan, *An American Life: The Autobiography* (New York: Simon and Schuster, 1990), 548, 594.

12. "Inaugural Address, January 21, 1985," *Public Papers of the Presidents: Ronald Reagan 1985* (Washington, D.C.: Government Printing Office [hereafter GPO], 1988), 58.

13. See, for example, Stephane Courtois, et al., *The Black Book of Communism* (Cambridge, Mass.: Harvard University Press, 1999).

14. "Inaugural Address, January 20, 1981," *Public Papers of the Presidents: Ronald Reagan 1981* (Washington, D.C.: GPO, 1982), 3.

15. Reagan, *An American Life*, 237.

16. Michael A. Ledeen, *Perilous Statecraft: An Insider's Account of the Iran-Contra Affair* (New York: Scribner, 1988), 5.

17. *Soviet Military Power* (Washington, D.C.: Department of Defense, 1981), 9; Caspar W. Weinberger, "Policy, Strategy, and the Budget," *Defense* (May 1982), 15. Estimates of Soviet military spending, which held that the Soviets were devoting 12–16 percent of GNP to the military, were never better than well-informed guesses, owing to Soviet secrecy and the difficulty of translating the ruble into dollars. However, there can be no question that the Soviets placed much higher priority on military expenditures than did the United States; it is almost certainly true that if anything, CIA estimates *understated* the proportion of Soviet GNP devoted to the military, both because it underestimated such spending and because it overestimated the size of the Soviet economy. In the early 1990s, analysts with access to Soviet archives concluded that Soviet military spending had been closer to 30 percent of GNP. Furthermore, because Soviet state socialism owned all industry and because Soviet wages were so low, the Soviets could produce a tank or airplane for much less than American industry could have produced an identical item. Thus, a gap in spending often masked an even greater gap in output.

18. Caspar W. Weinberger, *Fighting for Peace: Seven Critical Years in the Pentagon* (New York: Warner, 1990), 79. On the defense buildup more generally, see 39–79.

19. R. Herman, "Rally, Speakers Decry Cost of Nuclear Arms Race," *New York Times*, June 12, 1982, A43. However, public support for the freeze was never as solid or as deep as its proponents maintained; see J. Michael Hogan and Ted J. Smith III, "Polling on the Issues: Public Opinion and the Nuclear Freeze," *Public Opinion Quarterly* (Winter 1991).

20. David D. Schmidt, *Citizen Lawmakers: The Ballot Initiative Revolution* (Philadelphia: Temple University Press, 1989), 163.

21. Pam Solo, *From Protest to Policy* (Cambridge, Mass.: Ballinger, 1988), 127.

22. For example, the M-1 tank began replacing the venerable M-60; new stealth aircraft technologies came on line; and laser-guided "smart" munitions became an important part of the air arsenal. For a discussion of the importance of technology to the U.S. buildup, see

Peter Schweizer, *Victory: The Reagan Administration's Secret Strategy That Hastened the Collapse of the Soviet Union* (New York: Atlantic Monthly, 1994).

23. "Ready for Action—Or Are They?" *U.S. News & World Report*, February 14, 1983, 23. For a detailed account of readiness improvements, see the whole report, 23–27.

24. By 1985, it was estimated that the FMLN was responsible for up to 70 percent of political killings in El Salvador. See "Sun Breaks through for U.S. in Central America," *U.S. News & World Report*, June 24, 1985, 29.

25. Ashley J. Tellis, "The Geopolitical Stakes in Central American Crisis," in *Central America and the Reagan Doctrine*, ed. Walter F. Hahn (Lanham Md.: University Press of America, 1987), 34; for elaboration, see 34–48.

26. Discovered in the Grenada documents and quoted in *The Challenge to Democracy in Central America* (Washington, D.C.: Departments of State and Defense, 1986), 13.

27. "A Turn for the Worse," *Newsweek*, December 12, 1983, 54–57.

28. "The Outcome in El Salvador," *Washington Post*, January 19, 1992, C6.

29. Weinberger, *Fighting for Peace*, 249–87.

30. Weinberger, *Fighting for Peace*, 219–48.

31. See Robbin F. Laird, "Soviet Nuclear Weapons in Europe," in *Soviet Foreign Policy in a Changing World*, ed. Robbin F. Laird and Erik Hoffmann (New York: Aldine de Gruyter, 1986). For the NATO perspective, see Hans-Dietrich Genscher, "Intermediate Range Missiles: Moscow Holds the Key to Disarmament," *NATO Review* (March–April 1983), 1–8.

32. For a discussion of Soviet involvement in the European peace movement, see Vladimir Bukovsky, *The Peace Movement and the Soviet Union* (New York: Orwell, 1982).

33. Henrik Bering, *Helmut Kohl* (Washington, D.C.: Regnery, 1999), 14.

34. For such predictions, see Thomas L. Hughes, "Up from Reaganism," *Foreign Policy* (Fall 1981).

35. Margaret Thatcher, "Reagan's Leadership, America's Recovery," *National Review*, December 30, 1988, 23.

36. "The Pitcher and the Catcher," *Newsweek*, January 9, 1989, 20.

37. Christopher C. DeMuth et al., *The Reagan Doctrine and Beyond* (Washington, D.C.: American Enterprise Institute [hereafter AEI], 1987), 3.

38. Barry M. Goldwater, *Why Not Victory? A Fresh Look at American Foreign Policy* (New York: McGraw-Hill, 1962), 39.

39. Cited by Joseph Shattan, *Architects of Victory: Six Heroes of the Cold War* (Washington, D.C.: Heritage Foundation, 1999), 245.

40. Reagan, *An American Life*, 238.

41. See Schweizer, *Victory*, 76–77, 81–82, 125–27, 130–32.

42. Herbert E. Meyer, "Discussant," in *President Reagan and the World*, ed. Schmertz, Datlof, and Ugrinsky, 126, 128.

43. Fitzhugh Green, *American Propaganda Abroad* (New York: Hippocrene, 1988), 193.

44. "The President's News Conference, January 28, 1981," *Public Papers of the Presidents: Ronald Reagan 1981* (Washington, D.C.: GPO, 1982), 57.

45. "Address at Commencement Exercises at the University of Notre Dame, May 17, 1981," *Public Papers of the Presidents: Ronald Reagan 1981* (Washington, D.C.: GPO, 1982), 434.

46. "Address to Members of the British Parliament, June 8, 1982," *Public Papers of the Presidents: Ronald Reagan 1983* (Washington, D.C.: GPO, 1983), 747–48.

47. "Remarks at the Annual Convention of the National Association of Evangelicals in Orlando, Florida, March 8, 1983," *Public Papers of the Presidents: Ronald Reagan 1983* (Washington, D.C.: GPO, 1984), 363–64.

48. "Address before a Joint Session of Congress Reporting on the State of the Union, January 26, 1982," *Public Papers of the Presidents: Ronald Reagan 1982* (Washington, D.C.: GPO, 1983), 78.

49. Cited in Shattan, *Architects of Victory*, 280.

50. Edmund Morris, *Dutch: A Memoir of Ronald Reagan* (New York: Random House, 1999), 473.

51. Anthony Lewis, "Onward, Christian Soldiers," *New York Times*, March 10, 1983, A27. See also "The Lord and the Freeze," *New York Times*, March 11, 1983, A30.

52. John Lewis Gaddis, "The Tragedy of Cold War History," *Foreign Affairs* (January–February 1994), 148.

53. Jack F. Matlock Jr., *Autopsy of an Empire* (New York: Random House, 1995), 589.

54. "Reagan and History," *National Review*, May 24, 1993, 20. See also Morris, *Dutch*, 474.

55. Andrei Kozyrev, "Russia: A Chance for Survival," *Foreign Affairs* (Spring 1992), 3, 13.

56. Schweizer, *Victory*, 126.

57. Schweizer, *Victory*, 243.

58. Schweizer, *Victory*, 190–91.

59. *Soviet Strategic Defense Programs* (Washington, D.C.: Departments of State and Defense, 1985), 12.

60. *Soviet Military Power 1987* (Washington, D.C.: Department of Defense, 1987), 45. It should be pointed out that "strategic offense" and "strategic defense" were American constructs; to the Soviets, there was only strategic offense, with a tactically offensive component (ICBMs, submarine-launched ballistic missiles, and bombers) and tactically defensive component (ballistic missile defense, civil defense, air defense).

61. As Reagan later argued, "if we stopped work on the SDI and they continued work on their system, it meant we might wake up one morning to learn that they alone had a defense against missiles. We couldn't afford that." Reagan, *An American Life*, 677.

62. Pam Solo, *From Protest to Policy: Beyond the Freeze to Common Security* (Cambridge, Mass.: Ballinger, 1988), 148. See also Dinesh D'Souza, *Ronald Reagan: How an Ordinary Man Became an Extraordinary Leader* (New York: Free Press, 1997), 179.

63. Anatoly Dobrynin, *In Confidence* (New York: Times Books, 1985), 528.

64. For an analysis of the strategic and economic implications of SDI to the Soviet Union, see Ilya Zemtsov and John Farrar, *Gorbachev: The Man and the System* (New Brunswick, N.J.: Transaction, 1989), 181–83; and Schweizer, *Victory*.

65. McGeorge Bundy, George F. Kennan, Robert S. McNamara, and Gerard Smith, "The President's Choice: Star Wars or Arms Control," in *The Reagan Foreign Policy*, ed. Hyland, 165.

66. McGeorge Bundy, "Arms Control, Not Competition," *New York Times Magazine*, April 5, 1987, 46–47.

67. Zemtsov and Farrar, *Gorbachev*, 182–83.

68. See Eduard Shevardnadze, *The Future Belongs to Freedom* (New York: Free Press, 1991), 80–81; Bessmertnykh made this point at a conference at Princeton University in February 1993, cited in *National Review*, March 29, 1993, 12. Gorbachev claimed in 1994 that SDI had had no positive impact on Soviet reform; Richard Ned Lebow and Janice Gross Stein, "Reagan and the Russians," *Atlantic Monthly*, February 1994, 35–37. However, Bessmertnykh not only disputes this interpretation but argues that Gorbachev had privately admitted that SDI was important.

69. Robert M. Gates, *From the Shadows* (New York: Touchstone, 1996), 266.

70. Reagan, *An American Life*, 548.

71. Mark Lagon, *The Reagan Doctrine: Sources of American Conduct in the Cold War's Last Chapter* (Westport, Conn.: Praeger, 1994), 154.

72. See Stephen S. Rosenfeld, "The Guns of July," in *The Reagan Foreign Policy*, Hyland.

73. "Address before a Joint Session of Congress on the State of the Union, February 6, 1985," *Public Papers of the Presidents: Ronald Reagan 1985* (Washington, D.C.: GPO, 1988), 135.

74. George Shultz, "America and the Struggle of Freedom," address to the Commonwealth Club of California, San Francisco, February 22, 1985, 2–4.

75. Lagon, *The Reagan Doctrine*, 87.

76. William R. Bode, "The Reagan Doctrine," *Strategic Review* (Winter 1986), 26.

77. "Remarks on Soviet–United States Relations at the Town Hall of California Meeting in Los Angeles, August 26, 1987," *Public Papers of the Presidents: Ronald Reagan 1987* (Washington, D.C.: GPO, 1989), 979.

78. George Shultz, "Low Intensity Warfare: The Challenge of Ambiguity," address to the National Defense University, Washington, D.C., January 15, 1986, 3.

79. Charles Waterman, "Making Covert Aid to Rebels Overt," *Christian Science Monitor*, April 21, 1986, 12. See also Rosenfeld, "The Guns of July."

80. "What Goes Around," *U.S. News & World Report*, August 30–September 6, 1993, 48.

81. For a detailed discussion of the Reagan administration's secret strategies in Afghanistan, see Schweizer, *Victory*.

82. George Shultz, *Turmoil and Triumph: My Years as Secretary of State* (New York: Scribner, 1993), 1123.

83. Robert T. Huber, "Perestroika and U.S.-Soviet Relations: The Five-Year Plan No One Devised," in *Five Years That Shook the World*, ed. Harley D. Balzer (Boulder, Colo.: Westview, 1990), 162.

84. David K. Willis, "Rebels Deal Setback to USSR in Third World," *Christian Science Monitor*, February 19, 1986, 12.

85. Carl Bernstein and Marco Politi, *His Holiness: John Paul II and the Hidden History of Our Time* (New York: Doubleday, 1996).

86. See Schweizer, *Victory*.

87. Schweizer, *Victory*, 250.

88. Donald Devine, "Legacy Taking Shape," *Washington Times*, May 3, 1999, A17.

89. Dorothea Cypher, "Grenada: Indications, Warning, and U.S. Response," in *American Intervention in Grenada*, ed. Peter M. Dunn and Bruce W. Watson (Boulder, Colo.: Westview, 1985), 48.

90. "Address to the Nation on Defense and National Security, March 23, 1983," *Public Papers of the Presidents: Ronald Reagan 1983* (Washington, D.C.: GPO, 1984), 440.

91. See Constantine Menges, *Inside the National Security Council* (New York: Simon and Schuster, 1988), 80–82; Robert J. Beck, *International Law and "Urgent Fury,"* Ph.D. dissertation, University of Virginia, 1989, 239–42; Ralph Kinney Bennett, "Grenada: Anatomy of a 'Go' Decision," *Reader's Digest*, February 1984, 75–76.

92. Secretary of Defense Caspar Weinberger later pointed out that the Cubans were "organized in military fashion into 'Company A and B, Mortar Company, and Machine Gun Company'" and were "equipped with AK-47 automatic assault rifles and heavy weapons." *Fighting for Peace*, 124.

93. Cited in Frank Gregorsky, *What's the Matter with Democratic Foreign Policy?* (Washington, D.C.: Republican Study Committee, May 1984), 51–57. The latter collection of statements were made by, respectively, Rep. Pete Stark, Rep. Charles Schumer, Rep. Don Bonker, Rep. Ed Markey, George McGovern, Rep. Major Owen, Rep. Don Edwards, and Rep. Ted Weiss.

94. See *Grenada Documents: An Overview and Selection* (Washington, D.C.: Departments of State and Defense, 1984), esp. doc. 23.

95. See "'Enough Guns to Arm a Division,'" *U.S. News & World Report*, November 7, 1983, 34.

96. Margaret Daly Hayes, "Not What I Say, But What I Do: Latin American Policy in the Reagan Administration," in *United States Policy in Latin America: A Quarter Century of Crisis and Challenge, 1961–1986*, ed. John D. Martz (Lincoln: University of Nebraska Press, 1988), 117.

97. Shultz, *Turmoil and Triumph*, 344.

98. Jeane J. Kirkpatrick, "Dictatorships and Double Standards," *Commentary* (November 1979).

99. Dankwart A. Rustow, "Democracy: A Global Revolution?" *Foreign Affairs* (Fall 1990), 75.

100. R. Bruce McColm, "The Comparative Study of Freedom House, New York, 1992–1993: Our Crowded Hour," *Freedom in the World* (New York: Freedom House, 1993).

101. "Human Rights: Now the Hard Part," *New York Times*, December 30, 1989, I24.

102. See "Soviet Noncompliance with Arms Control Agreements," Special Report 122, United States Department of State, February 1, 1985; "Soviet Noncompliance with Arms Control Agreements," Special Report 163, United States Department of State, March 1987.

103. Michael Dobbs, "Soviets Acknowledge Breach of ABM Pact," *Washington Post*, October 24, 1989, 1.

104. Strobe Talbott, *Deadly Gambits* (New York: Knopf, 1984), 80–81.

105. See also Paul C. Warnke, "'Zero' May Mean Nothing," *New York Times*, January 26, 1983, A23.

106. Matlock, *Autopsy on an Empire*, 669.

107. Kenneth L. Adelman, "United States and Soviet Relations: Reagan's Real Role in Winning the Cold War," in *President Reagan and the World*, ed. Schmertz, Datlof, and Ugrinsky, 90.

108. Matlock, "Discussant," 124.

109. Remarks by Frank J. Fahrenkopf Jr., "The Conservative Agenda," in *Ronald Reagan's America*, ed. Schmertz, Datlof, and Ugrinsky, 290.

110. Beth A. Fischer, *The Reagan Reversal: Foreign Policy and the End of the Cold War* (Columbia: University of Missouri, 1997). Reagan himself details the multiple personal diplomatic initiatives he took with Brezhnev, Yuri Andropov, and Konstantin Chernenko. *An American Life*, passim.

111. John Lewis Gaddis, *The United States and the End of the Cold War* (New York: Oxford University Press, 1992), 123, 130.

112. I. M. Destler, "Reagan and the World: 'An Awesome Stubbornness,'" in *The Reagan Legacy: Promise and Performance*, ed. Charles O. Jones (Chatham, N.J.: Chatham House, 1988), 260.

113. Shevardnadze, *The Future Belongs to Freedom*, 80–81.

114. Shevardnadze, *The Future Belongs to Freedom*, 84.

115. Schweizer, *Victory*, 198.

116. Harrison Salisbury, "USSR: What's Ahead," *Denver Post*, November 1982, 3D.

117. Trofimenko made this remark on April 22, 1993, at a panel on Ronald Reagan's foreign policy at the Ninth Presidential Conference at Hofstra University. Morris, *Dutch*, 659.

118. "This Week," *National Review*, July 26, 1999, 12.

119. Lebow and Stein, "Reagan and the Russians," 35–37.

120. Matlock, *Autopsy on an Empire*, 669–70.

121. Matlock, *Autopsy on an Empire*, 672.

122. Indeed, the Democratic national platform of 1984 called for a cutback in the planned defense buildup; a freeze on nuclear weapons testing, production, and deployment; resubmission of SALT II to the Senate; an end to draft registration, to support for the Nicaraguan Contras, and to U.S. military exercises in Central America; and the imposition of virtually unmeetable conditions on aid to El Salvador.

123. Salisbury, "USSR: What's Ahead," 1D.

124. See William Greider, *Who Will Tell the People: The Betrayal of American Democracy* (New York: Simon and Schuster, 1992), 362–63; Richard Reeves, "Was the Cold War Necessary," *The Record*, August 5, 1990.

125. Adelman, "United States and Soviet Relations," 88.

126. "Address to Members of the British Parliament, June 8, 1982," 744.

127. Schweizer, *Victory*, 126.

128. John Kenneth Galbraith, "A Visit to Russia," *The New Yorker*, September 3, 1984, 60.

129. See Jean-Francois Revel, *Democracy against Itself* (New York: Free Press, 1993), 14. See also Seweryn Bialer, "Reagan and Russia," *Foreign Affairs* (Winter 1982–1983), 249–71.

130. Mary McGrory, "A Campaign That Has Ignored the Impact of Japan and Russia," *Denver Post*, November 11, 1982, 2B.

131. Strobe Talbott, "Rethinking the Red Menace," *Time*, January 1, 1990, p. 69.

132. Charles Krauthammer, "The Greatest Cold War Myth of All," in *Backward and Upward: The New Conservative Writing*, ed. David Brooks (New York: Vintage, 1995), 300.

133. John B. Ullman, "Ronald Reagan and the Illusion of Victory in the Cold War," in *President Reagan and the World*, ed. Schmertz, Datlof, and Ugrinsky, 90.

134. D'Souza makes the same point in *Ronald Reagan: How an Ordinary Man Became an Extraordinary Leader*, 132.

135. Revel, *Democracy against Itself*, 70.

136. Reagan, *An American Life*, 715.

8

Reagan, Coalition Building, and the Politics of Limited Government

ONE OF THE DEFINING POLITICAL CHARACTERISTICS of the 1980s was the way that Ronald Reagan forged and energized an effective new political coalition on behalf of conservative ideas. It was this endeavor that promised to translate those ideas into practical power, and that held the promise of implementing a new public philosophy after Reagan had left the scene. This political component, the third leg of his strategy, was consequently intertwined with the components of philosophy and policy.

Indeed, it is not clear whether this chapter should be the last in this book or one of the first. Reagan had to build the coalition in order to gain office and implement policy. Yet Reagan's discourse and original positioning on policy issues preceded and contributed to his election, just as subsequent policy helped solidify his coalition after 1980. In other words: without a coalition, no policy; without policy and discourse, no coalition. However, it is possible to discuss discourse and policy without discussing their coalitional impact, whereas it is not possible to discuss coalitional politics without first understanding the discourse and policy that shaped it. Accordingly, the coalition comes last—in order of consideration, though not necessarily in order of importance.

Though the old-time New Deal coalition of white southerners, urban ethnics, blacks, and liberals had fractured irremediably in 1968, a looser grouping of forces existed on the Left with sufficient strength to continue promoting effectively the expansion of government. There were two broad components to this coalition, one dating from the 1930s and one from the 1960s. Organized labor, a survivor of the New Deal coalition, represented millions of Americans and remained steadfastly Democratic. Out of the 1960s came a set of new groups and movements, the purpose of which were to protect Great Society benefits, promote the social causes of the 1960s, or apply the antiwar analysis of Vietnam to new foreign policy issues. This second strand added millions of citizens to the coalition of big government (though it also diluted the effect of the unions, many of whose members were not sympathetic to it).

While widely divergent in their issue focus, these groups shared certain common themes. For the most part, they were characterized by a common antipathy to the tradition of limited government. For the constituent members of this coalition, liberty was not the primary value; rather, some combination of egalitarianism and economic or social security was the value they most sought to advance. (In foreign policy, the strand emerging from the '60s preferred egalitarianism and conflict avoidance.) The point is not that the participation of these groups in American politics should be disdained. They represented the perceived interests and honestly held beliefs of a large number of Americans; in many cases, they arose and were sustained in response to genuine shortcomings in American society. From the standpoint of supporters of limited government like Reagan, however, the crucial concern was that American politics before the 1980s had been largely dominated by a coalition held together by consistent willingness to subordinate liberty to other concerns.

If the expansion of government in the twentieth century began in the ideas and policies of progressives and New Dealers, it was sustained by the coalition of organized interests that resulted from the consequent distribution of federal largesse. Curtailing that expansion, let alone reversing some of it, required the formation of a new electoral coalition that could compete with the old. This was a difficult task; the intensely concentrated benefits of government programs tend to be more salient than the widely distributed and often hidden costs of those programs, even when the costs are quite high.

Reagan sought to produce such a coalition. He built a winning coalition in the mass electorate. He also sought to cultivate an alliance of organized forces that could serve as a solid base for a conservative Republican Party. His successes on both scores led to three consecutive presidential victories in the 1980s: his solid 1980 victory against incumbent Jimmy Carter in a three-way race; a 1984 landslide against Democratic challenger Walter Mondale, who won only one state and the District of Columbia; and a strong (though not overwhelming) victory in 1988 by Reagan's vice president, George Bush, against Michael Dukakis of Massachusetts. Reagan's success in putting together an organized coalition was also important to governing between elections, as it gave him some means of balancing the weight of the permanent interests pressuring government for more benefits and more regulations.

The Reagan Countercoalition in the Electorate

Conventional opinion portrays the Reagan era as a time when voters were bedazzled by political vacuity, slick television ads, and empty and mean-spirited attacks. As a starting point in examining this charge, it bears pointing out that political campaigns have been accused of lacking content since long before the 1980s. Presidential scholar Paul Boller observes that "from almost the beginning, America's quadrennial confrontation was in part a circus, carnival, vaudeville show, pageant, extravaganza, spectacle, the Greatest Show on Earth."[1] In comparison, the campaigns of the 1980s seem positively serious. The election of 1980 was conducted in a climate of crisis, as candidates debated the best way to tame stagflation and restore American strength abroad. Subsequent analysis by respected public opinion experts like Everett Carll Ladd and Daniel Yankelovich indicated that while Reagan's victory was not a wholehearted public endorsement of conservatism, it was more than a simple rejection of Jimmy Carter; rather, it was a deliberate rejection by the electorate of the liberal economic strategy of the previous half-century.[2] The 1984 campaign featured a debate on taxes, national security and arms control, the future of the Supreme Court, and the proper role of religion in politics. Those issues went to the heart of the proper size and role of government in society, the proper role and strategy of the United States in the world, the meaning of the Constitution, and the role of the judiciary. The retrospective element of the election invited voters to compare systematically the first four years of Reagan with the four Carter-Mondale years, something that voters were qualified to do from experience. By most possible standards, that comparison revealed a significant improvement since 1980 on both domestic policy and foreign policy. As political analyst Michael Barone pointed out, the "morning in America" advertisements widely derided by Democrats and many in the media "worked only if their minimal words and images evoked the viewer's own genuine experiences and emotions."[3] After the troubles of the 1960s and 1970s, for many Americans it seemed that it *was* morning in America.

In the campaign of 1988, the election was decided on the basis of three factors. First, it was a referendum on the Reagan presidency and on the state of the nation in 1988. To political scientist Gerald M. Pomper, Bush's victory was "an electoral valedictory for Ronald Reagan."[4] Second, to a larger degree than the elections of 1980 and 1984, the Republican candidate won in a campaign that explicitly emphasized his "conservativeness" and his opponent's "liberalness." As hard as Michael Dukakis tried to make it something else, the election of 1988 became a contest between two broad philosophies of government and sets of values, or at least the voters' understanding of them.[5]

Finally, the election hinged on specific issues—taxes, crime, and foreign policy chief among them. Bush's approach to these issues—particularly the "no new taxes" pledge and an aggressive attack on crime—drew vehement criticism from some quarters. Yet in light of the complete failure of Bush's 1990 budget deal to reduce the deficit, it is hardly self-evident that his tax promise in 1988 was ill conceived. As for crime, the story of Willie Horton had first been told by then-senator Albert Gore in the New York Democratic primary, and the outraged focus group used by the Bush campaign to test the issue had never been informed that Horton was black. The presumption that race was the "real" subterranean agenda is simply not supported by fact.[6] In the end, the tax pledge and the Horton ad prove the Bush campaign to have been empty and vicious only if limited government and public safety are not real issues. Altogether, political scientist Larry Bartels has demonstrated that while voters expressed more satisfaction with the 1992 campaign than the 1988 campaign, "the tone of ads and press coverage was not much different [and] prospective voters learned less about the candidates' issue stands" in the 1992 campaign than in 1988.[7]

Indeed, there is considerable evidence that voters knew quite well what they were doing throughout the 1980s. Pollster Burns Roper pointed out in late 1983 that contrary to the oft-repeated notion that voters liked Reagan but not his policies, "Reagan's job rating is noticeably better than his personal rating"—in other words, the public liked Reagan's job performance more than they liked him as a person.[8] Other analysts noted that his positions on many issues (like tax cuts, school prayer, crime, the death penalty, busing, and racial quotas) were much more popular than he was. Even on issues for which he received an unfavorable rating in the abstract, voters in 1984 still rated Reagan more favorably than Mondale. For example, while voters disapproved of Reagan's handling of the deficit, they still believed him better able to deal with it than Mondale, by a margin of forty-six to thirty-two; similarly, despite reservations, voters expressed greater confidence in Reagan's Central America policy than Mondale's, by a score of forty-one to thirty-five.[9]

In a more general sense, public opinion had moved substantially in the conservative direction by 1980. In 1964, only 42 percent of the public agreed with the statement that "the government has gone too far in regulating business and interfering with the free enterprise system" (39 percent disagreed); by 1981, 65 percent agreed. Similarly, as late as 1973, Americans disagreed with the statement "the best government is the government that governs least," by a fifty-six-to-thirty-two margin; by 1981, Americans agreed with that statement by a fifty-nine-to-thirty-five margin, a total reversal in only eight years.[10] By the early 1980s, 77 percent of poll respondents believed that the federal government created more problems than it solved, and by a forty-nine-to-fifteen margin they agreed that the government in Washington was too powerful.[11] These views contrasted with the wide support Americans continued to give to many current and proposed government programs. They were consistent, though, when viewed in the context of the propensity of self-described conservatives consistently to outnumber self-described liberals in the electorate by ratios of approximately three to two, or even two to one, for twenty years or more.[12] Altogether, three factors indicated conservatism in the electorate—conservative-versus-liberal self-identification, increasing support for the philosophical principle of limited government, and conservative presidential election victories—while one factor indicated a sort of half-liberalism, the continued "operational liberalism" of the electorate in respect to many specific programs. As many political analysts have rightly pointed out, this is not to say that most Americans are hard-edged ideological thinkers when it comes to politics and voting. It is to say, more modestly, that there is no good reason to believe that Reagan's or Bush's electoral victories in the 1980s depended on personality, or popular delusion. Even columnist Richard Reeves, a frequent critic of Reagan, conceded that his 1984 election landslide was a triumph of ideas, not simply of image. "It was a spectacular personal triumph," Reeves argued, "but that did not make it a triumph of personality. What came to be known as 'Reaganism' was at least as much the triumph of conservative intellectuals who . . . [after 1964] gradually affected the way Americans thought about themselves and their relationship to government. . . . Americans voted for and against ideas in 1964, and they did the same thing in 1984."[13]

Reagan produced these electoral results, by constructing a viable electoral coalition in favor of conservative ideas of limited government and traditional values. At its simplest, this meant bringing together economic conservatives (or if one prefers, advocates of economic liberalism in the classical sense) and social conservatives. To be more precise, given the relatively nonideological nature of the decisive bloc of American voters, it meant bringing together voters who were sympathetic to economically conservative arguments and those who were sympathetic to socially conservative arguments, two sets of voters who oftentimes inhabited very different electoral worlds. In particular, it was the attachment of social conservatism to the traditional Republican base of economic conservatism that, in the view of Nathan Glazer, "brings to the Republican coalition a kind of strength it has not had for sixty years. . . . [U]nder President Reagan, Republicans can now make an appeal to lower-status Evangelicals and Fundamentalists who were once solidly in the Democratic camp."[14] This feat by itself took notable political skill, and it was achieved by Reagan with the use of innovative strategies. These included emphasizing different themes sequentially, as well as shifting the debate to local levels of government, or to the alternative venue of proposed constitutional amendments.[15] Yet this analysis, while essentially correct, is too simple.

One attempt to fill in the complexities was made by Andrew Kohut and Norman Ornstein, utilizing data from a 1987 *Times-Mirror* survey that broke voters into groups not demographically but on the basis of their "underlying values." According to Kohut and Ornstein, Reagan's winning coalition included two "rock-solid" Republican groups, the "enterprisers" (roughly speaking, economic conservatives) and the "moralists" (religious conservatives), but these were not enough to produce victory. The coalition also included two independent groups, the "upbeats" (who were young and optimistic) and the "disaffecteds" (who were alienated and attracted to outsiders). These latter groups turned the coalition into a majority, but they also made it "unstable."[16]

Another effort to explain the Reagan coalition was made by political scientists Benjamin Ginsberg and Martin Shefter, who noted in 1990 that "to secure election and reelection and to govern effectively, presidents must create linkages to constellations of interest groups and social forces. . . . Since gaining control of the White House in 1980, the Reagan and Bush administrations have sought to sever the ties between Democrats and their major constituencies and to fashion enduring connections between important interests in American society and the Republican party."[17] Ginsberg and Shefter's analysis is worth exploring in detail.

In their view, substantially shared by Aaron Wildavsky, Reagan's policies of tax reductions, tax reform, spending limits, and deregulation had the effect of disrupting the Democratic coalition by limiting what government could or would do on behalf of pro-Democratic constituency groups. The new climate of fiscal restraint meant that Democratic interests had to fight one another for limited resources, and Democratic politicians had to pick winners and losers within their coalition.[18] In essence, Reagan took away the tools Democrats had traditionally used to cement the loyalties of their voters.

Ginsberg and Shefter went on to argue that Reagan had undertaken to build a new coalition on the ruins of the old, disrupted Democratic coalition. His goal was to "transform the political identities of established groups, to create new political forces by dividing existing groups, to construct new interests by uniting previously disparate elements."[19] In particular, Reagan's Republicans sought, largely successfully, to shift the identities and allegiances of four major groups during the 1980s.

First, Reagan tried to unify the business community, by bridging the gap between big business and small business. Before 1980, big business had largely accommodated itself to the welfare state, while small business, chafing under the burden of government, continued leaning Republican. In the 1980s, Reagan took advantage of the dissatisfaction of big business with high taxes and growing regulation to reattach it to small business as part of the Republican coalition.

Second, Reagan successfully exploited the numerous trends that had in the 1960s and 1970s gradually turned the suburban middle class against Democrats. The key element to this strategy was tax reduction and continued emphasis on the tax issue, as well as the fight against inflation. On the basis of the tax and inflation issues, Reagan succeeded in turning this group from an orientation of government program beneficiaries to an orientation of taxpayers. Once members of the suburban middle class began to think of themselves primary as taxpayers rather than tax consumers, Republicans were naturally positioned to gain enormously. In 1984, Reagan won solidly in every income group above fifteen thousand dollars.[20] Among college-educated professionals, who had given substantial support to Democrats throughout the 1970s, Republicans in the 1980s continued losing those employed in the public sector but gained large majorities among those in the private sector.[21]

Third, Republicans under Reagan made great inroads into the working class ethnic vote. The ties that bound that group to Democrats—"trade unions, political machines, and urban service bureaucracies"—were undermined, by both Reagan administration policies and independent trends. As a substitute, Reagan and Bush made a largely successful appeal on the basis of cultural issues and patriotism. The move of the Democratic Party toward cultural McGovernism had provided an opening for this approach, which Republicans used in the 1980s to reorient this group's identity from being workers to patriots. In 1984, Reagan won a majority of Catholic voters and nonunion blue-collar households, as well as 46 percent of the union vote.[22]

Finally, white southerners had long been a crucial and monolithic component of the Democratic coalition but had been shaken loose in the 1960s by a combination of civil-rights and cultural issues. In the 1980s, Reagan succeeded in appealing to this group not as southerners but as religious evangelicals, on the basis of moral and cultural conservatism. Indeed, he won 78 percent of the "white born-again Christian" vote in 1984.[23] The degree to which this theme of social conservatism was common to Republican appeals to both white southerners and blue-collar ethnics also laid the groundwork for nascent political cooperation between evangelical churches and the Catholic Church, two forces historically at odds.[24] Another issue at work in both venues, though it was not as openly proclaimed, was race. Reagan strongly denounced racism, and there is no reason to doubt his sincerity. What Reagan advanced was, rather, a "racial conservatism" consisting of opposition to forced busing and racial preferences, an opposition on principled grounds of equality under the law and of limited federal and judicial power. These stands resonated in South Boston no less than South Carolina. Additionally,

Republicans used foreign policy and defense spending as mobilizing issues in the South, appealing to both the South's patriotism and its heavy economic reliance on military expenditures.[25]

What Reagan accomplished in 1980 and 1984 among all four groups was substantially repeated by George Bush in 1988, demonstrating that Reagan's personality was not the sole factor holding the coalition together. In his victory over Michael Dukakis, Bush maintained business support; continued capitalizing on the tax issue with the middle class; copied Reagan's performance among Catholic, nonunion blue-collar, and union households (though at slightly lower levels of support); and actually increased his percentage among "white born-again Christians" (to 81 percent).[26]

There was another theme of Reagan administration policy—unmentioned by Ginsberg and Shefter—that undoubtedly added strength to the Republican coalition over time, though its effect was more general and diffused. Throughout his presidency, Reagan promoted policies that enhanced individual self-reliance. Policies establishing individual retirement accounts like IRAs and 401(k) plans made millions of Americans more self-reliant as they looked to retirement, and they created an entirely new class of tax-wary small investors along the way. Spending cuts in federal programs also reduced dependence on government. On this score, Aaron Wildavsky recounted a conversation overheard in Berkeley during the 1980s: "It would be a great idea to do such and such. Wonderful. Let's get a government grant. Yeah. Oh, well, with Reagan around that's impossible. Do you suppose we could sell the service and do this ourselves?" As Wildavsky pointed out, "Although the uncoordinated efforts of millions of people moving to take care of themselves are not heard at a single time and place (so they are not recorded as events), they add up to a transformation of expectations, and, therefore, of practice in a self-reliant direction."[27] In the short run, the citizens deprived of government largesse in this way undoubtedly resented their deprivation; in the long run, the "transformation . . . of practice in a self-reliant direction" almost certainly added strength to the electoral coalition favoring limited government.

To point out the coalitional consequences of policy does not require us to believe that policy was devised primarily for purposes of coalition building. It is clear that Reagan pursued tax cuts, deregulation, domestic spending limits, an assertive foreign policy, and themes of patriotism and cultural conservatism because he believed they were right for the nation. But it is also clear that those policies and themes appealed to crucial groups in the American electorate, groups that had only recently become unmoored from the Democratic coalition. In some respects, the coalition constructed by Reagan and inherited by Bush was the one urged by Goldwater strategists in 1964 and later by strategists for Richard Nixon—the "sunbelt strategy" of fusing the individualistic West and the culturally conservative South. In 1969, analyst Kevin Phillips predicted an "emerging Republican majority" based on the sunbelt strategy plus the newly plausible appeal to blue-collar ethnic voters. In that sense, Reagan was building on groundwork laid by others.

Geographically, the Reagan coalition was not terribly different from the alignment of states that had elected and reelected Richard Nixon in 1968 and 1972. It differed, however, in other important ways. It explicitly appealed to evangelical Christians. It was built on a deliberate and extensive attempt not only to win votes for Reagan but to induce a durable shift in the way crucial groups of voters thought of themselves. Actual policy was, to a greater extent than before, an instrument of this attempt. If successful, the attempt held forth the prospect of changing the face of American politics for the foreseeable future. Further, it represented the first substantially successful attempt to build an electoral coalition with the express purpose of serving as a long-term counterweight to the constellation of forces that had for fifty years pushed for the expansion of government. As political analyst William Schneider said in 1988, "The Reagan revolution changed the coalition structure of American politics. Reagan brought together a variety of interests united by a distaste for big government."[28] The reunification of business was spurred by a reaction against perceived overtaxation and overregulation; the suburban middle class similarly came to see itself as a collection of besieged taxpayers; blue-collar workers and southern whites alike reacted against the heavy-handed social engineering of elected liberals and unelected judges, as well as against the aggressive strides of foreign communists. Altogether, Reagan's was the first successful electoral coalition of the twentieth century built explicitly around a defense of freedom.

Furthermore, while Reagan appealed to these groups, his appeals sought to strengthen rather than weaken their ties to the broader national community. While some accused Reagan of encouraging simple selfishness, his coalition was really built on a broader understanding of self-interest, a conception held together by reference to the common good. To put it another way, Reagan sought to counteract the bias toward larger government that is engendered by the strength of particularistic interests by strengthening more general interests and by convincing Americans to view themselves as part of a greater whole. Larger business was melded to smaller business in a common pursuit of national "competitiveness" and an even more basic defense of free enterprise. Middle-class suburbanites were taught to add up the hidden and disaggregated costs of particularistic programs. Blue-collar ethnics focused on national unity rather than class, while white southerners looked away from regional identity toward identification with a national community of moral norms. In each case, interests were redefined upward, toward a broader community.

Consequently, when Reagan won his reelection landslide in 1984, Richard Reeves contrasted Walter Mondale's "political tactics of dividing the nation into narrow constituencies" with the president's ability to reach voters "in every region and imaginable demographic group with themes of American nationhood."[29] Yankelovich polls confirmed that by a two-to-one margin Americans were more likely to think that Walter Mondale was indebted to "special interests."[30] A few months later, Democratic senator Edward Kennedy implicitly conceded the effectiveness of Reagan's appeal, urging his fellow Democrats to understand that "there is a difference between being a party that cares about labor and being a labor party. . . . There is a difference between being a party that cares about women and being the women's party. And we can and we must be a party that cares about minorities, without becoming a minority party. We are citizens first and constituencies second."[31]

The Organizational Base of the Reagan Countercoalition

The loose electoral coalition envisioned and constructed by Reagan was paralleled by a more structured organizational base. It is crucial to understand that he came to power as the culmination of a quarter-century of growth in the conservative movement. That movement began in a coherent fashion in the mid-1950s. By 1964, it was able to take control of the Republican Party and gain the nomination of Barry Goldwater, though it was unable to win the presidency. In 1980, the movement finally had gained enough strength to win the presidency, and it added grassroots organizational strength to Reagan's popularity. In that sense, Reagan's three victories in the 1980s were a testament to the success of one of the most broadly based and long-lasting political movements in the history of the United States.

When the conservative movement arose in an organized sense, it was composed of three basic strands. A strand of libertarian conservatism emphasized economic freedom and, more generally, the danger of domestic government becoming too powerful. The second strand was concerned primarily with the struggle against communism. A third strand of "traditionalists" viewed liberalism as a "disintegrative philosophy which, like an acid, was eating away at the ethical and institutional foundations of Western civilization."[32] By the 1980s, the old traditionalism had been augmented by a populist "religious Right." In the view of George H. Nash, "Whereas the traditionalists of the 1940s and 1950s had largely been academics in revolt against secularized, mass society, the New Right was a revolt by the masses against the secular virus and its aggressive carriers in the nation's elites."[33]

Throughout the 1980s, the organization of the conservative movement continued growing. At the intellectual level, dozens of new conservative think tanks arose. The Heritage Foundation, which was founded in 1973, expanded its budget to nearly twenty million dollars and served as model for many smaller efforts.[34] In the realm of more practical politics, numerous organizations—not all of them reliably conservative—joined Reagan's effort to promote conservative principles. Reagan clearly benefited from this organization of conservative sentiment, but he also helped inspire it. As Nash argued, Reagan "performed an emblematic and ecumenical function" for the conservative movement in the 1980s.[35] Martin Anderson concurred, writing that while Reagan was not responsible for the rise of the conservative movement, he "was an extremely important contributor to the intellectual and political movement that swept him to the presidency in 1980. He gave that movement focus and leadership."[36]

Across a broad front, organized activity supporting conservative causes expanded in the Reagan years, to some extent inspired by him. An antitax network was engendered through the organizational effort required to place dozens of antitax proposals on state ballots, requiring millions of signatures.[37] The antitax effort was bolstered by the National Taxpayer's Union, which saw its already-significant membership grow by one-third in the 1980s.[38]

On business issues, the National Federation of Independent Business, the U.S. Chamber of Commerce, and the National Association of Manufacturers—not openly conservative, but representing businesses of all sizes—were typically reliable allies in Reagan's budget, tax, and regulatory battles, with the exception of the tax reform of 1986 and some trade issues (on which they were divided). Throughout the Reagan years, the NFIB maintained well over half a million members, while the U.S. Chamber of Commerce more than doubled the number of business enterprises that were members between 1980 and 1985. The administration saw the organized business community as an asset in the fight for the budget and tax bills of 1981, the heart of the Reagan economic policy. During that struggle, the White House Office of Public Liaison played an active and successful role in mobilizing business on behalf of the president's program.[39] Other organizations within the Reagan coalition aimed at the maintenance of constitutional limits in other areas. Most notably, the National Rifle Association, which aimed to protect the right to keep and bear arms, more than doubled from 1980 to 1990.[40]

The governing value of this coalition of organizations, and of the looser coalition of voters it paralleled, became obvious when Reagan gave televised speeches calling on Americans to pressure Congress to vote for his economic program. According to presidential scholar Samuel Kernell, the speeches produced "waves of mail, telegrams, and phone calls that overwhelmed Congress. . . . Reagan's public appeals generated about 15 million more letters than normally flowed into congressional mailrooms each session."[41] That public mobilization was essential to the ultimate passage of the program.

Many organizations also supported Reagan's defense and foreign policies, including the American Security Council (which gained almost a hundred thousand members in the first half of the 1980s),[42] the Coalition for Democracy in Central America (which was founded in the early 1980s to support aid to El Salvador and the Nicaraguan resistance), and High Frontier (supporting the Strategic Defense Initiative). Large veterans groups like Veterans of Foreign Wars and American Legion provided important support for Reagan and many of his national security policies.

Finally, a loose collection of organizations objecting to the permissive drift of society grew in strength in the 1980s. While focused on a variety of separate specific issues, together they formed a complex that could be called the "cultural Right." Analysts unsympathetic to the aims of the cultural Right have frequently accused it of possessing undemocratic tendencies and a goal of imposing a controversial morality on an unwilling nation. Consequently, while it is clear that this component of conservatism in the 1980s sought to preserve traditional morality, further explanation is required of the sense in which the cultural Right could be considered part of a broader coalition for freedom.

The answer to that question is twofold. First, the forces of social conservatism were activated primarily as a defensive reaction against the social engineering of federal courts and bureaucracies, as well as against the aggressive social incursions of the counterculture. Courts, often utilizing questionable constitutional reasoning, introduced the issues of school prayer, pornography, and abortion, while feminists and homosexual activists seemed to signal an intention of using state power to alter the form of the American family. Organizationally, the rise of the "religious Right" is traced by several students of American politics to a reaction against rules proposed by the IRS in 1978 (never promulgated) that were perceived as threatening the very survival of numerous Christian private schools.[43] Where secular liberals saw the inexorable grinding-on of progress, these Americans were less sanguine, perceiving instead an unprovoked, wholesale, and undemocratic assault on the moral basis of American society generally and on their own cultural attachments specifically. In most cases, the call for cultural conservatism was made by way of a defensive argument for decentralization or community liberty, not for hegemony.[44]

Second, as was discussed in chapter 6, free society does not presuppose the annihilation of moral norms. To the contrary, conservatives argued—not without reason—that free societies have greater need of moral norms, or self-regulation, than do unfree ones. Yet Americans attracted to the cultural Right perceived that the moral norms underpinning America's free society were in danger of being critically undermined by many of the trends emanating from the 1960s. In one way, political organization would seem an improbable means of combatting this problem. Still, changes in the law had arguably contributed to the problem, and it seemed to many Americans unlikely that solutions were to be found that completely eschewed the law as an instrument. If nothing else, they hoped to undo through the law what the law had done, exercising political power to restore the legal status quo ante. In short, the mainstream of the cultural Right was committed to the traditional view of freedom as ordered liberty, and it was accordingly committed to shoring up what it saw as the social and moral foundation of American democracy.

The highly contentious issue of abortion can provide an insight into this frame of reference. Though often criticized as attempting to impose morality, invade the privacy of the bedroom, or "tell women what they can do with their bodies," advocates of the anti-abortion position could claim to be advancing the cause of ordered liberty in at least four ways. First, in their view, abortion represented a violation of the fundamental right to life, the protection of which had been established by John Locke and the Declaration of Independence as one of the chief purposes of government. Consequently, it was entirely consistent to urge restrictions on abortion while supporting the principle of limited government, just as limited government and the abolition of slavery had not been inconsistent. Second, utilitarian violations of the right to life in one case could undermine, over time, the rights of the born as well as the unborn. Third, in the anti-abortion view, easy abortion had the effect of divorcing people's actions (casual sex) from the consequences of those actions (pregnancy) in a way that not only nurtured a culture of promiscuity, with all of its attendant negative social consequences, but also weakened the principle of responsibility more generally. From this vantage point, abortion on demand was closer to libertinism than to genuine liberty, which must, in the end, rest on an ethos of responsibility. Finally, anti-abortion activists were troubled by the undemocratic means by which abortion on demand had been imposed on the nation by judicial fiat and hence saw the issue as one of consent of the governed as well as of rights. However these arguments might be evaluated, they cannot simply be dismissed. Taken together, they demonstrate both senses in which cultural conservatism more generally was connected to the coalition of freedom: opposition to abortion was mobilized as a defensive reaction against judicial overreaching, and it based its case on a theoretical defense of ordered liberty.

Organizationally, there were at least three overlapping components of the resurgence of cultural conservatism. First, a women's movement arose in the

1970s opposing ratification of the Equal Rights Amendment that by 1982 had defeated it. This movement comprised at least two major organizations, which continued growing rapidly through the 1980s: the Eagle Forum, directed by Phyllis Schlafly, and Concerned Women for America, headed by Beverly LaHaye.[45]

Second, the pro-life movement continued its grassroots growth and organizational diversification through the 1980s. The movement ranges from religious traditionalists of both Protestant and Catholic persuasions to pacifists, to a small coterie of feminists who consider abortion a negation of feminist values of nonviolence. It is, however, more conservative, more religious, and more Republican than otherwise. The pro-life movement expanded considerably in the 1980s; membership in the National Right-to-Life Committee grew by a million members from 1980 to 1985, when it stabilized for the remainder of the Reagan years. At least eight other pro-life organizations utilized a variety of approaches, from quiet education to civil disobedience.[46] Throughout the 1980s, annual pro-life rallies in Washington on the January 23 anniversary of the *Roe v. Wade* decision attracted no fewer than twenty-five thousand and as many as sixty-seven thousand marchers.[47] In 1988 and 1989 alone, civil disobedience led to approximately twenty-four thousand arrests of pro-life activists in Operation Rescue blockades.[48]

The third overlapping organizational strand of cultural conservatism was the Christian (or sometimes, religious) Right. By the 1980 elections, it had become "a virtual labyrinth of political action committees, lobbies, educational and research foundations, publications, television programs, and churches . . . some ninety organizations."[49] In the Reagan years, the Moral Majority, headed by Rev. Jerry Falwell, and Christian Voice were the chief organizational manifestations of the movement. In 1988, Rev. Pat Robertson's presidential campaign mobilized large numbers of new voters and contributors. He received almost 1.1 million votes in primaries and finished first in three caucus states. The year Reagan left the White House, Robertson shifted gears from the presidential campaign to build the Christian Coalition, an effort that had substantial impact in the 1990s. In all, the Christian Right drew millions of Americans into political activity.

The increasingly heavy affiliation of Republicans with organizations on the cultural Right carried risks as well as benefits. The organizations and leaders of the Christian Right or the pro-life movement were often much less popular than were the positions they espoused. Some analysts argued that the positions themselves, if pushed too much to the exclusion of other issues, had the potential of alienating the upper-income, more socially liberal, half of the Republican equation.[50] This sort of dilemma, however, is inevitable in any coalition in American politics that is large enough and broad enough to contest seriously for majority status.

The Reagan Coalition and the Young

Another important element of the Reagan coalition should be mentioned. Throughout the 1980s, political observers noted the (to them) surprising tendency of younger voters to move away from the Left and toward Reagan. The percentage of college freshmen declaring themselves to be on the left of the political spectrum fell from 51 percent in 1972 to only 21 percent ten years later.[51]

To critics of Reagan and the 1980s, this movement was merely further evidence of the self-centered and apathetic nature of students of the time. In comparison to students in the 1960s, students in the 1980s reported placing a higher emphasis on getting well-paying jobs and a lower emphasis on finding meaningful philosophies of life and on changing the world. In 1968, 85 percent said they hoped to develop a philosophy of life; by 1985, only 44 percent did, while a majority hoped their education would help them "earn a lot of money" or "become financially well off." As Barbara Ehrenreich saw it, there was "almost a 50 percent decline in idealism and a 100 percent increase in venality."[52]

Ehrenreich's interpretation was called into question, however, by surveys that showed that the young valued family, friends, career fulfillment, and financial security much more highly than having "lots of money."[53] Another set of surveys consistently showed that among supposedly materialistic young people in the 1980s, there was a minirevival of organized religion.[54] In fact, the trend line of caring about political activity and philosophies of life started going down, and the trend line of caring about being "well off financially" started going up, in 1973—not coincidentally, the year of the Vietnam peace accords and the OPEC embargo—and crossed during the Carter years.[55] Economists Frank Levy and Richard Michel argued in 1985 that the material concerns of young people were directed more at economic security than opulence: "What we are witnessing may not be so much a shrinking of young consciences as a shrinking of young wallets."[56]

To some extent, the criticism leveled at students of the 1980s undoubtedly reflected the view shared by many members of the 1960s generation that ignorance and apathy were the most likely reasons that any young person might not want to emulate them. Yet many students of the 1980s looking at the counterculture of the 1960s saw as its consequences moral chaos at home and defeat abroad; their chief attitude toward the student movement of the 1960s was one not of apathy but of positive repugnance. At the least, as *The New Yorker* put it in 1985, "Students . . . sense that idealism expressed as radicalism is 'old hat' and a throwback."[57]

As Georgetown University history professor Philip Gold pointed out in 1985, it is impossible to gauge "a generation's moral quality . . . by the

visibility and decibel count of its protestations."[58] Even by that flawed standard it is clear that the actual level of political activity on college campuses
throughout the decade was much greater than is often understood. Large
numbers of students participated in the presidential campaigns of Gary Hart
and Jesse Jackson. Hart's upset victory in the New Hampshire primary was
made possible by "mostly student volunteers"; news reports observed that
Hart was "attracting a large and enthusiastic army of young volunteers estimated by aides at 10,000 nationwide . . . [who] have helped turn the 1984
Democratic presidential campaign upside down."[59] Many of the groups that
fought U.S. policy in Central America had chapters on college campuses.
There was also a major expansion of the movement to impose strict trade
sanctions on South Africa, particularly in the form of divesting university-
owned stock in companies that did business with the apartheid government.[60]

What made student politics in the 1980s different, though, was that so much
of it was mobilized on behalf of conservative candidates and causes. The case of
the College Republicans provides an example of this development. In 1980, there
were approximately two hundred College Republican chapters around the
United States; by mid-decade, they had leveled off at around a thousand. The
CRs doubled their membership from below fifty thousand in 1980 to a hundred
thousand by the end of the decade—at a time when college enrollment increased
by only 9 percent.[61] Similarly, the Young Republicans (generally nonstudents
from age eighteen to forty) grew from three hundred thousand in 1980 to five
hundred thousand by decade's end. By comparison, the Young Democrats
(which included both students and nonstudents) grew from 115,000 in 1980 to
two hundred thousand in 1990, one-third the size of the CRs and YRs combined.

Additionally, Young Americans for Freedom, which was started by William
F. Buckley in 1960 and had participated heavily in Barry Goldwater's 1964
presidential campaign, grew from fifty-five thousand members in 1980 to
ninety thousand, with 650 chapters, in 1985, at which point it stabilized for
the rest of the decade, despite widely reported leadership disputes. Similarly,
the Young America's Foundation, started in 1969 to furnish guest speakers and
other educational resources to conservatives on college campuses, reported a
"geometric increase in interest in conservative speakers in the 1980s."[62] Numerous other conservative student organizations sprang up nationwide. Students For America was founded in 1983 and grew to a membership of 110,000
on 110 campuses by 1986.[63] By 1990, it had 150 steady chapters; in peak election years, the organization reported activity on upward of three hundred
campuses. Students for a Better America started at the University of Colorado
in 1981 and established up to twenty chapters in several states. Third Generation, a group for under-thirty-five conservatives in Washington, D.C., started
in 1984 and quickly claimed six hundred members.

Other organizations were devoted to particular issues. For example, the Coalition for Democracy in Central America was active on college campuses. American Collegians for Life was organized in 1982 and grew to five thousand members in 350 local chapters. The Young Conservative Foundation claimed a thousand activists at a hundred schools, focusing on divestment from the Soviet Union.[64] Other groups were formed to promote the Strategic Defense Initiative, decry the Soviet occupation of Afghanistan, and oppose divestment in South Africa.

At the beginning of the 1980s, there were only a handful of conservative publications on campus; the next ten years saw unprecedented growth in the number of college campuses having a conservative newspaper or journal. Among the most famous of these was the *Dartmouth Review*, which started in 1980 and served as a model for numerous imitators. The number of conservative campus newspapers reached at least eighty by 1990.[65] The importance of this development to campus conservatism cannot be overstated. A 1985 *New Republic* article reported that "the most prominent tool in the 'war of ideas' [on campus] . . . has been the campus conservative newspaper."[66]

In 1984, the College Republicans and others mobilized large numbers of student volunteers for Reagan; nationwide, 60 percent of the eighteen-to-twenty-four-year-old vote went for Reagan. Throughout the fall of 1984, the eighteen-to-twenty-four age group gave Reagan his largest margin in opinion polls, and some of his most enthusiastic receptions came on college campuses.[67] Observers noted that Reagan's standing ovations on campuses were most raucous whenever he mentioned the liberation of Grenada and pointed out that his administration had not lost "one square inch of territory to communist aggression."[68] In 1988, George Bush won 62 percent of the eighteen-to-twenty-five-year-old vote, his largest margin in any age cohort.[69] In the view of Michael Barone, "If the youngest voters were protesting, their targets were not 'the establishment' or right-wing patriots but the doomsayers of the left and the policymakers of the Carter administration. . . . [W]hen these voters looked about them they saw not a nation of failures and limits and alienation but one of peace and prosperity and resilience; and they voted for the candidates whose words and deeds comported with what they saw."[70]

By the late 1980s, polls were showing that eighteen-to-twenty-nine-year-olds had the most confidence in the nation's future, gave Reagan the highest approval ratings of any age cohort, were the only group other than those over seventy-eight to identify themselves as Republicans, and were the age cohort that said most often that the Republican Party best represented its ideas about how the United States should be governed.[71] One suspects that it was this phenomenon more than any other factor that led to accusations of apathy by critics like former 1960s radical Abbie Hoffman, who was driven in 1984 to say that he did not trust anyone under thirty.[72] It was not that the young had no politics; it was that they had too much of the wrong kind of politics.

The journal *The Progressive* called youthful conservatives of the 1980s "sleepers without dreams," but their activism should not be dismissed merely because it did not conform to the 1960s model of radical—and often radically uncivil—leftism.[73] They simply dreamed a different dream than that of *The Progressive*—one that was typically grounded in respect for America's founding principles, a love of freedom above other competing values, a belief in the essential goodness of America, and a distaste for the despots confronting America in the world. Speaking for many, Reagan speechwriter Peggy Noonan captured the idealism of the time: "Every generation gets a president. My grandmother's was FDR. . . . For my parents, it was JFK. . . . For me and the young people I worked with in the White House, it was Reagan. We came to Washington because of him. He moved us. We loved him."[74]

In one sense, young Americans were not a pivotal part of the Reagan coalition; citizens aged eighteen to thirty had among the lowest voting-turnout rates of any group in American society. In other ways, though, they were crucial. They added hundreds of thousands of votes that would not have been available to a conservative candidate a decade before. They provided energy to the Reagan coalition out of proportion to their numbers. They, more than any other group, demonstrated that American politics need not move inexorably to the left. They proved that a message of freedom, optimism, and patriotism could still inspire large blocs of voters, even blocs long considered provinces of statism and anti-Americanism; indeed, they proved that idealism could be reconceived in a manner that made conservatism appealing. Not least, though the voting cohort of 1980s youth was not cemented by Republicans and still oscillates between the parties, the conservative activists of that age group will undoubtedly exert a growing influence on American politics as the years progress. For the most part, they were the "upbeats," the voters declared by Andrew Kohut and Norman Ornstein to constitute one of the four legs of the Reagan coalition.[75]

Reagan's Coalition of Freedom: Evaluations

Altogether, Reagan's extensive coalition building in the 1980s accomplished two things. First, it put Republicans in a much stronger position than they had enjoyed before the Reagan era. They were now nationally competitive, especially for the presidency (where they were indeed dominant) and the Senate, and they had added considerably to their strength in governorships and state legislatures. It could no longer be said that Republicans were the clear minority party. Second, Reagan's coalition building made the Republican Party more clearly and avowedly a conservative party than before. The issues that held his coalition together were conservative issues, and his political success attracted emulation from within his party.[76]

For years, political scientists struggled with the question of whether Reagan's coalition indicated the onset of a partisan "realignment," a durable shift in majority support from one party to the other. By the end of the 1980s, it was clear that Republicans had fallen short of that coveted realignment, at least in the classical sense. Democrats remained a substantial majority in the U.S. House of Representatives, had recently regained a smaller majority in the U.S. Senate, and continued to predominate in state legislatures. While Republicans had drawn much closer to Democrats in voter identification, that drive, too, had stalled short of a majority. In 1992, Republicans were driven from their last bastion in the federal government, the presidency. Clearly, 1980 was not 1932.

On the other hand, some analysts argued that a different type of realignment had occurred. In their view, it did not make sense to hold analyses of political change hostage, as it were, to patterns established in a different America. For example, realignment is typically triggered by crisis. Since the crisis of 1979–80 had been less severe than the crises of 1860 or 1932, it might make sense to expect a different magnitude of realignment to come out of it. Additionally, the institutions of the 1980s were not the same as those of the 1860s or 1930s; the power of congressional incumbency made it more difficult to translate the impulse for change into electoral results. Furthermore, it is important not to forget the centrality of the "solid South," one of the most thoroughly entrenched features of American politics, to the Democrats before 1980. The Republican realignment after 1860 had been possible only because the South seceded; the Democratic one of 1932 was possible because Democrats already controlled the South. Any nascent partisan realignment in the 1980s had to work against, not with, the South's disposition to favor Democrats in elections below the level of the presidency. Despite all of these obstacles, Reagan clearly accomplished something of significance. Two alternative notions of realignment have consequently been offered.

First, many observers have argued that America in the 1980s experienced not a typical partisan realignment but a political or policy realignment. In other words, while domination of political institutions largely continued to elude Republicans, they had significantly shifted the policy outcomes and terms of debate in a conservative direction. Aaron Wildavsky framed this phenomenon as "getting the Democrats to support Republican issues."[77]

Second, some analysts have suggested the possibility that Reagan had set in motion a "rolling realignment." In this conception, victory in the presidency had been a first step that would be followed by victories down the ballot. The heightened resistance of American institutions to change could only be over-come gradually, but as time passed, fewer Americans would be able to sustain the dissonance of supporting Republican presidents while still considering themselves Democrats or independents. By 2000, there was considerable evi-dence supporting both of these interpretations (which were not mutually exclusive).

The Reagan coalition was clearly weakened by George Bush the elder, who lost the tax and quota issues and whose economic inattention during the re-cession of 1990–91 cost him significant support among blue-collar workers and the young. Additionally, the winning of the Cold War reduced the salience of patriotic and nationalist appeals and of anticommunist foreign policy. Ross Perot and Bill Clinton took full advantage of these openings, Clinton by mov-ing the Democratic Party to the right, and Perot by stripping away large parts of the coalition with his anti-Washington populist rhetoric. To put it another way, Clinton won the "upbeats," while Perot took the "disaffecteds."

Even so, the Reagan coalition was not destroyed. The South, at least, has provided an example of rolling realignment; Republicans there are now clearly the majority. Observant Catholics remain amenable to Republican arguments, and middle-class suburbanites remain sensitive to the tax issue. The Reagan coalition, declared dead by many pundits after 1992, proved itself quite alive in the 1994 elections. Essentially the demographic coalition that had appeared at the presidential level in 1980, 1984, and 1988 reappeared in 1994 to give Re-publicans control of both houses of Congress for the first time in forty years, control that they retained (albeit by somewhat narrower margins) throughout the 1990s. The coalition also proved powerful enough to block most major ex-pansions of government, or (when that failed in the 1990 and 1993 tax in-creases) to exact a sharp revenge, first against George Bush and then against congressional Democrats. Indeed, much of what the supporters of activist government have called "stalemate" or "gridlock" over the last twenty years has been a consequence of the continuing power of Reagan's new coalition to bal-ance and stymie the old coalition's appetite for bigger government. A com-parison of 1961–80 and 1981–2000 is instructive. In the twenty years before Reagan's inauguration, Republicans were completely shut out of all three elected departments of the federal government (president, House, Senate) for twelve years; in the following twenty years, they were shut out for only two. To look at it another way, they controlled the three institutions an aggregate eight out of sixty years from 1961 to 1980; from 1981 to 2000, they controlled an even thirty of sixty years (see table 8.1). The elections of 2000 affirmed the staying power of the Reagan coalition, as George W. Bush reassembled most of the coalition at the presidential level, and as Republicans (barely) retained control of Congress.

TABLE 8.1
Years of Republican Control of Elected Branches, 1961–1980 versus 1981–2000

	1961–1980	1981–2000
Shut out	12	2
Presidency	8	12
Senate	0	12
House of Representatives	0	6
Cumulative Presidency, Senate, House	8/60	30/60

Reagan's coalition-building efforts did not bring the unambiguous results he and his supporters obviously would have preferred, but the claims of critics like Anthony S. Campagna that Reagan "never took the time or made the effort to make the coalition that elected him into a permanent force"[78] were not accurate. William Schneider, more perceptively, held that the Reagan coalition would not disappear when Reagan left office. "The fact that a coalition is defeated does not mean it has been destroyed," Schneider argued in 1988. "The Reagan coalition would only come to an end if the various groups that comprise it no longer feel they have a mutual interest in limited government. . . . The antigovernment revolt that brought Reagan and the GOP to power in 1980 is over. But we have come out of it with a new institutional order, one based on low taxes and limited government. That new order does not lack for defenders."[79] Reagan brought about a coalition that has become a more or less durable feature of American politics and that has substantially changed the direction of America.

This political and partisan accomplishment was, needless to say, good for Republicans and conservatives, but it was also, more generally, good for America. One does not need to be a conservative or a Republican to perceive that the expansion of government will not stop itself. American government may be influenced by constraints established by public philosophy, but in practical terms, the outcome of political battles is determined by the relative strength of opposing forces. The interests organizing to advocate the expansion of government, like most organized interests, do not typically engage in unilateral restraint. They are prevented from moving farther only when they meet an opposing force of equal or greater strength. Consequently, there is not necessarily a natural end point to the accretion of state power, short of Tocqueville's "democratic despotism." If Americans want power to check power—and there is every reason to believe that most do—they are, whether they know it or not, agreeing to the necessity of a strong counterweight to the powerful coalition supporting big (and ever bigger) government. Reagan formed that counterweight. The alternative, stripped of euphemism, was to leave the road open to the gradual inevitability of what Reagan called the "silent form of socialism" and extensive social engineering conducted by the ambitious remnants of and successors to the 1960s counterculture. Before 1980, America lacked a strong electoral coalition for limited government. By 1988, it had one.

Notes

1. Paul F. Boller Jr., *Presidential Campaigns* (New York: Oxford University Press, 1985), xii–xiii.

2. Everett Carll Ladd, "The Reagan Phenomenon and Public Attitudes Toward Government," in *The Reagan Presidency and the Governing of America*, ed. Lester M. Salamon and Michael S. Lund (Washington, D.C.: Urban Institute, 1984); Daniel Yankelovich, "Comments: When Reaganomics Fails, Then What?" in *The Reagan Presidency*, ed. Salamon and Lund.

3. Michael Barone, *Our Country: The Shaping of America from Roosevelt to Reagan* (New York: Free Press, 1990), 644.

4. Gerald M. Pomper, "The Presidential Election," in *The Election of 1988: Reports and Interpretations*, ed. Gerald M. Pomper (Chatham, N.J.: Chatham House, 1989), 129. Pomper points out that the statistical correlation of Ronald Reagan's 1984 vote and George Bush's 1988 vote was "the highest of any two candidates in American history." Pomper, 132. See also Paul R. Abramson, John H. Aldrich, and David W. Rohde, *Change and Continuity in the 1988 Elections*, rev. ed. (Washington, D.C.: Congressional Quarterly, 1991), chaps 6–7.

5. See Pomper, "The Presidential Election."

6. In fact, there were two Horton ads. One was run by the Bush campaign and did not show Horton's face. The other was run by an independent pro-Bush organization and did include a (rather menacing) picture of Horton. It was the latter ad, the one not run by the Bush campaign itself, that received the greatest negative comment. Critics tended not to acknowledge the distinction.

7. Larry M. Bartels, "Campaign Quality: Standards for Evaluation, Benchmarks for Reform," paper prepared for presentation at the Annual Meeting of the American Political Science Association, Washington, D.C., August 1997, 45.

8. Burns Roper, "Presidential Popularity: Do People Like the Actor or His Actions?" *Public Opinion* (October–November 1983), 44.

9. William C. Adams, "Recent Fables about Ronald Reagan," *Public Opinion* (October/November 1984), 6–9.

10. See Robert Y. Shapiro and John M. Gilroy, "The Polls: Regulation: Part I," *Public Opinion Quarterly* (Summer 1984), 531–42.

11. "Opinion Roundup," *Public Opinion* (March–April 1987), 25.

12. See John Robinson and John A. Fleishman, "Ideological Identification: Trends and Interpretations of the Liberal-Conservative Balance," *Public Opinion Quarterly* (Spring 1988), 134–45.

13. Richard Reeves, *The Reagan Detour* (New York: Simon and Schuster, 1985), 10, 14.

14. Nathan Glazer, "The 'Social Agenda,'" in *Perspectives on the Reagan Years*, ed. John L. Palmer (Washington, D.C.: Urban Institute, 1986), 28.

15. Aaron Wildavsky, *The Beleaguered Presidency* (New Brunswick, N.J.: Transaction, 1991), 219.

16. Andrew Kohut and Norman Ornstein, "Constructing a Winning Coalition," *Public Opinion* (November–December 1987).

17. Benjamin Ginsberg and Martin Shefter, "The Presidency, Interest Groups, and Social Forces: Creating a Republican Coalition," in *The Presidency and the Political System*, ed. Michael Nelson, 3rd ed. (Washington, D.C.: Congressional Quarterly, 1990), 335.

18. Ginsberg and Shefter, "The Presidency, Interest Groups, and Social Forces," 336–39; Wildavsky, *The Beleaguered Presidency.*

19. Ginsberg and Shefter, "The Presidency, Interest Groups, and Social Forces," 339.

20. Stephen J. Wayne, *The Road to the White House 1996* (New York: St. Martin's, 1996), 270–71.

21. Ginsberg and Shefter, "The Presidency, Interest Groups, and Social Forces," 343.

22. Wayne, *The Road to the White House 1996*, 270–71.

23. Wayne, *The Road to the White House 1996*, 270.

24. Glazer, "The 'Social Agenda,'" 19–20.

25. Ginsberg and Shefter, "The Presidency, Interest Groups, and Social Forces," 339–47.

26. Wayne, *The Road to the White House 1996*, 270–71.

27. Wildavsky, *The Beleaguered Presidency*, 216–17.

28. William Schneider, "The Political Legacy of the Reagan Years," in *The Reagan Legacy*, ed. Sidney Blumenthal and Thomas Byrne Edsall (New York: Pantheon, 1988), 57.

29. Reeves, *The Reagan Detour*, 95.

30. "The Heat of the Kitchen," *Time*, October 8, 1984, 24.

31. Paul R. Abramson, John H. Aldrich, and David W. Rohde, *Change and Continuity in the 1984 Elections*, rev. ed. (Washington, D.C.: Congressional Quarterly, 1987), 293.

32. George H. Nash, *The Conservative Intellectual Movement in America since 1945* (Wilmington, Del.: Intercollegiate Studies Institute, 1996), 330.

33. Nash, *The Conservative Intellectual Movement in America since 1945*, 331.

34. William Rusher, *The Rise of the Right*, rev. ed. (New York: National Review, 1993), 241.

35. Nash, *The Conservative Intellectual Movement in America since 1945*, 332.

36. Martin Anderson, *Revolution* (New York: Harcourt Brace Jovanovich, 1988), 7.

37. James Ring Adams, *Secrets of the Tax Revolt* (New York: Harcourt Brace Jovanovich, 1984); David C. Schmidt, *Citizen Lawmakers: The Ballot Initiative Revolution* (Philadelphia: Temple University Press, 1989), 39, 125–45.

38. The NTU grew from 114,000 in 1980 to 150,000 in 1990. For subsequent organizational membership and chapter figures, unless otherwise cited, see Nancy Yates and Denise S. Akey, eds., *Encyclopedia of Associations 1980*, 14th ed. (Detroit: Gale Research 1980); Denise S. Akey and Katherine Gruber, eds., *Encyclopedia of Associations 1985*, 19th ed. (Detroit: Gale Research, 1985); Deborah M. Burek, Karen E. Koek, and Annette Novallo, eds., *Enyclopedia of Associations 1990*, 24th ed. (Detroit: Gale Research, 1990).

39. Joseph A. Pika, "Reaching Out to Organized Interests: Public Liaison in the Modern White House," in *The Presidency Reconsidered*, ed. Richard Waterman (Itasca, Ill.: Peacock, 1993), 155.

40. The NRA grew from 1.2 million in 1980 to three million in 1990.

41. Samuel Kernell, *Going Public: New Strategies of Presidential Leadership*, 2nd ed. (Washington, D.C.: Congressional Quarterly, 1993), 131.

42. The ASC grew from 226,000 at the beginning of the 1980s to 325,000 by mid-decade.

43. Rusher, *Rise of the Right*, 221; Godfrey Hodgson, *The World Turned Right Side Up: A History of the Conservative Ascendancy in America* (New York: Houghton Mifflin, 1996), 176–77.

44. Glazer, "The 'Social Agenda.'"

45. The Eagle Forum, which had been started in 1975, grew to fifty thousand by the mid 1980s and reached eighty thousand by 1990. CWA was formed in 1979 and had grown to 550,000 in 2,500 local chapters by the end of the 1980s.

46. These included Americans United for Life, the American Life League, Feminists for Life, American Life Lobby, the Christian Defense Coalition, Operation Rescue, the Let's All Protect a Child Fund, and the Pro-Life Nonviolent Action Project. See Connie Paige, *The Right to Lifers* (New York: Summit, 1983); Barbara Hinckman Craig and David M. O'Brien, *Abortion and American Politics* (Chatham, N.J.: Chatham House, 1993).

47. See Craig and O'Brien, *Abortion and American Politics*, 51; the only exception was in 1987, when an unusually bad storm reduced the crowd to five thousand.

48. Victoria Johnson, "The Strategic Determinants of a Countermovement: The Emergence and Impact of Operation Rescue Blockades," in *Waves of Protest: Social Movements since the Sixties*, ed. Jo Freeman and Victoria Johnson (Lanham, Md.: Rowman & Littlefield, 1999), 253.

49. Samuel S. Hill and Dennis E. Owen, *The New Religious Political Right in America* (Nashville, Tenn.: Abingdon, 1982), 69.

50. Edward G. Carmines and Geoffrey C. Layman, "Issue Evolution in Postwar American Politics: Old Certainties and Fresh Tensions," in *Present Discontents: American Politics in the Very Late Twentieth Century*, ed. Byron E. Shafer (Chatham, N.J.: Chatham House, 1997), 121.

51. Lewis H. Lapham, "The New Patriotism," *Harper's*, June 1984, 7.

52. See Barbara Ehrenreich, *The Worst Years of Our Lives: Irreverent Notes from a Decade of Greed* (New York: Pantheon, 1990), 32.

53. "College and Changing Values: Two-Year and Four-Year Institutions," *Change* (September–October 1988), 21–25.

54. Evidence for this shift is discussed in detail in chapter 6. Paradoxically, this change, which in some ways contradicts the lack of interest in "finding a meaningful philosophy of life," also can help to explain it. Students who were grounded in the Christian or Jewish religious traditions did not need to "find a meaningful philosophy of life"; they already had one.

55. "Idealism's Rebirth," *U.S. News & World Report*, October 24, 1988, 40. See also Frank Levy and Richard Michel, *Are Baby Boomers Selfish?* working paper 2081-01 (Washington, D.C.: Urban Institute, January 1985), 7; "College Students' Big Goal Today: Earn A Living," *U.S. News & World Report*, December 30, 1974, 54–55; "Away from the Barricades, Back to the Books," *U.S. News & World Report*, December 2, 1974, 70–71. As early as 1976, pundits had declared students the "new silent generation." R. J. Bresler, "The New Silent Generation," *Intellect* (May 1976), 549.

56. Levy and Michel, *Are Baby Boomers Selfish?* 12.

57. "Notes and Comments," *The New Yorker*, November 18, 1985, 42.

58. Philip Gold, "A Holocaust View from the Young," *Detroit News*, May 5, 1985, 13A.

59. John W. Mashek, "Fluke or Real Threat?" *U.S. News & World Report*, March 12, 1984, 22; Kenneth T. Walsh, "The Young Army behind Gary Hart," *U.S. News & World Report*, March 19, 1984, 25.

60. "A New Breed of Activism," *Newsweek*, May 13, 1985, 61.

61. Phone interview with the College Republicans' executive director, George Fondren, September 17, 1993.

62. Phone interview with Young America's Foundation executive director, Jim Taylor, September 17, 1993.

63. "Campus Conservatives on the Offensive," *U.S. News & World Report*, January 13, 1986, 20–21.

64. "Campus Conservatives on the Offensive," 20–21.

65. "New Voices Come from the Right," *U.S. News & World Report*, January 13, 1986, 21; Michael Hirschorn, "Little Men on Campus," *The New Republic*, August 5, 1985, 14; telephone interview with Chris Long, vice president, Intercollegiate Studies Institute, February 15, 1994.

66. Hirschorn, "Little Men on Campus," 14.

67. "Reagan's Youthful Boomlet," *Time*, October 8, 1984, 25.

68. Richard Brookhiser, "The Great Baby Boom Bust," in *Beyond the Boom*, ed. Terry Teachout (New York: Poseidon, 1990), 23.

69. Abramson, Aldrich, and Rohde, *Change and Continuity in the 1988 Elections*, 124.

70. Barone, *Our Country*, 646.

71. See "Sorting Out Age Differences," *Public Opinion*, November–December 1986.

72. "Sleepers without Dreams," *The Progressive* (October 1984), 10–11.

73. "Sleepers without Dreams," 11.

74. Peggy Noonan, *What I Saw at the Revolution: A Political Life in the Reagan Era* (New York: Random House, 1990), xii–xiii.

75. Kohut and Ornstein, "Constructing a Winning Coalition," 42.

76. Paul Allen Beck, "Incomplete Realignment: The Reagan Legacy for Parties and Elections," in *The Reagan Legacy: Promise and Performance*, ed. Charles O. Jones (Chatham, N.J.: Chatham House, 1988).

77. Wildavsky, *The Beleaguered Presidency*, 215–20.

78. Anthony S. Campagna, *The Economy in the Reagan Years: The Economic Consequences of the Reagan Administrations* (Westport, Conn.: Greenwood, 1994), 58.

79. Schneider, "The Political Legacy of the Reagan Years," 58–59.

Conclusion

THE 1980S WERE NOT EVEN OVER YET when many observers rushed to label them the "decade of greed." In many respects, however, the 1980s represented an American renaissance after two very difficult decades. While many factors contributed to that recovery, it was held together by Ronald Reagan and his goal of promoting American freedom. Reagan reinvigorated America's historic political discourse of limited government, constitutionalism, democratic accountability, and individual responsibility. At the same time, his policies bolstered important constitutional principles of limited government. Political institutions like the presidency and political parties were strengthened, as was patriotism and public confidence in American institutions, through the agency of Reagan's leadership. Altogether, Reagan cultivated a rejuvenation of the sense—central to the American identity—that the nation was meant to run the government, not the other way around. Talk of a "Second American Revolution" was hyperbolic, but it was also grounded in reality.

Reagan also promoted a policy of enhanced economic freedom as the remedy for nearly a decade of economic stagnation, declining real incomes, and inflation. After suffering a severe recession in 1981–82, the United States experienced what was to that point the longest peacetime period of economic growth in its history. In that economic expansion, America resumed growth rates resembling those that had been customary from 1950 to 1973, created twenty million jobs, and brought inflation under control. Real household income increased in every quintile, and poverty declined in every year from 1983 on. Despite widely held concerns about "deindustrialization," American manufacturing rebounded, and productivity gains were, as one *New York*

Times analysis put it, "almost unbelievable."[1] Furthermore, despite the relatively short and mild recession of 1990–91, these productivity gains put the
American economy on a strong competitive foundation for the future. Indeed, the American economy in the 1980s became the envy of much of the
world. Given the state of the economy at the end of the 1970s and the contemporary prognosis for continued stagflation, this record was little short of
amazing. At the end of the 1980s, the question of whether capitalism could
survive was seldom entertained by serious thinkers.

After twenty years of deterioration, many crucial indicators of social health
either stabilized or improved during the Reagan years: crime, drug use, alcohol abuse, the divorce rate, the abortion rate, participation in community associations, voluntarism and charitable giving, Scholastic Aptitude Test scores,
and high school dropout rates all improved, some dramatically. These improvements were underscored by two broader cultural developments: a significant revival of religion, and a turn in the intellectual atmosphere away
from the permissiveness of the 1960s and 1970s. Reagan encouraged and contributed to a shift of law and culture, putting his administration behind an attempt to fortify the social basis of democracy. In particular, the idea of a
strong civil society, represented by a meaningful independent sector, was an
important part of his political thinking.

Abroad, the United States and the West produced, through concerted effort, a striking reversal of international fortune. At the beginning of the
1980s, Soviet troops were in Kabul, American hostages were in Tehran, and
America's adversaries were able to claim that the "correlation of forces" was
moving decisively in their favor. The danger of war, or of strategic defeat
without war, was significant and growing. At the end of the 1980s, Reagan's
global strategy had brought the Soviet Union to the edge of ruin. Catastrophic war had been averted, the Cold War had been won, democracy was
advancing around the world, and the United States was on the verge of
being the only superpower on earth. To British historian Paul Johnson, the
significance of the Reagan years lay largely in the fact that the United States
had snapped out of its "suicide attempt" that had characterized the years
from 1968 on. In his view, "with the 1980s, there came a great wind of
change in the affairs of mankind that, gathering momentum throughout
the decade and beyond into the 1990s, swept all before it and left the global
landscape transformed beyond recognition. The 1980s formed one of the
watersheds of modern history"—a watershed favoring liberty and the rule
of law.[2] Thus, the United States and the West brought to a successful conclusion what amounted to the Third World War—the seventy-year struggle
between Leninist totalitarianism and liberal democracy, a struggle that had
claimed millions of lives and had been waged in virtually every corner of

the globe, utilizing every means but general war between the United States and the USSR.

The public spirit of the times, rallied by Reagan, not only reflected these successes but helped to produce them. After the demoralization of the previous two decades, the American sense of national purpose revived, a fact upon which most observers agreed. At the end of the 1980s, Americans by and large thought that the future belonged to America. Political analyst Michael Barone, in *Our Country: The Shaping of America from Roosevelt to Reagan*, summarized the 1980s with a single word: Resilience.[3]

Finally, Reagan turned his philosophy into policy by forging a long-term political coalition capable of advancing the claims of liberty against the powerful coalition whose first values were egalitarianism and economic security. Made up of big and small business, middle-class taxpayers, working-class patriots, evangelicals, the self-reliant and the young, Reagan's coalition was the only enduring coalition of the twentieth century built around a defense of limited government.

As many commentators have correctly pointed out, the Reagan years were hardly without flaws. The poverty rate declined for most of the decade but remained higher than it had been in 1978. Homelessness was a problem, though one that was consistently exaggerated, politicized, and attributed to implausible causes. Manufacturing jobs were lost, though the American manufacturing sector regained its place in the world. There were scandals in and out of government. Illegitimacy rates continued to climb, and while the growth of violent crime slowed dramatically, that violence seemed to become more random and youthful. With a few exceptions, popular culture continued its descent into nihilism. The deficit grew in the first half of the decade, though it fell again at the end to levels not much different than in 1980, as a proportion of the economy.

The thread that best defined the Reagan presidency, however, was the promotion of the architecture of freedom as conceived by the American Founders, Alexis de Tocqueville, the conservative movement of the last half of the twentieth century, and, of course, Reagan himself. Consequently, the 1980s are best understood as a decade not of greed but of liberty. They were a decade of enhanced economic liberty, a decade of political liberty and limited government that left room for civil society to regain its vitality, a decade of consideration about the institutional and rhetorical supports necessary for liberty, and a decade when American strength helped to secure the global victory of liberty against totalitarianism. In almost every particular, Reagan pursued a course calculated to make America and the world more free and more capable of sustaining freedom. More than any president in recent history, Reagan appreciated both the enormous power of freedom and the structural requirements of a free society. He consistently used the authority of his office to strengthen that structure and to harness that power.

Indeed, the four crises that faced America in 1980 were fundamentally crises of freedom: a crisis of the free-market economy, a crisis of free political institutions, a crisis in the social foundation that makes possible a free society, a crisis in the free world's struggle for survival. Altogether, the 1970s represented what Paul Johnson referred to as "the decade of collectivism," a cresting of the statism that had been on the move at home and abroad since at least the 1930s.[4] In 1937, commentator Walter Lippman had described that change, observable even then in the United States and to a greater extent around the world, as the replacement of an older faith by a newer one. The older faith, "born of long ages of suffering under man's dominion over man," held that "the exercise of unlimited power by men with limited minds and self-regarding prejudices is soon oppressive, reactionary, and corrupt"; the newer operated on the presumption that "there are no limits to man's capacity to govern others and that, therefore, no limitations ought to be imposed upon government."[5] Benito Mussolini put the choice more starkly, proclaiming in 1935 that while the nineteenth century had been an era of liberalism and the individual, "this is the century of the 'collective,' and hence the century of the State."[6]

At the beginning of Reagan's presidency, the outcome of that contest hung in the balance. Eight years later, Lippman's "old faith" had found new strength. By the end of Reagan's presidency, the political, economic, and international crises had largely been overcome, and more progress had been made on the social crisis than at any time since it had emerged in the 1960s. In short, Reagan and Americans halted, at least for a time, their nation's headlong but largely inadvertent slide into Tocqueville's "democratic despotism." Both at home and abroad, Reagan showed that history did not have to march inexorably toward collectivism and statism; when he left office, the United States and the world were freer (and not incidentally more prosperous and more peaceful) than he had found them.

A measured view must take care not to exaggerate these points. First, many of the tendencies toward greater freedom in the 1980s did not originate with Reagan. The tax revolt began in California and Congress in 1978, when Proposition 13 and a capital-gains tax cut passed. Richard Nixon had begun the talk of reining in judicial activism and restoring federalism, though his vision of federalism was clearly different from Reagan's. Likewise, it was Jimmy Carter who first appointed Paul Volcker head of the Federal Reserve Board, started deregulation, launched the defense buildup, and threw down the gauntlet to the Soviets in Afghanistan. The spirit of patriotism was kindled in late 1979 with the onset of the Iranian hostage crisis. Even abroad, leaders like British prime minister Margaret Thatcher and Pope John Paul II attained their positions before Reagan, heralding a broader sea change of which he was only one part. Indeed, on some issues, like deregulation and the defense buildup, Reagan inherited a bipartisan consensus, only to see that consensus crumble midway through his presidency. It is likely that consensus would have evaporated with or without Reagan—it was, in many respects, an aberration that belied the natural sentiments and interests of the contending parties—in which case Reagan's stubborn refusal to trim his sails in the face of renewed opposition was the only option that held the prospect of success. However, the question will always present itself as to whether Reagan himself squandered the consensus by pushing too far, too fast.

Second, it is impossible to prove beyond question that Reagan's strategy of freedom was actually responsible for the generally benign results of the 1980s, as opposed to merely coinciding with them. It is possible that the dramatic improvement in the economy had nothing to do with the dramatic change in economic policy brought by Reagan, or that the collapse of Soviet power was entirely unrelated to the adoption of a novel policy that aimed for the first time to bring about that very collapse, or that the reversal of many social indices that had deteriorated since the 1960s owed nothing to the gradual reversal of the legal and cultural climate during the Reagan years. Even if one rejects this scenario as implausible—as indeed it is—one must still grapple with the more difficult question of *how much* Reagan mattered to the outcome. For that question, there are no easy answers.

Furthermore, many if not most of Reagan's triumphs were incremental, partial, and subject to potential reversal. The growth of the federal government was limited, but government did not shrink. Reagan did not come close to balancing the budget. He had little success on some of the social issues that were particularly important to some of his supporters. His emphasis on constitutionalism restored federalism incrementally and enumerated powers metaphorically, but there was no comprehensive federalism reform. Many important court cases after he left office were decided by a narrow margin, showing that one or two retirements in the judiciary could undo the entire movement in Reagan's direction. No concept of enumerated powers limited federal action from 1989 until 1995, when the 104th Congress tried, with only limited success, to write a budget recognizing those limits. In the early 1990s, patriotism and confidence in institutions fell back, economic policy included two large tax increases, and the political coalition that Reagan developed survived only in a weakened condition. These shortfalls led to harsh criticism by many of Reagan's erstwhile allies, like New Right figures Paul Weyrich and Howard Phillips.[7] Compared to the expectations they had in 1980, Reagan's presidency did not do much to advance the cause of ordered liberty—though he may have done a great deal in comparison to what could actually have been done. These analysts, however, have difficulty explaining why Reagan should be judged against the standard of their expectations rather than against the standard of the possible.

The disappointment of allies was, of course, only one form of attack Reagan has suffered. In the early 1990s, the media gave significant attention to accusations—later proved groundless—that SDI tests had been rigged, that the CIA had helped Nicaraguan Contras run illegal drugs to major American cities, or that Reagan had conspired with the Ayatollah Khomeini to delay release of the hostages so he could win the 1980 election. Historians used their academic credentials to place a stamp of mediocrity over one of the most popular and successful presidents of the twentieth century—so popular and successful that a small movement was launched in the late 1980s to add his face to Mount Rushmore—because they found his policies disagreeable. Others ridiculed Reagan for sleeping in cabinet meetings, vacationing too much, and lacking intellectual capacity.

Some objections to the Reagan years can easily be dismissed as products of partisanship or reflexive ideological hostility. First, it was in the manifest interest of one of the two major political parties in America to discredit them. In 1990–91, a pollster for Bill Clinton, Stanley Greenberg, wrote a series of articles in *The American Prospect* outlining this strategy. In order for Democrats to be successful in the 1990s, Greenberg argued, it was necessary for them to "create an imagery" of the 1980s that "supersedes the Carter years and impeaches the credibility of conservative governance for middle America." The definition of the 1980s was hence "a critical political arena where Democrats have the opportunity to disrupt the Republicans' hold on the middle class." Greenberg's redefinition would have emphasized the themes that the rich got richer while the middle class suffered, that the 1980s had been dominated by values of greed, and that the decade "undercut notions of common citizenship."[8] This strategy was executed by Bill Clinton in his 1992 campaign for the presidency and during his subsequent administration. Thus, some portion of the attack on Reagan was a systematic partisan effort, openly declared by Democratic strategists, to redefine the past in order to secure an electoral future. In that sense, Reagan was not far from the truth when he observed that declarations that his presidency represented an "era of greed" usually came "from those who really mean that taxes are too low and government is too small."[9]

Other critics have made claims so devoid of factual support or common sense as to render them nearly as meaningless as the openly partisan ones. Barbara Ehrenreich, for example, simply asserted that the Reagan years were the "worst years of our lives."[10] In order for this to be true, they would have to have been worse than the 1970s, which had been the decade of OPEC, stagflation, Watergate, malaise, Iranian hostages, Afghanistan, and evacuations from Saigon rooftops; worse than the 1960s, the decade of Vietnam, of assassinations, of Bull Connor, riots, and bombings, of families divided in the maelstrom of the counterculture, and of the rapid deterioration of many crucial social indicators; worse than the 1950s, the years of Korea, of rampant corruption in the Truman administration, of Southern lynchings, of duck-and-cover drills, of Stalin and Khrushchev, of the treasonous Rosenbergs and the often slanderous McCarthy; worse than the 1940s, when over one million Americans had been killed or wounded in war, and when much of the rest of the world was devastated; worse even than the 1930s, the decade of the Great Depression and 25 percent unemployment, demagogues like Huey Long and Father Coughlin, the rise of the Axis powers, the Spanish civil war, and Stalin's purges. It is fair to surmise that few Americans share that appraisal.

Similarly, Sidney Blumenthal submitted that the Reagan era had been "a period of political fantasy," ridiculing Reagan (and Americans) for believing that "tax revenues would rise when taxes were cut. The Russians would be stopped in their tracks by the conquest of Grenada. The terrifying paradoxes of deterrence would be abolished by building an astrodome in outer space."[11] Yet what Blumenthal defined as fantasies are accomplished facts. Tax revenues *did* rise by 27 percent in real terms during the 1980s, more than in the 1970s. The Russians *were*, in a sense, stopped in their tracks in Grenada; in retrospect, October 24, 1983, represented the high-water mark of the Soviet empire. Rather than being abolished by a deployed SDI, the paradoxes of deterrence were made largely irrelevant by the mere threat of it, in that it hastened the Soviet collapse.

Unlike Blumenthal, who called things that did happen "fantasy," others have called things that did not happen facts. For example, Cornel West said about the 1980s that "an undeniable decline in the quality of life set in—with increased crime, violence, disease (e.g., AIDS), tensions over race, gender, and sexual orientation, decrepit public schools, ecological abuse and a faltering physical infrastructure."[12] In actuality, as we have seen, the crime rate declined by 2 percent, the murder rate declined by 8 percent, the overall violent crime rate grew at only one-third the pace of the 1970s and one-sixth the pace of the 1960s, majorities of both whites and blacks agreed that America had become less racist in the 1980s, SAT scores went up, and the National Wildlife Federation declared that air and water quality had improved and that "we have made steady progress against ills recognized in 1968."[13] The spread of AIDS, while real enough, owed more to the legitimization of promiscuity and drugs in the 1960s and 1970s than to anything that was done (or not done) in the 1980s.

It would be too easy, however, to focus exclusively on the intemperate claims of overly zealous or overly partisan commentators, even if they are widely representative. Other more intellectually serious objections almost uniformly revolved around the question of freedom. Indeed, for some critics, their fundamental quarrel was with the idea of ordered liberty that Reagan espoused.

There were some areas in which a good argument could be made that Reagan's policy actually contradicted the administration's own conception of liberty. The expansion of presidential power reinvigorated separation of powers in one sense, by preventing Congress from pushing its prerogatives any farther. Yet carried too far, this aggrandizement of the presidency carried its own dangers. Bill Clinton's use of executive orders to bypass Congress and his frequent deployments of U.S. forces without congressional consultation had precedents in the Reagan era. Similarly, numerous commentators across the political spectrum raised legitimate concerns that Fourth Amendment protections were unduly curtailed and that the war on drugs was prosecuted with so much vigor as to threaten important constitutional guarantees.[14] Some even perceived, though with more questionable reasoning, a general challenge to the rule of law emanating from the Reagan administration.[15] However, even granting for a moment the validity of some of these concerns, the critical question is whether, *on balance*, Reagan contributed to the advance of liberty as he understood it. When the issue is put that way, it is difficult to answer no.

One must distinguish between claims that particular Reagan policies enhanced state power in contradiction to Reagan's own principles of limited government—assertions that can be assessed on their merits on a case-by-case basis—and the claim that his attempt to revivify the moral basis of democracy was inherently dangerous because it refused to accede the principle of radical individualism. For homosexual rights activists, feminist supporters of abortion on demand, and others who conceived of liberty as simply the removal of any remaining barriers to "self-actualization," the Reagan years could never be satisfactory. More generally, many of a libertarian bent were never fully convinced that the swing toward social conservatism was compatible with liberty. From their point of view, the Reagan administration, while advancing limited government in the economic realm, was undermining liberty in the social realm by supporting greater police power, limits on abortion, school prayer, and the social constraints of religion and traditional morality. It is true that the administration's social policy was a mixture of support for school choice and a greater reliance on private charity and voluntarism, with more vigorous control of crime, drugs, pornography, and abortion. Yet the picture was always more complicated than that, resting ultimately on the question of whether a valid distinction can be made between liberty and license. It was the position of the Reagan administration that the social architecture of freedom requires something more than freedom itself; it requires enough popular virtue and enough physical and moral order to prevent a slide into anarchy, upon which despotism would inevitably follow. That architecture can sometimes require bolstering in the law or the culture, meaning that the long-term end of a free society can sometimes be in tension with the short-term means of greater constraint, of either a legal or social nature. Reagan's critics on this score were right to illuminate this tension, but it is far from clear that they had better insight than Reagan did into how to manage it.

From another philosophical perspective, it was possible to argue that if Reagan advanced the cause of liberty, he did so only at the expense of other important values, especially equality. Whether there is some truth to this objection depends on how one conceives of equality. By the Founders' conception of equality—a natural equality of moral standing and equality under the law—liberty and equality are complementary, and Reagan promoted both. However, by another conception, rooted in Rousseau and Marx, equality means equality (or at least equalization) of condition or result. Many of the attacks on Reagan have been products of this latter notion, which takes the form of what social scientist Aaron Wildavsky has called "radical egalitarianism." This egalitarian impulse holds equalization of material condition and social status to be the chief aim of the polity. Wildavsky argued that this radical egalitarianism has attained an unprecedented place of prominence in American politics since the 1960s, that it has come indeed to be the "great contemporary divide" defining the two parties.[16] Commentator Mickey Kaus, himself a liberal, agreed in his 1992 book *The End of Equality* that the goal of equality of income and wealth had become a fixation among liberals.[17] From this egalitarian impulse flows an appreciation for highly progressive taxation, for a centralized and activist government unlimited by the constraints of enumerated powers, for regulation, redistribution, and collectivism.

Radical egalitarianism also defines itself by what it is against: the elevation of property rights, economic or social meritocracy, individualism, and autonomous civil society—in short, anything that might inhibit the onset of the egalitarian society. The egalitarian ideal leads its adherents to consider inequality of condition as the worst of national shortcomings. To these critics, since the Reagan years saw a rise in income inequality, and since Reagan himself was committed to a public philosophy that preferred to accept that inequality rather than accept the expansion of government that would arguably be necessary to reverse it, his presidency was by definition objectionable.

A particularly audacious species of egalitarianism goes farther and seeks to redefine liberty itself. At the end of the Reagan presidency, Walter Karp wrote a tome purporting to show that American liberty was "under siege" from the "tyranny" of "reaction" and "oligarchy" represented by Reagan and conser-vatism.[18] In a less incendiary manner, legal scholar Jennifer Nedelsky argued in her book *Private Property and the Limits of American Constitutionalism* that the Founders had been mistaken in their belief that "the acquisition and use of property were essential elements of liberty." As Nedelsky describes it,

> The egalitarian vision is practically a reversal of this founding conception: whether the inequality of property is the result of liberty or not, it stands in the way of liberty and justice for all. The freedom to use and acquire property and the security of one's acquisitions are no longer defining elements of liberty and jus-tice, but the potential objects of regulation and redistribution—aimed at assuring justice and liberty. . . . Far from requiring respect for the boundaries defined by property, the egalitarian conception of liberty and justice requires incursions on traditional property rights. What once defined the limits to governmental power becomes the prime subject of affirmative governmental action.
>
> The problem egalitarianism poses for American constitutionalism is not merely that the egalitarian vision entails conceptions of liberty and justice fundamentally different from those on which our tradition was built, but that this vision is incompatible with the property-based conception of limited government.[19]

To the Karp and Nedelsky arguments that liberty really consists of the most unlimited and powerful government and the most dependent population possible, nothing much can be said. The complete conflation of liberty and equality—or to be more precise, the complete subordination of liberty to equality under the guise of a "new" liberty—leaves little room for meaningful dialogue. It can be said that Nedelsky is right that there is little or no basis in the Constitution or in the thought of the Founders for governmental efforts to equalize incomes. Also, as Nedelsky intimates, no president who values the principle of limited government can embrace such efforts to the satisfaction of the radical egalitarians. However, the record of bloodshed left behind by the confluence of radical egalitarianism and unlimited government in the last century hardly inspires confidence that conflicts between the competing prin-ciples should be resolved in favor of egalitarianism instead of the Constitution and limited government.

A more modest manifestation of this argument—that equality and liberty are distinct, that they are both important, and that Reagan shortchanged equality in favor of liberty—is the more supportable and interesting charge. In its favor, it can be argued that while Reagan and his administration gave enormous consideration to the principles of freedom, they gave relatively lit-tle thought to how to sustain a basic level of social equality. Policies were de-signed to advance limited government, with minimal concern for the effects of those policies on notions of equality beyond equality under the law.

On the other hand, to Reagan and others in his administration, equality under the law and the opportunity it provided helped to guarantee an equitable society, though not one characterized by equality of result. In any event, the effects on material equality of Reagan's emphasis on liberty were far less serious than his critics maintained. While income inequality grew in the 1980s, most analysts attributed little of the change to Reagan policies (Kaus estimated perhaps one-fifth).[20] Furthermore, the distribution of household consumption (as opposed to income) did not become more unequal, and several studies have indicated that economic mobility remained high.[21]

In a broader sense, it can be persuasively argued that in 1980 the pursuit of equality of condition was not the vector of American politics requiring dramatic reinforcement. A century and a half before, Alexis de Tocqueville had predicted that democratic nations, including America, would give equality of condition a higher priority than liberty, thus endangering freedom over the long run.[22] History has seemed to vindicate him. By the time Reagan was elected to the presidency, American politics had been dominated for fifty years by the pursuit of equalization of condition; no president in five decades had given an unambiguous preference to the value of liberty. If Reagan focused too exclusively on rebuilding the foundations of American freedom, it was undoubtedly because he perceived that egalitarians had spent most of the twentieth century neglecting (or even undermining) those foundations in their pursuit of redistributing wealth and eliminating social distinctions through governmental activism.

We are now faced with interlocking questions: How much of Reaganism survived Reagan? What was the long-term success of Reagan's attempt to bolster America's architecture of freedom? Did Reagan succeed in his goal of establishing a new dominant public philosophy in America? At the time Reagan left office, supporters like Martin Anderson argued that the president had fundamentally shifted the terms of debate in American politics and that the shift was likely to be long-lasting. Anderson predicted that "whether the new administration in January 1989 is Democrat or Republican, it will be largely irrelevant to the major policy changes that will likely dominate this republic for the next decade or so. What Reagan and his comrades have done is to shape America's policy agenda well into the twenty-first century."[23] Some scholars have seconded that assessment, claiming that there was a "philosophical realignment" in the 1980s.[24] Others, including many journalists and academics, held that his influence was limited and likely to be ephemeral. Richard Reeves argued as early as 1985 that the nation had experienced a "Reagan detour" and would probably not be long in returning to something resembling its prior course. Scholars like Hugh Heclo and John Palmer maintained that Reagan had mostly served to consolidate the welfare state rather than dismantle it;

they agreed that he had largely failed in his goal of establishing a dominant new "public philosophy."[25] Economist Isabel Sawhill, taking a more nuanced view, argued that there would probably be a rejection of particular policies in the short term but that Reagan had nevertheless heralded a longer-term shift toward generally more conservative economic policies.[26]

More than a decade has now passed since Reagan's departure, and some things can be said with greater certainty. The most important successes of the 1990s, from the long economic expansion to the balanced budget to the continued improvement of numerous social indicators, had their roots in the Reagan years. Two of Reagan's legacies particularly stand out. First, the free-market economic policies of the Reagan administration, including anti-inflationary monetary policy, relatively low marginal tax rates, deregulation, free trade, and limits on the growth of federal spending, have continued mostly intact—indeed, with the election of George W. Bush in 2000, seemed likely to enter a new phase—and almost certainly contributed to the economic expansion of the 1990s. Major expansions of government have been defeated, the small-investor class has grown in size and influence, and the technology revolution has been protected from the potentially stifling straightjacket of "industrial policy." The downward path of the deficit that started in Reagan's second term was broken only briefly by the recession of 1990–91; it continued until a surplus was reached in 1998. Welfare was reformed in 1996 along lines that Reagan presaged with the welfare reform of 1988. Overall, the economic expansion that began in 1983 continued for parts of at least nineteen consecutive years. As a measure of how thoroughly the conservative economic critique has become intellectually dominant, Lester Thurow, previously known for his advocacy of government industrial policy, published a book in 1999 entitled *Building Wealth* in which he acknowledged the centrality of creative entrepreneurship and the failures of big government. Thurow's turnaround led one reviewer to refer to *Building Wealth* as "a final victory marker for the Reagan revolution."[27]

Second, the winning of the Cold War was a monumental achievement for Reagan, for America, and for humanity (including, not least, the peoples of the former Leninist states). Throughout the 1990s, adversaries like Iraq, North Korea, and Serbia proved that the West's victory over communism was not also a victory over human nature or the historical scourges of hatred, territorial aggrandizement, and war. Greater tensions with China and Russia loomed on the horizon. Yet victory in the Cold War made the 1990s the first decade since the 1920s free from the shadow of global conflagration or totalitarian conquest. The benefits of that victory were incalculable, but they surely included the freedom and safety of millions, the end of fears of approaching Armageddon, and greater economic prosperity. No one can say how long the *Pax*

Americana will endure, but it is clear that Reagan's assumptions undergirded it: America is a force for good in the world; American military, political, diplomatic, and economic power can be applied successfully; and fortune favors the brave.

Reagan's broader goal of reinforcing the political and social architecture of freedom has had more mixed success over time. To be fair, he set for himself a difficult task. Americans have become highly reliant on government largesse since 1932. Even more, the success of Reagan's project depends to some extent on the ability of Americans to think institutionally about politics, and on the willingness of citizens and politicians sometimes to place the integrity of the structure of freedom ahead of their preferred substantive policy outcomes. A skilled orator and confident figure like Reagan could ask such a thing, but most other political leaders who try find themselves facing an uncomprehending public and demagogic opponents who can score easy points by confusing content and process (e.g., opposing federal education programs on federalism grounds is to court being labeled anti-education).

Nevertheless, even outside of foreign and economic policy, Reagan left a deeper and longer-lasting imprint than most presidents. By 1970, it was difficult to see much evidence that Dwight Eisenhower—to whom Reagan was frequently compared, especially by critics who thought his popular support was explained purely by his genial personality—had ever been president. Even much of his own party had rejected the philosophical direction he had laid out for it. Nothing of the sort could have been said about Reagan at the turn of the century.

Constitutionally, Reagan's view of issues such as separation of powers, federalism, the enumerated powers, and equality under the law all advanced incrementally in the elected branches and the judiciary. Indeed, the continued revival of some important constitutional principles in court decisions represented the long-awaited fruits of Reagan's judicial appointments. Institutionally, despite President Clinton's impeachment, the presidency as an office has not fallen to the level of ineffectiveness that was seen before 1980; Reagan's restoration of the presidency has endured.

Similarly, numerous social themes championed by Reagan in the 1980s continued and picked up strength in the 1990s. The civil society movement arose. Family was strengthened, as divorce and abortion rates both continued declining; the teen pregnancy rate declined, and the illegitimacy rate stabilized, for the first time since the 1960s. Aggressive community policing, policies of zero tolerance for disruptive behavior in public spaces, and tougher sentencing laws—all with their antecedents in the Reagan years—combined to drive crime rates to a thirty-year low. The educational innovation of the 1980s also continued into the 1990s, centered on decentralized experiments like charter schools, vouchers, and home schooling. Also, the revival of religion seemed to grow. A booming Christian subculture became one of the most dynamic features of American society, and large faith-based organizations like Promise Keepers and True Love Waits engaged millions of Americans. Indeed, the Columbine High School shooting in April 1999 both exposed and strengthened a nascent religious awakening among young people.

The importance of traditional political discourse in American politics has fallen on harder times but has not reverted to pre-1980 levels. Where Reagan averaged nearly four references to the American political tradition in his major addresses, George Bush averaged only one such reference, and Bill Clinton fewer than two and a half.[28] Yet in the 1994 elections, scores of congressional candidates promised to take seriously constitutional limitations on federal authority. Bill Clinton invited the criticism of the Left by appropriating Reagan's discourse of personal responsibility, just as he attempted to connect himself to the American political tradition by paying extensive homage to Thomas Jefferson in a way his two Democratic predecessors had largely avoided.[29] Though suffering in comparison with Reagan, Clinton referred to the American political tradition in his major addresses twice as often as Nixon, nearly three times as often as Johnson, and more than four times as often as Carter.

Finally, Reagan continued to dominate the landscape politically. Every Republican vied to be known as a "Reagan Republican." The coalition he built, weakened by the end of the Cold War and the mistakes of the first Bush administration, lost control of the presidency for eight years before regaining it in 2000, but it won control of Congress and seemed likely to remain competitive there for some time. In 2000, three-fifths of the nation's governors were Republicans. Even President Clinton felt compelled to declare the end of the era of big government.

Indeed, Bill Clinton served a pivotal if ironic role in the post-Reagan era. In order to win in the relatively conservative political environment nurtured by Reagan, Clinton had to adopt numerous themes from the 1980s; by adopting them, he gave them a bipartisan stamp and turned them from topics of intense debate into new portions of the national consensus. That consensus included wide agreement in favor of economic growth rather than a zero-growth conception of economics, deregulation of certain industries, a balanced budget, a partial restoration of federalism, support for the family as an institution, an emphasis on rebuilding civil society, the promotion of voluntarism as a social policy, stringent crime control measures, work-based and time-limited welfare reform, a discourse of personal responsibility, and even some form of ballistic missile defense as a serious option (though the scope of such a system remains a venue of controversy). Prior to the 1980s, most of these notions were hardly even on the table; during the Reagan years, they were the source of heated contention; in the 1990s, they became common wisdom.

Thus Clinton, in spite of his inclinations and some of his policy departures, nevertheless consolidated the legitimacy and general policy direction of the 1980s, much as Dwight Eisenhower consolidated the New Deal and Richard Nixon consolidated large portions of the Great Society. As Dinesh D'Souza observed in his study of Reagan, Clinton will most likely be recalled by future generations "as the reluctant custodian of the Reagan revolution, and the man who reconciled the Democratic party to the new political landscape created by Reagan."[30] While D'Souza might be accused of partisanship—he served in the Reagan White House—respected presidential scholar Bert Rockman concluded much the same thing, when he argued that "Like Eisenhower, Clinton may be known for having put a tepid but confirmatory seal of approval on popular policies of the other party."[31]

So, when all is said and done, did Reagan establish the dominance of a new public philosophy based on the politics of freedom? In the important elements of a public philosophy—discourse, coherent policy, control of the terms of debate, and consistent electoral success—one can see major Reagan successes, but also indications the success was incomplete. From 1980 to 2000, Americans never entrusted the whole federal government to the Republicans at one time, and their victory in 2000 was clouded by Al Gore's narrow lead in popular votes, the disputes in Florida, and the loss of congressional seats. Furthermore, Reagan's attachment to the American founding and the principles of limited government has not been replicated among candidates of either party. The discussion of "first principles" has again become submerged. The position that "government is the problem" also fails to find a voice among candidates and no longer stirs voters, though this is arguably because twenty years of Reaganism in some form—full-blooded or watered down, presidential or congressional—has succeeded in making it less true. On the other hand, Reagan fundamentally changed the center of gravity of American politics. He changed the questions that were asked, and not infrequently he changed the answers. His policy innovations remain largely intact. He forced Democrats to talk like Republicans in order to win, one of the surest signs of a new public philosophy. His coalition is still alive—sometimes winning and sometimes losing, but consistently competitive. The new policy and political regime he ushered in established, in essence, a two-decade-long moratorium on the creation of significant new government programs—a success few would have predicted in 1980, or 1988. Reagan's goal of enhancing the value that Americans placed on liberty as opposed to equalization of condition was largely successful.

Altogether, two decades after Reagan's election to the presidency, the disappointments of supporters seem increasingly analogous to the disappointments voiced by many of Franklin Roosevelt's liberal supporters before they were able to perceive clearly how much he had actually accomplished. The claims of Reagan's most vehement contemporary opponents increasingly appear shrill and disconnected from reality. Many of Reagan's accomplishments are looming larger over time, while the greatest failings of the Reagan years—including Iran-Contra, the savings and loan breakdown, and the trade and budget deficits—are, for a variety of reasons, receding into footnotes.

The ultimate significance of the Reagan years, of course, will also depend on events and decisions that have not yet taken place, including electoral decisions by voters, policy decisions by elected officials, and decisions by the ever-changing body of federal judges. The onset of the federal surplus papered over, but did not resolve, the deep-seated conflict between what Americans want from government and what they are willing to pay for it. At least two dangers loomed. The surplus seemed, ironically, to endanger the fiscal discipline that had brought it into being, by threatening to unleash a new explosion of uncontrollable spending. On the other hand, if the new norm of balanced budgets that Reagan promoted becomes the preeminent value of policy makers, it might collide with Reagan's other (and more crucial) economic prescriptions. In the tax debate of 2001, one could hear legislators argue that George W. Bush's tax cut should be scaled back because the economy was slowing and surplus projections might fall—an inversion of economic logic that Reagan himself rejected. Taken to an extreme, the subordination of economic growth to the goal of balanced budgets could have harsh economic consequences. A political discourse of limited, constitutional, and accountable government depends on both political leadership and public receptivity, neither of which can be taken for granted. Political cynicism grew for much of the 1990s, reopening the question of whether Americans could sustain their democratic form of government.

Furthermore, most measurements of social health remained far worse in 2000 than they had been in 1960; in many ways, American society was engaged in an uncertain race between deterioration and recovery. By virtually all accounts, the "culture war" has only grown more intense. Presidential scholar Paul F. Boller has argued that "Reagan's landslide victory [in 1984] meant that the eighties was somehow getting even with the sixties."[32] But the strength of the counterrevolution against the counterculture means that we now have dual cultures, ever wider apart: a 1960s culture that was chastened but hardly dispersed in the 1980s, and an anti-1960s culture that was significantly bolstered but not triumphant in the 1980s.[33] To cite just two examples, conflicts between committed religion and aggressive secularism, as well as between multiculturalism and a more traditional conception of American nationhood, have stirred ever greater passions and led some observers to wonder aloud whether national unity can be preserved.[34] The elections of 2000, split so clearly along a cultural divide that separates coastal metropolitan America from middle America, could only exacerbate those concerns, though Reagan's principle of strengthening federalism and local autonomy also offered a means of defusing conflict.

Needless to say, if the peace and prosperity of the 1980s and 1990s continue largely unbroken for a number of years, Reagan's legacy will be stronger. If peace proves short-lived, or if the economy slides into a severe and prolonged time of trouble, the long-term significance of his presidency will be more limited, especially if economic conditions lead Americans to abandon his free-market approach. Ultimately, Reagan may have advanced America's freedom, but only Americans can determine whether they will maintain their freedom and exercise it in a manner that brings happiness and honor to their country. Liberals will be tempted to ignore the lessons that Reagan taught, conservatives to apply them too rigidly. Consequently, while we know that Reagan strengthened America's architecture of freedom in the 1980s and beyond, it is not yet possible to know whether the Reagan years and their immediate aftermath will prove to have been a historical turning point of American renewal, a long detour from a future of overweening government and long-term economic and social decline, or even, in the worst case, a notable milepost on the road to civil disintegration.

No study of Reagan could fail to note that he would undoubtedly have found the first outcome most probable, and not only because his legacy is at stake. More than the intellectuals, the pundits, or the politicians of his time, Reagan believed in America and in what use Americans could make of their freedom. In the 1980s, at least, his confidence was not misplaced. To Reagan, the most important lesson of America's history was that freedom works. The record of the Reagan years, for the most part, confirmed the validity of that lesson. Whatever the future may hold, the bold claim of Ronald Reagan's second inaugural address—that the 1980s were golden years for America when freedom gained new life—was far closer to the truth than his critics have cared to admit to themselves or to the nation.

Notes

1. Sylvia Nasar, "American Revival in Manufacturing Seen in U.S. Report," *New York Times*, February 5, 1991.

2. Paul Johnson, *Modern Times: From the Twenties to the Nineties*, rev. ed. (New York: HarperCollins, 1991), 697.

3. Michael Barone, *Our Country: The Shaping of America from Roosevelt to Reagan* (New York: Free Press, 1990), 597.

4. Johnson, *Modern Times*, 659.

5. Walter Lippman, *An Inquiry into the Principles of the Good Society* (Boston: Little, Brown, 1937), 40.

6. Benito Mussolini, *The Doctrine of Fascism* (Florence, Italy: Vallenchi Editore Firenze, 1935), 36–37

7. Godfrey Hodgson, *The World Turned Right Side Up: A History of the Conservative Ascendancy in America* (New York: Houghton Mifflin, 1996), 248–49.

8. Stanley Greenberg, "From Crisis to Working Majority," *The American Prospect* (Fall 1991), 104–17.

9. "Remarks at the Annual Dinner of the Knights of Malta in New York City, January 13, 1989," *Public Papers of the Presidents: Ronald Reagan 1988–89* (Washington, D.C.: Government Printing Office [hereafter GPO], 1991), 1734.

10. Barbara Ehrenreich, *The Worst Years of Our Lives: Irreverent Notes from a Decade of Greed* (New York: Pantheon, 1990).

11. Sidney Blumenthal, *Our Long National Daydream* (New York: Harper and Row, 1988), xiii–xiv.

12. Cornel West, "The '80s: Market Culture Run Amok," *Newsweek*, January 3, 1994, 48.

13. "20th Environmental Quality Index," *National Wildlife* (February–March 1988), 38–39.

14. James Bovard, *Lost Rights: The Destruction of American Liberty* (New York: St. Martin's, 1994), 199–216; David R. Henderson, *The Truth about the 1980s* (Palo Alto, Calif.: Hoover Institution, 1994), 3–4.

15. Lincoln Caplan, "The Reagan Challenge to the Rule of Law," in *The Reagan Legacy*, ed. Sidney Blumenthal and Thomas Byrne Edsall (New York: Pantheon, 1988).

16. Aaron Wildavsky, *The Rise of Radical Egalitarianism* (Washington, D.C.: American University Press, 1991), 61.

17. Mickey Kaus, *The End of Equality* (New York: Basic, 1992).

18. Walter Karp, *Liberty under Siege* (New York: W. W. Norton, 1991).

19. Jennifer Nedelsky, *Private Property and the Limits of American Constitutionalism* (Chicago: University of Chicago Press, 1990), 261–62.

20. Kaus, *The End of Equality*, 29.

21. Richard McKenzie, *What Went Right in the 1980s* (San Francisco: Pacific Research Institute for Public Policy, 1994), 157–60; Marvin Kosters, "The Rise in Income Inequality," *The American Enterprise* (November–December 1992), 32.

22. Alexis de Tocqueville, *Democracy in America* (New York: Vintage, 1945), vol. 2, 99–103.

23. Martin Anderson, *Revolution* (New York: Harcourt Brace Jovanovich, 1988), 438.

24. John E. Chubb and Paul E. Peterson, "Realignment and Institutionalization," in *The New Direction in American Politics*, ed. John E. Chubb and Paul E. Peterson (Washington, D.C.: Brookings Institution, 1985).

25. Hugh Heclo, "Reaganism and the Search for a Public Philosophy," in *Perspectives on the Reagan Years*, ed. John L. Palmer (Washington, D.C.: Urban Institute, 1986); John L. Palmer, "Philosophy, Policy, and Politics: Integrating the Themes," in *Perspectives on the Reagan Years*, ed. Palmer.

26. Isabel Sawhill, "Reaganomics in Retrospect," in *Perspectives on the Reagan Years*, ed. Palmer.

27. Kevin A. Hassett, "We Are All Reaganites Now," *American Enterprise* (September–October 1999), 74.

28. Bush's memoirs were similarly bereft of serious consideration of the Constitution or key figures of American political thought. In both of the books that serve the role of memoirs for Bush, there is one mention of Abraham Lincoln and none of the Constitution, constitutional principles, Jefferson, Madison, or Washington. See George Bush and Brent Scowcroft, *A World Transformed* (New York: Knopf, 1998); George Bush, *All the Best, George Bush: My Life in Letters and Other Writings* (New York: Scribner, 1999).

29. On the former point, see Jacinda Swanson, "Clinton's Rhetoric of Responsibility," paper prepared for delivery at the Midwest Political Science Association annual meeting, April 1999. On the latter point, Clinton launched his presidency with a pre-inaugural visit to Jefferson's Virginia home, Monticello.

30. Dinesh D'Souza, *Ronald Reagan: How an Ordinary Man Became an Extraordinary Leader* (New York: Free Press, 1997), 259.

31. Bert A. Rockman, "Cutting with the Grain: Is There a Clinton Leadership Legacy?" in *The Clinton Legacy*, ed. Colin Campbell and Bert A. Rockman (Chatham, N.J.: Chatham House, 1999), 293.

32. Paul F. Boller Jr., *Presidential Campaigns* (New York: Oxford University Press, 1985), 373.

33. See Gertrude Himmelfarb, *One Nation: Two Cultures* (New York: Knopf, 1999).

34. See James Hunter, *Before the Shooting Begins: Searching for Democracy in America's Culture Wars* (New York: Free Press, 1994).

Bibliography

"1993 National Estimates of Electrocutions Associated with Consumer Products." Consumer Product Safety Commission, September 10, 1996 <www.cpsc.gov/>.

20th Century. New York: Kids Discover, 1999.

"20th Environmental Quality Index." *National Wildlife*, February–March 1988.

"60th Anniversary Report." *U.S. News & World Report*, October 25, 1993.

Abels, Jules. *The Truman Scandals*. Chicago: Regnery, 1956.

"About the Publisher: Coalition for Democracy in Central America." *Freedom Fighter in Central America*, October 1984.

Abramson, Paul R., John H. Aldrich, and David W. Rohde. *Change and Continuity in the 1988 Elections*. Rev. ed. Washington, D.C.: Congressional Quarterly, 1991.

———. *Change and Continuity in the 1984 Elections*. Rev. ed. Washington, D.C.: Congressional Quarterly, 1997.

"Acceptance Speech by Governor Ronald Reagan." Republican National Convention, Detroit, Michigan, July 17, 1980.

Adams, James Ring. *Secrets of the Tax Revolt*. New York: Harcourt Brace Jovanovich, 1984.

Adams, William C. "Recent Fables about Ronald Reagan." *Public Opinion* (October/November 1984).

"Address at Commencement Exercises at the University of Notre Dame, May 17, 1981." *Public Papers of the Presidents: Ronald Reagan 1981*. Washington, D.C.: Government Printing Office [hereafter GPO], 1982.

"Address before a Joint Session of Congress Reporting on the State of the Union, January 26, 1982." *Public Papers of the Presidents: Ronald Reagan 1982*. Washington, D.C.: GPO, 1983.

"Address before a Joint Session of Congress on the State of the Union, January 25, 1984." *Public Papers of the Presidents: Ronald Reagan 1984*. Washington, D.C.: GPO, 1987.

"Address before a Joint Session of Congress on the State of the Union, February 6, 1985." *Public Papers of the Presidents: Ronald Reagan 1985*. Washington, D.C.: GPO, 1988.

"Address before a Joint Session of Congress on the State of the Union, February 4, 1986." *Public Papers of the Presidents: Ronald Reagan 1986*. Washington, D.C.: GPO, 1988.

"Address before the 43rd Session of the United Nations General Assembly, September 26, 1988." *Public Papers of the Presidents: Ronald Reagan 1988*. Washington, D.C.: GPO, 1990.

"Address to Members of the British Parliament, June 8, 1982." *Public Papers of the Presidents: Ronald Reagan 1983*. Washington, D.C.: GPO, 1983.

"Address to the Nation on Defense and National Security, March 23, 1983." *Public Papers of the Presidents: Ronald Reagan 1983*. Washington, D.C.: GPO, 1984.

Adelman, Kenneth L. "United States and Soviet Relations: Reagan's Real Role in Winning the Cold War." In *President Reagan and the World*, edited by Eric Schmertz, Natalie Datlof, and Alexej Ugrinsky. Westport, Conn.: Greenwood, 1997.

Akey, Denise S., and Katherine Gruber, eds. *Encyclopedia of Associations 1985*. 19th ed. Detroit: Gale Research, 1985.

Akron v. Akron Center for Reproductive Health, 1983.

Akst, Daniel. "The Real 1980s." *Los Angeles Times Magazine*, November 13, 1994.

Allen, Martha Sawyer. "Survey: Church a Blessing for Teens." *Rocky Mountain News*, February 19, 1994.

Amaker, Norman C. "The Reagan Civil Rights Legacy." In *Ronald Reagan's America*, edited by Eric J. Schmertz, Natalie Datlof, and Alexej Ugrinsky. Vol. 1. Westport, Conn.: Greenwood, 1997.

———. *Civil Rights and the Reagan Administration*. Washington, D.C.: Urban Institute, 1988.

Ambrose, Stephen E. "Reagan's Foreign Policy: An Overview." In *President Reagan and the World*, edited by Eric Schmertz, Natalie Datlof, and Alexej Ugrinsky. Westport, Conn.: Greenwood, 1997.

"America at War." *Newsweek* Commemorative Edition, Spring–Summer 1991.

"Americans Return to Church and Temple." *U.S. News & World Report*, January 5, 1987.

"America's Youth in Search of a Cause." *U.S. News & World Report*, April 16, 1984.

Anderson, Curt. "Despite Cuts, Overall Tax Intake Highest since World War II." *Denver Rocky Mountain News*, April 9, 2000.

Anderson, Lorrin. "Good Intentions." *National Review*, June 21, 1993.

Anderson, Martin. "When the Losers Write the History." *National Review*, August 31, 1992.

———. *Revolution*. New York: Harcourt, Brace, Jovanovich, 1988.

Apple, R. W., Jr. "New Stirrings of Patriotism." *New York Times Magazine*, December 11, 1983.

Archer, Bill. "Who's the Fairest of Them All?" *Policy Review* (Summer 1991).

Armey, Richard K. "Economic Revisionism." *Commonsense* (Winter 1994).

"Away from the Barricades, Back to the Books." *U.S. News & World Report*, December 2, 1974.

"Back to That Oldtime Religion." *Time*, December 26, 1977.

Baily, Martin N. "Boom vs. Boom: '90s Beat the '80s." *Wall Street Journal*, February 25, 2000.

Baker, Russell. "Flagging Enthusiasm." *New York Times Magazine*, September 23, 1984.

Barlett, Donald L., and James B. Steele. *America: What Went Wrong?* Kansas City, Mo.: Andrews and McMeel, 1992.

Barna, George, and William Paul McKay. *Vital Signs: Emerging Social Trends and the Future of American Christianity.* Westchester, Ill.: Crossway, 1984.

Barnes, Fred. "Revenge of the Squares." *New Republic,* March 13, 1995.

Barone, Michael. "1983: Falling Walls, Rising Dreams." *U.S. News & World Report,* October 25, 1993.

———. *Our Country: The Shaping of America from Roosevelt to Reagan.* New York: Free Press, 1990.

Barone, Michael, and Grant Ujifusa. *The Almanac of American Politics 1998.* Washington, D.C.: National Journal, 1997.

Barro, Robert J. "A Gentleman's B- for Bush on Economics." *Wall Street Journal,* September 30, 1992.

Barron, John. *KGB Today: The Hidden Hand.* New York: Reader's Digest, 1983.

Bartels, Larry M. "Campaign Quality: Standards for Evaluation, Benchmarks for Reform." Paper prepared for the annual meeting of the American Political Science Association, Washington, D.C., August 1997.

Bartley, Robert L. *The Seven Fat Years . . . and How to Do It Again.* New York: Free Press, 1992.

Beam, David R. "New Federalism, Old Realities: The Reagan Administration and Intergovernmental Reform." In *The Reagan Presidency and the Governing of America,* edited by Lester M. Salamon and Michael S. Lund. Washington, D.C.: Urban Institute, 1984.

Beck, Paul Allen. "Incomplete Realignment: The Reagan Legacy for Parties and Elections." In *The Reagan Legacy: Promise and Performance,* edited by Charles O. Jones. Chatham, N.J.: Chatham House, 1988.

Beck, Robert J. *International Law and "Urgent Fury."* Ph.D. Dissertation, University of Virginia, 1989.

Beer, Samuel. "In Search of a New Public Philosophy." In *The New American Political System,* edited by Anthony King. Washington, D.C.: American Enterprise Institute [hereafter AEI], 1978.

Benda, Peter M., and Charles H. Levine. "Reagan and the Bureaucracy: The Bequest, the Promise, and the Legacy." In *The Reagan Legacy: Promise and Performance,* edited by Charles O. Jones. Chatham, N.J.: Chatham House, 1988.

Bennett, Ralph Kinney. "Grenada: Anatomy of a 'Go' Decision." *Reader's Digest,* February 1984.

Bennett, William J. *The Index of Leading Cultural Indicators.* Vol. 1. Washington, D.C.: Heritage Foundation and Empower America, 1993.

Berger, Renée A. "Private Sector Initiatives in the Reagan Era: New Actors Rework an Old Theme." In *The Reagan Presidency and the Governing of America,* edited by Lester M. Salamon and Michael S. Lund. Washington, D.C.: Urban Institute, 1984.

Bering, Henrik. *Helmut Kohl.* Washington, D.C.: Regnery, 1999.

Bernasek, Anna. "What's Really behind the Boom." *Fortune,* January 24, 2000.

Bernstein, Carl, and Marco Politi. *His Holiness: John Paul II and the Hidden History of Our Time.* New York: Doubleday, 1996.

Bialer, Seweryn. "Reagan and Russia." *Foreign Affairs* (Winter 1982–83).

"Biggest Shock Yet." *U.S. News & World Report,* January 14, 1980.

"The Black Middle Class." *Business Week*, March 14, 1988.

Blakesly, Lance. *Presidential Leadership from Eisenhower to Clinton*. Chicago: Nelson Hall, 1995.

Block, Fred, and Robert Heilbroner. "The Myth of a Savings Shortage." *The American Prospect* (Spring 1992).

Block, Michael K., and Steven J. Twist. "Lessons from the Eighties: Incarceration Works." *Commonsense* (Spring 1994).

Blumenthal, Sidney. *Our Long National Daydream*. New York: Harper and Row, 1988.

———. "Reaganism and the Neokitsch Aesthetic." In *The Reagan Legacy*, edited by Sidney Blumenthal and Thomas Byrne Edsall. New York: Pantheon, 1988.

Bode, William R. "The Reagan Doctrine." *Strategic Review* (Winter 1986).

Boller, Paul F., Jr. *Presidential Campaigns*. New York: Oxford University Press, 1985.

Bonafede, Dom. "Presidential Scholars Expect History to Treat the Reagan Presidency Kindly." *The National Journal*, April 6, 1985.

Boorstin, Daniel J. *The Genius of American Politics*. Chicago: University of Chicago Press, 1953.

Bovard, James. *Lost Rights: The Destruction of American Liberty*. New York: St. Martin's, 1994.

Bowman, Ann O'M., and Richard C. Kearney. *The Resurgence of the States*. Englewood Cliffs, N.J.: Prentice Hall, 1986.

Bowsher v. Synar. 1986.

"Brave New Economy." *U.S. News & World Report*, March 31, 1986.

"Breakdown of the Justice System." *U.S. News & World Report*, January 17, 1994.

Bresler, R. J. "The New Silent Generation." *Intellect* (May 1976).

Brewster, Lawrence G., and Michael E. Brown. *The Public Agenda: Issues in American Politics*, 3rd ed. New York: St. Martin's, 1994.

Broder, Davis S. "The Invalids Are Sitting Up." *Washington Post*, February 9, 1983.

———. *The Party's Over: The Failure of Politics in America*. New York: Harper and Row, 1972.

———. "A Party's Soldier." *Washington Post*, October 20, 1985.

———. "The Words Do Mean Something." *Washington Post*, January 30, 1983.

Brookhiser, Richard. "The Great Baby Boom Bust." In *Beyond the Boom*, edited by Terry Teachout. New York: Poseidon Press, 1990.

Brown, Stuart Gerry. *Conscience in Politics: Adlai E. Stevenson in the 1950s*. Syracuse, N.Y.: Syracuse University Press, 1961.

Broyles, William, Jr. "At Last, Loyalty Makes the Headlines." *U.S. News & World Report*, June 30, 1986.

Bryant, Adam. "They're Rich (and You're Not)." *Newsweek*, July 5, 1999.

Budget of the United States Government Fiscal Year 1994, Budget Summary. Washington, D.C.: Office of Management and Budget, 1993.

Budget of the United States Government Fiscal Year 1994, Historical Tables. Washington, D.C.: Office of Management and Budget, 1993.

Budget of the United States Government Fiscal Year 1998, Historical Tables. Washington, D.C.: Office of Management and Budget, 1997.

Budget of the United States Government Fiscal Year 2000, Historical Tables. Washington, D.C.: Office of Management and Budget, 1999.

Budget of the United States Government Fiscal Year 2001, Historical Tables. Washington, D.C.: Office of Management and Budget, 2000.

Bukovsky, Vladimir. *The Peace Movement and the Soviet Union.* New York: Orwell, 1982.

Bundy, McGeorge. "Arms Control, Not Competition." *New York Times Magazine,* April 5, 1987.

Bundy, McGeorge, George F. Kennan, Robert S. McNamara, and Gerard Smith. "The President's Choice: Star Wars or Arms Control." In *The Reagan Foreign Policy,* edited by William G. Hyland. New York: New American Library, 1987.

Burek, Deborah M., Karen E. Koek, and Annette Novallo, eds. *Encyclopedia of Associations 1990.* 24th ed. Detroit: Gale Research, 1990.

Burgess, Susan R. *Contest for Constitutional Authority: The Abortion and War Powers Debates.* Lawrence: University Press of Kansas, 1992.

Burnham, Walter Dean. "The Reagan Heritage." In *The Election of 1988: Reports and Interpretations,* edited by Gerald M. Pomper. Chatham, N.J.: Chatham House, 1989.

Busch, Andrew E. "Ronald Reagan's Public Philosophy: Strands of Jefferson and Hamilton." In *Ronald Reagan's America,* edited by Eric J. Schmertz, Natalie Datlof, and Alexej Ugrinsky. Vol. 1. Westport, Conn.: Greenwood, 1997.

Bush, George. *All the Best, George Bush: My Life in Letters and Other Writings.* New York: Scribner, 1999.

Bush, George, and Brent Scowcroft. *A World Transformed.* New York: Knopf, 1998.

"Bush vs. Bush vs. Clinton." *National Review,* November 19, 1992.

Button, Graham. "Topping Out." *Forbes,* June 21, 1993.

By Our Own Bootstraps: Economic Opportunity and the Dynamics of Income Distribution. Dallas: Federal Reserve Bank of Dallas, 1995.

Campagna, Anthony S. *The Economy in the Reagan Years: The Economic Consequences of the Reagan Administrations.* Westport, Conn.: Greenwood, 1994.

"Campus Conservatives on the Offensive." *U.S. News & World Report,* January 13, 1986.

"Can Capitalism Survive?" *Time,* July 14, 1975.

Cannon, Lou, *President Reagan: The Role of a Lifetime.* New York: Simon and Schuster, 1991.

Caplan, Lincoln. "The Reagan Challenge to the Rule of Law." In *The Reagan Legacy,* edited by Sidney Blumenthal and Thomas Byrne Edsall. New York: Pantheon, 1988.

Carmines, Edward G., and Geoffrey C. Layman. "Issue Evolution in Postwar American Politics: Old Certainties and Fresh Tensions." In *Present Discontents: American Politics in the Very Late Twentieth Century,* edited by Byron E. Shafer. Chatham, N.J.: Chatham House, 1997.

Carroll, Richard J. "Clinton's Economy in a Historical Context, or Why Media Coverage on Economic Issues Is Suspect." *Presidential Studies Quarterly* 26, Summer 1996.

Carter, Jimmy. *Keeping Faith.* New York: Bantam, 1982.

Carter, Stephen L. *The Culture of Disbelief: How American Law and Politics Trivialize Religious Devotion.* New York: Basic, 1993.

Ceaser, James W. "As Good as Their Words: Reagan's Rhetoric." *Public Opinion* (June–July 1984).

———. "Political Parties: Declining, Stabilizing, or Resurging?" In *The New American Political System*, edited by Anthony King. 2nd version. Washington, D.C.: AEI Press, 1990.

———. "The Reagan Presidency and American Public Opinion." In *The Reagan Legacy: Promise and Performance*, edited by Charles O. Jones. Chatham, N.J.: Chatham House, 1988.

———. "The Theory of Governance of the Reagan Administration." In *The Reagan Presidency and the Governing of America*, edited by Lester M. Salamon and Michael S. Lund. Washington, D.C.: Urban Institute, 1984.

Cetron, Marvin, and Owen Davies. *American Renaissance: Our Life at the Turn of the 21st Century*. New York: St. Martin's, 1989.

The Challenge to Democracy in Central America. Washington, D.C.: Departments of State and Defense, 1986.

Chandler, Clay. "A Market Tide That Isn't Lifting Everybody." *Washington Post National Weekly Edition*, April 13, 1998.

Chavez, Linda. *Out of the Barrio*. New York: Basic, 1991.

Chubb, John E., and Paul E. Peterson. "Realignment and Institutionalization." In *The New Direction in American Politics*, edited by John E. Chubb and Paul E. Peterson. Washington, D.C.: Brookings Institution, 1985.

Citizens Against Government Waste statement, Washington, D.C., February 22, 1994.

Citrin, Jack, and Donald Philips Green. "Presidential Leadership and the Resurgence of Trust in Government." *British Journal of Political Science* 16, part 4 (October 1986).

Citrin, Jack, Donald Green, and Beth Reingold. "The Soundness of Our Structure: Confidence in the Reagan Years." *Public Opinion* (November–December 1987).

Clecak, Peter. "Saved from the Sixties." *Commonweal*, May 7, 1982.

Clinton, Bill. *Putting People First: A National Economic Strategy for America*. N.p.:1992.

Cogan, John F., and Timothy J. Muris. "The Great Budget Shell Game." *The American Enterprise* (November–December 1990).

Cohen, Roger. "Europe's Recession Prompts New Look at Welfare Costs." *New York Times*, August 9, 1993.

"College and Changing Values: Two-Year and Four-Year Institutions." *Change* (September–October 1988).

"College Students' Big Goal Today: Earn a Living." *U.S. News & World Report*, December 30, 1974.

"The Competition of Ideas." *The American Enterprise* (January–February 1990).

Conlan, Timothy. *From New Federalism to Devolution*. Washington, D.C.: Brookings Institution, 1998.

———. *New Federalism: Intergovernmental Reform from Nixon to Reagan*. Washington, D.C.: Brookings Institution, 1988.

Cornuelle, Richard C. *Reclaiming the American Dream: The Role of Private Individuals and Voluntary Associations*. New Brunswick, N.J.: Transaction, 1993.

Council of Economic Advisers. *Economic Report of the President 1991*. Washington, D.C.: GPO, 1991.

Courtois, Stephane, et al. *The Black Book of Communism*. Cambridge, Mass.: Harvard University Press, 1999.

Craig, Barbara Hinkson, and David M. O'Brien. *Abortion and American Politics.* Chatham, N.J.: Chatham House, 1993.

Crandall, Robert W. "Relaxing the Regulatory Stranglehold on Communications." *Regulation* (Summer 1992).

Cribb, T. Kenneth. "Discussant." In *Ronald Reagan's America,* edited by Eric J. Schmertz, Natalie Datlof, and Alexej Ugrinsky. Vol. 1. Westport, Conn.: Greenwood, 1997.

Crovitz, L. Gordon, and Jeremy A. Rabkin. *The Fettered Presidency.* Washington, D.C.: AEI, 1989.

Cypher, Dorothea. "Grenada: Indications, Warning, and a U.S. Response." In *American Intervention in Grenada,* edited by Peter M. Dunn and Bruce W. Watson. Boulder, Colo.: Westview, 1985.

Dallek, Robert. *Ronald Reagan: The Politics of Symbolism with a New Preface.* Cambridge, Mass.: Harvard University Press, 1999.

Davis, Tami R., and Sean M. Lynn-Jones. "Citty Upon a Hill." *Foreign Policy* (Spring 1987).

DeMuth, Christopher C., et al. *The Reagan Doctrine and Beyond.* Washington, D.C.: AEI, 1987.

Denison, Edward F. *Accounting for Slower Economic Growth.* Washington, D.C.: Brookings Institution, 1979.

Denton, Robert E., Jr., and Dan F. Hahn. *Presidential Communication: Description and Analysis.* New York: Praeger, 1986.

Dentzer, Susan. "How to Reinvent Washington & Co." *U.S. News & World Report,* September 13, 1993.

Derthick, Martha. "American Federalism: Madison's Middle Ground." *Public Administration Review* 47, no. 1 (January–February 1987).

Derthick, Martha, and Paul J. Quirk. *The Politics of Deregulation.* Washington, D.C.: Brookings Institution, 1985.

Destler, I. M. "Reagan and the World: 'An Awesome Stubbornness.'" In *The Reagan Legacy: Promise and Performance,* edited by Charles O. Jones. Chatham, N.J.: Chatham House, 1988.

Detlefsen, Robert R. "Affirmative Action and Business Deregulation: On the Reagan Administration's Failure to Revise Executive Order No. 11246." In *Presidential Leadership and Civil Rights Policy,* edited by James W. Riddlesperger and Donald W. Jackson. Westport, Conn.: Greenwood, 1995.

Devine, Donald. "Legacy Taking Shape." *Washington Times,* May 3, 1999.

———. *Reagan's Terrible Swift Sword.* Ottawa, Ill.: Jameson, 1991.

DiClerico, Robert E., *The American President.* 4th ed. Englewood Cliffs, N.J.: Prentice-Hall, 1995.

DiIulio, John J., Jr. "New Crime Policies for America." In *The New Promise of American Life,* edited by Lamar Alexander and Chester E. Finn Jr. Indianapolis: Hudson Institute, 1995.

Dionne, E. J. *Why Americans Hate Politics.* New York: Touchstone, 1991.

Dobbs, Michael. "Soviets Acknowledge Breach of ABM Pact." *Washington Post,* October 24, 1989.

Dobrynin, Anatoly. *In Confidence.* New York: Times, 1985.

Drew, Elizabeth. *The Corruption of American Politics.* Secaucus, N.J.: Birch Lane, 1999.

D'Souza, Dinesh. *Ronald Reagan: How an Ordinary Man Became an Extraordinary Leader.* New York: Free Press, 1997.

———. "The Decade of Greed That Wasn't." *Forbes,* November 3, 1997.

———. "How Reagan Reelected Clinton." *Forbes,* November 3, 1997.

Dunn, Robert M., Jr. "Bye-Bye, Supply Side." *Washington Post,* July 30, 1985.

———. "Don't Knock Reaganomics." *Washington Post,* July 24, 1988.

Eastland, Terry. *Ethics, Politics, and the Independent Counsel: Executive Power, Executive Vice 1789–1989.* Washington, D.C.: National Legal Center for the Public Interest, 1989.

Eberly, Don E. *America's Promise: Civil Society and the Renewal of American Culture.* Lanham, Md.: Rowman & Littlefield, 1998.

The Economist Book of Vital World Statistics. American ed. New York: Economist/ Times Books/Random House, 1990.

Edestein, David. "Somewhere over the Rambo." *Rolling Stone.* December 19, 1985– January 2, 1986.

Edwords, Frederick, "The Religious Character of American Patriotism." *Humanist* (November–December 1987).

Ehrenreich, Barbara. *The Worst Years of Our Lives: Irreverent Notes from a Decade of Greed.* New York: Pantheon, 1990.

Eisenstadt, Abraham S. "Political Corruption in American History." In *Political Corruption,* edited by Arnold J. Heidenheimer, Michael Johnston, and Victor T. Levine. New Brunswick, N.J.: Transaction, 1989.

Eisner, Robert. *How Real Is the Federal Deficit?* New York: Free Press, 1986.

Ely, Bert. "The Savings and Loan Crisis." In *Fortune Encyclopedia of Economics,* edited by David R. Henderson. New York: Warner, 1993.

Encyclopedia of Associations 1961. 3rd ed. Detroit: Gale Research, 1961.

England, Catherine. "Lessons from the Savings and Loan Debacle." *Regulation* (Summer 1992).

"'Enough Guns to Arm a Division,'" *U.S. News & World Report,* November 7, 1983.

"Exchange with Reporters, December 3, 1993." *Presidential Papers of the Presidents: Bill Clinton 1993.* Washington, D.C.: GPO, 1994.

Executive Order 12612 of October 26, 1987, "Federalism." *Federal Register* 52, no. 216.

Fagan, Patrick F. "Why Religion Matters: The Impact of Religious Practice on Social Stability." *Heritage Foundation Backgrounder,* no. 1064, January 25, 1996.

Fahrenkopf, Frank J., Jr. "The Conservative Agenda." In *Ronald Reagan's America.* Vol. 1. Edited by Eric J. Schmertz, Natalie Datlof, and Alexej Ugrinsky. Westport, Conn.: Greenwood, 1997.

Faludi, Susan. *Backlash: The Undeclared War Against American Women.* New York: Crown, 1991.

"Farewell Address to the Nation, January 11, 1989." *Public Papers of the Presidents: Ronald Reagan 1988–89.* Washington, D.C.: GPO, 1991.

Feinsilber, Mike. "Reagan Just a Mediocre President, Historians Say." *Rocky Mountain News,* December 10, 1993.

"Fighting Crime: Talk or Action?" *U.S. News & World Report,* April 21, 1986.

Fiorina, Morris. *Congress: The Keystone of the Washington Establishment.* New Haven, Conn.: Yale University Press, 1977.

Firebaugh, Glenn, and Kenneth E. Davis. "Trends in Anti-black Prejudice, 1972–1984: Region and Cohort Effects." *American Journal of Sociology* (September 1988).

Fischer, Beth A. *The Reagan Reversal: Foreign Policy and the End of the Cold War.* Columbia: University of Missouri, 1997.

Fisk, Margaret, ed. *Encyclopedia of Associations 1970.* 6th ed. Detroit: Gale Research, 1970.

Fowler, W. Gary, Donald W. Jackson, and James W. Riddlesperger Jr. "Reagan's Judges: A Latent Revolution?" In *Ronald Reagan's America,* edited by Eric J. Schmertz, Natalie Datlof, and Alexej Ugrinsky. Vol. 1. Westport, Conn.: Greenwood, 1997.

Fried, Albert. *The Jeffersonian and Hamiltonian Traditions in American Politics.* Garden City, N.Y.: Doubleday, 1968.

Fukuyama, Francis. *The Great Disruption: Human Nature and the Reconstitution of Social Order.* New York: Free Press, 1999.

———. "The Tragedy of Cold War History." *Foreign Affairs* (January–February 1994).

Gaddis, John Lewis. *The United States and the End of the Cold War.* New York: Oxford University Press, 1992.

Galbraith, John Kenneth. "A Visit to Russia." *The New Yorker,* September 3, 1984.

Gates, Robert M. *From the Shadows.* New York: Touchstone, 1996.

Geewax, Marilyn. "Class Distinctions Making Unwelcome Return to U.S." *Rocky Mountain News,* April 8, 1998, 40A.

Genscher, Hans-Dietrich. "Intermediate Range Missiles: Moscow Holds the Key to Disarmament." *NATO Review* (March–April 1983).

Gibbs, Nancy. "Land That They Love." *Time,* February 11, 1991.

———. "The Low Road to Revolution." *Time,* August 16, 1993.

Gilder, George. *Wealth and Poverty.* New York: Basic, 1981.

Ginsberg, Benjamin, and Martin Shefter. "The Presidency, Interest Groups, and Social Forces: Creating a Republican Coalition." In *The Presidency and the Political System.* 3rd ed. Edited by Michael Nelson. Washington, D.C.: Congressional Quarterly, 1990.

Gitlin, Todd. "Afterword." In *Reassessing the Sixties,* edited by Stephen Macedo. New York: W. W. Norton, 1997.

Glassman, James F. "It's Reagan's Economy, Stupid." *Rising Tide* (Fall 1997).

Glazer, Nathan. "The 'Social Agenda.'" In *Perspectives on the Reagan Years,* edited by John L. Palmer. Washington, D.C.: Urban Institute, 1986.

Gold, Philip. "A Holocaust View from the Young." *Detroit News,* May 5, 1985.

Goldwater, Barry M. *The Conscience of a Conservative.* Shepherdsville, Ky.: Victor, 1960.

———. *Why Not Victory? A Fresh Look at American Foreign Policy.* New York: McGraw-Hill, 1962.

"Goodbye Balanced Budget." *Newsweek,* November 16, 1981.

"Goodbye to the Gipper." *Newsweek,* January 9, 1989.

Grace, J. Peter. *War on Waste: President's Private Sector Survey on Cost Control.* New York: Macmillan, 1984.

Gray, C. Boyden. "Lessons." *Regulation,* no. 3 (1993).

The Great Debate: Interpreting Our Written Constitution. Washington, D.C.: Federalist Society, 1986.

Green, Fitzhugh. *American Propaganda Abroad.* New York: Hippocrene, 1988.

Greenberg, Stanley. "From Crisis to Working Majority." *The American Prospect* (Fall 1991).

Greenfield, Meg. "Patriotism and Disappointment." *Newsweek*, November 14, 1983.

Gregorsky, Frank. *What's the Matter with Democratic Foreign Policy?* Washington, D.C.: Republican Study Committee, May 1984.

Greider, William. *Who Will Tell the People: The Betrayal of American Democracy.* New York: Simon and Schuster, 1992.

———. *Secrets of the Temple: How the Federal Reserve Runs the Country.* New York: Touchstone, 1987.

Grenada Documents: An Overview and Selection. Washington, D.C.: Departments of State and Defense, 1984.

Greve, Michael S. *Real Federalism: Why It Matters, How It Could Happen.* Washington, D.C.: AEI, 2000.

Grover, Ronald. "Whatever Happened to the Grace Commission?" *Business Week*, June 16, 1986.

Habitat for Humanity International website, historical information <www.habitat.org/>.

Hager, George. "What the Budget Rules Say." *Congressional Quarterly Weekly Report*, May 2, 1992.

Hager, George, and Eric Pianin. *Mirage: Why Neither Democrats nor Republicans Can Balance the Budget, End the Deficit, and Satisfy the Public.* New York: Times, 1997.

Hall, David Locke. *The Reagan Wars: A Constitutional Perspective on War Powers and the Presidency.* Boulder, Colo.: Westview Press, 1991.

Hamilton, Alexander. *Federalist 70.* In *The Federalist Papers*, edited by Clinton Rossiter. New York: NAL, 1960.

"Hands across America Organizers Estimate Turnout at 5,442,960." *Washington Post*, May 30, 1986.

Hargrove, Thomas, and Guido H. Stempel III. "America Losing the Volunteer Spirit." *Rocky Mountain News*, December 28, 1993.

Harris v. McRae, 1980.

Hassett, Kevin A. "We Are All Reaganites Now." *American Enterprise* (September–October 1999).

Hayashi, Fumio. "Is Japan's Savings Rate High?" *Quarterly Review, Federal Reserve Bank of Minneapolis* (Spring 1989).

Hayes, Margaret Daly. "Not What I Say, but What I Do: Latin American Policy in the Reagan Administration." In *United States Policy in Latin America: A Quarter Century of Crisis and Challenge, 1961–1986*, edited by John D. Martz. Lincoln: University of Nebraska Press, 1988.

"The Heat of the Kitchen." *Time*, October 8, 1984.

Heclo, Hugh. "Reaganism and the Search for a Public Philosophy." In *Perspectives on the Reagan Years*, edited by John L. Palmer. Washington, D.C.: Urban Institute, 1986.

Heilbroner, Robert. "Does Capitalism Have a Future?" *New York Times Magazine*, August 5, 1982.

Henderson, David R. *The Truth about the 1980s.* Palo Alto, Calif.: Hoover Institution, 1994.

Herman, R. "Rally, Speakers Decry Cost of Nuclear Arms Race." *New York Times*, June 12, 1982.

Herrnson, Paul S. "National Party Organizations and the Postreform Congress." In *The Postreform Congress*, edited by Roger H. Davidson. New York: St. Martin's, 1992.

Hernandez, Roger E. "Hispanics Gained in Reagan Years." *Rocky Mountain News*, July 15, 1994, 35A.

Hill, Samuel S., and Dennis E. Owen. *The New Religious Political Right in America*. Nashville, Tenn.: Abingdon, 1982.

Himmelfarb, Gertrude. *The Demoralization of Society: From Victorian Virtues to Modern Values*. New York: Knopf, 1995.

———. *One Nation, Two Cultures: A Moral Divide*. New York: Knopf, 1999.

Hirschorn, Michael. "Little Men on Campus." *The New Republic*, August 5, 1985.

"Hispanic-Owned Businesses Are Growing." *The 1992 Information Please Almanac*. Boston: Information Please LLC, 1992.

Hodgson, Godfrey. *The World Turned Right Side Up: A History of the Conservative Ascendancy in America*. New York: Houghton Mifflin, 1996.

Hogan, J. Michael, and Ted J. Smith III. "Polling on the Issues: Public Opinion and the Nuclear Freeze." *Public Opinion Quarterly* (Winter 1991).

Holbrook, Stephen. *That Every Man Be Armed: The Evolution of a Constitutional Right*. Albuquerque: University of New Mexico Press, 1984.

Hougan, Jim. *Decadence: Radical Nostalgia, Narcissism, and Decline in the Seventies*. New York: Morrow, 1975.

Huber, Robert T. "Perestroika and U.S.-Soviet Relations: The Five-Year Plan No One Devised." In *Five Years That Shook the World*, edited by Harley D. Balzer. Boulder, Colo.: Westview Press, 1990.

Hughes, Thomas L. "Up from Reaganism." *Foreign Policy* (Fall 1981).

"Human Rights: Now the Hard Part." *New York Times*, December 30, 1989.

Hunter, James. *Before the Shooting Begins: Searching for Democracy in America's Culture Wars*. New York: Free Press, 1994.

Hutson, James H. *Religion and the Founding of the American Republic*. Washington, D.C.: Library of Congress, 1998.

"Idealism's Rebirth." *U.S. News & World Report*, October 24, 1988.

Immigration and Naturalization Service v. Chadha. 1983.

"Inaugural Address, January 20, 1981." *Public Papers of the Presidents: Ronald Reagan 1981*. Washington, D.C.: GPO, 1982.

"Inaugural Address, January 21, 1985." *Public Papers of the Presidents: Ronald Reagan 1985*. Washington, D.C.: GPO, 1988.

Ippolito, Dennis S. *Congressional Spending*. Ithaca, N.Y.: Cornell University Press, 1981.

"Is an Ugly Past Returning to Haunt America?" *U.S. News & World Report*, February 21, 1987.

Ivins, Molly. "Prosperity Bypasses the Masses." *Rocky Mountain News*, May 5, 1999.

Johnson, Haynes. *Sleepwalking through History: America in the Reagan Years*. New York: W. W. Norton, 1991.

Johnson, Paul. *Modern Times: From the Twenties to the Nineties*. Rev. ed. New York: HarperCollins, 1991.

Johnson, Victoria. "The Strategic Determinants of a Countermovement: The Emergence and Impact of Operation Rescue Blockades." In *Waves of Protest: Social Movements since the Sixties*, edited by Jo Freeman and Victoria Johnson. Lanham, Md.: Rowman & Littlefield, 1999.

Jones, Charles O. "Ronald Reagan and the U.S. Congress." In *The Reagan Legacy: Promise and Performance*, edited by Charles O. Jones. Chatham, N.J.: Chatham House, 1988.

Judis, John B. "Conservatism and the Price of Success." In *The Reagan Legacy*, edited by Sidney Blumenthal and Thomas Byrne Edsall. New York: Pantheon, 1988.

Kahn, Alfred E. "Change, Challenge, and Competition." *Regulation*, no. 2 (1993).

"Kahn Tells Airlines: Sit Tight, Cut Costs." *Aviation Week and Space Technology*, August 16, 1993.

Karp, Walter. *Liberty under Seige*. New York: W. W. Norton, 1991.

Kassop, Nancy. "The Rise of the Arrogant Presidency: Separation of Powers in the Reagan Administration." In *Ronald Reagan's America*, edited by Eric J. Schmertz, Natalie Datlof, and Alexej Ugrinsky. Vol. 1. Westport, Conn.: Greenwood, 1997.

Kaus, Mickey. *The End of Equality*. New York: Basic, 1992.

Kengor, Paul. "Reagan among the Professors." *Policy Review* (December 1999–January 2000).

Kernell, Samuel. *Going Public: New Strategies of Presidential Leadership*. 2nd ed. Washington, D.C.: Congressional Quarterly, 1993.

Kirkpatrick, Jeane J. "Dictatorships and Double Standards." *Commentary* (November 1979).

Klinkner, Philip A., and Rogers M. Smith. *The Unsteady March: The Rise and Decline of Racial Equality in America*. Chicago: University of Chicago, 1999.

Kohut, Andrew, and Norman Ornstein. "Constructing a Winning Coalition." *Public Opinion* (November–December 1987).

Kosters, Marvin H. "The Rise in Income Inequality." *The American Enterprise* (November–December 1992).

Kosters, Marvin H., and Murray N. Ross. "A Shrinking Middle Class?" *The Public Interest* (Winter 1988).

Kozyrev, Andrei. "Russia: A Chance for Survival." *Foreign Affairs* (Spring 1992).

Krauthammer, Charles. "The Greatest Cold War Myth of All." In *Backward and Upward: The New Conservative Writing*, edited by David Brooks. New York: Vintage, 1995.

Krugman, Paul. *The Age of Diminished Expectations*. Washington, D.C.: Washington Post, 1990.

——. "The Dishonest Truth." *New York Times*, February 23, 2000.

——. "Dynamo and Microchip." *New York Times*, February 20, 2000.

Kudlow, Lawrence, and Stephen Moore. "It's the Reagan Economy, Stupid," <www.clubforgrowth.org> February 2000.

Kuttner, Robert. *The End of Laissez-Faire*. New York: Knopf, 1991.

——. "Is There a Democratic Economics?" *The American Prospect* (Winter 1992).

Lacey, Marc. "Clinton Ranks in the Middle, But Falls Last on Morality." *New York Times*, February 21, 2000.

Ladd, Everett Carll. "The Reagan Phenomenon and Public Attitudes toward Government." In *The Reagan Presidency and the Governing of America*, edited by Lester M. Salamon and Michael S. Lund. Washington, D.C.: Urban Institute.

Lagon, Mark. *The Reagan Doctrine: Sources of American Conduct in the Cold War's Last Chapter*. Westport, Conn.: Praeger, 1994.

Laham, Nicholas. *The Reagan Presidency and the Politics of Race: In Pursuit of Color-blind Justice and Limited Government*. Westport, Conn.: Praeger, 1998.

Laird, Robbin F. "Soviet Nuclear Weapons in Europe." In *Soviet Foreign Policy in a Changing World*, edited by Robbin F. Laird and Erik Hoffmann. New York: Aldine de Gruyter, 1986.

Landy, Marc, and Sidney M. Milkis. *Presidential Greatness*. Lawrence: University Press of Kansas, 2000.

Lapham, Lewis H. "The New Patriotism." *Harper's* (June 1984).

Lasch, Christopher. *The Culture of Narcissism*. New York: W. W. Norton, 1978.

Lebow, Richard Ned, and Janice Gross Stein. "Reagan and the Russians." *The Atlantic Monthly* (February 1994).

Ledeen, Michael A. *Perilous Statecraft: An Insider's Account of the Iran-Contra Affair*. New York: Scribner, 1988.

Levy, Frank, and Richard Michel. "Are Baby Boomers Selfish?" Working paper 2081-01. Washington, D.C.: Urban Institute, 1985.

Lewis, Anthony. "Onward, Christian Soldiers." *New York Times*, March 10, 1983.

Lewy, Gunther. *Why America Needs Religion*. Grand Rapids, Mich.: Eerdmans, 1996.

Lindsey, Lawrence B. *The Growth Experiment*. New York: Basic, 1990.

———. "Taxpayer Behavior and the Distribution of the 1982 Tax Cut." Working Paper 1760. Cambridge, Mass.: National Bureau of Economic Research, Inc., October 1985.

Lippman, Walter. *An Inquiry into the Principles of the Good Society*. Boston: Little, Brown, 1937.

Lipset, Seymour Martin. "Feeling Better: Measuring the Nation's Confidence." *Public Opinion* (April–May 1985).

"Lobbyists File in with Welcome Mats as State Capitols Take Bigger Role." *Wall Street Journal*, May 30, 1990.

Lohr, Steve. "Little of $100 Billion Loss Can Be Retrieved." *New York Times*, February 20, 1992.

"The Long Shadow of the Deficit." *Newsweek*, January 9, 1989.

"The Lord and the Freeze." *New York Times*, March 11, 1983.

Lynn, Laurence E., Jr. "The Reagan Administration and the Renitent Bureaucracy." In *The Reagan Presidency and the Governing of America*, edited by Lester M. Salamon and Michael S. Lund . Washington, D.C.: Urban Institute, 1984.

Madison, James. *Federalist* 39, 51. In *The Federalist Papers*, edited by Clinton Rossiter. New York: NAL, 1960.

Magnet, Myron. *The Dream and the Nightmare*. New York: Morrow, 1993.

Marcuse, Herbert. "Dehumanization and Repression." In *American Political Radicalism*, edited by Gilbert Abcarian. Lexington, Mass.: Xerox College, 1971.

Marin, Peter. "The New Narcissism." *Harper's* (October 1975).

"Marriage: It's Back in Style!" *U.S. News & World Report*, June 20, 1983.

Marty, Martin. "Sailing through Waves of Patriotism." *The Christian Century*, July 16–23, 1986.

———. "What People Seek—and Find—in Belief." *U.S. News & World Report*, December 29, 1986–January 5, 1987.

Mashek, John W. "Fluke or Real Threat?" *U.S. News & World Report*, March 12, 1984.

Matlock, Jack F., Jr. *Autopsy of an Empire*. New York: Random House, 1995.

———. "Discussant." In *President Reagan and the World*, edited by Eric Schmertz, Natalie Datlof, and Alexej Ugrinsky. Westport, Conn.: Greenwood, 1997.

Maurer, Christine, and Tara E. Sheets, eds. *Encyclopedia of Associations 1999*. 34th ed. Detroit: Gale Research, 1999.

May, Clifford D. "In the Post-Greed Era: A Varoom at the Top." *Rocky Mountain News*, July 18, 1993.

Mayer, William G. *The Changing American Mind*. Ann Arbor: University of Michigan Press, 1992.

Mayhew, David R. *Congress: The Electoral Connection*. New Haven, Conn.: Yale University Press, 1974.

———. *Divided We Govern*. New Haven, Conn.: Yale University Press, 1991.

McClendon, McKee J. "Racism, Rational Choice, and White Opposition to Racial Change: A Case Study of Busing." *Public Opinion Quarterly* (Summer 1985).

McColm, R. Bruce. "The Comparative Study of Freedom House, New York, 1992–1993: Our Crowded Hour." *Freedom in the World*. New York: Freedom House, 1993.

McGrory, Mary. "A Campaign That Has Ignored the Impact of Japan And Russia." *Denver Post*, November 11, 1982.

McKenzie, Richard B. "Decade of Greed?" *National Review*, August 31, 1992.

———. *What Went Right in the 1980s*. San Francisco: Pacific Research Institute for Public Policy, 1994.

McLaughlin, John. "Military Love Affair." *National Review*, October 24, 1986.

McTeeter, Robert C., Jr. "Out on a New-Paradigm Limb." *The New Paradigm: Federal Reserve Bank of Dallas 1999 Annual Report*. Dallas: Federal Reserve Bank of Dallas, 1999.

Mead, Lawrence M. *Beyond Entitlement: The Social Obligations of Citizenship*. New York: Free Press, 1986.

Medved, Michael. *Hollywood vs. America*. New York: HarperCollins, 1993.

Meese, Edwin. *With Reagan*. Washington, D.C.: Regnery Gateway, 1992.

Menges, Constantine. *Inside the National Security Council*. New York: Simon and Schuster, 1988.

Meyer, Herbert E. "Discussant." In *President Reagan and the World*, edited by Eric Schmertz, Nancy Datlof, and Alexej Ugrinsky. Westport, Conn.: Greenwood, 1997.

Meyer, Jack A. "Social Programs and Social Policy." In *Perspectives on the Reagan Years*, edited by John L. Palmer. Washington, D.C.: Urban Institute, 1986.

Milkis, Sidney M. "The Presidency and Political Parties." In *The Presidency and the Political System*, edited by Michael Nelson. 3rd ed. Washington, D.C.: Congressional Quarterly, 1990.

Milkis, Sidney M., and Michael Nelson. *The American Presidency: Origins and Development, 1776–1990*. Washington, D.C.: Congressional Quarterly, 1990.

Miller, Arthur. "Is Confidence Rebounding?" *Public Opinion* (June–July 1983).

Mitchell, Daniel J. "Bush's Rasputin." *National Review*, December 28, 1992.

Mitchell, Jack. *Executive Privilege: Two Centuries of White House Scandals*. New York: Hippocrene, 1992.

Morris, Edmund. *Dutch: A Memoir of Ronald Reagan*. New York: Random House, 1999.

Muir, Donal E. "'White' Attitudes toward 'Blacks' at a Deep South University Campus, 1963–1988." *Sociology and Social Research* (January 1989).

Muir, William Ker, Jr. *The Bully Pulpit: The Presidential Leadership of Ronald Reagan*. San Francisco: ICS, 1992.

Muris, Timothy J. "Ronald Reagan and the Rise of Large Deficits: What Really Happened in 1981." *The Independent Review* 4, no. 3 (Winter 2000).

Murphy, Kevin. "The Education Gap Rap." *The American Enterprise* (March–April 1990).

Murphy, Walter F. "Reagan's Judicial Strategy." In *Looking Back on the Reagan Presidency*, edited by Larry Berman. Baltimore: Johns Hopkins University Press, 1990.

Murray, Charles. *Losing Ground: American Social Policy 1950–1980*. New York: Basic, 1984.

Mussolini, Benito. *The Doctrine of Fascism*. Florence, Italy: Vallenchi Editore Firenze, 1935.

Nadler, Richard. "Special(k)." *National Review*, April 19, 1999.

Nasar, Sylvia. "American Revival in Manufacturing Seen in U.S. Report." *New York Times*, February 5, 1991.

———. "Do We Live as Well as We Used To?" *Fortune*, September 14, 1987.

Nash, George H. *The Conservative Intellectual Movement in America since 1945*. Wilmington, Del.: Intercollegiate Studies Institute [hereafter ISI], 1996.

Nathan, Richard, *The Administrative Presidency*. New York: Wiley, 1983.

———. "Federalism: The 'Great Composition.'" In *The New American Political System*, edited by Anthony King. 2nd version. Washington, D.C.: AEI, 1990.

———. "Institutional Change Under Reagan." In *Perspectives on the Reagan Years*, edited by John L. Palmer. Washington, D.C.: Urban Institute, 1986.

"The Nation's Mood." *New York Times Magazine*, December 11, 1983.

Nedelsky, Jennifer. *Private Property and the Limits of American Constitutionalism*. Chicago: University of Chicago Press, 1990.

Nelson, Lars-Erik. "Family Values Are Now a Liberal Cause." *Denver Post*, November 7, 1993.

Nelson, Michael. "Evaluating the Presidency." In *The Presidency and the Political System*, edited by Michael Nelson. 3rd ed. Washington, D.C.: Congressional Quarterly, 1990.

Neuhaus, Richard. *Presidential Power and the Modern Presidents: The Politics of Leadership from Roosevelt to Reagan*. New York: Free Press, 1990.

———. "So Little Change, So Much Difference." *National Review*, March 24, 1989.

———. *Presidential Power: The Politics of Leadership from FDR to Carter*. 3rd ed. New York: Wiley, 1980.

"A New Breed of Activism." *Newsweek*, May 13, 1985.

"'New Patriotism' Called Dangerous." *USA Today*, August 1985.

"New Voices Come from the Right." *U.S. News & World Report*, January 13, 1986.

"The New Volunteerism." *Newsweek*, February 8, 1988.

Niskanen, William A. *Reaganomics: An Insider's View of the Policies and the People*. New York: Oxford University Press, 1988.

Nitze, Paul H. "Strategy in the Decade of the 1980s." *Foreign Affairs* (Fall 1980).

"Non-Fire Carbon Monoxide Deaths and Injuries Associated with the Use of Consumer Products: Annual Estimates." Consumer Product Safety Commission, December 10, 1997 <www.cpsc.gov/>.

Noonan, Peggy. *What I Saw at the Revolution: A Political Life in the Reagan Era*. New York: Random House, 1990.

"Notes and Asides." *National Review*, December 31, 1999.

"Notes and Comments." *The New Yorker*, November 18, 1985.

"The Numbers behind the Budget: Growing Deficits." *Washington Post*, August 29, 1990.

O'Brien, David M. "The Reagan Judges: His Most Enduring Legacy?" In *The Reagan Legacy: Promise and Performance*, edited by Charles O. Jones. Chatham, N.J.: Chatham House, 1988.

O'Neill, June E. "The Story of the Surplus." *Policy Review* (June–July 2000).

———. "An Argument against Comparable Worth." *Comparable Worth*. Washington, D.C.: U.S. Commission on Civil Rights, June 1984.

O'Neill, Tip. *Man of the House*. New York: St. Martin's, 1987.

Olsen, John B. "Assessing an Unfinished But Promising Experiment." In *The Reagan Presidency and the Governing of America*, edited by Lester M. Salamon and Michael S. Lund. Washington, D.C.: Urban Institute, 1984.

"Opinion Roundup." *Public Opinion* (March–April 1987).

"Opinion Roundup." *Public Opinion* (July–August 1987).

"Ordinary Millionaires." *U.S. News & World Report*, January 13, 1986.

"OSHA Enforcement Policy." U.S. House of Representatives. Hearings before a Subcommittee of the Committee on Governmental Operations, 98th Congress, November 9–10, 1983.

"The Outcome in El Salvador." *Washington Post*, January 19, 1992.

Pacelle, Richard L. *The Transformation of the Supreme Court Agenda from the New Deal to the Reagan Administration*. Boulder, Colo.: Westview Press, 1991.

Paige, Connie. *The Right-to-Lifers*. New York: Summit, 1983.

Palmer, John L. "Philosophy, Policy, and Politics: Integrating the Themes. In *Perspectives on the Reagan Years*, edited by John L. Palmer. Washington, D.C.: Urban Institute, 1986.

"Patriotism Is Back in Style." *U.S. News & World Report*, July 9, 1984.

Pemberton, William E. *Exit with Honor: The Life and Presidency of Ronald Reagan*. Armonk, N.Y.: M. E. Sharpe, 1998.

Peterson, Merrill D. ed. *The Portable Thomas Jefferson*. New York: Viking, 1975.

Peterson, Paul E., and Mark Rom. "Lower Taxes, More Spending, and Budget Deficits." In *The Reagan Legacy: Promise and Performance*, edited by Charles O. Jones. Chatham, N.J.: Chatham House, 1988.

Peterson, Wallace. *Silent Depression*. New York: W. W. Norton, 1994.

Phillips, Kevin. *The Politics of Rich and Poor: Wealth and the American Electorate in the Reagan Aftermath*. New York: Random House, 1990.

Pika, Joseph A. "Reaching Out to Organized Interests: Public Liaisons in the Modern White House." In *The Presidency Reconsidered*, edited by Richard Waterman. Itasca, Ill.: Peacock, 1993.

Pines, Burton Yale. *Back to Basics: The Traditionalist Movement That Is Sweeping Grass-Roots America*. New York: Morrow, 1982.

Pinkney, Alphonso. *The Myth of Black Progress*. New York: Cambridge University Press, 1984.

"The Pitcher and the Catcher." *Newsweek*, January 9, 1989.

Piven, Francis Fox, and Richard A. Cloward. *The New Class War*. New York: Pantheon, 1982.

Plunkert, Lois M. "The 1990s: A Decade of Job Growth and Industry Shifts." *Monthly Labor Review* 113, no. 9.

Pomper, Gerald M. "The Presidential Election." In *The Election of 1988: Reports and Interpretations*, edited by Gerald Pomper. Chatham, N.J.: Chatham House, 1989.

"The Poor Aren't Poorer." *U.S. News & World Report*, July 25, 1994.

Popenoe, David. "The Controversial Truth: Two-Parent Families Are Better." *New York Times*, December 26, 1992.

Porter, Bruce D. *The USSR in Third World Conflicts*. Cambridge: Cambridge University Press, 1984.

Pound, John, Kenneth Lehn, and Gregg Jarrell. "Are Takeovers Hostile to Economic Performance?" *Regulation* (September–October 1986).

Poverty in the U.S.: 1990 (Washington, D.C.: Bureau of the Census, August 1991).

"Presidential Timber: How Chief Executives Stack Up." *U.S. News & World Report*, November 27, 2000.

"The President's News Conference, January 28, 1981." *Public Papers of the Presidents: Ronald Reagan 1981*. Washington, D.C.: GPO, 1982.

"Proclamation 5576: National Family Week, 1986, November 21, 1986." *Public Papers of the Presidents: Ronald Reagan 1986*. Washington, D.C.: GPO, 1988.

"Psychic Shock for a Generation." *Newsweek*, February 18, 1991.

"The Public Assesses the Reagan Record on Foreign Policy." *Public Opinion* (Summer 1986).

Putnam, Robert D. "Bowling Alone: America's Declining Social Capital." *Journal of Democracy* (January 1995).

"Racism on the Rise." *Time*, February 2, 1987.

"Radio Address to the Nation on Family Values, December 20, 1986." *Public Papers of the Presidents: Ronald Reagan 1986*. Washington, D.C.: GPO, 1988.

"Radio Address to the Nation on the Federal Judiciary, June 21, 1986." *Public Papers of the President: Ronald Reagan 1986*. Washington, D.C.: GPO, 1988.

"Radio Address to the Nation on Independence Day and the Centennial of the Statue of Liberty." July 5, 1986." *Public Papers of the Presidents: Ronald Reagan 1986*. Washington, D.C.: GPO, 1988.

Rahn, Richard W. "A Settling of Accounts." *Wall Street Journal*, October 12, 1987.

Rainie, Harrison. "His Moment Arrives." *U.S. News & World Report*, January 30, 1989.

"Ready for Action: Or Are They?" *U.S. News & World Report*, February 14, 1983.

"Reagan and History." *National Review*, May 24, 1993.

"The Reagan Record: Five Continuous Years of Economic Growth." White House Office of Public Affairs, November 1987.

Reagan, Ronald. "Address Announcing His Candidacy for the Presidency, New York, November 13, 1979."

———. *An American Life: The Autobiography*. New York: Simon and Schuster, 1990.

———. "At the Investiture of Chief Justice William H. Renquist and Associate Justice Antonin Scalia at the White House, September 26, 1986, Washington, D.C." In *The Great Debate: Interpreting Our Written Constitution*. Washington, D.C.: Federalist Society, 1986.

"Reagan's Youthful Boomlet." *Time*, October 8, 1984.

Reeves, Richard. "The Ideological Election." *New York Times Magazine*, February 19, 1984.

———. *The Reagan Detour.* New York: Simon and Schuster, 1985.

———. "Was the Cold War Necessary?" *The Record*, August 5, 1990.

Reich, Robert. *The Resurgent Liberal.* New York: Times, 1989.

Reischauer, Robert D. "The Phantom Surplus." *New York Times*, January 28, 2000.

"Remarks Accepting the Presidential Nomination of the Republican National Convention in Dallas, Texas, August 23, 1984." *Public Papers of the Presidents: Ronald Reagan 1984.* Washington, D.C.: GPO, 1987.

"Remarks and a Question and Answer Session at a White House Reception for Participants in the Youth Volunteer Conference, November 12, 1982." *Public Papers of the Presidents: Ronald Reagan 1982.* Washington, D.C.: GPO, 1983.

"Remarks at the Annual Convention of the National Association of Evangelicals in Orlando, Florida, March 8, 1983." *Public Papers of the Presidents: Ronald Reagan 1983.* Washington, D.C.: GPO, 1984.

"Remarks at the Annual Convention of the National Religious Broadcasters, January 30, 1984." *Public Papers of the Presidents: Ronald Reagan 1984.* Washington, D.C.: GPO, 1987.

"Remarks at the Annual Dinner of the Knights of Malta in New York City, January 13, 1989." *Public Papers of the Presidents: Ronald Reagan 1988–89.* Washington, D.C.: GPO, 1991.

"Remarks at the Annual Meeting of the National Alliance of Business, October 5, 1981." *Public Papers of the Presidents: Ronald Reagan 1981.* Washington, D.C.: GPO, 1982.

"Remarks at the Bicentennial Celebration of the United States Constitution, September 16, 1987." *Public Papers of the Presidents: Ronald Reagan 1987.* Washington, D.C.: GPO, 1989.

"Remarks at an Ecumenical Prayer Breakfast in Dallas, Texas, August 23, 1984." *Public Papers of the Presidents: Ronald Reagan 1984.* Washington, D.C.: GPO, 1986.

"Remarks at a Luncheon Meeting with Members of the President's Task Force on Private Sector Initiatives, December 2, 1981." *Public Papers of the Presidents: Ronald Reagan 1981.* Washington, D.C.: GPO, 1982.

"Remarks at the 'We the People' Bicentennial Celebration in Philadelphia, Pennsylvania, September 17, 1987." *Public Papers of the Presidents: Ronald Reagan 1987.* Washington, D.C.: GPO, 1989.

"Remarks at a White House Briefing for the American Legislative Exchange Council, December 12, 1986." *Public Papers of the Presidents: Ronald Reagan 1986.* Washington, D.C.: GPO, 1988.

"Remarks by Governor Bill Clinton." Economic Club of Detroit, Detroit, Michigan, August 21, 1992.

"Remarks in Atlanta, Georgia, at the Annual Convention of the National Conference of State Legislatures, July 30, 1981." *Public Papers of the Presidents of the United States: Ronald Reagan 1981.* Washington, D.C.: GPO, 1982.

"Remarks on Soviet–United States Relations at the Town Hall of California Meeting in Los Angeles, August 26, 1987." *Public Papers of the Presidents: Ronald Reagan 1987.* Washington, D.C.: GPO, 1989.

"Remarks to the Winners of the Bicentennial of the Constitution Essay Competition, September 10, 1987." *Public Papers of the Presidents: Ronald Reagan 1987.* Washington, D.C.: GPO 1989.

"Rethinking Drugs." *The National Journal,* February 2, 1991.

"Rethinking Race." *The New Republic,* February 9, 1987.

Revel, Jean-Francois. *Democracy against Itself.* New York: Free Press, 1993.

"A Revival of Religion on Campus." *U.S. News & World Report,* January 9, 1984.

"Reviving the Energy Tax." *Washington Post,* July 6, 1993.

Rhoads, Steven E. *The Economist's View of the World.* New York: Cambridge University Press, 1985.

———. *Incomparable Worth: Pay Equity Meets the Market.* New York: Cambridge University Press, 1993.

Riccards, Michael. *The Ferocious Engine of Democracy: A History of the American Presidency.* Vol. 2. New York: Madison, 1995.

Rivlin, Alice M. *Reviving the American Dream.* Washington, D.C.: Brookings Institution, 1992.

Roberts, Paul Craig. "Coasting on the Reagan Boom." *Washington Times National Weekly Edition,* March 13–19, 2000.

———. "Debt, Lies, and Inflation." *National Review,* August 31, 1992.

———. *The Supply-Side Revolution.* Cambridge, Mass.: Harvard University Press, 1984.

Robinson, John, and John A. Fleishman. "Ideological Identification: Trends and Interpretations of the Liberal-Conservative Balance." *Public Opinion Quarterly* (Spring 1988).

Rockman, Bert A. "Cutting with the Grain: Is There a Clinton Leadership Legacy?" In *The Clinton Legacy,* edited by Colin Campbell and Bert A. Rockman. Chatham, N.J.: Chatham House, 1999.

Rodgers, Harrell R., Jr. "Fair Employment Laws for Minorities: An Evaluation of Federal Implementation." In *Implementation of Civil Rights Policy,* edited by Charles S. Bullock III and Charles M. Lamb. Monterey, Calif.: Brooks/Cole, 1984.

"Rolling Back Regulation." *Time,* July 6, 1987.

Roper, Burns. "Presidential Popularity: Do People Like the Actor or His Actions?" *Public Opinion* (October–November 1983).

Rose, Susan D. "Gender, Education, and the New Christian Right." *Society* (January–February 1989).

Rosenbaum, David E. "A New Heave in Tax Policy." *New York Times,* December 8, 1992.

———. "Prof. Moynihan Wakes the Class with Truth about Taxes." *New York Times,* January 24, 1990.

Rosenfeld, Stephen S. "The Guns of July." In *The Reagan Foreign Policy,* edited by William G. Hyland. New York: New American Library, 1987.

Ross, Shelly. *Fall from Grace: Sex, Scandal, and Corruption in American Politics from 1702 to the Present.* New York: Ballantine, 1988.

Rubenstein, Ed. "The Fading American Dream?" *National Review,* August 31, 1992.

———. "Race and Poverty." *National Review,* August 31, 1992.

———. "More Than McJobs." *National Review,* August 31, 1992.

———. "The Reregulation President." *National Review,* September 14, 1992.

Rubenstein, Edwin S. *The Right Data.* New York: National Review, 1994

Rusher, William. *The Rise of the Right.* Rev. ed. New York: National Review, 1993.

Rustow, Dankwart A. "Democracy: A Global Revolution?" *Foreign Affairs* (Fall 1990).

Sabato, Larry J. *Goodbye to Good-Time Charlie: The American Governorship Transformed.* 2nd ed. Washington, D.C.: Congressional Quarterly, 1983.

———. *The Party's Just Begun: Shaping Political Parties for America's Future.* Glenview, Ill.: Scott, Foresman, 1988.

Salamon, Lester M., and Alan J. Abramson. *The Federal Government and the Nonprofit Sector: The Impact of the 1981 Tax Act on Charitable Giving.* Washington D.C.: Urban Institute, 1981.

Salisbury, Harrison. "USSR: What's Ahead." *Denver Post,* November 1982.

Salisbury, Robert H. "The Paradox of Interest Groups in Washington: More Groups, Less Clout." In *The New American Political System,* edited by Anthony King. 2nd version. Washington, D.C.: AEI, 1990.

Salter, Stephanie. "There's No Boom in World of Have-Nots." *Rocky Mountain News,* May 26, 1998.

Samuelson, Robert J. "The Irony of Capitalism." *Newsweek,* January 9, 1989.

———. "Japan as Number Two." *Newsweek,* December 6, 1993.

———. "Racism and Poverty." *Newsweek,* August 7, 1989.

Sanches, Rene. "Survey of College Freshmen Finds Rise in Volunteerism." *Washington Post,* January 13, 1997.

Sanders, Elizabeth. "The Presidency and the Bureaucratic State." In *The Presidency and the Political System,* edited by Michael Nelson. 3rd ed. Washington, D.C.: Congressional Quarterly, 1990.

Savage, James D. *Balanced Budgets and American Politics.* Ithaca, N.Y.: Cornell University Press, 1988.

Sawhill, Isabel. "Reaganomics in Retrospect. In *Perspectives on the Reagan Years,* edited by John L. Palmer. Washington, D.C.: Urban Institute, 1986.

Scanlon, Bill. "If Longevity Is Your Goal, Go to Church." *Denver Rocky Mountain News,* May 19, 1999.

Schiller, Ronald, "How Religious Are We?" *Reader's Digest,* May 1986.

Schlesinger, Arthur M. Jr., *The Disuniting of America.* New York: W. W. Norton, 1992.

———. "The Ultimate Approval Rating." *New York Times Magazine,* December 15, 1996.

Schmidt, David D. *Citizen Lawmakers: The Ballot Initiative Revolution.* Philadelphia: Temple University Press, 1989.

Schneider, William. "The Political Legacy of the Reagan Years." In *The Reagan Legacy,* edited by Sidney Blumenthal and Thomas Byrne Edsall. New York: Pantheon, 1988.

Schuman, Howard, Charlotte Steeh, and Lawrence Bobo. *Racial Attitudes in America.* Cambridge, Mass.: Harvard University Press, 1985.

Schweizer, Peter. *Victory: The Reagan Administration's Secret Strategy That Hastened the Collapse of the Soviet Union.* New York: Atlantic Monthly, 1994.

"A Search for the Sacred." *U.S. News & World Report,* April 4, 1983.

Shapiro, Karl, and Joseph Satin, eds. *The 1950s: America's "Placid" Decade.* New York: Houghton-Mifflin, 1960.

Shapiro, Martin. "The Supreme Court from Early Burger to Early Rehnquist." In *The New American Political System,* edited by Anthony King. 2nd version. Washington, D.C.: AEI, 1990.

Shapiro, Robert Y., and John M. Gilroy. "The Polls: Regulation, Part I." *Public Opinion Quarterly* (Summer 1984).

Shattan, Joseph. *Architects of Victory: Six Heroes of the Cold War.* Washington, D.C.: Heritage Foundation, 1999.

Shevardnadze, Eduard. *The Future Belongs to Freedom.* New York: Free Press, 1991.

Shull, Steven A. *A Kinder, Gentler Racism? The Reagan-Bush Civil Rights Legacy.* Armonk, N.Y.: M. E. Sharpe, 1993.

Shull, Steven A., and Albert C. Ringelstein. "Presidential Rhetoric in Civil Rights Policymaking 1953–1992." In *Presidential Leadership and Civil Rights Policy,* edited by James W. Riddlesperger Jr. and Donald W. Jackson. Westport, Conn.: Greenwood, 1995.

Shultz, George. "America and the Struggle for Freedom." Address to the Commonwealth Club of California, San Francisco, February 22, 1985.

———. "Low Intensity Warfare: The Challenge of Ambiguity." Address to the National Defense University, Washington, D.C., January 15, 1986.

———. *Turmoil and Triumph: My Years as Secretary of State.* New York: Scribner, 1993.

Siminov, Vladimir. "The 'New Patriotism.'" *World Press Review,* December 1985.

Simon, James F. *The Center Holds: The Power Struggle inside the Rehnquist Court.* New York: Simon and Schuster, 1995.

Skinner, Kiron K., Annelise Anderson, and Martin Anderson. *Reagan in His Own Hand: The Writings of Ronald Reagan That Reveal His Revolutionary Vision for America.* New York: Free Press, 2001.

Skowronek, Stephen. *The Politics Presidents Make: Leadership from John Adams to George Bush.* Cambridge, Mass.: Belknap, 1993.

"Sleepers without Dreams." *The Progressive,* October 1984.

Sloan, John W. *The Reagan Effect: Economics and Presidential Leadership.* Lawrence: University Press of Kansas, 1999.

Smith, Adam. *The Roaring '80s.* New York: Summit Books, 1988.

Smith, Daniel. *Tax Crusaders.* New York: Routledge, 1998.

Smith, Tom W., and Paul B. Sheatsley. "American Attitudes toward Race Relations." *Public Opinion* (October–November 1984).

Smith, William French. "Independent Counsel Provisions of the Ethics in Government Act." In *The Fettered Presidency,* edited by L. Gordon Crovitz and Jeremy A. Rabkin. Washington, D.C.: AEI, 1989.

"A Sobering Decision." *U.S. News & World Report,* April 7, 1986.

"Social Welfare Expenditures Under Public Programs." *The 1992 Information Please Almanac.* Boston: Information Please LLC, 1992.

Solo, Pam. *From Protest to Policy: Beyond the Freeze to Common Security.* Cambridge, Mass.: Ballinger, 1988.

"Sorting Out Age Differences." *Public Opinion* (November–December 1986).

Sourcebook of Criminal Justice Statistics 1981. Washington, D.C.: Department of Justice, 1981.

Sourcebook of Criminal Justice Statistics 1991. Washington, D.C.: Department of Justice, 1991.

Soviet Military Power. Washington, D.C.: Department of Defense, 1981.

Soviet Military Power 1987. Washington, D.C.: Department of Defense, 1987.

"Soviet Noncompliance with Arms Control Agreements." *Special Report 122.* United States Department of State, February 1, 1985.

"Soviet Noncompliance with Arms Control Agreements." *Special Report 163*. United States Department of State, March 1987.

Soviet Strategic Defense Programs. Washington, D.C.: Departments of State and Defense, 1985.

"Special Report: The New Volunteers." *Newsweek*, July 10, 1989.

"The Spirit of Independence." *Inc.*, July 1988.

"The State of American Values." *U.S. News & World Report*, December 9, 1985.

"State of the Nation." *Public Opinion* (February–March 1984).

"State of the Union, January 25, 1988." *Public Papers of the Presidents: Ronald Reagan 1988*. Washington, D.C.: GPO, 1990.

Statistical Abstract of the United States 1992. Prepared by the Chief of the Bureau of Statistics. Washington, D.C.: GPO, 1992.

Statistical Abstract of the United States 1998. Prepared by the Chief of the Bureau of Statistics. Washington, D.C.: GPO, 1998.

Steibel, Gerald L. *Detente: Dilemma or Disaster?* New York: National Strategy Information Center, Inc., 1969.

Stein, Herbert. "The Middle-Class Blues." *The American Enterprise* (March–April 1992).

Stein, Herbert, and Murray Foss. *An Illustrated Guide to the American Economy*. Washington, D.C.: AEI, 1992.

"Stepping into the Middle of OSHA's Muddle." *Business Week*, August 2, 1993.

Steuerle, C. Eugene. *The Tax Decade*. Washington, D.C.: Urban Institute, 1992.

Stewart, Joseph, Jr. "Between 'Yes' and 'But': Presidents and the Politics of Civil Rights Policy-Making." In *The Presidency Reconsidered*, edited by Richard W. Waterman. Itasca, Ill.: Peacock, 1993.

Stockman, David. *The Triumph of Politics*. New York: Avon Books, 1987.

Stone, Joseph, and Tim Yohn. *Prime Time and Misdemeanors*. New Brunswick, N.J.: Rutgers University Press, 1992.

"Street Crime: People Fight Back." *U.S. News & World Report*, April 15, 1985.

Stuckey, Mary. *The President as Interpreter-in-Chief*. Chatham, N.J.: Chatham House, 1991.

"Sudden Rise of Hate Groups Spurs Federal Crackdown." *U.S. News & World Report*, May 6, 1985.

"Sun Breaks Through for U.S. in Central America." *U.S. News & World Report*, June 24, 1985.

"Suvorov, Viktor." *Inside the Soviet Army*. New York: Macmillan, 1982.

Swanson, Jacinda. "Clinton's Rhetoric of Responsibility." Paper prepared for delivery at the Midwest Political Science Association, April 1999.

Talbott, Strobe. *Deadly Gambits*. New York: Knopf, 1984.

———. "Rethinking the Red Menace." *Time*, January 1, 1990.

"Tax Cuts: How You Will Be Better Off." *U.S. News & World Report*, August 10, 1981.

Tellis, Ashley J. "The Geopolitical Stakes in Central American Crisis." In *Central America and the Reagan Doctrine*, edited by Walter F. Hahn. Lanham, Md.: University Press of America, 1987.

Texeira, Ruy A. *The Disappearing American Voter*. Washington, D.C.: Brookings Institution, 1992.

Thatcher, Margaret. "Reagan's Leadership, America's Recovery." *National Review*, December 30, 1988.

Theus, Kathryn T. "Campus-Based Community Service." *Change* (September–October 1988).

"This Week." *National Review*, March 29, 1993.

"This Week." *National Review*, July 26, 1999.

Thomas, Dana L. *Lords of the Land: The Triumphs and Scandals of America's Real Estate Barons: From Early Times to the Present.* New York: Putnam, 1977.

Thornburgh v. American College of Obstetrics and Gynecology, 1986.

"Those Budget Cuts: Who'll Be Hit Hardest." *U.S. News & World Report*, August 10, 1981.

Thurow, Lester. "The Great Stagnation." *New York Times Magazine*, October 17, 1982.

Tobin, James. "Current Controversies in Macroeconomics: The Four Schools." *Harvard Graduate School Newsletter*, 1990.

———. "Reaganomics in Retrospect." In *The Reagan Revolution*, edited by B. B. Kymlicka and Jean V. Matthews. Chicago: Dorsey, 1988.

Tocqueville, Alexis de. *Democracy in America.* 2 vols. New York: Vintage Books, 1945.

Transportation Research Board. *Winds of Change: Domestic Air Transport since Deregulation.* Washington, D.C.: National Research Council, 1991.

"Truth in Taxing." *New York Times*, March 10, 1983.

Tulis, Jeffrey L. *The Rhetorical Presidency.* Princeton, N.J.: Princeton University Press, 1987.

Ture, Norman B. "To Cut and to Please." *National Review*, August 31, 1992.

"A Turn for the Worse." *Newsweek*, December 12, 1983.

"Twisted Federalism." *Los Angeles Times*, November 16, 1986.

Ullman, John B. "Ronald Reagan and the Illusion of Victory in the Cold War." In *President Reagan and the World*, edited by Eric Schmertz, Nancy Datlof, and Alexej Ugrinsky. Westport, Conn.: Greenwood, 1997.

U.S. Advisory Commission on Intergovernmental Relations. *The Question of State Government Capability*, Report A-98. Washington, D.C.: Government Printing Office. 1985.

"The U.S. Family: Help!" *Time*, December 28, 1970.

U.S. News & World Report, December 30, 1985–January 6, 1986 (cover).

U.S. News & World Report, January 14, 1980 (cover).

"U.S. Prefers War to 'Amerika,' G.W. Survey Finds." Office of News and Public Affairs, George Washington University, February 20, 1987.

United States Department of Education. *The Nation Responds: Recent Efforts to Improve Education.* Washington, D.C.: GPO, 1984.

United States National Commission on Excellence in Education. *A Nation At Risk: The Imperative for Educational Reform: A Report to the Nation and the Secretary of Education, United States Department of Education.* Washington, D.C.: GPO, 1983.

Updike, John. "The '50s: Each Man Was an Island." *Newsweek*, January 3, 1994.

Vogelstein, Fred. "Greed is good again. Just don't tell anyone." *U.S. News & World Report*, December 15, 1997.

Waldrop, Judith, and Thomas Exter. "Legacy of the 1980s." *American Demographics* (March 1991).

Walker, David B. *The Rebirth of Federalism: Slouching toward Washington.* 2nd ed. Chatham, N.J.: Chatham House, 2000.

Waller, James. *Face to Face: The Changing State of Racism across America.* New York: Insight, 1998.

Walsh, Kenneth T. "The Young Army behind Gary Hart." *U.S. News & World Report,* March 19, 1984.

Wang, Charleston C. K. *OSHA Compliance and Management Handbook.* Park Ridge, N.J.: Noyes, 1993.

Warnke, Paul C. "'Zero' May Mean Nothing." *New York Times,* January 26, 1983.

Waterman, Charles. "Making Covert Aid to Rebels Overt." *Christian Science Monitor,* April 21, 1986.

Wattenberg, Ben J. "It's Time to Stop America's Retreat." *New York Times Magazine,* July 22, 1979.

Wattenberg, Ben. "GOP's Faith in Punishment May Not Have Been in Vain." *Rocky Mountain News,* August 30, 1993.

Wayne, Stephen J. *The Road to the White House 1996.* New York: St. Martin's, 1996.

Weinberger, Caspar W. *Fighting for Peace: Seven Critical Years in the Pentagon.* New York: Warner Books, 1990.

———. "Policy, Strategy, and the Budget." *Defense* (May 1982).

West, Cornel. "The '80s: Market Culture Run Amok." *Newsweek,* January 3, 1994.

West, John G., Jr. "George Washington and the Religious Impulse." In *Patriot Sage: George Washington and the American Political Tradition,* edited by Gary L. Gregg II and Matthew Spalding. Wilmington, Del.: ISI, 1999.

West, Thomas G. *Vindicating the Founders: Race, Sex, Class, and Justice in the Origins of America.* Lanham, Md.: Rowman & Littlefield, 1997.

"What Goes Around." *U.S. News & World Report,* August 30–September 6, 1993.

"When Presidents Take It Easy." *U.S. News & World Report.* March 19, 1984.

White, Joseph, and Aaron Wildavsky. *The Deficit and the Public Interest: The Search for Responsible Budgeting in the 1980s.* Berkeley: University of California Press, 1989.

Whitehead, Barbara Defoe. "Dan Quayle Was Right." *The Atlantic Monthly,* April 1993.

Wildavsky, Aaron. *The Beleaguered Presidency.* New Brunswick, N.J.: Transaction, 1991.

———. *The New Politics of the Budgetary Process.* 2nd ed. New York: HarperCollins, 1992.

———. *The Rise of Radical Egalitarianism.* Washington, D.C.: American University Press, 1991.

Will, George F. "Greenspan Tweaks . . ." *Washington Post,* February 20, 2000.

———. "How Reagan Changed America." *Newsweek,* January 9, 1989.

"Will the U.S. Stay Number One?" *U.S. News & World Report,* February 2, 1987.

Willis, David K. "Rebels Deal Setback to USSR in Third World." *Christian Science Monitor,* February 19, 1986.

Wills, Garry. *Reagan's America: Innocents at Home.* Garden City, N.Y.: Doubleday, 1987.

Wilson, James Q. *The Moral Sense.* New York: Free Press, 1993.

———. *Thinking about Crime.* Rev. ed. New York: Basic, 1983.

Wisensale, Steven K. "Family Policy during the Reagan Years: The Private Side of the Conservative Agenda." In *Ronald Reagan's America,* edited by Eric J. Schmertz, Natalie Datlof, and Alexej Ugrinsky. Vol. 1. Westport, Conn.: Greenwood, 1997.

Wolfe, Tom. "The Me Decade." *New York*, August 23, 1976

Wood, B. Dan. "Presidential Control of Intergovernmental Bureaucracies." In *The Presidency Reconsidered*, edited by Richard Waterman. Itasca, Ill.: Peacock, 1993.

Woods, Geraldine. *Drug Abuse in Society*. Santa Barbara, Calif.: ABC-CLIO, 1993.

Woodward, Kenneth L. "The Rites of Americans." *Newsweek*, November 29, 1993.

Woodward, Robert. *The Agenda: Inside the Clinton White House*. New York: Simon and Schuster, 1994.

Yago, Glenn. *How High-Yield Securities Restructured Corporate America*. New York: Oxford University Press, 1991.

Yakes, Nancy, and Denise Akey. *Encyclopedia of Associations 1980*. 14th ed. Detroit: Gale Research, 1980.

Yankelovich, Daniel. "Comments: When Reaganomics Fails, Then What?" In *The Reagan Presidency and the Governing of America*, edited by Lester M. Salamon and Michael S. Lund. Washington, D.C.: Urban Institute, 1984.

Yankelovich, Daniel, and Larry Kaagan. "Assertive America." In *The Reagan Foreign Policy*, edited by William G. Hyland. New York: New American Library, 1987.

Yarbrough, Tinsley E. "Reagan and the Courts." In *The Reagan Presidency*, edited by Dilys M. Hill, Raymond A. Moore, and Phil Williams. New York: St. Martin's, 1990.

Young, Cathy. *Ceasefire: Why Women and Men Must Join Forces to Achieve True Equality*. New York: Free Press, 1999.

Zemtsov, Ilya, and John Farrar. *Gorbachev: The Man and the System*. New Brunswick, N.J.: Transaction, 1989.

Zuckerman, Mortimer B. "Doing What Is Necessary." *U.S. News & World Report*, March 1, 1993.

Zycher, Benjamin. "Debt, Lies, and Reaganomics." *National Review*, December 14, 1992.

Index

abortion, 20, 40, 42, 169, 236–38; and Reagan, 24, 26, 41–42, 159–60, 174, 258

Adams, John, 12

Adarand Constructors v. Pena, 33

Adelman, Kenneth, 210, 215

affirmative action, 30, 33, 41–44; Reagan and, 9, 27–29, 41–42, 44, 228, 231

Afghanistan: invasion by USSR, xxv, 52, 54, 185–88, 241, 252, 254, 257; Carter and, 188, 201, 254; Reagan and, 201–5, 213

Aid to Families with Dependent Children (AFDC), 36, 103, 132

AIDS (Acquired Immune Deficiency Syndrome), xvii, 157, 257

alcohol abuse, 168, 172, 252; Reagan and, 37, 39, 158

Allen, Richard V., 195

American Association of Retired Persons (AARP), 68, 138

American Bar Association (ABA), 41–42

American Collegians for Life, 241

American Legion, 236

American Security Council, 236

Anderson, John, 130

Anderson, Martin, xv, 78, 124, 235, 261

Angola, 186, 213; Reagan and, 202–4; and UNITA, 202, 204

antifederalists, 33; and Reagan xx, 153

antinuclear movement, 190, 194, 199–200

antitax movement, 235, 254

antitrust policy, 88; Reagan and, 42, 80

arms control: INF Treaty, 210; Reagan and, 190, 200, 209–13; USSR and, 194, 200, 210–11, 213–14; Reykjavik summit, 200, 210–11; "Zero Option," 210, 213; SALT II, 187–88; START I, 210

Asian Americans in 1980s, 31, 101, 109

AT&T, breakup of, 88

Bakker, Jim, 171

Balanced Budget Amendment, 136–37

Beirut peacekeeping mission, 4, 53, 206, 212

Bennett, William, 172, 176

Bessmertnykh, Aleksandr, 201

Bishop, Maurice, 206

Black Panthers, 31

blacks in 1980s, xvii, 29–31, 100–102, 109

Bob Jones University, 28

Boem-Barwek, Eugene, 78

The Public Interest, 155
Third Generation, 240
Thomas, Clarence, 30
Times-Mirror survey of the electorate, and Reagan coalition, 230, 242
Tocqueville, Alexis de, xxii–xxiii, 164, 174, 245, 261; Reagan and, xxi–xxiii, 120, 153, 155, 173, 253–54
Tower, John, 60
trade deficit. *See* competitiveness; international
Truman Doctrine, 191
Truman, Harry S, 14; scandals, xviii, 257
Trump, Donald, xvi
Ture, Norman, 124
TV Marti, 196

unemployment, 75, 82, 101–2, 107
Union of Soviet Socialist Republics (USSR), xxiii, 185–88, 192–93, 209; collapse of empire, 185, 205, 212–17; and view of "détente," 187; economic weakness of, 198, 200, 204, 214–16; and internal reform, 200–201, 210, 213–15; military buildup of, 7, 186–87, 189–91, 194, 199, 213; Reagan view of, 12, 188–89, 196, 209, 216–17; reaction of to Reagan rhetoric, 197, 214; and third world anticommunist guerrillas, 202–5, 211, 213; and third world communist movements, 191–93; and treaty violations, 209, 213. *See also* arms control; Cold War; specific countries
United States Information Agency (USIA), 196
United States v. Lopez, 22
United States v. Morrison, 22

Veterans of Foreign Wars (VFW), 236
Vietnam War, 51, 53–54, 186–87, 189, 191, 207, 226, 239, 257; Reagan and, 189
Voice of America, 196
Volcker, Paul, 80, 106, 254

voluntarism, xix, 152, 165, 167–69, 175, 177, 264; G. H. W. Bush and, 160, 162, 177; G. W. Bush and, 177; Dukakis and, 176; Gore and, 177; Reagan and, 162–64, 167
voter participation, 51, 67–69, 242
Voting Rights Act Amendments of 1982, 30

Walesa, Lech, 197
War Powers Act of 1973, 23
Ward's Cove Packing v. Atonio, 28, 33
Washington, George, 5, 12, 57, 152
Watergate, 51, 53–54
Wattenberg, Ben, 154
Weidenbaum, Murray, 78
Weinberger, Caspar, 193, 205
welfare reform, 154–55, 262; of 1981, 37, 103; of 1988, 37, 103, 160–61; of 1996, 40, 103, 264; Clinton and, 103; Reagan and, 103
Weyrich, Paul, 255
White House Office of Public Liaison, 235
White House Office on Private Sector Initiatives, 163–64
White House Working Group on Families, 160, 162
Wilder, Douglas, 30
Williams, Polly, 162, 175
Wilson, James Q., 154
Wilson, Woodrow, xx, 13, 60, 176
women in 1980s, 29, 31–33, 101, 109
working class ethnics and Reagan coalition, 28, 231–33, 244, 253
Worldnet, 196

Yemen, 186–87; and Carter, 187
Young America's Foundation, 240
Young Americans for Freedom (YAF), 240
Young Conservative Foundation, 240
youth: liberal activism by, 240; and Reagan coalition, 230, 240–42, 244; values of, 239

Zaire, 186

About the Author

Andrew E. Busch is an associate professor of political science at the University of Denver, where he teaches American government. He is author of *Outsiders and Openness in the Presidential Nominating System* and *Horses in Midstream: U.S. Midterm Elections and Their Consequences, 1894–1998*. He is also coauthor of *The Perfect Tie: The True Story of the 2000 Presidential Election* and books on the 1992 and 1996 presidential elections. He received his Ph.D. in government at the University of Virginia in 1992.